The Longest Patrol

The Longest Patrol

◆

A U-Boat Gunner's War

Gregory L. Owen

WITH A FOREWORD BY
CDR PETER G. CHANCE, RCN (RET.)

iUniverse Star
New York   Bloomington

The Longest Patrol
A U-Boat Gunner's War

iUniverse Star
an iUniverse, Inc. imprint

iUniverse books may be ordered through booksellers or by contacting:

iUniverse
1663 Liberty Drive
Bloomington, IN 47403
www.iuniverse.com
1-800-Authors (1-800-288-4677)

ISBN: 978-1-60528-032-5 (pbk)
ISBN: 978-0-595-63580-1 (ebk)

Printed in the United States of America

To
Karl and Anneliese Baumann
for
their children and grandchildren

and to
Sheila D. F. Owen
1958-2008
My Beautiful Sheila

Day and night
We have not closed our eyes
On the great hunt on the high seas.
Behind binoculars
And wet to the bone,
The Watch peers out for tonnage,
The diesel engines sound, the sea grows rough,
The boat is so small
And the sea is so large,
Now it depends on every hand
From the captain to the last man.

—Translation of the U-boat sailors' song,
So Klein ist das Boot, und so Groß ist das Meer

Contents

Foreword
By
Peter Godwin Chance,
Commander, Royal
Canadian Navy (Retired)

Lieutenant, Navigating Officer, HMCS Skeena, 1943–1944

I feel highly honoured to be invited to write a foreword to Gregory L. Owen's *The Longest Patrol; A U-Boat Gunner's War.* It is a remarkable account of Karl Baumann's life and a most worthy complement, from a German submariner's point of view, to the long list of books written about the 1939 - 1945 war at sea. The author's thoroughness of the research is compelling in itself. His telling of the story is warm in regard to personal relationships, complete in the descriptions of the various stages of Karl's life, and dramatic, realistic and stark pertaining to his service at sea.

From a personal standpoint, I found this book astonishing and exciting, especially when I read of U-953's determined and brave attacks against ships of Escort Group 12 of which HMCS *Skeena* was one. I was her Navigating Officer at that time. During the day of 8 June 1944, Gnat homing torpedoes were launched against our four ships. Thanks to a simple but effective invention dubbed CAT [Canadian Anti Torpedo] gear we sustained no damage as the torpedoes were attracted to the frequency of CAT gear above that of our ships' propellers. It was particularly exciting when U-953's periscope passed in front of our ship's bow. Our Hedgehog ring of bombs was fired toward the fast disappearing U-boat when at the same time we saw a torpedo pass down our starboard side only to explode in the CAT gear streamed well astern.

My profound thanks to Karl Baumann for his splendid memoir and to Greg Owen for telling it so brilliantly.

Sidney, British Columbia
23 April 2006

Preface

The purpose of this book is to render a memoir of Karl Baumann's World War II experiences in strict accordance with his extraordinary memory, and to describe his experiences through his unique perspective as a former U-boat crewman and prisoner of war. Accordingly, a significant portion of the text is founded upon a single primary source: Mr. Baumann himself, who provided a wealth of information during numerous formal and informal interviews. The first interview was conducted on 13 March 1999 under the auspices of the Special Collections Oral History Project at James Madison University in Harrisonburg, Virginia, and the last informal meeting occurred on 19 January 2006. The majority of interviews and meetings were conducted at Karl's home in Stuarts Draft, Virginia.

During and after numerous informal sessions, Karl Baumann reviewed sections of text line-by-line to assure that his experiences were accurately and appropriately described. Afterward, he provided detailed written notes to the author that explained the need for any recommended changes to the text. Without exception, complete accuracy was the ultimate goal upon which both the main subject of the biography and the author insisted.

As a single illustration of the level of accuracy that continually was sought and subsequently achieved, the author initially wrote that while Karl was confined at a prison camp in France, "…a quart of soup was ladled into each man's mess kit," presumably by a captor or another prisoner. After Mr. Baumann reviewed the text, he noted and explained that *he* ladled the soup into his own mess kit. The sentence was amended accordingly for the final version of the text.

Significant supporting material establishes the context within which Mr. Baumann's experiences were related to the larger events of World War II. The most important primary source document was the original war diary of U-953, upon which Karl Baumann served during the Battle of the Atlantic. Footnoted entries indicate where information sources conflict with or augment his recollections, perspectives, or understanding of events.

It is hoped that the text adequately portrays the wartime experiences of a former enemy; and that when viewed from his unique perspective, the reader will gain greater understanding of the human tragedy that occurred during World

War II. Karl Baumann's memoir replaces the abstract designations of "we" and "they" with a human face.

Acknowledgements

I am very grateful for the kind assistance of the following individuals who gave their valuable time and expertise toward my writing effort, without which the completed work would not have been possible.

Above all, Karl and Anneliese Baumann of Stuarts Draft, Virginia, warmly opened their home and their extraordinary memory banks to me on countless occasions. Karl provided many hours of formal and informal interviews and discussions, reviewed every page of written text several times, and suggested detailed corrections to establish the highest level of accuracy. Mrs. Baumann provided delicious evening meals, entrusted this stranger with irreplaceable family photographs and documents, and provided many details of her own wartime experiences.

The late Galen Heatwole provided invaluable information regarding the German PWs and the Prisoner of War Camp in Lyndhurst, Virginia. Likewise, Harry Cooper of Sharkhunters, Inc. in Hernando, Florida, provided crucial information to assist my search for U-boat primary sources, as did John Taylor of the National Archives II Annex in College Park, Maryland.

David Benevitch of the U.S. Forest Service in Natural Bridge, Virginia, provided contemporary newspaper articles and invaluable transcriptions of several interviews he conducted in 1991 during his efforts to record the history of Camp Lyndhurst, which was situated in the George Washington National Forest in Augusta County, Virginia.

Leonard L. Lewane, Colonel, U.S. Army (Ret.), a gifted history instructor from Lexington, Virginia, first noticed I possessed some latent writing talent and directed me toward ultimate honors as a George C. Marshall Scholar by the George C. Marshall Foundation at Virginia Military Institute. The Foundation provided significant research and writing opportunities that gave me greater confidence to undertake the substantial effort necessary to produce a history work I trust will stand up to critical examination.

Gabrielle Lanier, Ph.D., of the History Department at James Madison University in Harrisonburg, Virginia; directed my History Honors Thesis, which became the basis for this book, during my pursuit of a BA degree in History, *Summa Cum Laude with Distinction in History*.

Robert L. Jobin, of Staunton, Virginia, translated German correspondence and the *Kriegstagebuch*, the official war diary of U-953. Donald E. Corbin, Ph.D., and Ashley Corbin of Harrisonburg, Virginia, kindly translated the French correspondence.

U-953 crewmember Karl-Heinz Patzer of Bad Sachsa, Germany, provided photographs from his personal collection, and U. Eduard Hartmann of Chicago, Illinois, graciously lent an album of photographs that belonged to his late father, U-953 navigator Eduard Hartmann. Lothar Kestler of Aberdeen, Scotland, kindly provided a U-boat postcard.

Alain Biard and fellow members of the La Rochelle, France, Kiwanis Club gathered and provided valuable historical information about their city and present day photographs of the U-boat bunker complex at nearby La Pallice.

The late William P. Albright, Ph.D., a former prisoner of war in Germany and my long-time friend, edited the initial text of this book with an English professor's critical eye until his spirit suddenly and unexpectedly was carried to the Heavens.

My brother, Steven D. Owen, Major, U.S. Army, conducted an exhaustive editorial review and advised me of the means required to win acceptance from critical readers of military history. In the wake of his efforts, I alone am responsible for any textual errors that may remain.

Other eyewitnesses to Karl Baumann's wartime experiences—Germans, Americans and Canadians alike—contributed their recollections, which lent crucial context to the story and helped give it life through the written word. I wish to pay special thanks to Peter Godwin Chance, Commander, Royal Canadian Navy (Retired), of Sidney, British Columbia; and Leighton Steinhoff of Kitchener, Ontario for their accounts of the attacks against HMCS *Skeena* on 8 June 1944, when their destroyer and U-953 battled each other in the English Channel.

Cecilia Cuevas coordinated all communications between iUniverse and this wary author, while editorial and design teams conducted a number of comprehensive reviews and evaluations that proved invaluable toward the successful production of the book.

Finally, my wife Sheila, figuratively, kept the home fires burning and endured untold hours of research and writing with patience and understanding while her husband sailed aboard U-953 and stood with Karl Baumann behind barbed wire enclosures inside America's PW camp network.

Gregory L. Owen
15 May 2006

Introduction

The late summer of 1944 produced the bloodiest fighting to date in five agonizing years of World War II. In the wake of the invasion of Normandy on the sixth of June the U.S. Army's VIII Corps slugged its way across the Brittany Peninsula with orders to destroy all German forces on the western coast of France. Despite vicious and determined efforts to impede their pursuers, the remnants of Adolf Hitler's Wehrmacht were driven into rapidly shrinking salients surrounding several Atlantic port strongpoints.

American troops laid siege to the city of Brest for more than four weeks, with its German naval base and massive submarine pens their ultimate objectives. Under the weight of U.S. manpower and materiel, the outcome never was in doubt. With no possibility for escape or reinforcement, the decimated German forces surrendered to the dogfaces of the 2nd, 8th and 29th infantry divisions on 18 September.

As haggard GIs stumbled over the rubble of the almost totally devastated city they discovered a battered entrance that led to an underground hospital. The scene inside bore witness to the brutal punishment German troops suffered from overwhelming American firepower. The last occupation troops to be maimed or killed for the city lay everywhere. Those who were able formed into groups to march quietly into captivity. Others too ill or badly wounded to move from their beds lay helplessly while American soldiers took stock of their prisoners. A severely wounded U-boat gunner, *Matrosenobergefreiter* Karl Baumann, watched the events unfold before him and with weary acceptance awaited the inevitable moment of captivity. He knew beyond any doubt that, for himself, the deadly Battle of the Atlantic was over.

Among the growing volume of World War II history that has been written from the enlisted man's perspective, few works describe the war experiences of the common German soldier, sailor, or airman. Still fewer describe the war through the eyes of U-boat crewmen, because so few survived to record their experiences. The Kriegsmarine's U-boat force suffered a seventy-five percent mortality rate—the greatest percentage of deaths in the combat arms of all countries that fielded armies, navies, and air forces during the war. The memories and

1

insights of those who survived are important chronicles that underscore the human cost paid by the common man when nations wage war against each other.

Karl Baumann was a seasoned sailor—a *Matrose*—born during the desperate and tumultuous years of the 1920s in the Ruhr Valley of Germany. He was the child of a disrupted family, the Great Depression, and an abbreviated formal education. He also was an unenthusiastic member of the *Jungvolk* legion of the Nazi youth movement. His decision to become a sailor when he was fourteen years old was both fortuitous and fateful. He came of age at sea in the German civilian fleet and matured while a member of the Kriegsmarine's legendary U-boat force. He participated in several crucial battles on the high seas, as well as the fateful underwater counteroffensive to destroy the Allied invasion armada while it delivered troops onto the Normandy landing beaches.

Baumann was one of only ten thousand U-boat crewmen who survived the war, and the even smaller fraternity of captured submariners. As a prisoner of war, his personal struggle with his captors reached across the Atlantic and into the heart of the Shenandoah Valley of Virginia. Confined at Camp Lyndhurst near Sherando Lake in Augusta County, the nineteen-year-old was not a model prisoner by American standards. Karl Baumann's prisoner of war experience, however, produced life-transforming consequences he never could have contemplated before his capture and imprisonment in the land of his sworn enemy. This is Karl Baumann's wartime odyssey.

1

Karlchen

For more than six hundred years legions of hardy souls in the land of Westphalia descended long vertical mine shafts to attack the vast veins of coal that lay beneath the Ruhr Valley of northwestern Germany. In their dank, pitch black netherworld—save for scant traces of artificial light—men and boys expended shortened lives in stifling heat and blinding dust to extract the fossil fuel that propelled the industrial revolution in the region. Massive industrialization, in turn, scarred the mineral-saturated Ruhr Valley, blackened its rivers, darkened the sky with smoke, bore the heavy machinery of the modern technological age, and imprinted its character upon the bodies and souls of the people.[1]

By the tumultuous 1920s, once-placid Ruhr farmlands long had been overtaken by hundreds of mines, mills, and factories that yielded the lifeblood of Germany's economic power. One hundred million tons of coal alone trundled out of the mines in a normal year. Iron ore also was dug out of the flat terrain from quarries that competed for land surrounding the cities of Dortmund and Essen and their numerous suburbs. Steel, paper, cotton, and silk mills as well as gigantic railroad shops vied for space; as did dye, salt, and chemical works; tanneries and glass factories.[2]

Chief among all Ruhr industries was the massive Krupp works at Essen, whose eighty thousand workers smelted, forged, and hammered out a multitude of steel products around the clock. Krupp produced the essential commodities of the modern era: railroad engines and cars, farm implements, tools, ship frames and bridge steel—and the world's best heavy artillery. Until the end of the First World War, technicians test-fired every artillery piece that Krupp produced. The roar of cannon added a thunderous undertone to the cacophony of screeching

---

1. Frederick Simpich, "The Story of the Ruhr," *The National Geographic Magazine*, May 1922, 553-554.
2. Simpich, 553.

steam whistles, clattering conveyer belts, and rumbling machines that greeted each new day in the Ruhr.[3]

A network of railroads and inland waterways crisscrossed the region, clogged with the handiwork of the labor class. Scores of trains rolled out of the Ruhr every day; an enterprising analyst calculated a single train thirty miles long would be required to transport one day's finished goods. Hundreds of heavily laden barges and special river-sea steamers plied the murky Ruhr River to its junction with the Rhine, where the latter flowed toward the Dutch city of Rotterdam on the North Sea and the world's markets beyond.[4]

Hundreds of thousands of workers from the poor provinces of Germany and Eastern Europe had poured into the region over several generations to provide the hard labor that generated the productive output. With their families in tow, blue-collar laborers and a new middle class of white-collar workers filled neighborhoods that formed a solid procession of Ruhr communities.[5] Population density in some neighborhoods was as great as 1,800 per square mile by 1922 and was estimated at nearly four million for the entire industrial district, all in an area smaller than the state of Rhode Island. A contemporary visitor to the Ruhr wrote that the factory city of Essen was the sort of place one liked to see—once.[6] The people themselves looked with pride to their damaged landscape and the sprawling communities that delivered most of the prosperity and power the nation enjoyed, even as the storm clouds of desperate troubles formed upon the horizon. In the wake of Germany's disastrous defeat in the First World War, the Ruhr remained one of the most intensely developed and productive industrial regions in the world. It provided 80 percent of the nation's coal and steel supply in 1922 after another important industrial region, Upper Silesia, was wrested from Germany under the Versailles Treaty and ceded to newly created Poland.[7] Despite Germany's post-war progress and the productivity of the Ruhr during the first years of the 1920s, a significant undercurrent of public discontent always threat-

---

3. Simpich; 555, 558.
4. Simpich; 553, 554, 561.
5. Modris Eksteins, *Rites of Spring; The Great War and the Birth of the Modern Age* (Boston: Houghton Mifflin Co., 1989), 69.
6. Simpich; 553, 559. Anneliese Samhuber Baumann took exception to Mr. Simpich's observation, and emphasized that residents routinely washed the soot off the facades of their homes out of their sense of pride in themselves and their communities. Interview by author, March 2000.
7. William L. Shirer, *The Rise and Fall of the Third Reich; A History of Nazi Germany* (New York: Simon and Schuster, 1960), 61.

ened, and often erupted into, ugly demonstrations of seething anger. Citizens often expressed indignation over the terrible wartime losses in German lives and resources, the humiliation and nearly universal condemnation of Germany for prosecuting the war, and the reparations demanded by the victorious Allies under the Versailles Treaty. Moreover, the new Weimar government was the target of abject hostility over the acquiescent role it played in the crucial current events that challenged the country's hegemony.[8]

The Ruhr represented Germany's headlong transformation into the new and often frightening post-industrial world, where technology reigned and the relative value of individualism waned. German advances in physics, chemistry, engineering, and urban architecture largely shaped the modern industrial and urban landscape of the developed nations. While the Ruhr more than any region in Germany bore the scars of rapid and wholesale environmental change, its population suffered the psychic disorientation of that change. In mines, mills, and factories, the individual worker had become merely a single component in the larger-than-life mechanical production processes.[9]

In 1923 the Ruhr also served as the venue for one of the traumatic events that nearly destroyed Germany and further provoked the fearsome post-World War I economic, social, and political ferment that led ultimately to National Socialism and the catastrophe of the Second World War. Germany's payment of punitive war reparations under the auspices of the Versailles Treaty taxed the national economy nearly to the breaking point by 1922. Finally, the Weimar government asked France for a moratorium on payments when it defaulted on deliveries of timber to its age-old adversary and border sharing neighbor. Rather than grant relief, French Premier Raymond Poincare angrily responded to the German appeal with force.[10] The inhabitants of the Ruhr watched in stunned and bitter silence as long columns of French and Belgian infantry and armored units rolled over the border into the region on 11 January 1923. The two armies proceeded to occupy and control the land, if not the people, for three calamitous years.[11]

With open defiance toward their unwelcome overlords, and to protest the ignominy of occupation, the powerful Ruhr labor unions called a general strike that was taken up by rank and file workers everywhere across the industrial

8.   J. M. Winter, *The Experience of World War I* (New York: Oxford University Press, 1989), 213.
9.   Eksteins, 67-68.
10. Shirer, 61.
11. Richard Overy, *The Penguin Historical Atlas of the Third Reich* (London: Penguin Books, 1996), 116.

region.[12] Rather than see the profits of their labors confiscated by their long-standing enemy, the strikers completely shut down nearly every mining and manufacturing facility. An eerie silence soon replaced the thunderous sounds of production while the sky above was swept clean of industrial smoke. For all classes of employees and their families, uncharacteristic idleness replaced their legendary work ethic. Ahead lay a decade of unprecedented economic depression, temporary recovery, and heightened social, cultural, and political turmoil that cast a pall of gloom over all of Germany.

The foundations of a catastrophic economic depression began to descend upon Germany as early as 1921, when its currency value started losing ground against other currencies and ended the year at seventy-five *Reichmarks* to the U.S. dollar. In 1922 the exchange rate fell to four hundred for every dollar, and by the end of the year dove to seven thousand. When the French and Belgians occupied the Ruhr, the *Reichsmark* plummeted to eighteen thousand to the dollar. With production suspended throughout the industrial region, by July the strangled German economy forced the collapse of the *Reichsmark* to a rate of 160,000 to the dollar—then spiraled down to one million by the beginning of August. By November 1923 one dollar bought four billion *Reichsmarks*, and afterwards unimaginable trillions.[13] Fatalistic Germans repeated the story of one city dweller who left a large basket of *Reichsmarks* outside her door, only to discover later the pile of currency lying on the sidewalk and the basket missing.[14] The out of control money supply symbolized staggering inflation. *Reichsmarks* in circulation soared from 81.6 billion in 1920 to 496 trillion in 1923.[15] Currency and postage stamps in denominations of five million *Reichsmarks* and more were produced by the government and were not worth the paper upon which they were printed. The face values of newly printed bills and stamps could not keep pace with the inflation rate that increased by the minute, and higher denominations were overprinted on currency and *Briefmarke* before they were issued.[16] The life savings of hardworking middle class and blue-collar families were wiped out virtually overnight and the purchasing power of salaries was reduced essentially to zero. Retail and wholesale merchants in turn closed their doors in financial ruin as the cycle of economic devastation encompassed most of German society. Financial chaos

---

12.   Shirer, 61.
13.   Shirer, 61.
14.   Robert T. Elson, *Prelude to War*, World War II (Alexandria, Virginia: Time-Life Books, 1976), 70.
15.   Overy, 123.
16.   Translation: *Briefmarke* are postage stamps.

reigned, and robbed vast numbers of Germans of all feelings of security, hope for a brighter future, and faith in their government and its institutions.[17]

German currency finally began to stabilize in 1924. Inflation soon was curtailed, war reparations were restructured, money poured in from the United States, and the French and Belgians began to pull out of the Ruhr.[18] Germany had barely survived its own destruction, but would thrive again, if only briefly. In the wake of economic depression strong psychological forces of defeat and powerlessness, combined with the fears and uncertainties of modernity, threatened to unravel the unifying fabric that bound the German people into a young nation of diverse states. Such was the enfeebled condition of Germany in 1924—the *Zeitgeist* into which Karl Baumann entered the world.

Karl Christian Wilhelm Baumann was born at the family home in the Dortmund suburb of Brambauer on 18 October 1924, the second child and only son of Christian and Antonia Kampe Baumann.[19] The elder Baumann was a *Kaufmann* who purchased wholesale foodstuffs for two stores the family operated in the nearby city of Bochum, where the family moved when Karl was a toddler. One of the Baumann's stores sold fresh produce and the other general grocery items. Karl's mother was the principal owner of the establishments, having earlier received formal clerical training in the merchant trade. Concerted effort sustained the small mercantile operation through the hard years of the decade's first economic calamity.

Bochum is an ancient community that lies between the larger cities of Dortmund and Essen. Its population swelled tenfold in little more than two generations after the coal and steel industries were established in the mid-nineteenth century. By 1906 Bochum's 22,844 miners had carved over five million tons of coal out of the nearby tunnels and established a way of life for the common man. The prosperous city soon incorporated a number of smaller towns into its juris-

---

17. Shirer, 61.
18. Shirer, 112.
19. Karl Baumann, interviews by Author, 13 March 1999 through 14 April 2006, Author's collection. Recorded interviews augmented by the author's handwritten notes from numerous informal meetings provided all primary source material that relates directly to Karl Baumann and the Baumann family, unless otherwise noted. All interviews were conducted at Mr. Baumann's home in Stuarts Draft, Virginia. The master recording and transcript for the first 1.5 hours of interviews are available from the Special Collections section of the Carrier Library at James Madison University, Harrisonburg, Virginia.

diction and would swell the population to 321,000 by 1929, another dreadful year for the German economy.[20]

The continued economic recovery that stabilized the *Reichsmark* during the mid-1920s restored appreciable vigor to the wary public psyche. Then, on 29 October 1929, the crash of the New York Stock Exchange signaled the beginning of the Great Depression, which soon spread throughout the industrialized world. Fewer than five years after the first economic catastrophe of the decade had subsided, Germany faced another financial crisis of dire proportions.

The Great Depression brought financial ruin to the young Baumann family and deprived the parents of any hope or plans to rear daughter Ilse, son Karl-lchen—Little Karl, as he was called—and toddler Helga with middle-class comforts obtained through the efforts of their entrepreneurship. With the financial collapse many desperate customers begged Antonia to extend credit for them to purchase food and other essential wares. Young Mrs. Baumann could not resist their pleas and acquiesced out of the goodness of her heart, but to the peril of her own livelihood, her home and her family.

The Depression deepened during the autumn and winter of 1929, and with too little income and too many uncollectible accounts the Baumanns soon lacked sufficient working capital to pay the rent for their storefronts and to restock their shelves with merchandise. Financial disaster was imminent, and the family could do nothing to stop it.

The Christmas season of 1929 was a melancholy affair for families facing ruin. Nonetheless, enough of the spirit of togetherness prevailed for the Baumann family to make the twenty-kilometer train journey to spend the holidays at Antonia's mother's house on the outskirts of Brambauer. There Karl's *Oma,* Lina Kampe, unquestionably ruled her domain, which included seven children who still lived at home. *Oma* had become a widow in 1912, when her husband was killed in an accident in one of the nearby mines. Five-year-old Karl enjoyed visits to *Oma's,* especially for the playful attention he received from several uncles, though they were young adults. When Karl's family returned to Bochum at the end of the holidays he stayed with *Oma* for an extended visit.

One cold January day a few weeks later, the little boy suddenly, inexplicably was seized by the greatest apprehension that something at home was terribly wrong. He hurried to his *Oma* and with flowing tears implored to be taken home. *Oma* assured him that he could go; soon Karl and his Uncle Wilhelm were en

---

20. "Facts About Bochum" (Internet website: www.bochum.de/english/boallg.htm., 1999).

route by train to Bochum and the boy's home. When they arrived there they were shocked to find Antonia confined to bed and very gravely ill, though no one had yet notified the family in Brambauer. The youngster's intuition proved fatefully accurate, whether merely by coincidence or through some extraordinary perceptive connection between a loving mother and child. An ambulance was summoned to rush her to the local hospital, where doctors would quickly determine she suffered from some form of internal bleeding. During the interminable wait for the ambulance, Antonia tried to assuage her son's fear and grief as he stood by her bedside. She pointed to a picture on the wall Karl always admired, a framed print of the Apostles of Jesus that she had received as a confirmation gift when she was a young girl.

"Karlchen," she whispered weakly while her son looked into her eyes, "when I come back you may have that picture." However, the young businesswoman and mother of three would never return home: she died a few days later at the age of twenty-nine.

The struggle to care for three small children and a failing business fell hard upon Christian. Still distraught over Antonia's death, and with growing desperation, he sent eight-year-old Ilse and her brother into the neighborhood to collect the credit accounts due from the stores' customers. Not surprisingly, the youngsters' efforts proved utterly fruitless, since former patrons were as destitute as the Baumanns themselves. Shortly thereafter, with nowhere to turn for financial assistance, Christian Baumann faced bankruptcy. To prevent creditors from seizing the family's household furniture, Christian gave their possessions to *Oma* and other family members. Virtually penniless and with little to call his own, the young widower was glad his wife did not have to witness the loss of the family's business, home and possessions.

Unable to find employment elsewhere, Christian had no recourse but to take a job as a *Reparationsarbeiter*—a reparations worker—in France. Under the auspices of the war reparations program that provided German workers to serve the victors of the Great War, he was sent to Alsace Lorraine as a laborer. There he joined a crew digging mine shafts in the French coalfields. His descent into the mines was particularly distasteful as he recalled the life he once had known, the death of his wife, and the children he was forced to leave behind. Just as profoundly, five-year-old Karl and his sisters hungered for the loving relationship and daily influence of their parents.

Five year-old Karl, wearing necktie, attends a local festival; Bochum, 1929.

With Christian's departure for France *Oma* Kampe welcomed the Baumann children to her small home on the edge of Brambauer. There the grandchildren shared cramped but loving surroundings. Under *Oma*'s judicious guardianship, Karl managed to experience a rather normal childhood in spite of the abnormal stresses that personal losses conspired to create. Throughout his youth, however, he suffered the emotional scars of significant loss—of his home, his mother's and father's physical presence, and their involvement in his life. Not surprisingly, as he grew older the manifestations of his early misfortune assumed some all-too-familiar forms. Of Karl and his younger sister Helga, *Oma* Kampe jocularly called them her "*Zwei kleine Teufel*"—two little devils

Truly devilish activity at the same time often was played out locally and in streets and town squares throughout Germany. Karl listened intently while his uncles relayed excited accounts of trouble they had encountered, either as onlookers or willing participants, during weekend forays into neighboring cities. Crime waves and pitched street fights between members of rival political parties were rampant as a plague. Political vandals defaced the walls of homes and businesses in Karl's own neighborhood. The letters *KPD*, painted in bold ugly brush strokes, announced frequent stealthy visits by the Communist Party of Germany in the dead of night. What was it going to take, the boy's elders pondered aloud, to stop the waves of crime and turmoil that had infected the soul of the German people and the *Vaterland*?

Despite the privations that marked the onerous passage of time during the global depression of the 1930s, people persevered and adapted to the prevailing conditions as best they could. Young Baumann and his sisters settled into the routine of life in their large extended family of grandmother, uncles, and aunts. With effort and cooperation the basic necessities of life always were provided, though extra comforts and luxuries were few. Everyone at home performed household chores in accordance with age and abilities.

In addition to gathering firewood, polishing shoes for the family, and pulling weeds—the one chore he hated—Karl's primary task during childhood was to search farm fields nearby for grasses to feed the family's goats and sheep, and dandelions to feed their rabbits. The work helped satisfy his boyish curiosity and sense of wanderlust. As he scoured the landscape he enjoyed the feeling of freedom, solitude, and discovery the rural countryside offered.

Karl seldom shirked his chores—that would have profoundly disappointed *Oma*—but frequently paused during his expeditions to relax and daydream, and during warm weather to swim in the large millpond beyond the woods behind *Oma*'s house. He fostered friendships at the pond with classmates and other boys from the neighborhood who gathered there to swim. With youthful abandon they shed their clothes and hid them under the thick canopy of wild ferns that populated the edge of the pond. The boys then charged into the cool water to escape the hot summer sun. Karl occasionally arrived with *Oma*'s dog in tow. With faulty canine logic the pooch invariably charged into the water to drag the splashing boy onto the shore to save him from drowning. Whenever patrolling policemen made their rounds the trespassing youngsters stealthily retreated from the water into the thick canopy of ferns that served as their sanctuary. The adrenaline rush from their narrow escapes and other simple pleasures of youth buoyed the boys' spirits.

The passage of time helped little to diminish the sense of tremendous loss Karl had carried in his heart since his mother's death, but rather exacerbated the effect of her absence in his life. Far too early in his youth, Karl began to seek solace and pleasure in alcohol. In the thralls of intoxicants he oftentimes was assaulted by an abject loneliness that only parental love and involvement could have appeased. During such low times the precious memories of an irretrievable past surged through him and unleashed a torrent of tears.

Karl received eight years of formal education at Brambauer's *Volkschule*, an experience akin to a love-hate relationship. He enjoyed learning new skills and achieving new levels of knowledge and understanding, but as he grew older his dislike for the rigid structure and discipline imposed upon students grew apace. During the Hitler era most educators down to the primary level were members of the Nazi party. Teachers routinely infused daily lessons with Nazi theory, history and philosophy, and an arduous brand of discipline born of the *Führerprinzip*—the top-down authority that flowed from Adolf Hitler to the lowest official functionary.[21] The *Führerprinzip* was put into practice when Adolf Hitler, the *Führer*, ascended to the Chancellorship of Germany on 30 January 1933.

The students at Karl's *Volkschule* were elated to spend 28 June 1934 outside of the classroom. Their excitement remained unabated as later that day they stood in the rain along the road leading to *Schloß* Buddenburg, near Brambauer. The castle was a leadership training center for the Reichsarbeitsdienst—the Reich Labor Service—and was prepared to receive a very important visitor.[22] On that day *Gauleiter* Josef Terboven, the governor of the Nazi district of Essen, was to be married.[23] The honored guest at the affair was Adolf Hitler, who made it a point to attend the weddings of long-time party leaders.[24] Since he was in the area, the *Führer* scheduled to visit the training center. The air was charged with excitement as the time approached for Hitler's entourage to pass through the throng that had gathered to catch perhaps only a fleeting glimpse of the Chancellor of Germany. After the appointed time had long passed, however, it became apparent that Hitler's plans had been altered. A matter of great importance obviously had intervened to prevent the *Führer* from passing through waves of smiling and shouting admirers with arms thrust out in the Hitler salute.

---

21. Norman Rich, *Hitler's War Aims; Ideology, the Nazi State, and the Course of Expansion* (New York: W. W. Norton & Co., 1973), 29.
22. The Reichsarbeitsdienst was a program of one-year compulsory labor service for eighteen year-old males—with the exception of those already engaged in government service.
23. Shirer, 220.
24. Herbert Walther, ed., *Der Führer; The Life & Times of Adolf Hitler* (London: Bison Books, 1978), 52.

Even as the disappointed crowd dispersed, Adolf Hitler was sequestered at a nearby office while he made a series of anxious telephone calls to his political and military cronies. Their unquestioned support was necessary, he believed, before he dared execute a bold, bloody attack he had planned against a number of party members and hacks—some of whom were his personal friends. The *Führer* was convinced that a cabal of party officials had conspired to remove him from power as Chancellor and leader of the Nazi party. Just two days later he would carry out the notorious Blood Purge that would result in the murder of as many as one thousand former supporters and unfortunate personal enemies of top Nazi party leaders. The most notable casualty of the purge was Hitler's personal friend, Ernst Röhm, who as leader of the Nazi party's private army—the *Sturm Abteilung*—had been instrumental in Hitler's rise to power.[25]

Notwithstanding his preoccupation with cleansing the party ranks, the *Führer* finally took time on 29 June to visit *Schloß* Buddenburg before his return trip to Berlin. For a second day Karl Baumann and his classmates excitedly converged along the roadside. This time the big Mercedes staff car bearing Adolf Hitler arrived to wade through the approving mass of admirers. The children were astounded to see the car stop for a moment directly in front of them; being no threat to safety, the *Führer's* entourage of bodyguards allowed the youngsters to swarm around the vehicle. Karl, too, was swept up in the excitement of the moment and enthusiastically joined the throng of young voices and waving arms that praised the savior-apparent of Germany. All around him men, women and the schoolchildren hailed the leader who by all appearances had put a stop to rampant crime, rid the streets of political agitators and put the German people back to work. Fewer than four feet from Karl Baumann, the *Führer* smiled and basked in the wild acclaim, possessed of the knowledge that within twenty-four hours most of his political enemies would be dead, and absolute control of Germany would rest firmly in his hands.

The draconian discipline imposed in the classroom contrasted dramatically with the discipline Karl received at home. *Oma* ruled her household with discipline and order born of familial love and respect, and her grandson never challenged her authority. Nonetheless, he sorely needed the time-consuming, ever-watchful day-to-day oversight that conscientious parents provide. As he grew older Karl realized that no one, not his aging grandmother nor his aunts and uncles, could fill the void in love, guidance or discipline that had emerged from

---

25. Shirer, 221. *Sturm Abteilung* members were variously known as the *SA* or Brown Shirts.

the loss of his parents' physical and emotional connectedness, and most especially his mother's love. The void remained even after Karl's father returned home from the French mines, when Christian wed his deceased wife's sister, Melitta. Try as she might, Melitta could not provide the selfless bond that Antonia naturally had developed with her son.

Significant religious instruction might have helped ameliorate Karl's loss, but like many in Europe his extended family did not attend regular weekly church services. Nevertheless, Karl was confirmed at age fourteen into Germany's Evangelical church after he completed several denominational training courses. Unlike American church services that include sermons to broach issues of individual moral integrity and matters of right and wrong as fundamental aspects of faith, European church services tended to emphasize traditional ceremonial elements that characterized their long and rich history of procession and prayer. While many Europeans officially belonged to a denomination, attendance at regular services typically was quite low; Karl was no exception in his attendance. Though he was not challenged by a formal religious upbringing to guide his daily life, *Oma* taught Karl and his sisters by example. She resolutely exhibited her strong religious background and lived by her faith, though she was unable to attend services due to acute health problems that confined her to her home. *Oma* influenced Karl always to be strongly aware of the continual battle between good and evil, and to live by the precepts of goodness.

Karl usually was well behaved during his years at *Volkschule* and only occasionally ran afoul of school or teachers' rules, whereupon he suffered the normal consequences for minor infractions. Classmate Anneliese Samhuber saw in Karl a shy, good boy who obeyed the rules at *Moltkeschule*-2 during their years there. Life seldom is always fair, however, and in one incident when he was twelve years old Karl was wrongly accused of being a member of a schoolboys' ad hoc smoking club. The guilty party was an older student named Karl Baumann who attended *Moltkeschule*-1, to which young Baumann's *Volkschule* was an annex. Flush with testosterone and the air of fledgling adulthood, the elder boys loitered around the schoolyard before classes and puffed, coughed, and wheezed on forbidden cigarettes. School authorities soon discovered the untoward activity and chafed at the intolerable breakdown of discipline. When the name Karl Baumann surfaced as one of the teenaged conspirators the administrators suspected young Karl was the guilty smoker. In short order the startled boy was removed from his classroom and harshly interrogated by a teacher. Time and again he vehemently denied any involvement in the club, and with each denial Karl's interrogator slapped him hard across the face. Despite the abuse, he would never admit guilt to the unfounded accusations. Shaken by his harsh treatment and frightened that the punishment would continue, Karl fled the *Volkschule* without permission as soon as he was able. He breathlessly ran home to find his father, and explained how he had been unjustly accused, interrogated, and punished. The elder Baumann returned his son to the school to confront his tormenters and soon persuaded them that the young boy was wholly innocent of the accusation. Shortly afterward, however, with a mind-numbing demonstration of bureaucratic intransigence, a school administrator informed Karl that when he ran home to report his cruel interrogation he breached the sacrosanct rule that forbade a student to leave the school grounds without permission. Karl received an official reprimand on his school report for the serious rule violation, without regard to the extenuating circumstances that had prompted his desperate action.

Karl never forgot the humiliation he felt when he received the stinging assaults from the errant teacher. Worse, in keeping with the nature of German bureaucratic efficiency, throughout his eight years of schooling his behavior was rated along with his grades on a single report card that contained his entire academic history. The existence of the official reprimand for a single six-month reporting period thereafter would become known to any prospective employer Karl would face during adulthood, whenever he was compelled to submit his academic history for review. Karl regretted that at the conclusion of his eight years at *Volkschule* his academic report did not bear the notation, *Ohne Tadel*—without reprimand—that job-seekers and employers alike coveted.

By his fourth year at *Volkschule* Karl had developed an irrepressible desire to pursue life with the greatest measure of enjoyment that the conditions of his early travails would allow. His free-spirited disposition was severely challenged in 1934, though, by the power and influence of the vastly expanding National Socialist youth movement. The overarching Nazi youth organization was known generally as the *Hitler Jugend*—Hitler Youth—though the name also properly referred to the largest group designed for boys between the ages of fourteen and eighteen.[26] The thoroughly apolitical Karl was by his very nature disinclined to join even friends and fellow classmates, no less millions throughout Germany, who sought membership in one of several age-and sex-specific *HJ* groups. Friendly but relentless persuasion by his teacher and classmates at *Volkschule* eventually coerced reluctant Karl to join the local unit of the *Jungvolk*, the Nazi youth organization for boys ten through thirteen years of age. Nonetheless, the

26. Dr. Christian Zentner, ed., *Hitler-Jugend* (Hamburg: Verlag für geschichtliche Dokumentation GmbH, 1978), 17.

JV, and by extension the Nazi party, never was able to assert its authority over Karl, cultivate his abiding loyalty, or elicit more than unenthusiastic and grudging participation in the organization.

Hitler Youth membership was voluntary until 1936. Although official compulsion was lacking, other means of coercion would drive young people to join. Before Hitler became Chancellor in 1933, more than ten million young people had belonged to one or more of the hundreds of thriving youth-oriented civic, religious, political, and social groups across Germany. At the time, slightly more than one hundred thousand were members of the Hitler Youth, which had been formed in 1926.[27] By 1936, all other youth organizations would be almost entirely outlawed or incorporated into the Nazi youth movement. Large numbers of young people would follow previously established peer groups into the *HJ* and swell its ranks to nearly six million in 1934, nearly twice its 1933 membership. Jewish and communist youth organizations alone would be excluded from the wide-sweeping fiat.[28] Though they hoped to exert complete control over German youth, the Nazi leadership never achieved their impossible objective to win the heart and mind of every young person.[29] Karl Baumann's attitude toward the *Jungvolk* was emblematic of their failure.

A long enduring myth developed and promoted by Hitler's propaganda ministry held that the whole of German youth willingly and happily participated in the Nazi youth movement. Actual membership numbers convey the reality: many thousands of young Germans either resisted membership outright or, like Karl, participated only marginally.[30] After membership became compulsory in 1936 many young people were intimidated, cajoled, jailed in special youth prisons, and otherwise forced into the *HJ,* sometimes into special units reserved for miscreants and other wayward youth.[31] Karl's resistance to the *Jungvolk* was not an anomaly, but instead was a common reaction by a significant minority of young people who resented the intrusion of the Nazi state into their lives.

Traditionally, the *Volkschule* in Brambauer held classes six days every week during the school year. By 1934, however, the boys and girls who joined, respectively, the *Jungvolk* and the *Jungmädelbund* were excused from Saturday classes so they could attend *Staatsjugendtag*—the day of training and drill that youth con-

---

27. Shirer, 252-253.
28. Overy, 30-31.
29. Daniel Horn, "Coercion and Compulsion in the Hitler Youth, 1933-1945," *The Historian* 41 (August 1979): 643.
30. Horn, 642.
31. Horn, 655.

tributed to the state. Eventually Karl and several other boys in his class stood alone to resist membership. The last holdouts and their frustrated teacher were required to attend class since the *JV* had not otherwise appropriated their time. Entrapped by the recalcitrant boys who prevented him from taking the day off, the teacher spent most Saturday class hours trying to convince them to join the *Jungvolk*. He extolled the virtues and benefits of membership: the fellowship with friends and classmates, the rigorous physical training and sports activities, the military drills, and the charitable work in which the *JV* was engaged. For the teacher at least, relentless coercion eventually paid off as the obstinate boys finally yielded their resolve to remain outside the Nazi youth movement. Mostly to avoid the tedious hours of Saturday classes, Karl finally joined the local *Jungvolk* unit.

The *Jungvolk* was organized along rigid military organizational lines, and encompassed its own hierarchy of ranks—from lowly *Pimpf* to exalted *Jungbannführer*. Despite the younger age group involved, *JV* rank and unit structures were parallel with, and not subservient to, those of the *Hitler Jugend* proper, the organization for boys between the ages of fourteen and eighteen. Members wore the *JV* uniform during regular *Staatsjugendtag* meetings and special events.[32]

The overarching purpose of the *Jungvolk* and the *Hitler Jugend* was physical preparation for soldiering and war. Likewise, girls and young women of the *Jungmädelbund* and the *Bund Deutscher Mädel*, respectively, developed or enhanced the habits of good health and exercise, all for the express purpose of becoming strong and healthy mothers of future soldiers for the *Reich*. Nazi propaganda emphasized the traditional role for girls and young women of the *JMB* and *BDM*: *Kinder, Kirche, Küche*—children, church, and kitchen.[33] The Nazi youth organizations paid much less attention to educational pursuits and political indoctrination than to physical exercise, outdoor activities, group games, and stirring music to inculcate the Aryan spirit.[34]

Karl long retained his lack of enthusiasm for the *JV*. His temperament failed to mesh with the organization's regimentation, its activities and training routine, or its leadership structure. He objected to being led, ordered about, and drilled by mere children, including erstwhile friends who had risen to command the unit in

---

32. Zentner, 17.
33. Overy, 31. Also, Anneliese Samhuber Baumann, interview by Author, 28 December 2004. For some reason the *Kinder, Kirche, Küche* emphasis never was strongly pursued by the leaders of the *BDM* unit in Brambauer to which *Fräulein* Samhuber belonged.
34. Horn, 646.

accordance with the organization's leadership doctrine. Consequently, the lowly and unhappy *Pimpf* missed probably more meetings than he attended. While his unit drilled rank and file to high-pitched commands of *Rechts* and *Links,* the recalcitrant Baumann spent Saturdays exploring the woods behind his home or sitting in the sun reading adventure books about courageous seafarers and their exploits.[35]

"Are you a *Jungvolk*," the local cinema manager inquired one day when she saw Karl walking alone past the neighborhood movie house.

Karl's affirmative reply drew an admonition from the proprietress.

"You don't play with that boy again, that Jewish boy," meaning Felix Treidel, one of Karl's best friends and his closest neighbor.

"If you don't play with him again, I'll give you a pass for the cinema so you won't have to pay," the woman promised.

Karl voiced no response, but knew inwardly that he would not trade his friendship with Felix for a few free movies. Treidel was several years older but always treated Baumann with kindness; in return, Karl liked the boy immensely. There would be no tradeoff, *Jungvolk* membership or not.

Resistance to full and enthusiastic participation in the Nazi youth movement bore significant penalties, as many thousands of young people discovered to their misfortune and regret. The successes and failures of each member were duly recorded in a performance book that followed the child through the entire Nazi youth movement.[36] The book served either as a passport for future success or an indictment against the holder. Karl realized only too late that his indiscreet opposition to the dictates of the *Jungvolk* had produced far-reaching and lasting consequences.

Adolf Hitler understood that a concerted effort to indoctrinate the population was necessary to perpetuate the Nazi ideal.[37] The *Führer* tended to make important speeches at 10:00 in the morning; at the Brambauer *Volkschule*, students and teachers alike routinely convened in the music room to listen with rapt attention to the radio as Hitler's voice thundered across the airwaves. Radio news broadcasts extolled significant achievements in the reawakened and rearmed *Vaterland,* and were carefully crafted by the Propaganda Ministry to stir the patriotic and martial passions of listeners.

---

35. Translation: Right! Left!
36. Shirer, 253.
37. Overy, 42.

On 14 February 1939, barely two months before he finished his final school year, Karl and his classmates crowded near the school's radio as the christening ceremony for the battleship *Bismarck* crackled from the speaker. His mind's eye imagined the exciting scene of the giant warship sliding down the slipway at Hamburg's Blohm und Voß shipyard in the wake of an uncharacteristically short but electrifying fifteen-minute speech by Adolf Hitler. Many a schoolboy listened and fancied himself turned out with a crisp blue Kriegsmarine uniform, standing at attention on the main deck of the battleship while thousands cheered and rendered the Nazi salute toward *Bismarck's* towering bow.[38]

In April 1939, the last springtime of uneasy peace before the Second World War was unleashed upon Europe, fourteen year-old Karl Baumann completed his eighth year in *Volkschule* and bade farewell to a schoolboy's mundane existence. The strong-willed teenager resolved to become self-sufficient and eagerly left behind the classroom to pursue a technical trade that promised a comfortable and secure future. He confidently assessed his prospects for success amid the frenetic national and economic revival that symbolized the new Germany of Adolf Hitler and the Third *Reich*. The nation now seemed to surge with electricity, a miraculous transformation from the malaise of the 1920s and early thirties. The *Führer's* clarion call for all Germans to serve the Fatherland and dedicate *Alles für Deutschland* still failed to strike a responsive chord in young Baumann's heart and mind.[39] Though he sought privileges and responsibilities of adulthood, he enthusiastically embraced the less martial and more carefree distractions of youth.

The halcyon days of the radio era inspired Karl to pursue a vocational education in radio technology, from which he hoped to establish himself as a skilled radio technician. First he needed to locate a firm willing to hire him as an apprentice and teach him the skills necessary to build and repair radio transmitters and receivers. His initial search for an employer about a month before he was graduated from *Volkschule* revealed there were no such job openings in Brambauer. He then made inquiries and explored possibilities in neighboring communities. After several weeks he finally located a retail storefront in the neighboring town of Lünen that sold and repaired radios; the firm was willing to take him on as an apprentice. When Karl applied for a worker's permit at the Lünen employment office, however, his carefully crafted plan was obstructed by the bureaucratic vagaries of the totalitarian state. The National Socialist government operated

---

38. Robert D. Ballard, *The Discovery of the Bismarck* (Toronto: Madison Press Books, 1990), 16.
39. Translation: Everything for Germany.

under the philosophy that the general public was unable to rule itself either directly or indirectly, and thus forever and always was subject to the *Führerprinzip*. Conferred with such authority, the Lünen employment officer declared that he would not issue a worker's permit to allow the youngster from Brambauer to work outside his home community.

Karl returned home, frustrated that his goals for the future had been thwarted at the very outset. Armed with his required *Volkschule* report book, he shortly visited the Brambauer employment office to inquire about job openings in other fields and vocations. The employment officer performed a critical review of the official documents as he scrutinized the boy himself. Karl's *Volkschule* records duly revealed his single black mark—his untoward schoolhouse reprimand. The official handed back the school record book, then issued his decision flatly and with finality.

"Your father is a coal mine worker. On April first you come back here and we will give you a permit to work in a mine." The dreadful declaration struck Karl like a hammer blow. Stunned and embittered by the official's pronouncement, the dejected youth trod home to his grandmother's house, where he vented his displeasure over the failure his job-hunting efforts had wrought.

Fourteen year-old Karl Baumann, in pursuit of work, was ordered by a *Reich* bureaucrat to find a job in a Ruhr coal mine like the Victoria Mathias operation near Essen.

"Karl, come here. I have something to show you," *Oma* intoned as she held out a small news article she recently had cut out of the local newspaper. The boy read the bold title line of the clipping: "Who would like to be a sailor?" Karl scrutinized the details about a training ship used to educate would-be officers for a merchant shipping company, and realized a new opportunity might present itself if he was willing to pursue the possibility. He might not yet be condemned, he thought, to the dark drudgery of a coal mine and the distressing and back-breaking conditions that miners endured day after day.

Karl never contemplated living and working at sea until then, but desperately searched his memory for a background of experiences to justify pursuing the opportunity. He did not find much. He liked to read adventure books such as The Flying Dutchman and other exciting stories about sailing ships and rugged seafarers. He never had visited the ocean, but certainly he loved to swim and found the water at the mill pond very much to his liking. Karl then considered the costs of answering a call to the sea. He would leave the comforts of home and family for the first time in his life. No longer would he enjoy the long, carefree summer days when he swam and relaxed at the mill pond. He would regret parting from lifelong friends and schoolmates, among them his pal Felix and a little girl named Anneliese Samhuber he had known since the second grade. Despite the hardships he had endured, life in Brambauer had been predictable and generally pleasant after all. Regardless, he clearly realized he would have to begin a new life altogether to resist the reach and grasp of the Ruhr mines. Once again hopeful to begin a career of his own choice, Karl Baumann then and there affirmed his intention to become a sailor—a *Matrose*.

2

Cabin Boy

Karl wrote to the shipping company in Hamburg to request details of the selection process for the officer's training school, but the reply he eventually received described only the company's training program for cabin boys. Downcast but curious, he read through the program literature, and upon further consideration reluctantly concluded the program provided the only realistic opportunity for him to stay out of the mines. He was disappointed to learn, however, that boys accepted for the training program were required to pay tuition for their first year of study. The required thirty *Reichsmarks* seemed an almost insurmountable obstacle at the time, and might as well have been three hundred or three thousand *RM* instead. Karl's hopes again seemed to have been quashed, until one of his mother's sisters offered to pay the tuition. An even more formidable obstacle then emerged and appeared likely to derail his efforts to avert a shortened lifetime shoveling coal beneath the sandy Ruhr plain. The shipping company asked to see his *Jungvolk* records to determine his fitness for training within the constructs of the National Socialist precepts of duty and loyalty to the *Führer*.

Karl had no choice but to send the requested documentation, which clearly indicated his lack of enthusiasm and attendance in the Nazi youth movement. He waited anxiously to receive the verdict company officials had cast upon his patriotic deportment. In due course, a curt letter from the company stated the cabin boy training program was closed to him. Someone in the company either had determined Karl would be disinclined to pursue their training program with the requisite amount of interest and discipline, or in his own zeal for Nazi ideology had become perturbed with the boy's lack of loyalty to the *Reich*. The verdict depressed Karl but did not surprise him.

Fortunately, in short order he obtained a second opportunity to go to sea. By some means the Hamburg *Seemanns-Heuerstelle*, the official employment agency for merchant seamen, learned Karl was interested in seaman's work and mailed an offer to help him find work on one of the ships that sailed out of Hamburg.

The rapidly expanding armed forces had conscripted a considerable supply of manpower from the merchant fleets. The resulting shortage of merchant seamen was so worrisome that the *Reich* waived the rule that required one's local employment office to approve all employment arrangements. Karl replied at once, and accepted the offer with gratitude for the opportunity he had been given. Within days the agency had completed arrangements for him to travel to Hamburg.

On the morning of 1 May 1939, Karl Baumann emerged from the upstairs bedroom he had shared for years with one of his uncles. The two small suitcases he carried contained most of his few worldly possessions: several sets of clothes and the bedclothes he would need aboard ship. His last days at *Oma's* had been no different from any others, except that *Oma* had taught Karl how to wash his clothes. From now on he would be fully responsible to make sure to keep his mind, body, soul, and clothing clean and sanitary. Downstairs, his stepmother Melitta waited with her suitcase in hand to accompany him to Hamburg. Without formality and with few words, *Oma* and Karl bade each other goodbye; *Oma* knew her grandson was profoundly grateful for the love and support she had given him in his mother's absence, but did not expect a long and tearful farewell. Outside her home *Oma* talked with Melitta while Karl watched the approaching streetcar that would stop for them almost at his grandmother's front door. At last, his long journey into adulthood began as he and Melitta boarded the *Straßenbahn* and settled into their seats for the ten-kilometer trip to Dortmund's main train station. Karl glanced back to see *Oma* one last time as the streetcar pulled away from her house—his home—and felt the first of many conflicting emotions that attended his ascent into the new life he had chosen to pursue.

With third-class tickets in hand Karl and Melitta boarded the Hamburg-bound *D-Zug*, an express train, and found seats on the wooden benches in one of the compartments that divided the car into sections. Promptly at noon, the steam whistle screamed from the big engine in front of the train; as its echo resounded through the cavernous *Hauptbahnhof*, late arriving passengers burdened with luggage ran to board the cars. The train then lurched to a start and slowly pulled away from the Dortmund station. Within a few kilometers the *D-Zug* built up a head of steam that propelled it at high speed across the Ruhr plain toward Münster, Osnabrück, and Hamburg. Between the three two-minute stops along the route, Karl and his stepmother engaged in small talk as buildings and trees next to the tracks flashed by their compartment window. Karl felt a kinship with her, but as an aunt rather than a mother figure; after all, she was his late mother's sister. He could not bring himself to call Melitta *Mutter*, even after Karl was offered money if only he would confer that honor upon her. Rather, he and his sisters would continue to call her by her given name for most of her life. The train pulled into Hamburg's main station at 18:00 sharp. The tired travelers were glad their six-hour journey was over; the hard wooden benches quickly had become uncomfortable for the third-class passengers.

Hamburg existed largely because of its huge inland port—the second largest in Europe—on the Elbe River. Fully one third of its 1,200,000 residents worked in the shipping or export industries. A large network of railways terminated in the city and at the port, where hundreds of huge cargo cranes created a steel girder skyline around the harbor. The old city itself had been largely destroyed by a terrific fire during the mid-1800s, but had been rebuilt and regenerated as the life-blood of its conservative, hard-working populace.[1] The seafaring character of Hamburg projected a hard-edged courseness that was perceptible and often unsettling to newcomers.

Karl and Melitta trudged through the unfamiliar streets to find a hotel they could afford. Family money was so scarce that little was available for them to use during the trip. They finally located an old hotel not far from the harbor, but soon realized they had not stumbled onto a bargain. As Melitta settled into her bed that night the slats that had barely supported the bedsprings and mattress gave way and crashed to the floor. The levity of the moment helped alleviate some of Karl's apprehension over his new and inhospitable surroundings. Still, the sights and sounds of the bustling city that surrounded him were daunting. Four hundred kilometers now separated him from the familiar places and, except for his stepmother, those who knew and loved him. His eagerness to begin his new life was mitigated by fear of the unknown. The fourteen year-old struggled to find sleep that night.

The next morning Karl, with Melitta close at hand, reported to Hamburg's *Seemanns-Heuerstelle*. There he was interviewed, photographed, and sent to the agency's doctor for a physical examination. The doctor's office was located in the same building the *Heuerstelle* occupied, and in a few minutes the fledgling sailor was being probed, poked, and thoroughly evaluated to determine his fitness for the hard work that awaited him. One important test proved the boy was able to distinguish between red and green, the most important colors for nautical signals. With the physician's approval Karl returned to the *Heuerstelle* to complete his paperwork. *Heuerstelle* officials then set to work to find a ship in need of a cabin boy. In the meantime, Baumann had to attend to yet another bureaucratic

---

1.   Eugene Fodor, ed., *1936...On the Continent; An Entertaining Travel Annual* (New York: Fodor's Travel Guides, 1986), 519-523.

requirement the *Reich* had imposed. He visited the *HJ* office in Hamburg to request a transfer from his old *Jungvolk* unit. Since membership in the *Hitler Jugend* had become compulsory in 1936, he was required to join a local *HJ* unit while he lived in and sailed out of the port of Hamburg. He applied for and obtained an official transfer to the *Marine Hitler Jugend*, the natural choice for a young prospective seaman to satisfy his obligation to the state.

An *MHJ* official named Richelmann reviewed Karl's *JV* records as well as the rejection letter lately received from the shipping company. As Karl looked on he noticed the man wore a special lapel pin adorned with a golden-rimmed swastika; Mr. Richelmann was one of the first ten thousand members of the Nazi party.

"What do you have in mind to do when you get older?" the official inquired.

"Well, go to sea now, and when I'm old enough, join the Navy," Karl explained.

"No, you're not going to do that," the man declared to the boy's surprise and consternation. Would his past haunt him forever, Baumann wondered.

"I have something for you," Richelmann continued. "I have permission from Berlin to have the Hamburg-Finkenwärder fishing fleet give you the experience of twenty months on a sailing ship. When you have finished your twenty months, come back to me. I will give you a whaling ship for thirty-six months of steam-ship time you must have. Then, with the money you have saved, you can go to navigator's school."

Karl was relieved nearly beyond words. Good fortune seemed finally to have smiled upon him, and he enthusiastically accepted the *MHJ* official's offer of assistance. The plan seemed to guarantee success. Not only would he find work as a seaman, he concluded; he would become a career ship's officer with a secure income. Amid buoyed spirits and his celebratory mood for the good tidings he had just received, he could never have contemplated that a world war would intervene to forever disrupt his career plans—and sweep him into its whirlwind.

That evening Karl and Melitta checked into a *Seemannsheim*, a boarding house operated for merchant seamen and their families, where the *Heuerstelle* had arranged for them to have rooms. Karl shared his room with a young cabin boy from Southeast Asia who had arrived by ship. Their room overlooked the port of Hamburg, which that night glittered and glowed under the bright lights of the fish markets and warehouses that lined the quays, from the hundreds of ships that sat in the harbor, and from countless cranes, smokestacks, and ships' masts that jutted into the sky. Lights everywhere reflected off the gleaming surface of the Elbe River and created a mesmerizing panorama. The stirring scene fascinated the boys, who felt pride in the fact that they were to be even minor participants in the living land-and waterscape that spread so magnificently before them.

Karl reported to the *Seemanns-Heuerstelle* again on the morning of 3 May and learned that his employment had been secured for a ship of the fishing fleet on the harbor island of Hamburg-Finkenwärder. Shortly Karl and Melitta boarded a ferry to the island and found the vessel that had been appointed his home and workplace. Emblazoned on her bow was the registration number HF 186, which identified her homeport as Hamburg-Finkenwärder. Better known to her owners and her crew as *Flora*, HF 186 was a wooden two-masted sailing ship—actually a *Motorsegeler*—a motor-sailing ship fitted with a small, thirty-six horsepower engine to provide secondary propulsion on calm, windless days. Nearly out of money, Melitta was anxious to return home. With few words and little emotion, she bade Karl goodbye and good luck, then returned to the ferry and the *Hauptbahnhof* to catch the next train bound for Dortmund. As he stood on the dock in the shadow of HF 186, he felt dwarfed by its presence. Not quite a child and not quite an adult, now alone in the strange city, in several days the youngster would take on his first real job wholly unaware and unprepared for the tasks and responsibilities he would be ordered to perform aboard *Flora* and in port.

HF 186 was a small vessel by commercial standards, built and outfitted solely for fishing. She contained few creature comforts or amenities other than essential gear used to catch and haul large quantities of fish to market. Her deck was apportioned simply, with the wheelhouse at the stern, a lifeboat at the bow, winches to pull long rope fishing nets and to haul them in, and finally the nets themselves. A small area below deck was divided into living quarters for the ship's captain and his crew of three. When the ship was in her homeport the crewmen slept on board but usually dined nearby at the skipper's home, where his wife prepared the meals for them.

Karl Baumann, the newest and youngest member of the four-man crew, naturally filled the bottom rung in *Flora's* ladder of authority when he was hired on as a cabin boy on 5 May 1939. Officially he held the position of *Schiffsjunge*, the ship's boy. The next man up the ladder was Fritz Kuhn, a young Austrian from Wiener-Neustadt who was a *Leichtmatrose*, a civilian sailor for the *Reich*. Above Kuhn was a man named Bernhard, a rough, frightening character who perfectly fit the stereotype of the grizzled old seaman with a dark past who seemed to have lost his surname. Bernhard lived hard and was experienced in every aspect of the sailor's trade. The captain of the ship was a thirty-six year-old seadog named Walter Kröger, whose absolute authority was unquestioned by his crew. He had spent years at sea and led his ship and crew with a no-nonsense style that could be fearsome. The crew's first impression of Karl was not conducive to their immediate acceptance of the boy into their circle of trusted sailors, nor was Karl impressed by the men he would work with shoulder to shoulder on the ship.

Identification page from Karl Baumann's *Seefahrtsbuch*; Hamburg, 1938.

Karl reported to the *Seemannsamt* on the morning of 6 May, where his *Heuerstelle* documentation was reviewed and he was issued a *Seefarhtsbuch,* the official passport all German civilian sailors were required to possess before they put to sea.[2] The little book detailed the rights and obligations set forth for every man and boy who sailed under the German flag. Most importantly, the *Seefahrtsbuch* provided essential identification data for the sailor and traced his maritime employment history. A small black and white head and shoulders photograph of the very young-looking Baumann was stapled onto page two above his signature, while page three listed vital statistics for the blond-haired, gray-eyed youth. Succeeding pages briefly described each ship upon which the holder sailed and noted the seaman's service record aboard the respective ship.

Karl boarded HF 186 and presented his *Seefahrtsbuch* to Kröger, who informed him the cabin boy's primary job was to cook three meals each day and wash the dishes afterward, then help the other crewmen wherever and in whichever capacity he was needed. Karl was terrified by the news; not only had he no sailing experience whatsoever, he had never learned to cook during his childhood years. Nonetheless, he resolved to learn the requisite skills and perform his duties as well as his training and accumulated skills would allow. He did not know how intensely his perseverance would be tested over the coming hours, days, and weeks.

The crew prepared *Flora* to sail into the North Sea later that day. Every activity, every sight, and every sound was an entirely new experience for Karl. Even the dialect the men spoke was new and very difficult for the boy to understand. When Kröger finally took the helm and motored away from the dock, Karl felt utterly alone in a world wholly unfamiliar, unsympathetic, and friendless. The ship soon cleared the harbor entrance and was steered into the Elbe traffic channel that it would take to the sea.

No one offered to break the tension with small talk, but remained at arm's length from Karl until the *Kapitän* called him belowdeck to the galley. There, Kröger was hunched over a small cookstove. To the cabin boy's dread, the skipper informed him it was time to start the evening meal. He announced the menu the cabin boy would need to prepare, and explained where the ship's supplies were stored. A frying pan of sliced potatoes soon sat atop the little stove. The captain leaned over the sizzling pan and talked as he turned over the potatoes with a spatula. Karl watched and listened intently as the skipper briefly explained exactly how he wanted the potatoes prepared.

"Don't you forget to put pepper on them when you turn them," the captain called over his shoulder while he strode toward the ladder to return topside. Karl nodded his understanding, and was left alone to sit on a stool in front of the stove. He soon became lost in thought while he watched the potatoes pop and

---

2.   Translation: *Seefahrtsbuch* means, literally, sea-travel book. The *Seemannsamt* exercised bureaucratic authority over Germany's civilian sailors.

sizzle in the cast iron skillet and fish fry in another. Overwhelmed at the newness of his situation and all that was around him, he began to make mental journeys back home to the warm familiarity of family and friends. Some minutes later, while adrift in his daydreams, he failed to hear Kröger's approach behind him. Suddenly, out of nowhere, a resounding slap across the face brought Karl back to the reality of the present. The skipper had discovered his new cook lost in thought and clearly observed Karl's failure to follow express instructions.

"I told you to put pepper on those potatoes," Kröger bellowed as he gestured toward the frying pan. Shaken by the captain's harsh rebuke for such a trivial infraction, the *Schiffsjunge* thereafter focused all of his attention on a constant vigil over the stove. To ward off future assaults he turned the potatoes every few minutes and, as he did so, liberally blanketed them with pepper. The aroma of fried fish and potatoes soon wafted from *Flora's* galley and dissipated on the breeze that blew inland from the North Sea. When mealtime finally arrived, the hungry captain and crew bounded down to the steps to the galley. They congregated around the stove to stab at a pile of fried flounder and ladle fried potatoes onto their plates. With complete informality the ravenous men tore into their food, but their enthusiasm was quickly thwarted when the thickly peppered tubers unleashed an incendiary assault inside their mouths and throats. Streams of vulgarities immediately rang into the fledgling cabin boy's ears. Karl fought back tears as the men expressed outraged contempt for their new *Schiffsjunge*. Over succeeding weeks he would learn many such lessons of humility—and humiliation—aboard the little *Motorsegeler*.

Flora continued to chug her way slowly down the hundred-kilometer stretch of the Elbe between Hamburg and Cuxhaven on the North Sea coast. Kröger ordered Fritz Kuhn to strike the mainsail when dusk began to settle over the western horizon. Still chastened by his first upbraiding from the crew, Karl lent a hand to help Kuhn haul down and furl the heavy canvas. As he manhandled the sail he noticed a row of large houses perched high upon the sixty-meter bank that overlooked the river; the warm glow of interior lights twinkled and shined through their many windows. He stared at the placid scene and imagined families inside happily congregated in their kitchens, dining rooms, and parlors. The beautiful imagery represented everything that was good about life, love, family, and home. Almost suddenly a surge of emotion swelled forth from deep inside, and the youth helplessly burst into sobs of loneliness, fear, and homesickness. His own world had been reduced to the length and breadth of HF 186, and the ship's crew appeared to despise his intrusion into their lives. As he fought to regain his composure he was reeled around with a violent jerk. Bernhard, the crusty old seaman, had grabbed Karl by the shirt collar.

"You cry once more and I'm going to beat you!" Bernhard yelled as his rough hands tightly gripped the boy and scraped against his neck. Karl knew the old man meant what he said, but throughout the voyage he succumbed to gut-wrenching bouts of emotion. The accumulated anxieties crowded into Karl's thoughts and overwhelmed any confidence he had possessed before the voyage. Irrational in his grief, he convinced himself that his family had written him off as if he were lost at sea. Alone in the darkness below deck, he lay in his bunk at night and cried anguished tears while *Flora* creaked and rocked with the rough waves of the North Sea.

"Karl, go out and see who is shaking the ship," Bernhard ordered with a spiteful grin. The newest member of the crew would have to endure no small amount of hazing and similar indignities to earn his way into *Flora's* small fraternity. The adversarial climate became so depressing that even good-natured joking was a dreadful experience. The ribbing, seasickness, homesickness, and backbreaking work helping tend the heavy sails and long fishing nets finally conspired with such severity that he soon gave up all desire to become a seaman. He flatly announced to Fritz and Bernhard he wanted to go home. The men told him that if he quit his job, his allotted percentage of expenses for food and fuel would be deducted from the small amount of pay he would earn for the voyage. The boy would not have enough pay remaining to buy a train ticket back to Brambauer, they declared condescendingly. In desperation Karl asked the men to lend him the money he would need. Kröger sternly told the crewman that no one was to lend the boy any money; they should tell him instead that he needed to stay with the ship.

Out in the cold North Sea, *Flora* dragged long nets through schools of flounder during her weeklong voyage. Several times a day the crew hauled in the nets, sorted out and cleaned the edible fish, then dumped their catch into baskets that were stored in her large hold below deck. *Flora's* catch of sixty to eighty baskets of flounder was destined for the huge Hamburg-Altona fish market, where it would be weighed and sold. *Flora* sailed into the port of Cuxhaven at the end of Karl's first week at sea with a full load of fish in her hold. There Baumann resolved to leave the ship and her crew; in the depths of frustration and anxiety he felt they would never become his substitute home and family. He approached the skipper and declared his resignation from his lowly post; surprisingly, Kröger consoled the youth with empathy and an unusual prescription to overcome depression.

"Whenever you feel bad," the skipper said as he pointed to the top of the mast, "just climb up there and think things over. You will feel better." Desperate for relief but skeptical nonetheless, Karl took Kröger's strange advice and pulled himself up the steel O-rings that connected the sail to the tall wooden mainmast. A glorious panoramic view of the port of Cuxhaven spread out before him when he reached the top of the mast. Unexpectedly, after awhile the *Schiffsjunge* felt a glimmer of renewed hope and excitement. The numerous ships and crewmen below him created an intriguing scene of frenzied activity. He began to feel better about his present situation and somehow realized that in time his burden would be lifted as unfamiliar surroundings and people became familiar and more acceptable to him—and as they began to accept him. He clambered down the mainmast to the deck, resolved to stay aboard *Flora* and endure whatever hardships his shipmates and his work cast upon him. Though neither the captain nor his veteran crewmen had commended him for his early efforts, they could not avoid the conclusion that their cabin boy was proving himself to be a hard worker, highly intelligent, a quick study and astute observer.

Karl's gradually-won membership into *Flora's* crew was not without difficulty and setbacks. After his second voyage into the North Sea, *Flora* made port in late evening to unload the week's catch at the bustling fish market. The fish-laden ship nudged against a quay and her hawsers were quickly tied to the mooring posts. Darkness descended as haggard seamen toiled under the lights that illuminated the market area. Fritz quickly jumped into the cargo hold and told Karl to balance the crates of fish while a dockside crane lifted the catch through the hatchway. Using a foot-long hook to grapple a rope handle, the boy struggled to lean over the gaping opening to steady each sixty-pound crate as it emerged from the hold. Inevitably, he lost his tenuous balance with one of the containers, which seconds later tipped over and dumped sixty pounds of flounder directly onto Kuhn. Covered with slimy brine, Fritz exploded into a rage of expletives and berated the youngster for his incompetence. Kröger, having witnessed the accident just as he returned to the ship from dockside, overheard the commotion and quickly stepped into the fray.

Karl Baumann's first ship, *Flora* (HF 186), aboard which he worked as a
cabin boy; Hamburg-Finkenwärder, 1939.

"You should have given the easier job to Karl!" the *Kapitän* thundered as he
glared into Kuhn's squinting eyes. Karl realized then and there that Kröger had
begun to accept his *Schiffsjunge* as a bona fide member of the crew rather than a
hopeless fledgling to be scorned. When Kröger's temper had cooled sufficiently
he informed Karl that mail was waiting for him at their homeport in nearby
Finkenwärder. The news comforted the boy like a soothing balm. No matter that
Fritz had unleashed a stream of vitriol toward him; Karl's family had not forgotten their young son, grandson, and nephew. He soon retrieved two parcels—a
package of clothing and other welcome gifts as well as a letter that told him all
was well in Brambauer. The lifeline from home sufficiently mollified Karl's
immediate desire to abandon the fishing fleet; cash in his pocket also helped considerably.

After the men unloaded their weekly haul they met at the skipper's house, where each was paid a percentage of the sale price according to the total weight of the fish. Karl's pay was set at 2 percent of the total amount that had been paid for the catch. His first voyage had yielded twenty *Reichsmarks*—untold wealth and a new sense of well-being for a child of the Great Depression. With money that weighed heavily in his pocket, the next day Karl trod down the busy and once notorious Reeperbahn section of Hamburg, where street children routinely followed sailors and begged ten *Pfennings* for ice cream. At a seaman's clothing store he bought his first pair of bell-bottomed sailor's trousers, festooned with a double row of buttons in front. He then made his way to a small restaurant where he feasted on potato pancakes, potato salad, and milk with sugar. Basking in the glow of self-satisfaction, he fancied himself already a veteran sailor. With his spirits lifted, young Baumann vowed stubborn determination to persevere, learn, and succeed in his chosen vocation, and to adopt the rakish bearing and appearance of a *Matrose*.

Schiffsjunge Baumann remained with the little ship and rapidly perfected his cooking skills and sailing acumen to win his shipmates' grudging respect. His bouts of homesickness dissipated and eventually disappeared altogether, but would forever remain a distant unpleasant memory. He became thoroughly accustomed to the sailor's hearty existence after several months aboard HF 186. The seaman's ways of life became second nature; among other rituals he now washed his hands in a mixture of seawater and cod liver oil without hesitation. In turn, Kröger, Fritz and even Bernhard finally accepted him fully as a member of the crew. As a measure of growing fondness for the boy, Fritz and Bernhard gave Karl the nickname Kuddel.[3] The source of the strange moniker was a dialectical aberration by which the skipper, with his unique Hamburger accent, pronounced Karl as "Kardel." The nickname stuck. He made friends with other *Schiffsjungen* and enjoyed the company of his new teenaged companions, all of whom swapped seafaring experiences and entertained each other with adventures of their own creation. With his crewmates Karl worked hard, laughed heartily, and ate very well—duty free Danish sausages and creamery butter, for example—even when wartime rationing was invoked by the *Reich*. As he became fully comfortable with his new life he preferred the excitement of the port and the sea over the more mundane existence of home, family and friends he had left in Brambauer. He once intercepted the ship's mail and found a letter from one of his aunts; she appealed to the boy to return home for an overdue vacation and included money

---

3.   Kuddel is pronounced "Koo-dle."

for his train fare. Karl sent the money back, and explained untruthfully that the *Kapitän* would not give him time off work to make the trip.

Baumann toughened to the rigors of a seaman's life when he sailed with the North Sea fishing fleet.

While *Flora* bobbed peacefully upon the North Sea waves on 1 September 1939, the full might of German military power smashed into neighboring Poland in the opening phase of outright hostilities that quickly exploded into the Second World War. The greatest and most terrible catastrophe of the twentieth century had begun. Except when coastal waters north of Cuxhaven froze over and forced the fishing fleets to stay in port, *Flora* and her crew harvested a fish crop that helped feed both civilians and soldiers of a nation at war. Karl was not terribly surprised to learn that war had been declared; he had anticipated the announcement for two months. He recalled a conversation that had taken place at the end of a July voyage after *Flora* had delivered her latest catch to the fish market. As Kröger settled the sale transaction Mr. Richelmann, the *Marine Hitler Jugend* official who had found work for Baumann aboard *Flora*, boarded the ship. Fritz Kuhn had completed his twenty-month obligation aboard *Flora* and had asked

Richelmann to arrange a transfer to a whaling steamer for his thirty-six month training period. The *MHJ* official directed Kuhn's attention to the sleek 28,000 ton *Cap Arcona* of the Sud-Amerika Line as it slowly edged into a nearby dock. The majestic passenger liner had proudly plowed the high seas on long journeys throughout the world.

"Fritz, you see that ship there, the *Cap Arcona*? She won't go out anymore. We will have war! You need to stay here, on this ship."[4] When Karl overheard the conversation he could not believe the old Nazi's chilling war forecast. Certainly the *Führer* would not allow Germany to be embroiled in another war, he thought. All the same, he pondered the potential effects a war might have upon his own chances to transfer to a whaling steamer and then to navigator's school. He had good reason to speculate about the course of his future.

The Second World War came, and with it the new and terrifying tactic: *Blitzkrieg*. The Germans unleashed their Lightning War maelstrom across the Polish border and perfected it in the Low Countries and France. In the wake of the phenomenally successful campaigns, Germans everywhere rejoiced and praised the Wehrmacht and their *Führer*.[5] They first had hoped the war might end in 1940 with minimal casualties and disruption in their lives. Most had greeted the outbreak of war the previous September entirely without enthusiasm or fanfare, but by May even skeptics celebrated the brilliant and seemingly endless victories.[6] Radio reports, newspaper accounts, and movie newsreels exulted with news that the enemy had been thrown off the continent in utter defeat at the French coast town of Dunkirk. Only a miraculous seaborne rescue by a rag-tag armada of British navy and merchant vessels and numbers of small pleasure craft had saved more than 338,000 encircled British and French troops to fight another day.[7] A month later, Germans collectively breathed a sigh of relief when France was con-

---

4. The *Cap Arcona* did sail again—to her doom. The former luxury liner and the passenger liner Thielbek were transporting concentration camp inmates away from advancing Soviet forces when they were bombed and sunk in Lübeck Bay on 3 May 1945, by British fighter-bombers. The RAF pilots were unaware the ships' passengers were concentration camp inmates. Only a few of the 7,500 inmates aboard the ships survived the attack. See *The Holocaust; A History of the Jews of Europe During the Second World War*, by Martin Gilbert (New York: Holt, Rinehart and Winston, 1985), 806.
5. Translation: Wehrmacht referred to all German armed forces—the Heer (Army), Kriegsmarine (Navy), and the Luftwaffe (Air Force).
6. Shirer, 597.
7. Shirer, 737.

quered after the nearly total collapse of its huge but thoroughly demoralized army. As if caught in the eye of a terrible hurricane, Europeans that summer experienced a temporary and uneasy lull in fighting. All too soon the relative calm would be replaced by the unprecedented fury of total war.

Probably few were more surprised or elated by the unbroken string of German victories than Hitler himself. Indeed, with the British Expeditionary Force humiliated at Dunkirk and a seemingly irreplaceable wealth of heavy arms and equipment abandoned or destroyed on the beach, the *Führer* was convinced he could force England to sue for peace. Hitler and the naval High Command believed the Kriegsmarine could encircle the British Isles with an impregnable ring of U-boats and surface vessels to cut off the vital lifeline of food and commodities the island nation counted upon for its very survival. During a strategy conference late in May, however, Kriegsmarine Grand Admiral Erich Raeder persuaded Hitler to drive the English to their knees by a more daring and aggressive tactic: invasion.[8]

Raeder first broached the idea to invade Britain when the war in Europe began the previous September. Hitler had tabled the idea at the time due to its political and military impracticality, but now concluded that British forces had been so soundly beaten that he could destroy the Empire on its home island. With France conquered and occupied, the Wehrmacht controlled the necessary collection points for troops and equipment, ports of embarkation, and airfields along the coast to serve as a springboard for the invasion across the narrow English Channel. Tantalized by the strategic advantage he would achieve with the western front closed to attack, and the enormous prestige he would gain among friends and enemies alike, Hitler ordered his military chiefs to plan a massive operation to invade Britain. He set a target date for mid-September 1940, only a few short months away.[9]

Operation Sea Lion, as the cross-Channel invasion plan was called, was calculated initially to require forty Army divisions, about 800,000 men. The vast majority of the invasion force would make beachhead landings along the Southeast and Southern English coast from landing craft that would brave the treacherous waters of the Channel. The number of divisions committed to the landing operation later was reduced to thirteen, or 260,000 men, in the mistaken belief that the British could not mount a defense large enough to consume the energy

8. *Führer Conferences on Naval Affairs, 1939-1945* (Annapolis: Naval Institute Press, 1990), 110.
9. *Conferences*, 111, 115.

of forty divisions. With even thirteen divisions, Admiral Raeder faced a daunting task to assemble a large fleet to transport the invasion troops.[10]

In terms of men and equipment, his Kriegsmarine was by far the smallest military branch of the Third *Reich*. The burgeoning world power that wielded such fearsome military force possessed not one landing craft designed to disembark troops upon hostile shores. Hitler and his commanders-in-chief never contemplated their conquests would be purchased so cheaply and quickly. Consequently, they were largely unprepared and ill-equipped to mount a large-scale invasion of England in the summer months of 1940. The resourceful Raeder, however, resolved to assemble from any and all available sources the ships necessary to transport the invasion force. In so doing he stripped the seas, then the rivers and canals of the *Vaterland* and the occupied countries, of virtually every floating vessel that was deemed seaworthy.[11] Little HF 186 and her crew were called to war, but without *Schiffsjunge* Baumann.

On 18 August 1940, with *Flora* commandeered by the Kriegsmarine, Karl and his new crewmate Karl Voss were abruptly released from duty and told they should return home. Potentially in the midst of a terrific battle, the little fishing trawler would be no place for younger teenagers. With little ceremony the *Seemannsamt* collected the two boys' *Seefahrtsbüche*, gave them train fare to return home, and bade them farewell. A year and three months after he had left home Karl reluctantly returned from the sea. He had become a different person than the youngster his family and friends had remembered: more wise to the ways of the world, much more knowledgeable and confident of his own strengths and skills, and more physically mature.

Karl had welcomed Voss as a cabin boy for *Flora* in the late fall of 1939. Both boys hailed from northern Germany, so their similar backgrounds melded into immediate understanding and friendship. Young Voss was the same age as Baumann and was the product of a disrupted family; he too was fourteen years old when he left home for the sea but already was experienced far beyond his years. He had served as a cabin boy aboard the steamer *Cordoba*, which had been sailing off the Brazilian coast when war was declared on 1 September 1939. The steamer had proceeded in haste for Germany, via Spain, and the safety of home waters, but encountered a British naval blockade off the German coast. With skill and daring the ship and crew sailed under cover of darkness between a cordon of warships poised to demolish any German vessel foolish enough to attempt to run the

---

10. *Conferences*, 121.
11. Rich, 160-161.

blockade. Safely home, the skipper and his crew were celebrated and commended for their courageous feat. Voss was a decorated civilian sailor at the age of fourteen, which greatly impressed *Schiffsjunge* Baumann.

Karl Voss had transferred to *Flora* from a fishing trawler that now rested on the floor of the North Sea. He happily related how his grizzled old skipper had taken to fishing in restricted waters outside the established fishing lanes. One day as the trawler and her sister ship dragged long fishing nets through the sea in search of herring, Voss's boat snagged a large unrecognizable object. The skipper maneuvered the trawler into a wide circle that converged on the net so his crew could inspect their mysterious catch. The curious fishermen leaned over the railing to take a closer look at the object, which still was some distance from the boat.

In a blinding instant the sea erupted with a deafening roar as a geyser of water surged high into the air. The trawler had netted a giant naval mine, which exploded with such force that it ripped away the boat's stern. Cold North Sea waves quickly swamped the deck as Voss and the skipper tried frantically but unsuccessfully to release the lifeboat that was securely griped in the davits of its stowage cradle. When the deck disappeared underwater and he lost sight of the skipper, the *Schiffsjunge* jumped onto the mainsail that stretched to the top of the mast, and clambered up the canvas shroud as the boat's pilot house sank beneath the waves. During his headlong ascent his head slammed into an unseen rigging block, and his swirling consciousness nearly gave way to total darkness. Before he could regain his wits he then became entangled in the shroud line and was unable to release himself before the top of the mast disappeared into the North Sea. Nearly out of breath, he somehow broke free and bobbed to the surface near the floating skipper. Relieved still to be alive, the stunned duo floated silently in their life vests above the scene of the disaster and pondered their next move. Voss had been so terrified that he would later claim he sweated underwater while he frantically struggled to untangle himself from the shroud line.

The final act of the bizarre incident then became forever seared into Voss's memory. While the two gently rode the undulating waves, deep below them the buoyant wooden lifeboat on the sinking ship broke loose from its stowage cradle and rocketed toward the surface. As Voss kept his eyes glued upon the *Kapitän* to make sure the waves did not separate them in the vast expanse of sea, suddenly and without warning the lifeboat slammed into the old sailor from below. The terrific force of the blow flung the man completely out of the water and into the air, and with wildly flailing arms and legs the skipper then splashed ignominiously back into the brine. Coughing and sputtering, the skipper's senses returned enough that he pulled himself into the lifeboat that nearly killed him. He then stood up unsteadily and raised his arms high to the sky as he stared into the heavens. One finger had been ripped off and blood streamed down his lacerated face.

"What a comedy!" the battered and exasperated old skipper bellowed at the top of his lungs before he collapsed into the bottom of the boat. Voss clambered into the lifeboat, barely able to stanch his laughter despite his near-death experience.

Flora was one of the large number of fishing vessels ice-locked into the port of Cuxhaven during the coldest winter weeks of 1939-1940. Unable to net the fish that provided their livelihoods, seamen scoured the area to find work and earn at least a pittance for spending money. Baumann and Voss once were hired to unload coal from a boxcar, a backbreaking day's work in exchange for twelve *Reichmarks* the two divided evenly. Their pay was enough to sustain the boys and occasionally provide the luxury of an evening at the movies. In port Baumann, Voss, and other fellow *Schiffsjungen* gathered to pass the time and otherwise enjoy themselves with teenagers' diversions. One afternoon four or five of the boys met aboard *Flora* to give each other haircuts, after which they planned to go to the movies on the money saved by having avoided the barber's chair. Voss's turn for a haircut gave the other boys a golden opportunity for mischief.

The conspiracy commenced as Karl surreptitiously hid all of the mirrors from view while another boy trimmed Voss's hair on the top and sides. The hapless cabin boy was wholly unaware, however, that the wise guy had trimmed a large swastika into the hair on back of the head. Another member of the brotherhood secretly covered the palm of one hand with stove soot, then placed his hand squarely upon Voss's forehead while he trimmed the victim's eyebrows. With the prank successfully executed, the boys agreed to take in the latest movie at a nearby cinema. With no mirrors in sight to check his haircut, Voss donned his jacket and crammed a hat down onto his head, then joined the group as they walked to the movie house. No one en route or inside the theater noticed Voss's peculiar visage until the end of a wartime public service film that was shown before the main feature. The film had introduced a slow-witted character named Tran who, as the foil of the story, was oblivious to the reality of the world around him. When the lights were turned on in the auditorium during the intermission Voss stood up to put on his coat and hat to leave. People nearby soon began to giggle and snicker, which attracted the attention of others around them. In seconds a wave of laughter spread outward and reached every corner of the theater as all eyes focused upon poor Voss. The boy with the abused forehead and hair stood utterly dumbfounded by the laughter, stares and fingers pointed toward him. He soon charged out of the theater, but not before the instigators of the prank spontaneously gave Voss the nickname Tran.

In mid-August 1940 Karl Baumann, with Tran in tow, arrived at *Oma*'s house in Brambauer. Karl chuckled as he recalled his first homecoming visit, when he had arrived in the darkness of late night. Since the house was locked, he had retrieved a beanpole and tapped on a second floor window to arouse the inhabitants inside. His sister Helga soon opened the window to see who or what had interrupted the early morning silence. Through sleep heavy senses she was unable to recognize the mature baritone voice that called for her to open the door, so she refused to let her brother into the house. Karl was rescued only when *Oma* appeared in the window a moment later and recognized him. Now the long-absent youth anticipated another warm welcome back into the family fold, and would enjoy the gladness and glow of loved ones and home. Voss, too, would delight in the embracing welcome Karl's family would extend to him.

The homecoming was short-lived. Just short of a month later, and much to their surprise, the former *Schiffsjungen* were back at sea. They had just settled into the satisfying routine of living at *Oma*'s and working at the Hermann Göring Werke, a giant aluminum factory fully engaged in war production, when the Brambauer employment office summoned the erstwhile sailors back to Hamburg at the urgent request of the *Seemannsamt*. The boys were surprised and irritated to receive the unexpected directive. Both had resolved that their sailing days were over for the foreseeable future; anyway, wartime work at the aluminum factory promised good wages, shorter hours, and a regular paycheck.

Baumann and Voss reported to the employment office to explain that they could not return immediately to Hamburg. Karl declared that they were hardly one week into their new jobs and had not yet been paid. Presently they had no money even to pay for room and board at *Oma*'s, nor had they funds for train fare for the return trip to Hamburg. The employment officer was utterly unmoved by the teenagers' dilemma.

"Either you go back to Hamburg now, or you can go to the *Arbeitslager*," the official snarled as he pointed an admonishing finger at them.[12] The boys were shaken by the first direct threat they had received from a Nazi bureaucrat. They well knew that under the *Führerprinzip* the official could back up his threat with action. With absolutely no further discussion, the boys stretched out their arms in the required salute, thundered out their best "*Heil Hitler*," and fled the locus of their rank indiscretion.

---

12. Translation: Concentration Camp.

In short order Baumann and Voss packed their belongings, bade farewells to *Oma* and the rest of the family, and took the streetcar to the Dortmund *Bahnhof* where they caught the next train bound for Hamburg. Karl settled into his seat and sighed with dejection and disappointment. He sorely regretted that he had not taken the opportunity to call upon attractive, petite Anneliese Samhuber during his brief homecoming. She and Karl had much in common as children of miners, and had known each other since they had attended the second grade together at *Volkschule*. Karl had grown quietly fond of Anneliese with the passing years. He pondered whether she would still like him since he had become a man of means and no longer a child. He had intended to contact her, he told himself, but things just did not work out. Despite all rationalization and contrived excuses, he recognized an awful truth about himself: in terms of dating and romance he was a coward. He had forfeited a golden opportunity to contact Anneliese rather than risk the prospect that she might reject his attention.

Anneliese Samhuber, age 18, in a wartime portrait; Brambauer, 1943.

The *Seemannsamt* in Hamburg greeted the boys with their *Seefahrtsbüche* and new ship assignments. Their new charge was the *Motorsegeler Cremona*, a coastal sailing vessel of 586 tons that had hauled cement and other bulk commodities. During Karl's tenure on board, *Cremona* sailed under the *Reichsdienstflagge*, which identified the merchant ship as a government-chartered vessel and her crew as employees of the *Reich*.[13] Whereas little *Flora* had transported fish for consumption, *Cremona* regularly transported fish of steel bent on destruction. On each eastward voyage along the edge of the Baltic Sea, from Eckernförde to the submarine base at Kiel, then to Gotenhafen in East Prussia, the unarmed coastal sailing ship carried a hefty cargo of eighty-six torpedoes without warheads.

German forces early in the war had captured and occupied the Polish Corridor and its port city of Gdynia. The Corridor, which in the aftermath of the First World War gave the newly reconstituted Poland a land lifeline to the sea, was an aberration in geopolitical boundaries that was heartily despised by many, if not most, Germans. First, it was legislated into being by the Versailles Treaty; most importantly, however, the Corridor had cut off East Prussia from the rest of the *Reich*. After Hitler's conquest of Poland reclaimed the lands within the Corridor, Gdynia was renamed Gotenhafen. The waters offshore became the site for the German Navy's *Torpedoversuchsanstalt*, or *TVA*, as it was best known. Wearing leather Kriegsmarine coats, trousers, and gloves to ward off thick layers of grease that covered each torpedo, Karl and his crewmates guided their cargo out of special stowage racks in *Cremona's* hold while a crane operator deftly lifted them through the hatchway.

The *TVA* evaluated new torpedo designs and taught U-boat captains and crews the skills they needed to execute perfectly in order to direct their main armament into the hulls of enemy merchant and fighting ships. All new torpedoes also were test-fired six to eight times with a dummy warhead to determine their mechanical and electrical fitness before consignment to U-boats or S-boats for combat operations. Detailed record books accompanied torpedoes wherever they were transported; they provided technical analyses of running characteristics so combat launch crews could make compensating adjustments to the missiles' intricate guidance systems. *TVA's* dummy warheads contained locator lights so chase crews could follow and retrieve them for reuse. With no explosive charges to detonate, the warheads were completely harmless—except for one driven by a torpedo that plowed completely through the bow of a wooden-hull boat that was unlucky enough to cross directly into its errant course.

13.　Translation: *Reichsdienstflagge* was a Reich organization flag. Whenever the banner was flown, the ship was considered a vessel of the German government.

One day as the ship docked at Hamburg during low tide, Karl spotted a youngster waving broadly from the pier above him.

"Hey *Cremona*, I'm your new *Schiffsjunge!*"

Baumann climbed onto the dock and greeted the boy, who introduced himself as Egon Porta, and soon learned that Porta hailed from a neighborhood in Bochum about fifteen miles from *Oma*'s house.

"You know Engelmann's store?" Karl inquired about a little grocery and bakery in Porta's neighborhood that was owned by one of his aunts.

"Yeah, I buy our bread there. A girl works there who has a brother at sea. She said he likes it so well he never comes home."

"What is the girl's name?" Karl inquired, fully expecting the answer he received.

"Ilse Baumann," Egon replied.

"I am the brother who likes the sea so well he never comes home," Karl exclaimed with a chuckle.

Despite his worldly boastfulness, while *Cremona* steamed along the Baltic coast, Karl's thoughts often returned him home to Bochum and the people he knew and loved. Still stinging from the missed opportunity to call upon Anneliese, Karl finally had sent a postcard to her, a simple greeting that he ended with a request for the girl to write a letter to him. Though Anneliese was surprised and pleased to receive the postcard from her former classmate, she returned a simple greeting to Karl—on a postcard.

Life aboard *Cremona* involved long hours of tiring work. No longer a *Schiffsjunge*, Karl had signed on as a *Leichtmatrose*, and with several crewmates manhandled the heavy missiles either into or out of the ship's large hold. Then, after *Cremona* set sail each crewman in turn stood a four-hour watch. The man standing watch needed to remain fully alert for a variety of potential hazards both aboard ship and from the sea as the vessel plied the cold coastal waters in all weather conditions. He also was responsible to alert or awaken the next man scheduled to stand watch; if for any reason the next man did not report for duty, the unrelieved sailor was required to stand the next four-hour shift without a break or rest. Upon arrival at *TVA* in Gotenhafen, the crew reversed their loading process as a crane operator lifted the torpedoes out of the cargo hold. Regular work days in port or at sea included all of the hard work and tiresome routine that kept *Cremona* clean, trim, and in good repair for sailing.

Karl was promoted to *Matrose* on 30 June 1941, in recognition of the seamanship skills he had honed and perfected over the previous two years. By that time, however, he was thoroughly disenchanted with the seemingly endless hours of work aboard ship, which he considered nothing less than abusive. Karl resolved to leave *Cremona* and her crew for employment elsewhere; perhaps on another ship, he thought. His immediate superior and the ship's captain, one Wilhelm Haganah, in accordance with the *Führerprinzip* and under the constraints of wartime rules, refused the request by the young *Matrose* to terminate his employment. The only permissible option for a crewman to leave the ship permanently, the captain explained, was to join the Kriegsmarine. Military service, Karl thought, really would not be too foreign to him considering his work experience. He already had contributed to the war effort by helping transport U-boat and S-boat torpedoes. He also had experienced some of war's bitter handiwork as *Flak* exploded over Hamburg and giant searchlight beams stabbed the night sky in search of British bombers. Against the background of wailing air raid sirens and distant bomb blasts, he had dodged spent but still deadly shrapnel chunks from the *Flak* bursts high in the sky, which showered to earth and clattered onto the dock and *Flora's* deck.

On 20 December 1941, while *Cremona* lay in port at Gotenhafen, Karl and Tran walked to the *TVA* base and into the Kriegsmarine recruiting office. Just two weeks earlier the war had taken a stunning turn when the Japanese attacked the U. S. Navy's Pacific fleet in Pearl Harbor and four days later Germany declared war on the United States. Hostilities in the Atlantic Ocean were certain to multiply in intensity and violence, and the Kriegsmarine needed experienced sailors to join the ranks of its small fraternity. The two civilian sailors were desirable candidates for enlistment in view of their practical experience and seafaring knowledge. If conscripted, they would have been earmarked for Kriegsmarine service anyway; officially they belonged to Germany's seafaring population, the *seemännische Bevölkerung.*[14]

Inside the recruiting office the boys' sensibilities were assaulted by the unfamiliar hustle and bustle of military bureaucracy. Navy personnel worked amid a jumble of desks with piles of paperwork. Some rapidly hammered on typewriters while others answered phones that ceaselessly jangled. An unspoken sense of urgency permeated the office and seemed to affect all in its midst. The boys joined the group of prospective volunteers that sat against a wall on a row of benches. Those who did not sit in quiet introspection spoke loudly in nervous, animated tones. With each passing minute the crescendo of the banter increased

14. *Handbook on German Military Forces,* reprint of 1945 U.S. War Department Technical Manual TM-E 30-451 (Baton Rouge: University of Louisiana Press, 1990), 58.

until finally the voices merged into a cacophonous roar; the sailors now seemed to answer phones that didn't ring and type madly but silently on their typewriters.

"*Halt's Maul!!!*" a recruiter exploded as he glared at the young civilians with ill-disguised contempt.[15] The conversation from the benches stopped in mid sentence as the boys instantly sat in stony silence. The sounds of tapping typewriters and ringing phones suddenly returned and continued unabated. The unexpected outburst completely unnerved Tran. After a few seconds of agitated silence the *Schiffsjunge* sprang from his seat and snapped to attention.

"*Heil Hitler,*" Voss shouted in response as his right arm shot stiffly outward in a salute. Then in the blink of an eye he bolted from the recruiting office as if he had been set aflame. The incident left Karl dispirited and alone in the company of total strangers. He suddenly felt out of place and apprehensive about the immediate future, much as when he first had left home for the sea. He had resolved to join the navy, however, and would not allow the outburst to dissuade him. The young *Matrose* was interviewed by a recruiter, who completed a stack of paperwork as he queried the youth about his education, work experience, family background and genealogy, and religious heritage. When Karl returned to the port where *Cremona* was docked Tran was nowhere to be found; he did not return to the ship until much later that day. Downcast and in despair for having bounded out of the recruiter's office, Voss had temporarily soothed his self-loathing by visiting a small carnival that had set up in town.

Kapitän Haganah realized he could no longer prevent his *Matrose* from leaving *Cremona* when Karl returned with military enlistment papers in hand. With young Baumann's destiny no longer a personal matter, the skipper released Karl from duty; he also made arrangements for Karl to receive vacation time and his final pay. Since Karl was under the normal age for enlistment he first had to obtain his father's signature on the enlistment papers. He immediately penned a letter to explain why he had decided to join the Kriegsmarine and petitioned his father to sign the papers he enclosed with his letter to Brambauer. Christian Baumann shuddered when he received his son's letter. The veteran of ghastly trench warfare dreaded the thought that Karl might someday experience war's madness and inhumanity that he personally had witnessed.

"Karl, don't go; but if you insist, I will sign the papers," Christian implored in a long letter that accompanied the signed enlistment documents. Karl returned to the navy recruiting office to present the enlistment paperwork to the recruiting officer, and was formally inducted into the Kriegsmarine. The induction cere-

---

15. Translation: Shut up!!! (Literally, "Stop your mouth.")

mony affirmed Karl's legally established military obligation to the *Führer* that commenced the moment he recited the oath:

> I swear by God this holy oath that I will render unconditional obedience to the *Führer* of Germany and of her people, Adolf Hitler, the Supreme Commander of the Armed Forces, and that, as a brave soldier, I will be prepared to stake my life for this oath at any time.[16]

Though neither a Nazi nor one who ever was influenced by National Socialist dogma, Karl Baumann took up arms for the *Reich* and the *Vaterland* and embarked upon an unknown future amid the ferocity of the most wide-sweeping and destructive war in the history of the world. He was seventeen years old.

---

16. *Handbook*, 4.

3

Navy Recruit

Karl Baumann reported to the Kriegsmarine base in Gotenhafen on 5 January 1942 to begin his twelve-year enlistment of military service for the *Reich.* From the first moment he arrived at the entrance to the *Kaserne,* where mostly young boys were gathered in their last moments of civilian life, he began to second-guess his decision to join the armed forces. One after another, nervous recruits walked up to the forbidding *Wachhaus,* where a guard inspected enlistment papers, then motioned each man to proceed through the portal.[1]

Once inside the *Kaserne,* harsh reality immediately struck most new recruits: one could get inside, but not get out! Too late for the notion to matter, Karl felt a strange uneasiness as he reflected upon the life of freedom he had abandoned upon his own volition. Surely every workday aboard *Cremona* was long and difficult, he thought, but at least he could take leave of his employers afterwards and spend free time as he wished. The realization that all the freedoms he had recently enjoyed were now suddenly lost came into stark, cruel focus. "What did I do?" Karl ruefully asked himself time and again over the next few days at the *Kaserne* while he watched other souls—some forlorn, others carefree, everyone unknown to him—assemble for their introduction to military life. Silent, lonely apprehension prevailed as well when he and the other recruits later boarded a transport ship for the daylong journey to the naval basic training center on the Baltic seacoast at Libau, Latvia.

The twelve-week basic training course for Kriegsmarine recruits in Libau combined physical training, basic military exercises, and parade drills more appropriate for fledgling Army infantrymen than for sailors. Day after day the recruits wore down the parade grounds and exercise fields, where they marched rank and file, drilled close order, and strengthened their bodies with tough physical conditioning. Karl was grateful to discover that hard work aboard *Flora* and *Cremona*

---

1.   Translation: *Kaserne* is the term for a guarded military base or installation; a *Wachhaus* is a gatehouse.

had steeled him to the rigors of the navy's training program. Weapons training constituted an important component of basic training as well. The men memorized the nomenclature of the Mauser MK 98 rifle, learned to disassemble and reassemble the weapon with confidence and speed, and achieved proficiency in marksmanship on the firing range. Curiously, seamanship training such as emergency navigation, weather forecasting, and lifeboat drills was not included in the basic course curriculum.

Among other crucial skills in the art of warfare, trainees learned to fight as part of a team within assigned squads, platoons, and larger unit structures. Most significantly, the trainees learned complete obedience to the rules of military law and to the authority conferred by rank.[2] Trainees were expected to obey orders without delay and without question. Enlisted men were not to think, they were told; they were simply to obey and to react to their officers, who were paid to think. To underscore the point, German drill sergeants invoked a curious admonition, "You do not think! You are not a horse, and only horses think, because they have bigger heads!"[3]

Karl's longstanding distaste for deference to undeserved superiority presented the greatest obstacle to overcome during basic training. The privileges and obligations of military rank naturally extended to the lowest enlisted members of the training cadre. Karl heartily despised the protocol that required recruits to salute young *Matrosen* who were the same age as he, but whose few months of naval service conferred seniority within the rigidly structured hierarchy. Many were sailors in name only, mere landlubbers who had never actually lived and worked on the sea. Karl, on the other hand, was an experienced and knowledgeable *Matrose* in every practical respect, yet subordinate to them. The ludicrous reality reminded him of his *Jungvolk* days and the bitter contempt he held for adolescent peers who so thoroughly lorded their superior rank over less fortunate members of the group.

On 10 February 1942, during Baumann's second month of basic training, steel workers at the massive Blohm und Voß Shipyard in Hamburg laid down the keel of the submarine that ten months later would be commissioned U-953. The divergent paths of the boat and the young man were destined to meet fifteen months later, when they would sail together into a desperate war of pursuit, attack, evasion, survival—and ultimate defeat.

---

2.   *Handbook*, 4.
3.   Robert Witter, ed. "Rudolf Salvermoser, A Grossdeutschland Veteran" (Internet website: www.uwm.edu/~jpipes/interview6.html., 1999).

Despite his temperament against military protocol, Karl performed exceedingly well in basic training. The physical maturity he had developed and maintained through heavy labor at sea obviated the difficulties of physical conditioning that recruits tended to suffer. Flush with youthful confidence in himself, but against his better judgement, he volunteered to attend an advanced individual training course to become a Kriegsmarine drill instructor.

Karl Baumann as a seventeen-year-old navy recruit; Libau, 1942.

Drill instructor training in Hitler's navy was conducted in a separate compound of the large base at Libau. Unlike basic training, the advanced course for aspiring instructors was grueling and extensive, though still not oriented toward living and fighting on the sea. Physical conditioning and gunnery training were intensified and relentlessly pursued. Thorough knowledge and proficiency with infantry weapons was the objective in concentrated courses for rifles, machineguns, pistols, and grenades. A drill instructor had to exhibit complete confidence and unfailing competence whenever teaching gunnery or other combat skills; otherwise, the mantle of complete authority over recruits in his charge would be challenged by their disrespect. Likewise, the drill instructor needed to excel physically in all respects. A grueling obstacle course tested and extended the limits of the recruits' stamina and their ability to endure physical hardship. One dreadful part of the obstacle course was known as the sand hole, into which the men slogged and had to traverse at top speed. The deep sand gave way under each footstep, enveloped legs and arms, and yielded its almost deathly grasp only through extreme effort that exhausted muscles and lungs.

Fifteen trainees persevered and mastered their required technical skills through the three-month course. Karl, though, had determined unequivocally very early into the program that he did not want to serve the *Vaterland* as a drill instructor. The sea had become an essential element of his life, and he longed to return to its familiar rhythms, comforts, challenges, and dangers. He had realized too late that if he became a drill instructor he probably never would be assigned sea duty. In the serious business of waging war, however, the Kriegsmarine forbade any recruit merely to change his mind and quit an advanced individual training course. A confrontation between personal will and military authority clearly loomed for Karl on the near horizon.

The advanced training course ended with a final written examination early in July 1942, and a small ceremony was convened in the examination classroom to recognize the Kriegsmarine's newest drill instructors. The fifteen graduates stood at attention one last time as their chief instructor, a *Stabsoberbootsmann* with eighteen years of service, addressed them.[4] The men were praised for their hard work and challenged to commit all their mental and physical resources to the *Führer* and the *Vaterland*. With final remarks and congratulations duly rendered, the proud old boatswain's mate informed the newly minted instructors that each would be privileged to select the training unit to which he wished to be assigned. With that pronouncement Karl shuddered; the inevitable moment for decisive action had arrived. He hoped his pounding heart would stand up under the strain when the instructor at last faced him, eye to eye.

"Baumann, in which company would you like to be an instructor?" the Senior Chief Boatswain inquired.

"*Herr Stabsoberbootsmann*," Karl replied after he took a deep breath, "I would like to be on a ship!" In an instant the instructor's demeanor transformed from self-satisfaction to stunned incredulity. He could barely comprehend what he had just heard, after his beloved Kriegsmarine had expended an extraordinary amount of time, cost, and effort to make a drill instructor out of the young man that stood before him. That Baumann now did not want to discharge his duty was

---

4.   A *Stabsoberbootsmann* was equivalent to a chief petty officer in the U.S. Navy.

outrageous and beyond contempt. The *Stabsoberbootsmann* seethed in anger and fumbled for an appropriate response to the insubordination and lack of appreciation for one's obligation that the obstinate recruit had so callously exhibited.

"Melden Sie sich zum Scheiße fahren!" the instructor thundered, his face contorted with rage. Karl was dumbfounded, having been ordered to report to the company garden to haul wheelbarrows of manure as if he were an unskilled laborer, and shaken to his core by the instructor's vicious upbraiding. Disconsolate over the prospects of myriad punishments he was certain to suffer, Karl quickly reported to the company *Oberbootsmann* and repeated the orders the instructor had pronounced. The petty officer was wholly unsympathetic.

"Go to the garden, take a spade, and turn up the ground until we come and tell you what to do," the *Oberbootsmann* ordered tersely.

For several hours Karl shoveled and tilled the garden soil during the pleasant summer day, all the while contemplating the dark fate the navy had in store for him. The *Reich* and its military forces, he well knew, were not institutions to be casually reckoned with or confronted lightly. The approach of footsteps along the path in front of the garden suddenly diverted his thoughts. He looked up from his work and instantly snapped to attention before his commanding officer. In the manner prescribed for German enlisted men, Karl stated his identity and the duty in which he presently was engaged.

"Matrose Baumann meldet sich bei der Gartenarbeit!" Karl declared with a rigid vocal cadence.[5] *Oberleutnant* Dr. Maywald, who in civilian life was a Hamburg attorney, acknowledged the young sailor and continued his brisk pace past the garden. The officer then hesitated, looked over his shoulder and returned to Karl, who was about to resume work. The young man on garden detail again snapped to attention.

"Aren't you supposed to be a drill instructor?" Maywald inquired. "What happened?" Given the opportunity, Baumann fully explained the chain of events that had unfolded upon his graduation from the advanced training course, and his desire to serve aboard a warship at sea.

"What is your occupation?" the commanding officer asked.

"I am a sailor!" Karl declared with obvious pride.

The *Oberleutnant* nodded his head approvingly, perhaps as his own memories of the huge Hamburg docklands entered his foremost thoughts.

"Tomorrow morning, come to the company office to do some other work."

---

5.   Translation: "Sailor Baumann reports himself at garden work!"

"*Ja wohl, Herr Oberleutnant*," Karl responded, as he suddenly felt the weight of the world lifted from his shoulders. Obviously, any punishment his insubordination might incur would be short-lived. Even more significantly, his chance encounter with the commanding officer set into motion an altogether different future and fate.

Karl reported to the office of the Funfte Schiffstammabteilung the next morning as ordered.[6] For the next six months he worked wherever he was needed in the post office and as a headquarters clerk. He also served as orderly for *Oberfeldwebel* Kelle, the chief enlisted man in the company.[7] As far as land duty was concerned, the young sailor was most fortunate. He was promoted to *Matrosengefreiter* while assigned to the company.[8] The work environment also was congenial and pleasant; being indoors was no small comfort against the bitterly cold winter temperatures and the frigid winds that blew in from the Baltic Sea.

Karl's navy life settled into a thoroughly enjoyable routine, especially whenever he worked for Kelle. The *Oberfeldwebel*, like Karl, hailed from Westphalia and spoke the same dialect. When the chief was away from the base, Karl relaxed in the chief's room, slept in the chief's bed, and helped himself to the chief's cigarettes. The comfortable existence he led in Hitler's navy was such that most enlisted men could not share or even imagine. Nonetheless, Karl continued to suffer the irresistible call of the sea, and sought shipboard duty at the sacrifice of all the creature comforts he knew and enjoyed.

To the disbelief of contented comrades, Karl wrote to the admiral of the Baltic Fleet to request a transfer to submarine duty. He did not remotely like the prospect of sailing beneath the waves aboard an *Unterseeboot*, but had been told that no other opportunities existed for sea duty. By 1943 the Kriegsmarine's small surface fleet had been battered by heavy losses and relegated to a very limited role in the war. The commander of the Baltic Fleet eventually notified the Funfte Schiffstammabteilung that Baumann's request for transfer to submarine duty had been approved, pending a thorough medical examination.

A Kriegsmarine doctor conducted an excruciatingly complete physical examination to determine Karl's fitness for submarine duty. In the process of the pushing, pulling and peering, he discovered scar tissue on the patient's eardrum, the

---

6.   Translation: The Fifth Fleet Headquarters.
7.   A Kriegsmarine *Oberfeldwebel* was equivalent to a German Army (*Heer*) *Hauptfeldwebel*. See Internet website: www.feldgrau.com/ranks.html. The rank also was equivalent to a World War II U.S. Navy Chief Petty Officer.
8.   A *Matrosengefreiter* was equivalent to a World War II U.S. Navy Seaman 1st Class.

residual effect of a puncture Karl suffered from an ear infection during early childhood. The pressing need for U-boat crewmen overrode caution, and the doctor certified Karl for submarine duty, though on a restricted basis.

Back at the office, *Oberfeldwebel* Kelle pored over Karl's medical report and noted the conditional approval his orderly had received for submarine duty.

"Well, Baumann, you're not going yet!" he declared with a grin; but two weeks later Karl received transfer orders to report to a submarine training school. Happiness was tinged with apprehension and a melancholic awareness that he probably never again would see the many good comrades that personified his pleasantly memorable first months of service. Intuitively, he also realized the comfortable life to which he had grown accustomed in the Kriegsmarine soon would become a remote memory.

Matrosengefreiter Baumann entered U-boat basic training with the Erste Unterseeboots-Lehrdivision in Pillau, a harbor city on East Prussia's Baltic coast, in March 1943.[9] The twelve-week course for trainees was conducted aboard the *KdF Schiff Robert Ley*, a former passenger liner built and operated under the *Kraft durch Freude* program established by the *Reich* before the war.[10] The young sailor was fascinated by the ship's opulence. Before the war, working class Germans who otherwise had been unable to afford to vacation aboard commercial ocean liners could travel in memorable and low-cost luxury aboard a *KdF* ship. The *Robert Ley* was a sleek, fast, diesel-electric vessel of 27,288 tons that was a propagandist's dream. Crowds of smiling passengers once swarmed over her decks to enjoy life before the lenses of *Reich* photographers and newsreel cameramen, and showed the world Hitler's new Germany.[11] The necessities of war cast aside all luxury and glamour and relegated the liner to serve first as a hospital ship, then as a floating Kriegsmarine classroom where future U-boat crewmen received general training for submarine duty.

Though the U-boat trainees were destined for war service aboard the navy's work-horse U-boat, the Type VIIC, all but one week of training was conducted aboard the *KdF* ship. Karl at last was reintroduced to basic maritime skills that included the fundamental uses of ropes and knots, signals training using Morse code and semaphore flags, and ever-present physical training. He was gratified to discover his latest training course was largely a refresher for the seamanship he had learned aboard *Flora* and *Cremona*.

---

9.   Translation: The First U-boat Training Division.
10.   Translation: Strength through Joy.
11.   Shirer, 265-266. *KdF* ships were off-limits to Germany's Jewish citizens.

Karl's practiced skills proved fortuitous on more than one occasion. A visiting admiral once called an inspection of U-boat trainees to gauge their progress in the training program. To the approval of the beaming admiral, Karl deftly displayed his knot-tying expertise, which actually he had perfected much earlier as a civilian sailor.

The training course was designed to discipline the mind to react to orders with an immediate response. Every aspect of training aboard the *Robert Ley* was necessarily planned to prepare future U-boat crewmen to perform their specific duties or functions with maximum speed and efficiency. In the harsh reality of submarine warfare, a crewman's instantaneous and competent reaction to a given order might mean the difference between survival and death for the U-boat and her entire crew. Time and again, day after day, the trainees were tried and tested on their abilities to carry out commands under a variety of stressful circumstances and conditions. Mealtimes even required obedience and regimentation; each training class entered the mess hall and was segregated at specified tables. The students then stood at attention, sat, ate, and returned to their classrooms under the express orders and watchful eyes of their commanding officers. Another rite of passage for fledgling submariners was the *Kostumfest*. Upon command and without forewarning, trainees had to rush to their lockers at breakneck speed, change into a different uniform, then scramble to a specified deck level where their overall comportment was scrutinized to the smallest tolerances.

Baumann experienced his first taste of life aboard a U-boat just prior to graduation, while on a weeklong cruise with a small, 250-ton training submarine—probably a Type IIa—that sailed out of Pillau. Nerves tightened and hearts pounded as ten trainees watched the U-boat's crew confidently perform the methodical, mechanical dive procedures with practiced synchronization. First, watertight hatches clanged shut and were tightened down; then began a confusion of crisp commands and choreographed responses that were marked by a score of mysterious sounds that varied in pitch, tempo, and dynamic range.

A strange sensation of unnatural movement soon overcame the students as the small, cramped U-boat sliced into the Baltic and sank beneath the surface. The training regimen then began, though most students and a few regular crewmen alike soon fought against the dread surge of seasickness. Karl did not submit to the terrible malady; long ago he had grown sea legs and a cast-iron stomach aboard the little *Flora* while she heaved, dipped, and pitched against the choppy North Sea waves. As the lowest of the low among the ranks of *Ubootfahrer*, the students—whether seasick or not—helped prepare and serve all daily meals to the regular crewmen.[12] On at least one occasion Baumann sat utterly alone and happily peeled potatoes while his nine green-faced companions in training succumbed to seasickness and begged early death to relieve their boundless agony.

The training cruise introduced the fundamentals of U-boat operation by practical application. The unique environment of the boat, when submerged, required special attention to the crucial aspects of buoyancy, balance, and trim; to underwater communications; and to the methods and rules of navigation. Karl was fascinated by the intricate knowledge each crewman possessed, and by the demands that were placed upon skill and experience simply to survive in an underwater world even when absent the perils of combat. He completed the training cruise with greater confidence in himself and his ability to withstand all the rigors and stresses a U-boat crewman was certain to encounter.

Baumann finished basic U-boat training and, either by chance or by necessity, was ordered to attend a six-week course for anti-aircraft gunners. In June 1943 he traveled by train to the Baltic coast town of Swinemünde to begin the intensive course in gunnery. Again, the locus for the training course was a ship, an anti-aircraft vessel that bristled with a variety of *Fliegerabwehrkannonen*—flak weapons—designed to bring down enemy aircraft. Karl and his fellow *Matrosen* were required to learn to operate and maintain a variety of anti-aircraft batteries installed on the fleet submarines they would sail into battle. Their primary objective was to understand every aspect of the thirty–seven millimeter deck gun and several configurations of single and multiple-barreled twenty-millimeter cannon.

The watchword for gunnery training was, as always, speed. The men learned by rote trial and error how to man their battle stations with maximum efficiency and minimum wasted motion; to load, aim, track, fire, and reload their weapons without the slightest hesitation that otherwise might prove fatal when defending themselves against attacking planes. They learned and lived by the oft-repeated phrase, "*Flaklehrgang ist Flitzer Lehrgang.*"[13] In live fire exercises each man was required to man a gun position, either to fire at moving targets or to load heavy canisters of ammunition into his weapon. Under the stern and watchful gaze of gunnery instructors, every function a trainee performed was timed and critiqued. The high level of innervating stress under such trying conditions became almost palpable. On several occasions Karl nearly lost his composure during crucial tests of the fundamental skills he was required to master to become a U-boat gunner.

---

12.   Translation: *Ubootfahrer* means literally U-boat driver, but was the name used for all U-boat crewmen.
13.   Translation: "Flak learning is speed learning."

The gunnery course seemed much longer in duration than six weeks, as harried sailors at the end of each grueling day collapsed into their hammocks aboard the floating boarding school. Their misery was exacerbated by modest and uninviting conditions, including the dining regimen in the enlisted mess. The men routinely pounded loaves of hard black navy bread on the edge of a countertop to knock off the cockroaches that scurried across the crust.

Graduation from the anti-aircraft gunnery course came not one minute too early to satisfy *Matrosengefreiter* Baumann. He never looked back as he boarded a train that soon departed Swinemünde for the huge and familiar naval base at Kiel, where in mid-July of 1943 he was temporarily assigned to a personnel replacement unit. He reported for duty there and simply rested and relaxed until all the required transfer paperwork and travel orders were prepared for him. Two days later he and four other new *Ubootfahrer* received their paperwork and were issued carbines to protect themselves during their journey through the occupied Low Countries and France. Laden with weapons and seabags, the men boarded a special train, operated by the Befelshaber der Uboote (BdU), destined for permanent assignments aboard U-boats operating out of French coast ports.[14]

Travel attire for the men was the regulation dress-blue Navy uniform. To signify his *esprit de corps* with the Kriegsmarine and to indicate he no longer was a mere recruit, Karl adopted several popular though unauthorized uniform components. Whereas U.S. Navy enlisted men wore their hats tilted at a radical, jaunty angle to signify their passage from recruits to full-fledged sailors, their German counterparts inaugurated a two-part ritual for their dress blues. They replaced the short ribbon that dangled from the back of the dress hat with a streamer often two feet long; the wearer draped the long ribbon across his shoulder and down the front of his uniform jacket. Next, the bell-bottomed uniform trousers were widened at the cuff far beyond their regulation cut. Non-commissioned officers on the *KDF Schiff Robert Ley* had carried rulers to measure the width of trouser bottoms. They forbade trainees to wear non-regulation uniforms. As a fully inaugurated *Ubootfahrer*, Karl now could express his successful passage into the fighting ranks of the Kriegsmarine.

The train pulled out of Kiel and rolled toward a number of stops at Kriegsmarine bases situated across northern Germany. It then headed south across the Dutch border to Amsterdam, then through Belgium, and finally into France. The young sailor first saw German-occupied Paris as his train nosed into *Gare du*

---

14. BdU (*Befehlshaber der Unterseeboote*) referred simultaneously to the Commander-in-Chief of U-boats, *Konteradmiral* Karl Dönitz, and to his headquarters and staff.

Nord, the main terminal through which trains bound for the Atlantic coast were routed.

Gare du Nord was a hive of non-stop activity. French civilians and German troops in all manner of Wehrmacht uniforms and gear trod about the platforms between arriving and departing trains. Dim lights punctuated the expanse of the great terminal which, with echoes of dissonant shouts and the shrill hissing and clanking of steam locomotives, rendered a melancholy presence that was at the same time bustling, mysterious, and exciting. The men's official travel orders allowed no time to explore the enticing venues of Paris; the celebrated City of Light was merely a transit point for most German occupation forces. Every transient soldier, sailor, and airman doubtless promised himself to return to Paris on leave and surrender either to its grand cultural allure or its hedonistic delights.

The BdU train left Paris late in the afternoon and headed toward the Brittany peninsula and the port cities of Brest, Lorient, and St. Nazaire. Karl studied the French landscape that sped by the window of his passenger coach during the final leg of his long rail journey. The alternating vistas of towns, tree-lined roads, and rural farmlands fascinated him even as he contemplated his uncertain future and the war he was about to enter. At no point did he consider that Germany might lose the global war; of ultimate victory he was certain. Unbeknownst to Baumann, and to most Germans, the Battle of the Atlantic already was irretrievably lost. The Ubootwaffe had been mortally wounded since mid-May 1943, when the U-boat war turned decisively in favor of the Allies. Many more U-boats and their brave crews would be lost to the sea war before the fighting would end two years later.[15]

Despite efforts to keep U-boat losses a secret, the tragic toll was widely known among the crewmen at every French coast base. By July, three out of every five U-boats dispatched to patrol the Atlantic were sunk in the Bay of Biscay. The British owned the skies over the Bay, and on 24 June alone the RAF had sunk four U-boats.[16] In a meeting with Adolf Hitler at the *Führer's* mountaintop retreat at Berchtesgaden on 5 June 1943, Admiral Dönitz decried the loss of fully one-third of all U-boats on combat patrol during May. The majority of losses were attributed to Allied aircraft, whose presence was hardly disturbed by the Luftwaffe, much to the consternation of the Navy Commander-in-Chief.[17] Despite the turn

---

15. Michael Gannon, *Black May; The Epic Story of the Allies' Defeat of the German U-boats in May 1943* (New York: Harper Collins, 1998), 381.
16. Herbert A. Werner, *Iron Coffins; A Personal Account of the German U-boat Battles of World War II* (New York: Holt, Rinehart and Winston, 1969), 144. Werner was the second commander of U-953, the boat upon which Karl Baumann sailed.

of the tide against the Atlantic U-boat fleets, Dönitz declared his intention to continue the submarine war even if great successes were no longer possible. The *Führer* wholeheartedly agreed and further admonished:

> There can be no talk of a let-up in submarine warfare. The Atlantic is my first line of defense in the West, and even if I have to fight a defensive battle there, that is preferable to waiting to defend myself on the coast of Europe. The enemy forces tied up by our submarine warfare are tremendous, even though the actual losses inflicted by us are no longer great. I cannot afford to release these forces by discontinuing submarine warfare.[18]

The hard fighting and dying in the Atlantic campaign would escalate with every passing month until the end of the war. Hundreds of U-boats would sail out of their giant coastal bunkers on long, hazardous missions from which they would never return. At no time during his U-boat training and service was young Baumann informed of the terrible odds against his survival.

At each scheduled stop along the route toward the train's terminus at Bordeaux, new U-boat crewmen and officers shuffled among war-weary veterans of the Battle of the Atlantic. Whether one's bearing reflected anxiety for combat not yet experienced or the post-traumatic stress of having seen the face of war, those among each group of sailors usually were distinguishable from their opposite numbers. The BdU train shuddered to a stop the next morning at the large and ornately adorned *Gare* at La Rochelle, where Karl's gear-burdened travel party quickly exited their coach. Nearby lay the sub pens of La Pallice, the homeport of the Dritte Unterseebootsflottille to which the men had been assigned.[19]

The new arrivals gathered on the station platform, with orders to walk to Flotilla headquarters. Karl-Heinz Schlüter, Franz Band, Helmut Aue, Gerhard Ahrendholz, and Karl Baumann slung their rifles around their necks and hefted their heavy seabags onto their shoulders. When they had determined their bearings they set out to find the Kriegsmarine base situated in an old *Kaserne* on the northern edge of town. With the *Gare* to their backs they walked down the beautiful tree-bordered Avenue de Strasbourg, which was lined by fine large homes that lent an air of sophistication to the historic town. Shortly they arrived at the old harbor. The soft breeze that wafted about them carried the peculiar pungent

---

17. *Conferences*, 332-333. Dönitz replaced Grand Admiral Erich Raeder as Commander-in-Chief of the Kriegsmarine in January 1943.
18. *Conferences*, 334-335.
19. Translation: Third U-boat Flotilla.

smell of seacoast towns: an admixture of seawater, fish, stale tobacco smoke, and dog feces.

La Rochelle was an ancient walled seaport with large defensive towers that had guarded both sides of the narrow entrance to the old harbor for several centuries. The towers long had been the unmistakable symbol of the *Ville*. Passengers and provisions destined for the New World once had passed between the medieval stone towers in tiny sailing ships to begin their perilous, months-long journeys in search of new lives in the American wilderness. The two sentinels now stood as silent reminders of the dangers the sea held for sailors who still risked their lives and fortunes upon and, with twentieth century warfare, beneath the vast unforgiving waters of the Bay of Biscay and the open Atlantic beyond.

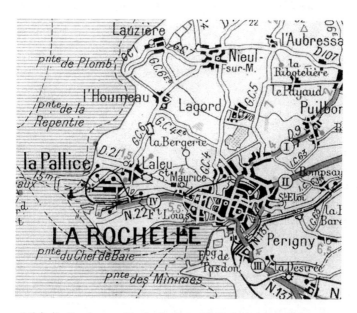

Michelin Roadmap of La Rochelle in 1945 shows the rail line the Kriegsmarine used to transport its men between the *Kaserne* on the northern perimeter of the town and the U-boat base that dominated the harbor at La Pallice.

The men stopped at the first café they encountered, and there rested their backs as each soaked up an apertif. Afterward they trod past the arcaded storefronts of Place de Verdun—the old town square—and shortly located the former French *Caserne* that had been commandeered by the Kriegsmarine for Third Flotilla headquarters.[20] Ahrendholz, who had been entrusted with the transfer papers for the five replacements, presented the documents to the personnel officer on duty. Each new *Ubootfahrer* was to be assigned to a U-boat where his individual advanced training skills were required. As it happened, all five were posted to U-953, a boat that had recently arrived at the Biscay base from her maiden mission and was in need of anti-aircraft gunners and other personnel.

Karl and his companions were escorted across the grounds of the *Kaserne* to one of several large houses where U-953's crew lived. The properties had been confiscated from some of the well-heeled of La Rochelle. Karl was pleased to find a large swimming pool behind the house, and looked forward to swimming there during off duty hours. The new men walked into a living room where U-953 crewmen lounged and congregated around a large bowl of cold cuts. Together with these men Karl Baumann would live, work, fight, and quite possibly die for the *Vaterland*. He saw no reason to approach the veteran *Ubootfahrer* with hesitation; besides, he was hungry. Without formality, he confidently strode up to the cold cuts and helped himself while his travel companions held back—unsure whether Karl had violated some protocol that prohibited such displays of premature familiarity.

The reconstituted crew of fifty-six made the appropriate rounds of introductions. The new crewmen were gratified to be cordially welcomed into the circle of sailors whose fates had converged on the coast of France. Conversation topics naturally involved hometowns, sweethearts, wives, children, training experiences, and preferred drinking establishments in La Rochelle. Hard facts were liberally spiced with rumors about the conduct of the war, and both circulated freely among the group. A harsh reality weighed most heavily upon the veterans' shoulders: their first war patrol and the death of one of their own. Several men related their recent experience to the new *Kameraden*.

U-953 had arrived at La Pallice on 22 July at the end of her first combat patrol. Her seventy-one day roundabout journey from Kiel on the North Sea had followed a course between the Faroe Islands and Iceland in the North Atlantic, then west and southwest into the warmer climes of the mid-Atlantic. With a change of course on 13 June they sailed due east toward Southern Morocco, then northward on 3 July from a point just above the Canary Islands. The final leg of the patrol followed a wide sweeping course along the shipping lanes that ran along the Spanish and French coasts. U-953 at last entered the Bay of Biscay and

---

20.   Translation: *Caserne* is the French equivalent to the German *Kaserne*, a guarded military installation. Thus, upon the German occupation of La Rochelle, the *Caserne* thus became a *Kaserne*.

her new homeport of La Pallice.[21] Boat and crew arrived as combat veterans, having received their baptism of fire from both the sky and the sea.

U-953's crew assembled in Germany for *Baubelehrung*, the time period to become acquainted with the brand new boat before she was commissioned and underwent operational trials. The boat officially entered service with the Kriegsmarine on 13 May 1943. Note that *Oberleutnant zur See* Karl-Heinz Marbach, front row center, did not yet wear the U-boat commander's distinctive white hat cover.

The first week of the patrol had proceeded quietly, with endless hours and calm seas punctuated mainly by mealtimes, duty shifts, and test dives. Then, on the evening of 20 May, U-953 made her first hostile contact. A distant Allied aircraft had appeared twice and sent the boat into an emergency dive. The Commanding Officer, *Oberleutnant zur See* Karl-Heinz Marbach, peered through his periscope and spotted ten to fifteen columns of oily black smoke from an enemy convoy on the northwestern horizon. Meanwhile, Asdic signals pinged loudly in the German sound technician's ears.[22] The convoy was too far away for the submerged U-953 to close in and launch an attack, so it sailed unscathed into the

---

21. *Kriegstagebuch U-953* (United States Nation Archives and Records Administration; College Park, Maryland). Roll 3379 of Mircofilm Publication T1022, 13 May–22 July 1943. Known as the *KTB*, this document is the official war diary that was produced daily aboard U-953.

22. Asdic was the acronym for the sound detection system, similar to U.S. Navy sonar, developed by the Allied Submarine Devices Investigation Committee.

night. Nonetheless, all *Ubootfahrer* had felt the first pangs of excitement, anticipation, and fear that accompanied their first enemy contact.

A half-hour after midnight, barely an hour after the convoy smoke had disappeared, watch party members atop the boat's bridge spotted an American-built B-24 Liberator in the dim twilight of the clear sky. Another crash dive safely hid the boat from the long-range anti-submarine patrol bomber. Then, at 01:30, a PBY Catalina flying boat from of an American or British base probably in Iceland closed in at three thousand meters while U-953 ran on the surface to recharge her electric batteries. Unable to dive, the men trapped on the bridge braced themselves for attack. On the skipper's orders the helmsman quickly steered the boat hard to starboard, perpendicular to the aircraft, to present the smallest possible target. Seconds later the German gunners opened fire on the lumbering flying boat as it flew directly overhead. Only one hundred meters above the U-boat, gunfire poured down upon the vessel while five small bombs tumbled from the Catalina's bomb bay. The hail of bullets kicked up small geysers of seawater and slammed against the conning tower but caused no serious structural damage. The bombs harmlessly erupted into large waterspouts twenty to fifty meters off the starboard side of the boat. The PBY then slowly droned away as its crew launched four red star shells into the sky to mark U-953's location. The boat also fled from the area as fast as her huge diesels could propel her, but could not dive for another hour until her batteries had been fully recharged. No one had been wounded or killed during the attack, but the men clearly had seen the face of war and were chastened by its immediacy and its harsh reality.[23]

More than six weeks passed without further contact with the enemy. U-953 often was attached to one of several *Gruppen,* or wolfpacks, that prowled the Atlantic for convoy traffic. On 6 July and twice the following day, lookouts spotted single American-built light bombers off the coast of Portugal, but the boat had escaped detection.[24] The presence of the patrol bombers was a portent of the deadly aerial threat the Fates had decreed would be visited shortly upon the U-boat and her crew.

While she sailed along the Portugese coast at 02:00 on the morning of 9 July, U-953 monitored radio messages that two U-boat *Gruppen* were under heavy enemy aircraft surveillance or attack, but the boat remained safely submerged on her slow northward course toward the Bay of Biscay. At 02:30 in the afternoon the skipper ordered U-953 to the surface to better observe the horizon. Though skies

23. *KTB*, 21 May 1943.
24. *KTB*, 6-7 July 1943.

were only 30 percent overcast, low clouds hung over the ocean surface. Twenty minutes later a B-24 suddenly plunged through a cloud bank five thousand meters toward the southwestern horizon. The young U-boat skipper watched the approach of the bomber for several seconds while he considered whether to flee underwater or fight on the surface—the only two options at his disposal. His life-and-death decision was firm and final: U-953 would stay and fight. On Marbach's orders both 20mm anti-aircraft guns opened fire on the B-24 at about 2,500 meters. The gutsy pilot quickly dove his Liberator to between fifteen and twenty meters above the Atlantic and pressed his attack toward the boat's stern. U-boat officers and watch party members piled on top of each other against the armored bridge wall atop the conning tower, but had no protection against the attack. Seconds later the big bomber roared overhead nearly close enough to touch. German gunners raked the B-24 with 20mm anti-aircraft rounds, of which at least twenty to thirty seemed to hit the plane without effect. The Liberator's gunners simultaneously poured streams of fifty-caliber bullets into the U-boat and her conning tower. The bomber climbed and then disappeared into the nearest cloud bank. The only material damage to the boat was to the severed Metox antenna, which dangled by its cable alongside the conning tower.[25]

Human flesh had not been so impervious. The *Ubootfahrer* on the bridge quickly untangled themselves from their huddle and looked around to assess the cost of the skipper's decision to stand and fight. *Bootsmaat* Helmut Hentschel gripped his bloody right arm and stared blankly at his bullet-shattered elbow. *Matrosenobergefreiter* Herbert Raschewski lay on the deck with four bullet wounds in each leg; miraculously, the large missiles had passed cleanly through the limbs without hitting any bones and arteries, and he would recover to sail again aboard U-953.[26] As the bomber droned unseen inside distant clouds, the unharmed men rushed to the aid of their wounded *Kameraden*. Hentschel and Raschewski were hastily picked up and carried to the main hatch, then lowered down the ladder into waiting hands.

"*Flieger Alaaarrrm!!! Auf Tiefe gehen,*" Marbach ordered.[27] The remaining bridge watch and gun crewmen stormed down the hatch, less one man; *Matrose*

---

25. *KTB*, 9 July 1943. Metox was a rudimentary radar system developed by the French. Because of its shape, the Metox antenna also was known as the *Biskaya Kreutz*—Biscay Cross.

26. *KTB*, 9 July 1943.

27. Translation: *Auf Tiefe gehen* was the command issued to dive the U-boat; literally, "Go to depth." *Wintergarten* was the name given the upper gun deck that was located directly aft of the conning tower bridge on most U-boats.

Egon Döring was missing. The skipper frantically looked over the bridge to the gun mounts on the *Wintergarten*, but young Döring was nowhere to be seen. Reluctantly, Marbach jumped through the main hatch, pulled the heavy cover closed and spun the locking wheel tight even as the boat began her plunge below the Atlantic waves.

With practiced perfection U-953's crew skillfully submerged their boat into the depths. As the boat sank seventy-five meters below the surface the men clearly heard five heavy splashes, then the teeth-clenching eruptions of bombs nearby. The boat reached for the deep Atlantic and finally leveled out at two hundred meters, where the extreme pressure of the depths threatened to implode the boat's superstructure. U-953 remained at depth for nearly seven hours to escape any lingering threat that might have assembled in the wake of the boat being sighted and attacked.[28]

U-953 broke onto the surface at 19:50, while daylight still threatened to expose the boat to enemy observation. When the watch party manned their positions they made a horrifying discovery. *Matrose* Doring's lifeless body lay crumpled and wedged into the leading edge of the *Wintergarten,* where the gun deck was joined to the conning tower. Eighteen year-old Döring's first combat mission had been his last; his body was torn by ghastly fifty-caliber bullet wounds in the heart, chest, and back. Death, at least, had been instantaneous. Several crewmen removed the trapped body and carried it below deck, where it was sown into a section of canvas sailcloth. Then, without ceremony or formal proceedings, the body was dropped over the side of the U-boat to rest forever beneath the waves. Details of Döring's burial at sea were not recorded in U-953's *Kriegstagebuch*, but forever would mar the memories of the crewmen with whom the youngster had served.[29]

U-953 continued to be dogged by aircraft sightings as she made her way slowly into the Bay of Biscay, but managed to avoid further attacks from the air. The masts of an Allied destroyer appeared over the horizon on the evening of 14 July and sent the *Ubootfahrer* to battle stations. Within minutes each vessel had locked onto the unique sound signature of her adversary. The submerged U-boat

---

28. *KTB*, 9 July 1943.
29. *KTB*, 9 July 1943, and Herbert Raschewski. Details of the discovery of Döring's body and his burial at sea were given to Karl Baumann by Herbert Raschewski of Kassel, Germany in a telephone conversation on 8 November 2004. According to Mr. Raschewski U-953 surfaced about two hours after submerging, at which time Döring's body was found, rather than after seven hours underwater as recorded in the *KTB*.

remained at torpedo depth and tracked the southward course of the onrushing destroyer until the skipper determined he could not launch an attack against the nimble ship. Marbach ordered the boat to the depths as the destroyer maneuvered onto a straight course of attack. The ship plowed directly overhead at 19:43; the sound of her churning propellers was fearfully amplified through the water and the hull of the U-boat. Seconds later the Germans heard the muffled splash of five depth charges that slowly descended toward their steel underwater chamber. The five *Wabos* exploded nearby with fearsome violence but without effect, save for frayed nerves and shaken psyches in the wake of the crew's first depth charge attack. Inexplicably, the destroyer failed to press the attack and sailed on after her unsuccessful first attempt against U-953.[30]

Early postwar map of La Pallice.

On 18 July Marbach received a radio message from the commanding officer of the U-boat force in the western theater of operations. The communication ordered U-953 to proceed to La Pallice rather than Bordeaux, her original destination. The boat was to be rebuilt at the navy shipyard to counter the increased and substantial threat posed by Allied aircraft, a problem already well known to the submarine commander and his crew. Marbach was completely surprised by

---

30.   *KTB*, 14 July 1943. Translation: *Wabos* were depth charges, or *Wasserbomben*.

the unexpected order, and recorded his incredulity in the boat's *Kriegstagebuch* with the idiomatic exclamation, "*Nanu!*"[31] Accordingly, on 22 July U-953 was carefully maneuvered into an empty *Boxe* inside the massive concrete submarine bunker at La Pallice. The chief of the Third U-boat Flotilla was on hand to greet the boat when she arrived with her recently tested and bloodied veteran crew.[32]

If the flotilla commander privately felt little hope for U-953's long-term survival, he had good reason. The Kriegsmarine's legendary Happy Time—when U-boats owned the seas at the Allies' great peril—had ended and never would return. As the war ground on, veteran *Ubootfahrer* tended to view their future with pessimism or pure fatalism that was entirely justified. By July 1943 the average survival rate for U-boat officers and crewmen in combat was six to seven months.[33] The vaunted Ubootwaffe already had begun to sail headlong and irreversibly toward total, catastrophic defeat.

Through shared experiences, adventure and danger, U-953's crewmen had quickly developed bonds of mutual affection akin to love. The strength of those bonds was hardened by their reliance upon each other for survival. There were exceptions to the rule, however. The original *Leitender Ingenieur* of U-953 was an arrogant young man named Heinemann who lorded rank over his subordinates but lacked the experience, skills, and polish of a veteran *Ubootfahrer*.[34] His haughty attitude and annoying traits, such as being the only man on board who slept in pajamas, invited silent derision and scorn from many who sailed with him. The *Leitender* was just the kind of man Karl always found so annoying, and that critical view was not lost on Heinemann. Both men mutually disliked each other.[35] Marbach found his chief engineer difficult to stomach as well; finally, with U-953's first mission completed, the skipper employed the time-honored method used by commanding officers the world over to rid themselves of unwanted subordinates: promotion. The skipper arranged for Heinemann to attend a service school that was certain to direct the *Leitender's* career advancement far away from U-953, which in Heinemann's case would be assignments to U-883 and U-3036.[36]

31.   *KTB*, 14 July 1943. Translation: "Well, I never!"
32.   *KTB*, 22 July 1943.
33.   Werner, 158.
34.   The *Leitender Ingenieur*—L.E.—was the Chief Engineering Officer of the U-boat.
35.   Albert Bechtel, telephone conversation with Karl Baumann, 1 May 2000. Mr. Bechtel reminded Karl that the mutual dislike between Karl and Heinemann was known by other crewmen.
36.   Internet website: www.ubootwaffe.net/crews.

Officers and crew form up on U-953's deck while *Leitender Ingenieur* Heinemann walks toward the camera.

Karl listened with interest to the veterans' accounts of his boat's first war patrol and Döring's death. Possessed with the youthful confidence of a veteran seaman himself, he simply could not contemplate or comprehend the possibility that he had cast his lot to fight for a lost cause and, statistically at least, he most likely would be killed, wounded, or captured before the war's end. The evening ended as tired men drifted off to their rooms to catch a few hours of sleep. The veterans would introduce the replacements to U-953 the next morning when they reported for duty in port to prepare their boat for her next mission. Karl Baumann's long and circuitous journey back to sea finally was over.

His wartime odyssey was about to begin.

4

U-boat Gunner

Shortly after the next day's dawn, the men of U-953 lined up for morning formation and roll call in front of their quarters. When all officers and crewmen had been accounted for, the group marched rank and file about ten minutes to a little railroad station next to the *Kaserne*. The brilliant morning sun unleashed its summer fury as the sailors stood next to the tracks. Waves of heat radiated off the brick wall that ran alongside the boarding platform and excited several small lizards that skittered up, down and across its rough surface. A small train operated by the Kriegsmarine soon chugged into the station and stopped in front of the platform. The men quickly boarded the cars and settled onto wood-slatted seats; a moment later the train's engineer signaled the start of the four-mile run to the coast with a staccato blast of the high-pitched steam whistle and a slight jolt as power was transferred to the engine's drive wheels. Kriegsmarine guards toting MP40 machine-pistols pulled themselves aboard the slowly moving cars to fend off any attempts by the French Resistance to attack the train and the unarmed U-boat crewmen.

The little train wound its way westward out of La Rochelle and a few moments later rolled through La Pallice, a hard scrabble town of mostly ancient two-story houses and storefronts attached one to another. La Pallice now was largely a ghost town; most of its citizens had abandoned their homes to escape the Anglo-American bombing raids on the German U-boat base that dominated the nearby harbor. The U.S. Eighth Army Air Force's VIII Bomber Command had sent its first force of B-17 Flying Fortresses from England on 18 November 1942 to bomb La Pallice and two other U-boat bases on the Bay of Biscay. Nineteen of the heavy bombers had lined up their Norden bombsights on St. Nazaire, thirteen on Lorient, and another nineteen on La Pallice. The Forts had made another bomb run over the port on 29 May 1943 and a third on the Fourth of July, several weeks before *Matrosengefreiter* Baumann arrived for his combat assignment.

Eighth Air Force intelligence reports characterized the 4 July bombing as being extremely accurate.[1] The Allies would have been sorely disappointed had they viewed the actual bomb damage. The five-hundred-pounders that landed squarely on the huge concrete U-boat bunker caused no appreciable damage. The aerial bombs used early in the war had no ability to inflict damage on the Third Flotilla U-boats that hid inside the bunker's ten *Boxen*—three wet docks and seven dry docks. *Organization Todt*, the construction branch of the Wehrmacht, had built the main bunker in 1941. The *OT* was responsible for many stark concrete edifices often of mammoth proportions that symbolized Hitler's power and domination across Nazi-controlled Europe. Built entirely of reinforced concrete, the main bunker complex was 195 meters long, 165 meters wide, and nineteen meters high.[2] The roof that protected boats and men from direct bomb hits ranged from twenty-one to twenty-four feet thick. The geometric patterns of walls and roof edges were designed to deflect falling ordnance and dull their explosive effects. Huge armored blast doors closed off the interior docks from outside perils.[3] The huge sub pen was surrounded by smaller, yet still massive, concrete torpedo bunkers and ancillary structures—all of which cast sinister otherworldly shadows across the landscape. However, the complex was a beautiful and welcome sight to exhausted and spent *Ubootfahrer* who returned from combat patrols in the Bay of Biscay or the depths of the Atlantic. The cavernous bunker provided cover and protection for the flotilla's U-boats while they were refitted and overhauled between missions. Near the armored entrance, twisted chunks of steel shrapnel as much as two feet long lay about as silent ugly reminders that the Allies had La Pallice plotted on their bomb groups' target boards.

Baumann strode with his crewmates into the bunker and down a long corridor that sharply amplified the echoes of their footsteps and animated voices; the musty odors of continually damp concrete assaulted the men's nostrils. The *Ubootfahrer* then turned onto a dockside of a *Boxe* that opened to the waters of the Bay. The yawning entrance at the front end of each long *Boxe* resembled the opening to a cave. Nudged against the dock was a long hulking monster of steel that lay silently in wait for her handlers to arouse to life. Two armed crew-

1. Kit C. Carter and Robert Mueller, *The Army Air Forces in World War II; Combat Chronology 1941-1945* (Washington, DC: U.S. Government Printing Office, 1973); 60, 140, 153.
2. In English dimensions, the bunker was approximately 640 feet by 542 feet, and sixty-two feet high.
3. Karl-Heinz Schmeelke and Michael Schmeelke, *German U-boat Bunkers Yesterday and Today* (Atglen, PA: Schiffer Publishing, Ltd., 1999), 28-34.

men—one who stood dockside and the other on the boat deck—had arrived earlier to take their turn at guard duty. In the yellow glare of electric light bulbs that hung inside the manmade cavern, U-953 resembled a menacing shark. Karl's mind raced as it absorbed his first sight of the warship that would become either his protector from harm or the instrument of his destruction.

U-953 was one of 665 Type VIIC U-boats and their variant models commissioned by the Kriegsmarine between 1940 and 1945. Each 220-foot boat displaced 871 tons when submerged and was the workhorse of Hitler's U-boat fleet. The Type VIIC may have been the best-integrated combat system developed by German engineers until the radically improved Type XXI U-boat was introduced late in the war.[4] While cruising speed was marginally slower than other U-boat types and she operated over a shorter cruising range, the small VIIC could dive faster than other boats and was more agile both on the surface and when submerged, which prolonged the lives of many crews in combat. Type VIIC boats fought in virtually every corner of the world, from the South Atlantic to the Arctic Circle and the eastern shores of the Americas, and across the Indian Ocean to the Pacific and the Japanese home islands.

U-953 was launched into the Elbe River at Hamburg's Blohm und Voß shipyard on 28 October 1942. Kriegsmarine inspectors scoured her structural integrity for nearly two months before they certified the boat for delivery to the naval service. *Oberleutnant zur See* Karl-Heinz Marbach then became U-953's first commander during her commissioning ceremony on 17 December 1942. Assigned to the Funfte Ausbildungsflottille—the Fifth Training Flotilla—in Kiel, Marbach put his new boat and his newly assembled crew through an intensive shakedown program that was completed on 31 May 1943.

Karl-Heinz Marbach was born in 1917 and began his naval career at age nineteen as a *See-Kadett*. He served aboard two of the surface fleet's light cruisers until he volunteered for the U-boat forces in the autumn of 1940. He entered the U-boat training program after serving a year as a staff officer, and from March to November 1941 he served aboard U-101 on three combat patrols. During the patrols U-101 sank three enemy ships and taught Marbach the intricacies of actual submarine warfare. An excellent service record aboard U-101 later qualified Marbach for nomination to the training school in Kiel for new U-boat commanders. He completed the course and remained there six months longer to command the school boats U-28 and U-29. Command of U-953 signified the next step in the young *Oberleutnant's* naval career and his return to the Battle of

---

4.   Gannon, 6.

the Atlantic. During eight war patrols that would span 223 days—until August 1944—the skipper would guide U-953 and his crew through long days and weeks of extreme boredom, with occasional interruptions of combat.

The Kriegsmarine ensign is hauled up the mast of the new U-boat while ObLt. Karl-Heinz Marbach salutes.

Contrary to both wartime and postwar stereotypes that U-boat men were ruthless Nazis who possessed the worst traits of sharks and wolves, *Oberleutnant* Marbach was the antithesis of the hardened U-boat captain of legend and lore who wielded brutal discipline over his crew. He did expect technical perfection and dedication from every man who sailed with him, but trusted each to perform his critical duties with utmost skill to assure the boat's success and survival. The twenty-six year-old skipper possessed a relaxed, informal demeanor that displayed casual confidence in his own abilities. His coveted white U-boat commander's hat was a battered affair wholly in keeping with the informal hand salute that became his trademark—several fingers casually spread apart rather than stiffly straight in the formal manner. His easy grin implied a wise and calculating mind driven by genuine cheerfulness seemingly entirely out of character with the job he was trained to perform. His crew, in turn, responded well to the skipper and dedicated themselves to his able command.

Oberleutnant zur See Karl-Heinz Marbach, commander of U-953; La Pallice, 1943.

During U-953's initial shakedown each crewman acquainted himself with the new boat to perfect his skills, forge a cohesive fighting team and operate with maximum efficiency. *Kater* was inspected bow to stern as well, to make necessary adjustments and repairs to her complex machinery. Every mechanical and electrical component was required to operate in synchronized perfection for the boat to submerge, remain underwater for many hours, and return to the surface with the greatest degree of safety for the crew. Gunners and torpedo specialists also honed their fighting skills aboard the boat that would carry them into harm's way. All the resources expended by the *Reich* to train, assemble, equip, and deploy the warship on combat patrols were for naught if gunners and torpedo technicians could not confidently deliver their deadly ordnance against enemy ships, aircraft, and shore installations.

Two general categories of crewmen were assigned to every U-boat: seamen and technicians. Seamen included gunners, helmsmen, cooks, and others who protected, steered, and maintained basic operational control over their vessel. Technicians were specialists who operated torpedo launch systems, radio and sound detection gear, and the diesel and electrical power plants.[5] Diesel machinists kept their giant MAN engines running under the watchful eye of a petty officer, the *Obermachinist*, who used a series of loud whistle signals to issue commands above the engine room noise. Naturally, technicians and seamen alike considered their own group members and responsibilities superior to the others. Baumann and his fellow seamen referred to their technician friends as *Bilgekrabbe*—bilge crabs.

The bow compartment of a Type VIIC U-boat, looking forward, with four torpedo launch tube hatches in the center. The spare torpedo rack in place, left, prevents crew bunks from being used.

The main armament aboard U-953 was five torpedo tubes, four in the bow and one in the stern. Type VIIC boats normally carried fourteen torpedoes, five of which were loaded directly into the tubes at the port before each combat patrol. The bow torpedo room also served as crew sleeping quarters, where two spare torpedoes were chained into loading positions that prevented the hinged bunks from being lowered for use. After one of the first four spares was loaded into the launching tube the crew manhandled one of eight remaining spares out of the storage hold beneath the bow compartment floor. Using hand cranks they hoisted, pulled, and pushed the huge grease-covered torpedo into the vacant loading position. The monstrous *Aale* always vied against their human overseers for the limited living space on board and held absolute priority over all minimal

5.   Gannon, 36-37.

creature comforts the men otherwise enjoyed. U-boat crewmen invariably hoped to make early contact with the enemy and launch their complement of torpedoes during the first days into each *Feindfahrt,* which spanned as many as twelve weeks.[6] The ratings then could lower the hinged bunks to rest and sleep rather than continue to stake claims on lengths of walkway where others constantly had to step over and around them. Free space and privacy inside the cramped, buoyant sphere were among the rarest of commodities.

The enlisted ranks could expect no solitude or seclusion from their *Kameraden* during a war patrol. Little wonder Marbach and other U-boat commanders allowed crewmen to express their individuality through the clothes they wore at sea. The men of U-953 went to war and lived and fought in all manner of non-regulation attire. Many outfitted themselves at the *Bekleidungskammer,* a Kriegsmarine clothing storehouse at La Pallice, where piles of military and civilian clothes from captured or destroyed Allied ships had been stacked. The sailors variously sported British dungarees and loud plaid shirts to straw hats like those worn by French singer-actor Maurice Chevalier, all of which they combined with parts of their navy-issued work uniforms.

U-953 now was structurally unique among most of the many hundreds of Ubootwaffe boats. The conning tower had been rebuilt during the first required overhaul to accommodate three gun platforms. The towers of six other Type VIIC Biscay-based boats had undergone the same or similar conversions, all of which were designated *U-flak* to identify them as anti-aircraft gunboats. U-953 now bristled with specialized weapons to take on the Allied fighter planes and patrol bombers that swarmed over the Atlantic and the Bay. Eight 20mm automatic cannon in two quadruple mounts and a 37mm semi-automatic cannon were crowded onto the new gun platforms. The prime responsibility of the *U-flak* was to protect less well armed U-boats while they crossed the treacherous Biscay toward the open Atlantic and their assigned patrol sectors. To carry out their dangerous assignments, *U-flak's* sailed on the surface as decoys to invite attack by hostile aircraft. Theoretically, pilots who took the bait would be subjected to a concentrated and withering stream of anti-aircraft fire. Caught in the maul of such massed firepower, the attacking aircraft would be destroyed while the escorted U-boats remained unmolested.

---

6.   Translation: Torpedoes were referred to as *Aale*—eels. A *Feindfahrt* was an operational war patrol.

U-441, shown above, along with U-256, U-621 and U-953 were
converted to *U-flak* anti-aircraft gunboats in mid-1943 after their towers
were lengthened to accommodate multiple gun mounts. The *U-flak*
concept quickly proved fatally flawed, and U-953 was reconverted back
to its attack boat configuration after only one mission

U-953's conversion to a *U-flak* was a work in progress when Karl climbed
aboard the boat for his first workday as a crewmember. The conning tower,
which resembled a shark's dorsal fin and encompassed the bridge where crewmen
stood watch, had been substantially lengthened to accommodate the three elevated gun platforms. Mounted on the forward platform was a *Flakvierling* 38, a
four-barreled twenty-millimeter anti-aircraft gun that fired up to eight hundred
high explosive or armor-piercing rounds per minute. The gun was positioned to
provide a 180-degree zone of fire starboard to port across the bow of the boat,
and in a skyward arc to ninety degrees above the boat. A second *Flakvierling* 38
was mounted on the slightly higher *Wintergarten,* the platform immediately aft of
the bridge, to provide concentrated firepower abeam. The third gun platform was
located below the aft *Flakvierling* and mounted a single *Flakvisier* 37, a thirty-
seven-millimeter anti-aircraft gun that also protected the boat against attacks
from astern. The semi-automatic weapon fired larger high explosive and armor-
piercing projectiles a greater distance than the twenty-millimeter cannon, but at a
slower rate of eighty rounds per minute.[7] The crew's six gunners were thoroughly
trained on each weapon and in combat could man any of the three interchange-
ably. The essential yet unspoken element required to invite air attacks upon U-

---

7.   *Handbook*, 346-348.

953 was to place Baumann and his fellow gunners in the line of enemy fire as human bait.

Crewmen busied themselves in the daily dockside routine of mundane tasks that were part of the normal process of overhaul and repairs that each boat underwent between operational patrols. U-boats were complex machines that suffered tremendously from the effects of weather, the corrosive sea, and the men who lived aboard them for extended periods of time. After an extremely difficult *Feindfahrt,* for example, the Chief of one U-boat itemized nearly five hundred repairs that were necessary to return the boat to maximum trim.[8] The heavy work to overhaul U-boats and return them to the ocean war was performed by teams of specialists and engineers from the navy yard. The procedure to completely overhaul the boat was to remove all moving parts and hoist the stripped-down superstructure into dry-dock.[9] After two months at sea U-boats returned home covered with streaks of rust that gave them a derelict appearance. In order to minimize deterioration, repair personnel scraped and sanded the entire exterior surface of the dry-docked boat and applied a new heavy coat of gray paint. Battle damage and shortages of replacement parts sometimes lengthened repair and overhaul procedures to eight weeks or more.

The *Ubootfahrer* tackled mostly simple equipment repairs and cleaning chores aboard their boat. The work was easy and consumed excess energy, and was for some a balm that soothed stressed nerves. *Matrosenobergefreiter* Karl-Heinz Patzer performed his mundane cleaning routine with such relish that he was given the moniker *P-Drei,* a reference to the P-3 solvent he used to restore a factory-new sheen to every mechanical component he could find.

The crewmen universally savored overhaul and dry-dock time, during which they could travel home or elsewhere on extended leave. Those who remained on shore duty enjoyed short workdays and long evenings to pursue whatever degree of rest, relaxation, and revelry they chose. To make time ashore even more enticing and fruitful, U-boat officers and men could request to receive their monthly pay in advance since money was worthless during long combat patrols from which they might never return. Many well-paid *Ubootfahrer* sailed into combat with barely a *Reichspfenning* to their names.

Karl settled into the daily routine of shore duty at La Pallice, and in short order discovered the cafe and bar scene during off-hours in La Rochelle. The young boys and men whom the unnatural milieu of war had thrown together

---

8.   Werner, 228.
9.   Werner, 61.

inside conquered France strove to sort out their private fears and passions with the assistance of comrades and alcohol. German occupation troops were paid in French currency rather than in *Reichsmarks*. Stacks of *Francs* changed hands every payday, which returned to the local economy through merchants, restaurants, bars, brothels, and girlfriends. Baumann received a *Matrosenobergefreiter's* monthly salary of 112.5 *Reichmarks* in regular and war service pay after his latest promotion in rank, plus additional pay for undersea duty.[10] While the Kriegsmarine automatically sent part of Karl's pay home, where Christian Baumann deposited the funds into a savings account for his son, the U-boat gunner survived well on the payments he received in cash: the equivalent of five *Reichsmarks* bought twenty shots of cheap, powerful and plentiful cognac. While thick nighttime fog enshrouded the ancient seaport town, La Rochelle's bars and restaurants rumbled inside with raucous laughter and raunchy conversation—all lubricated by massive alcohol consumption—and U-boat men who swayed to the sound of blaring band music. At the same time, melancholy accordion strains set a somber and contemplative mood for lone Germans who populated the town's small cafes to drown out homesickness or the loss of friends whose boats had disappeared while on patrol in the Biscay or the Atlantic.

In the depths of the brutal world war the German sailors in La Rochelle were unwelcome and hated occupiers who personified the Nazi juggernaut that had destroyed French sovereignty after only six weeks of *Blitzkrieg*. The large number of French citizens who refused to submit to Hitler's authority had formed a vast network of loosely organized fighters that waged unconventional warfare against local German forces. The friendly merchant or waitress might also be a member of one of the feared guerilla units generally referred to as the French Resistance. Rumors about Resistance activity around La Rochelle were frequent and terrifying, so every member of the Wehrmacht was constantly wary of attackers who could strike without warning. Unseen assailants might lurk behind any doorway or in any shadow to ambush unsuspecting sailors, then disappear into the thick evening fog that rolled in from the Bay. Karl Baumann always armed himself with a double-edged Kriegsmarine dagger whenever he left the relative safety of the *Kaserne* to visit the surrounding streets of La Rochelle.

---

10. See *Handbook of German Military Forces*, 9-10, for a detailed table and explanation of Wehrmacht pay scales. One *Reichsmark* was valued unofficially at $0.40 in 1945.

Karl Baumann inside the *Kaserne* at La Rochelle; whenever he ventured into town he carried a dagger to fend off any attack from the French Resistance.

The German forces that occupied La Rochelle had good reason to look over their shoulders. The town's revered elderly mayor, Léonce Vieljeux, had led resistance to the occupation since the Wehrmacht first arrived on 23 June 1940. His refusal to fly the swastika over city hall or to post official occupation edicts and propaganda had marked him as a dangerous troublemaker. Occupation authorities relieved Vieljeux of his mayoral duties on 22 September, and in 1941 expelled him from the town. Vieljeux had returned in secret to his beloved La Rochelle, however, and had become the proud symbol of the city's refusal to become a subdued German enclave. The Germans would arrest and execute the former mayor in 1944, but his armed resistance fighters would remain a deadly, threatening presence until the final days of the war in Europe—never conquered by the Wehrmacht's superior arms.[11]

Though the prospect of death was never far over the horizon, Karl sought solace only in drinking and directed his life wholly outside of his religious orientation. He never thought to attend public chapel services inside the *Kaserne* or to pray for guidance and salvation within the privacy of his heart. He did not remotely consider the prospect that he and his drinking companions had offended their spiritual dimensions when they requested passes to leave the compound early on Sunday mornings to attend a church in town, but instead visited their favorite downtown watering holes. Nor could he truthfully have claimed he simply had followed the crowd; in every respect he was a prominent member of the crowd, if not a leader and instigator of frequent off-duty mischief. The eighteen year-old had grown up quickly and early; according to the statistics for his service, most likely he would die young. He was determined to eke out the minor pleasures each day held.

One nondescript evening Karl decided to join drinking companions who earlier had ambled into town for a few rounds. When he swung open the door of his armoire to retrieve his dress uniform he discovered that one of his roommate's had surreptitiously requisitioned his one available navy blouse, leaving behind only Karl's neckerchief. Karl was both annoyed and amused at his predicament, but remained determined to meet up with his friends. A short time later he made his way to the bar and took a seat with several *Kameraden.* He appearance was noteworthy only in having not removed his bulky navy overcoat in the warm, sailor-packed saloon. The evening's festivities ramped up to their normal state of exuberance as young *Ubootfahrer* expressed themselves with volleys of boisterous laughter and animated conversation against the backdrop of loud, live band music. At some point the conversation around one table turned to whether anyone was man enough to lift over his head one of their drinking party, a very large Kriegsmariner. The challenge quickly traveled from table to table until Karl's circle of friends prodded and taunted him to attempt the feat. Bolstered by the flow of cognac, the brawny youth from Brambauer confidently accepted the test of strength, and word of the contest quickly spread throughout the bar. The band stopped playing when the roomful of sailors crowded around Karl's table. Wagers raced from man to man, and tension mounted as Karl took a final sip of cognac. The decibel level of competing conversations dropped precipitously and attention was focused upon the young man bundled in his heavy coat as he finally slid

---

11. Louis Desgraves, *Visiting La Rochelle*, English edition (France: Editions Sud Ouest, 1998), 13. On 1 September 1944, Vieljeux was murdered—executed by an SS firing squad at the Struthof concentration camp near Strasbourg, France.

back his chair and rose to his feet. Then, with a trace of theatric melodrama he flung off his overcoat. The room instantly exploded into lusty howls and guffaws of laughter. Young Baumann had worn only an undershirt beneath his regulation neckerchief. Laughter then turned to raucous cheers as Karl placed his taut frame beneath the giant sailor and hefted him high overhead into the smoke-laden air.

For more than two months U-953 was overhauled and refitted at a steady pace. Karl continued to assimilate himself thoroughly to the responsibilities of a gunner aboard the submersible weapons platform. In that role he would man his primary battle station only when a *Flieger Alarm* announced the approach of enemy planes. If the *Alarm* sounded with Karl standing watch on the bridge, he would leave the watch party immediately to man his weapon. Otherwise, the gunners would ready their weapons for action as soon as the boat surfaced, then return down below to stand ready until ordered to battle stations. In an extreme emergency the boat then could crash dive without risking the gunners' lives or those of the men on watch. With the boat submerged during an *Alarm*, Karl would assist other crewmen in any manner possible and at any location help was needed. Finally, at the very least he would be useful as ballast—a realistic assessment and crucial function despite the derogatory implication of uselessness that was conveyed whenever a superior spat out the familiar submariners' admonition.[12]

The new crewman's introduction to the interior of the Type VIIC U-boat was a sobering experience. The fact that one adapted to her cramped otherworldly confines and thrived in the narrow cylindrical vessel was an amazing feat of human willpower and endurance. Pipes, ducts, handwheels, valves, gauges, and all manner of mechanical instrumentation vied for space in every direction and crowded the low ceiling of the narrow walkway that ran from bow to stern. Low watertight hatches presented more head-banging opportunities when men passed—sometimes at breakneck speed—through the steel bulkheads that separated the boat's four pressurized compartments.

Every day Karl reported for duty he became more comfortable with U-953's confined spaces and intricate mechanical systems. An emotional bond soon developed between the new *Ubootfahrer* and the slender steel marvel of engineering into which he would place all hopes for survival at sea and in combat. His pulse quickened every time he walked across the gangplank from the dockside onto the boat's main deck. From the wooden-slatted outer deck, Karl would climb the lad-

---

12. Werner, 13. U-boat crewmen disdained the comment, "At least you'll be useful for ballast!"

der that ran alongside the conning tower to the steel-railed *Wintergarten* just behind the U-boat's bridge, then step around the tall attack periscope that dominated the cramped bridge deck atop the tower. The main hatch through which the crew normally entered and exited the boat was located between the attack periscope and the bridge's semi-circular armored steel forward wall.

The men stationed topside during any combat emergency had to flee the bridge in mere seconds when the U-boat began her crash dive. The entry maneuver was so critical that every crewman practiced it whenever he entered the boat in port or at sea. Thus, Karl jumped feet-first through the small circular main hatch onto a rung of the ladder that descended to the tower compartment deck. An instant later he gained his balance, released his foothold and raised his arms above his head in a single coordinated motion, and rapidly fell through the hatch. The narrow portal proved a formidable barrier to plunge through at breakneck speed. Karl, as did many others, sometimes sported ghastly bruises and abrasions under his arms after striking the hatch rim during the virtual free fall into the tower compartment. As he approached the deck below he gripped the vertical ladder rails to stop his descent. He then immediately repeated the procedure to drop through the tower deck hatch onto the ladder that led down into the *Zentrale*, the U-boat's centrally-located main control room. Karl landed with a muffled thud on the lower deck, atop a folded life raft that lay beneath the ladder to soften the impact of landing and absorb the sound. Finally, he swung himself off the raft and away from the ladder without delay, lest others scrambling down the hatch behind him land in a heap of heartily cursing bodies.

A narrow walkway led from the *Zentrale* to the bow, through the forward bulkhead, past the radio and sound operators' rooms, then through the captain's nook. The captain's territory contained a felt-curtained bunk where the U-boat commander occasionally would catch a few precious moments of solitude and sleep. The nook also contained a desktop, around which the skipper frequently met with his officers to work and relax.

Accommodations for the U-boat crew followed in descending order of rank toward the forward torpedo room in the bow. The next compartment past the captain's nook housed the sleeping quarters, mess, and wardroom table for the other officers. The walkway passed through another bulkhead hatch and the quarters for the chief warrant officers. It then skirted a tiny compartment on the port side that contained the forward toilet and washroom, and terminated in the bow compartment and forward torpedo room.

The bow compartment housed the enlisted crew's sleeping quarters. At the beginning of each long combat patrol the narrow bow compartment usually was jammed with provisions and spare torpedoes; enlisted crewmen crawled on hands and knees to maneuver about the compartment. Storage areas were so compact and stuffed with supplies that tinned food was stacked even in the aft washroom; under such conditions only the smallest personal items and trinkets found their way on board. Little space was allocated to sleeping quarters for the enlisted men, so the twelve available bunks were constantly in use. Men relieved of duty at the end of their shifts crawled into "hot bunks" that had just been vacated.

The aft section of the U-boat was similarly apportioned to utilize every inch of space. From the *Zentrale*, the rear bulkhead led to the walkway that passed through the petty officers' quarters and into the galley, followed by the aft toilet and washroom. The next compartment housed two large six-cylinder, 1160-horsepower diesel engines that provided the fastest cruising speed for the boat. The stern bulkhead at the end of the diesel room led to the motor room, the last compartment in the stern. The motor room contained the crucial dynamotors that powered the lights and electrical equipment the crew relied upon for survival underwater. The electric motors also provided silent propulsion while the boat was submerged. Additional critical equipment located in the motor room included air compressors to flush the ballast tanks of water in order to surface. Finally, a single torpedo tube was located at the rear of the compartment. Storage compartments located beneath both the forward and aft walkways held spare torpedoes, ammunition for the anti-aircraft guns, and two giant lead-acid batteries that ran the electric motors.

The U-boat's interior was fully encased in a cylindrical steel pressure hull that provided buoyancy and prevented the submerged vessel from collapsing against the tremendous forces of pressure the sea exerted in the depths. The steel-plated exterior surface encompassed and protected the pressure hull, the huge ballast tank that ran beneath the pressure hull, and the fuel tanks that rode along the length of boat like side-saddles.[13]

When the men made final preparations for a *Feindfahrt* they laid in a large supply of foodstuffs and drinking water. A day or more was required to adequately stock the boat with food, supplies, and munitions before each long patrol. Since a war patrol might span twelve weeks or more, the interior of the U-boat was stuffed with rations. From the ceiling of each already cramped compartment and walkway, mesh hammocks sagged under the weight of vegetables, eggs, fruit; and loaves of *Kommissbrot*—hard black navy bread. Sausages and hams hung by the score from overhead pipes. The elite group of warriors who sailed

---

13. Gannon, 33-35.

their iron coffins thousands of miles to scour the Atlantic for enemy ships was the best-provisioned troops in Hitler's Wehrmacht.[14] The abundant provisions offered exceedingly better fare at the outset of a patrol than toward the final days or weeks. Crates of eggs and other foods prone to spoilage were eaten early because very little refrigerator space was available. The boat's harried cook fried eggs to order for the grateful men. By the end of every long patrol the cook was forced to subject his mates to vile-tasting potatoes and canned bread. Large sacks of spuds usually were stored in the engine room, where after several weeks they absorbed the strong taste and smell of diesel fuel. No manner of cooking or preparation completely camouflaged the potatoes for their assault upon the already abused senses.

Shortly after dawn on 2 October 1943, those who would take U-953 again to war lined up for morning formation and roll call in front of their quarters. Karl Baumann and his young *Kameraden*, some of whom had barely learned to shave, appeared for all the world like a college fraternity or members of a sports club; their navy uniforms—the parts they chose to wear—alone disclosed the martial purpose for which they had been gathered at the *Kaserne* in La Rochelle. They had arisen early to prepare themselves for an extended journey into the Atlantic warfront. They had savored the limitless supply of hot water and soap that momentarily left them cleaner than they would find themselves for the next six, eight, or perhaps twelve weeks. They had consumed mountains of freshly prepared breakfast foods in the mess hall, along with countless cigarettes that clouded the air with low hanging smoke. Many had written hasty last letters home to family, friends and lovers, and deposited them in stacks at the *Feldpost*. They had wrestled all their belongings into their seabags as ordered, and now stood at attention with them while the boat's officers checked off names from their crew rosters. The young warriors' faces variously revealed a curious fusion of conflicting emotions: excitement, nonchalance, bravado, trepidation, anticipation, and tinges of unspoken but very real fear.

With all officers and crewmen present and accounted for, the group was marched rank and file about ten minutes to the railroad station next to the *Kaserne*. The morning sun unleashed its blinding light with early autumn intensity as the men stood squinting, waiting impatiently on the station platform. The timbre of conversation was subdued. Quiet tension surrounded the *Ubootfahrer* when they finally boarded the small train that delivered them a few minutes later to the U-boat pens at La Pallice. The men formed up and marched to a large con-

---

14.   Gannon, 10.

crete storage bunker, inside which they deposited their seabags. In the not-unlikely event their boat was reported sunk during the mission or simply never heard from again, the contents of the seabags simply would be gathered up and shipped to each crewman's family. The macabre implication from such brutal efficiency neither helped reinforce morale nor engendered great confidence that the mission would be successfully concluded. Under the present circumstances, however, the policy was wholly practical and realistic. With only the smallest personal articles in hand or stuffed inside pockets, the men then marched into the gaping entrance of the U-boat bunker and down its seemingly endless corridors to their docked boat.

U-953, completely overhauled and provisioned, converted to a *U-flak* gunboat and gleaming with a new coat of gray paint, waited at her berth for her crew to commence their second *Feindfahrt*—Karl Baumann's first. A final flurry of activity completed the pre-mission preparations while the last of the crewmembers milled dockside, where they smoked, fidgeted, and relished the last moments of solid ground under their feet.

A short time later Marbach arrived and ordered the entire crew onto the main deck. Crewmen flicked their cigarettes into the water and ran across the gangplank to fall into line on the main deck. The men inside the boat scrambled out of the bridge hatch and onto the deck where comrades already stood at attention. After the officers rechecked their personnel rosters and accounted for the entire crew the skipper queried his section chiefs on preparations and conditions of the boat, then briefed the men on the final procedures for departure. At no time, however, did Marbach reveal any specifics about their patrol assignment or their ultimate destination. Security measures were required to subvert the work of spies known to number among the French civilians who worked in and around the concrete fortress. The commander would divulge the mission details to his officers only after the boat was underway. German military protocol mandated that enlisted men had no business to know any details of the mission, and none dared ask. At sea the radio operator would tune his receiver to the BdU frequency at predetermined times every day to pick up coded radio messages for each boat on patrol. U-953 was subject to every order issued to the boat code-named *Kater*—a moniker young crewmen wholeheartedly approved because it connoted the independent nature and carnal prowess of the male feline.[15]

U-boats received patrol assignments that plotted their destinations by a system of grid squares. The entire Atlantic Ocean and contiguous seas were divided into

---

15. Translation: Tomcat.

a series of imaginary squares that measured approximately 486 *Seemeilen* or nautical miles per side, along the fifty degrees latitude line. These squares, the largest in the grid system, were given alphabetical designations AD, BB, CH, and so on. Each grid square was subdivided into nine smaller unnumbered squares of 162 *Seemeilen* per side. Each unnumbered square then was subdivided into nine smaller grids of fifty-four *Seemeilen* per side and given double-digit identification numerals from eleven to ninety-nine. Each small numbered grid was finally subdivided into numbered squares the size of a *Marinequadrat,* an area approximately 4.25 *Seemeilen* on each side or eighteen square nautical miles.[16]

Before each patrol, the U-boat commander ordered his navigator to obtain sets of maps and charts from flotilla headquarters. The crew was never informed which section of the vast ocean was their patrol destination, so unofficial news and occasional revelations about the grid square maps observed on-board set off rounds of furious speculation and rumor. The men had to be prepared to live and fight amid the wide vagaries of Atlantic Ocean weather. One hundred percent humidity turned the interior of a boat into a sweltering oven in the warm ocean climes, while the cold North Atlantic turned U-boats into damp and sometimes icy refrigerators. Lightweight clothing, rubberized rain slickers, and bulky insulated leather trousers and coats jammed storage spaces in the claustrophobic environs of the boats.

The skipper ordered the crew to their duty stations for departure. One at a time—barely—the men scrambled up to the main hatch atop the tower, then down into the belly of the steel beast. Dockhands simultaneously pulled away the gangplank and untied U-953 from her moorings. As he stood on the bridge with the First Officer, *Leutnant zur See* Gustav Bischoff, Marbach ordered electrical power to the twin screws that propelled the vessel. As a member of the first watch party, Karl stood at his station on the bridge. The boat slowly pulled away from the dock at 19:45 without a sound.[17] Had Marbach ordered diesel power the immense bunker would have reverberated with the rumble of the two big diesels being kicked to life; reeking fuel exhaust also would have lingered so heavily inside the *Boxe* that large fans would have been required to suck out the noxious gas from the bunker.[18]

In stark contrast to the departure of U-boats during the legendary Happy Times, subdued fanfare hailed *Kater* when she left her concrete sanctuary at

---

16.   Gannon, 50. Grid squares usually were referred to as a *Quadrat,* or *Qu.*
17.   *KTB,* 2 October 1943.
18.   Schmeelke, 37.

19:49 to silently creep into the evening dusk. By autumn 1943 there was little to rejoice or celebrate. From the moment the boat emerged from her *Boxe* until she returned to the safety of the bunker she was vulnerable to attack from Allied air and naval forces. Marbach, Bischoff, and the *Erstewache* or *I. Wache*—the men assigned to the First Watch—stood on the cramped bridge high above the water as the boat gracefully slid past the harbor's artificial breakwater, through a canal lock, and into the Bay of Biscay.

U-953's prow cuts into the Bay of Biscay at the 200 meter depth line west of La Pallice, France, with the setting sun dead ahead. The U-boat soon will overtake a French fishing boat and a German patrol boat guarding the harbor entrance.

The boat trailed a converted trawler that served as an armed escort to direct her safe passage through the German minefields that surrounded the harbor entrance. German warships often shared the coastal waters with tiny civilian fishing boats and sailboats that bobbed atop the gentle Biscay waves. On at least one occasion a sailboat was captured after radio transmission gear and weapons were spotted on board. The French Resistance had used the vessel to report the presence of outbound U-boats to Allied naval and air forces headquarters. In the aftermath of the obliteration of the sailboat and its crew, French and German sailors eyed each other warily whenever their paths crossed in the shallows of the harbor.

The U-boat finally cleared the mined areas. Her first escort returned to La Pallice while a second German vessel led the *U-flak* toward a location designated *2A plus 20*, where the depth of the Bay sank to two hundred meters. U-953 arrived at the 200-meter line at 08:40 on 3 October, where Marbach and crew had taken their boat for deep dive tests five days earlier.[19] When en route to an assigned patrol area in mid-ocean, the first priority for the skipper was to get his boat and crew there safely and secretly. Thus, U-boat commanders preferred to traverse the Biscay in darkness for stealth while running on the surface at maximum speed.

All through the night a Watch Officer stood on the bridge as his team of lookouts scanned the sea and sky in every direction. One of four watch parties—*Erstewache, Zweitewache, Drittewache,* and *Gefechtswache*—constantly held vigil over U-953 whenever she rode the surface.[20]

Most seamen among the crew, including gunners, were assigned to one or more watch parties. A Watch Officer commanded each *Wache* and was assisted by a petty officer, both of whom scanned the sea and sky in all directions. One of four seamen was responsible for each ninety-degree zone that comprised the 360-degree radius around the boat, the bow of which represented zero degrees and the stern 180 degrees. A *Steuermann* sat high inside the conning tower and steered the boat on orders from the submarine commander on the bridge or, in the skipper's absence, the Watch Officer.[21]

Baumann was assigned to the *Erstewache* and the *Gefechtswache,* always to the zone ninety degrees to 180 degrees starboard. The rules of conduct for the *Wache* were strict and uncompromising. During their four-hour shifts, the four seamen on watch never moved their gazes away from their assigned ninety-degree zones or their eyes away from their large, powerful navy binoculars. Not surprisingly, the effort proved extremely difficult. After the first hour muscles ached, boredom crept into the mind, and the sweet allure of sleep was never far from its stealthy approach. To fend off these afflictions Karl frequently raised himself up on the balls of his feet and concentrated upon balancing himself in that position for a

---

19. *KTB*, 2-3 October 1943.
20. Translation: First Watch, Second Watch, Third Watch, Attack Watch.
21. Translation: Helmsman.

moment. He then lowered his heels back to the deck and repeated the exercise as often as necessary to remain alert.[22]

Lookouts searched for any trace of enemy activity: a pinprick of light that gave away a plane's still-silent approach, the masts of a lone cargo vessel, or smoke belching from the stacks of an entire convoy of Liberty ships. Though the *U-flak* gunners were prepared to pour streams of lethal fire into any fighter plane or patrol bomber that dared attack out of the morning sun, no one spoiled for a fight. The veterans of U-953's first patrol had only to recall the swiftness with which death came for one of their own.

At the 200 meter line Marbach ordered the six-man *Wache* to clear the bridge. The watch party leapt through the main hatch as the skipper leaned over the speaking tube that ran between the bridge and the control room below.

"*Auf Tiefe gehen!*" the skipper shouted. A second later the submarine commander jumped onto the ladder inside the main hatch, then pulled the hatch cover closed. His timing had to be perfect, for even as he spun the handwheel that tightened down the hatch cover seawater began to lap over the bridge and spray through the hatch. The amazing choreography of the dive procedure already was fully underway. Working with the perfect coordination of a skilled crew, the fast-diving Type VIIC could plunge more than forty-two feet in thirty seconds.[23]

Beneath the surface a U-boat was suspended in calm smooth waters even during the worst of storms, safe from any tempest wreaking havoc above. In their pressurized steel chamber the men worked, slept, relaxed, daydreamed, and ate the food the skipper ordered the boat's cook to prepare. Type VIIC U-boats comfortably remained underwater up to only twenty-four hours until underwater breathing devices were installed on some boats beginning in 1944. During extreme wartime emergencies U-boats sometimes remained underwater many hours longer. Submerged for an extended length of time, the electric motor batteries began to wear down, and the air below deck became thin and even more stale than the putrid atmosphere the men normally endured. They eventually had to surface to recharge their batteries under diesel power, vent out the foul air, restore the oxygen-starved crew to vitality, and repressurize the living space.

---

22. See Lothar-Gunter Buchheim, *U-Boat War* (New York: Bantam, 1979), 56: "Four straight hours of incessant vigilance—it can seem an eternity in any kind of bad weather. Every seagull will turn into an attacking aircraft, every scrap of cloud rising above the horizon will look like a trail of smoke, the contours of distant waves will seem outlines of ships."

23. Gannon, 6.

On Marbach's dive order the *Leitender Ingenieur* ordered crewmen to vent the main ballast tanks as he shoved his hand against the dive bell. The dive alarm sounded to set the crew into immediate action at their respective stations. With skilled precision, twenty-four technicians in the control room, the engine room, and the maneuvering room methodically turned red and black valve wheels, pulled levers, and flipped panel switches in the prescribed order to plunge the boat to the depths. The U-boat's mechanical responses were similarly precise. The external ballast tanks opened and tons of seawater displaced the buoyant air. Air intake vents and diesel exhaust valves were cut off and sealed against the inflow of water as the electrical motors replaced diesel power supply to propel the boat slowly and silently underwater.[24] When the dive procedure was performed perfectly the submerged U-boat quickly but smoothly descended at a gradual downward angle—bow first—then leveled off at the prescribed depth. If any part of the dive procedure was not properly executed, or if the weight of the boat was not evenly distributed, the boat might inadvertently dive stern first or bow first at a dangerous angle. If exterior vents were not properly closed the interior of the boat could be quickly swamped with cascades of seawater. If the dive procedure was executed perfectly but not quickly enough, the boat might remain on the surface several seconds too long to escape a disastrous attack by Allied aircraft or warships. The survival of the U-boat and her crew was based purely upon the absolute knowledge, precision, and honed skills of every crewman, non-commissioned officer, and officer who directed or operated the myriad mechanical and electrical systems.

U-953 submerged to maximum depth to undertake a series of final tests to determine the boat's sea-worthiness. Throughout the day the complex combat, diving, and life-sustaining systems were checked and rechecked while the mechanical integrity of the boat was scrutinized. While all systems either passed their tests or were repaired on board, two serious mechanical problems came to Marbach's attention by a signal from U-573, which had trailed *Kater* to *2A plus 20*. The *Wache* on U-573's bridge had noticed a porous weld running along U-953's conning tower and oil patches over the spot where the boat had submerged. Marbach deliberated his options in consideration of the reported mechanical faults. Either problem, if not thoroughly repaired, could compromise the safety of the mission, the boat, and the crew. A weak welded seam could collapse under the extraordinary water pressure to which the boat would be subjected during underwater operations. Floating oil spots on the ocean surface might tip off

---

24. Gannon, 33.

Allied ships or aircraft to the location of the submerged boat. In any case, the potential for disaster was too great; Marbach ordered U-953 back to La Pallice for repairs, and at 04:05 on 4 October the boat moored inside Bunker 2. Later that morning U-boat maintenance specialists tested the reported problem areas and confirmed the need for repairs. By evening the mechanics and welders had completed their work. The crew was corralled and ordered back to the boat, and at 19:50 U-953 again eased out of the Bunker and followed a barrage- and mine-laying vessel out of the port and into the eastern Biscay.

Another Type VII U-boat accompanies U-953 into the Bay of Biscay and the Battle of the Atlantic.

Marbach ordered the escort vessel dismissed after *Kater* successfully concluded a deep dive test on the morning of 5 October. Momentarily, the *U-flak* submerged and plodded slowly westward, farther into the Bay. The boat and it's crew settled into a routine that for the next four days consisted of diving at the break of dawn to avoid visual detection by enemy ships and aircraft, sailing underwater during daylight, then surface running at high speed at night to recharge the huge electric batteries. The weather each day remained[25] largely unchanged, with moonlit nights, clear days and unobstructed visibility.

At night the boat sliced through the waves of the open bay. Survival depended upon crossing as much of the Biscay as possible before daybreak, though blessed

---

25. *KTB*, 3-9 October 1943.

darkness alone no longer protected U-boats or surface warships from detection. By the war's fourth year British and American naval and air forces possessed stronger radar, better signals intelligence, and aircraft equipped with searchlights to track down U-boats in the busy traffic lanes of the Bay even in the pitch black of moonless nights. German engineers worked equally hard to develop counter-measures against the Allies' latest innovations, but no defenses had been found to give the technological advantage back to the U-boat fleet.[26]

The main thrust of all U-boat activity originated from five submarine bases strategically located on the Bay of Biscay at the French ports of Brest, Lorient, St. Nazaire, La Pallice, and Bordeaux. By the spring of 1943 more than one hundred U-boats had traversed the Bay each month heading north, west, or south toward assigned positions in the Atlantic from Iceland to South America, or on return trips from increasingly unsuccessful undersea patrols. The Allies knew well that the highest concentrations of U-boats were to be found in the Bay within a zone that ran three hundred miles south from Brest and roughly two hundred miles west where the waters of the Bay met the Atlantic.[27] To the British and Americans the area was a kill zone. They concentrated large anti-submarine forces in the Bay with devastating results. Aircraft accounted for the great majority of U-boats destroyed during the first half of 1943. The fortunate boats that safely reached Atlantic waters markedly increased their chances for survival; nonetheless, by June 1943, 65 percent of U-boat losses had occurred to those en route to their assigned positions or while they lay in wait to attack Allied convoys. The remainder of losses occurred in near proximity to targeted convoys and their escort ships.[28]

26. *Conferences*, 339-340.
27. Gannon, 94.
28. *Conferences*, 331-332.

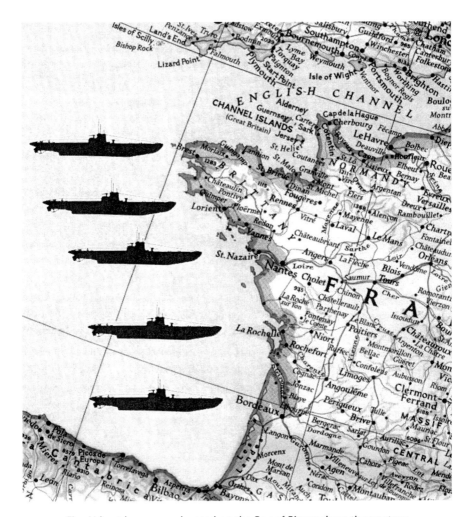

Five U-boat bases were located on the Bay of Biscay along the western coast of France; at Brest, Lorient, St. Nazaire, La Rochelle/La Pallice, and Bordeaux. Karl Baumann was based first at La Rochelle/La Pallice; then nearest to the English Channel at Brest, to await the Allies' long-expected invasion of France.

Grand Admiral Karl Dönitz, chief of the U-boat force, invoked three resolute duties upon U-boat skippers and their crews: pursue, attack, and destroy.[29] With only thirty-nine operational boats in service at the beginning of the war, their skippers had located and sunk an astounding number of enemy ships almost at

29. Werner, 48.

will. While the war progressed and escalated, however, the ability of U-boats to locate, stalk, and kill their prey became exponentially more difficult as the British and later the Americans developed new anti-submarine tactics and equipment. By 1943 large numbers of veteran skippers and crews had been killed or captured. Experienced and skilled fighters were replaced by younger, less experienced or untried officers and men who were essentially sacrificed for an already-lost cause. To be sure, success and long-term survival were products of hard-won experience. Only thirty U-boat commanders out of a total of 1,411 would account for more than 30 percent of all merchant ships sunk during the war. More than 850 U-boats—over 75 percent of the boats commissioned by the *Reich*—failed to damage a single merchant vessel. Slightly more than 50 percent of all U-boats engaged in combat operations would sink or damage an enemy ship of any type. In the waning months of the war, a great number of U-boat sailors never would see an Allied convoy or fire a shot at the enemy before they were killed on their first combat patrols.[30]

Shortly after midnight on 10 October Marbach received a message from BdU that warned all U-boats to be on the lookout for an aircraft carrier last observed in grid square BD 96, about 600 nautical miles west of U-953's position. The message reported that four days earlier several planes from the carrier had heavily attacked four German vessels. Since Marbach's assigned area of operations included the area where the carrier might have sailed, the skipper decided to proceed underwater during the day to the farthest boundary of his operational area. He then would run on the surface at night along a zigzag course that would be determined by any subsequent messages reporting later sightings of the carrier. By midnight on 12 October the *U-flak* had crossed the western line of the Biscay and entered the Atlantic Ocean. The boat surfaced at 03:37 into completely overcast skies.[31]

While *Kater* rode the surface *Matrosengefreiter* Willi Schmall fell asleep during watch duty atop the bridge, one of the most potentially consequential acts of dereliction a submariner could commit during a combat patrol. An unseen aircraft or warship could have suddenly appeared on the horizon in Schmall's unwatched sector and in minutes or seconds launched a fatal attack against the unsuspecting boat. So serious was the offense that German military law considered the act a capital crime.[32] Unfortunately for Schmall, the Watch Officer noticed the seaman's binoculars tilted in a peculiar downward angle as they remained pressed

---

30. Gannon, 227.
31. *KTB*, 10-12 October 1943.

against his eyes. The officer quietly stepped up to the youngster and waved his hand in front of the binoculars to confirm his suspicions. Schmall did not flinch until he was roughly shaken out of his exhausted stupor.

"You were asleep on watch!" the enraged officer thundered. "Your binoculars were pointed at the water."

"I was—watching the dolphins," the frightened lookout explained hopelessly. The Watch Officer reported the incident to Marbach, who requested the details of Schmall's dangerous infraction. The skipper considered the gravity of the crime, then ordered the desperate young sailor into a hammock, to sleep without interruption, for the remaining five weeks of the combat patrol. Schmall was permitted to leave his bunk only to use the toilet, and was forbidden to speak or read. His *Kameraden* were forbidden to talk to him, and could only hand plates of food to him and retrieve the empty plates. In addition to the stinging humiliation he suffered from his punishment, Schmall was utterly terrified by the nearly certain prospect that he would stand trial at flotilla headquarters and face a firing squad. The severe object lesson was not lost on Karl Baumann or any other *Wache* member.

Ten days out of La Pallice, U-953 had not encountered a single Allied aircraft or ship. Boredom began to encroach upon the men's collective mood, which was little relieved by the absence of fear. Early into their *Feindfahrt*, the best food that provisioned the boat still was plentiful and still helped salve the crew's growing restiveness. *Ubootfahrer* often preferred duty to time off; the hours passed faster while they worked, when their attention could be turned toward crucial tasks and mental stimulation.

Karl Baumann preferred work over leisure time, especially when tasks required the skill and acumen of an experienced seaman. He realized soon after his arrival aboard U-953 that, despite being one of the youngest crewmen, he possessed more practical knowledge of the sea and seamanship than any other member, with the probable exception of former civilian sailors Marbach and Bischoff. Because of his youth and training as a gunner, he seldom was called upon to ply the skills he had perfected aboard the sailing ships *Flora* and *Cremona*, a fact he quietly resented.

Life aboard a U-boat was never entirely pleasant. The exuberance of youth and camaraderie, the momentary excitement and terror of rare combat, and the even

32. Germany was not alone in meting out the death penalty for sailors who fell asleep on watch; during World War II the United States Navy also prescribed the death penalty for its sailors found guilty of the crime. See *The Bluejackets' Manual, United States Navy, 1943* (Annapolis: U.S. Naval Institute, 1943), 63.

more rare combat victory did little to interrupt the otherwise endless plodding hours of tedium the men endured. Living conditions overall were unsavory throughout the boat. The limited amount of fresh water taken aboard before each patrol was used only for drinking. Each man was allotted one cup daily to brush his teeth, but most men chose to drink the water instead. No one could shave or shower while at sea, so after two to twelve weeks on patrol the boat's atmosphere hung heavy with a malodorous blend of bodily secretions, unbrushed teeth, sweat-drenched clothing, oven fumes, oil, grease, rotten food, battery acid, and more—all incubated in 100 percent humidity. Baumann and his crewmates tried to subdue their foulness by liberally bathing themselves in either *Kolibri* or *Kölnischwasser* 4711 colognes, which in such large volume added to the noxious aroma that forever would scar veterans' memories. After even a short duration many foodstuffs exposed to the air absorbed the odors that permeated the interior of the boat; as a consequence, food tasted like the U-boat smelled.[33]

U-953 reached the western boundary of her present operational area—about 650 nautical miles due west of La Pallice—by noon on 14 October, where she surfaced and was prepared to operate as a *U-flak* gunboat. Crewmen worked feverishly to overhaul deck guns fouled by seawater and floating debris. The precision-made weapons were no match for the brutal ocean environment; roiling waves had snapped some of the heavy springs that balanced the 37mm cannon and the 20mm anti-aircraft guns on their mounts.[34] Unfortunately for the *U-flak* mission, the gunners were ill-equipped to repair the crew-served weapons. The damaged and broken balance springs did not render the deck guns useless, but reduced their effectiveness since the gunners could no longer easily raise and lower the weapons to sight and track their targets.

An eight hour surface run brought no sight of enemy air or sea activity, so Marbach issued the dive order and took advantage of stealth to change his position about twenty-five nautical miles due west with a slow seventeen hour underwater trek. The boat surfaced into dim, fog-filled daylight and a low cloud ceiling that during the Happy Time would have afforded comforting protection from enemy observation. Now the weather that closed around U-953 might conceal the approach of a radar-bearing long-range antisubmarine bomber. Binocular lenses misted over and made *Wache* members edgy as they stood at their posts

33.   Gannon, 34; and Karl Baumann. U-953 crewmen seemed partial to the *4711* brand of cologne.
34.   *KTB*, 14 October 1943.

atop the conning tower. Finally, with the setting sun and worsening weather, U-953 sought solace among the calm underwater currents of the eastern Atlantic.[35]

Karl Baumann, center, and fellow members of the *I Wache* returned to La Pallice from Baumann's first combat patrol, 17 November 1943.

Kater again surfaced in the early morning hours of 16 October, nearly 650 miles from the repair shops at La Pallice. The skipper at last sent two coded messages to notify BdU that his guns had been damaged seven days earlier, and that no reserve parts were on board. A few minutes after midnight on 17 October, BdU ordered Marbach to rendezvous with *Oberleutnant* Peter-Arthur Stahl,'s U-648 a short distance from his present location at 10:00 the following day. U-953 remained in the general area of the rendezvous point throughout the day, then late at night sailed on a westerly course toward BE 5922. The boat rode heavy seas the next morning and the weather worsened with each passing hour. Moonlight gave way to overcast skies, then hail. As visibility diminished, Marbach ordered the boat below the surface, still more than twenty nautical miles north of the assigned meeting point. 10:00 came and passed, then noon and the afternoon hours as U-953 slowly plowed toward her rendezvous coordinates. The boat's clock read midnight when finally the *U-flak* reached BE 5922, twelve hours behind schedule. U-648 was nowhere in sight, and *Kater's* radio operator had received no signals from the elusive vessel. Even if the rendezvous had been made on schedule, high waves recorded at that time and location would have made delivery of the replacement parts impossible.[36]

35. *KTB*, 14-15 October 1943.

The U-boat rolled and bucked with surface waves that crashed onto her deck and against the conning tower. Each member of the *Wache* wore a heavy cotton belt around his waist to tether himself to a similar cotton belt that was attached to the inside wall of the bridge. Without the tether, high breaking waves could sweep up and wash away a man in the blink of an eye—sacrificed to the sea without a trace. The watch party wore rubberized hats and suits with their life jackets during rough weather and high seas. The bulky suits protected them only marginally against tall waves and wind-driven spray. Cold seawater routinely poured down Karl Baumann's back after it found its way inside the collar of his slicker, and made the endless hours of the *Wache* drag along with greater misery.

With her long cruising range the U-boat might be ordered to patrol the warm South Atlantic and find beautifully calm seas, then set sail to a location in the frigid North Atlantic under perilous weather conditions. In the worst storms, those on the bridge witnessed the surreal beauty and unbridled power of the seas. Under the worst conditions massive angry waves alternately blotted out the sky and slammed down upon the boat from astounding heights, then opened momentary chasms far below the bow. The leading edge of the boat would alternately disappear into the roiling sea, then pitch into the air before it smashed back down into the underside of the next wave.[37] Tethered to the bridge wall, the men outside at least could observe the boat's harrowing pitch and yaw and brace themselves for the stomach-churning ride. The unfortunate *Ubootfahrer* below-deck had no visual perspective to gird themselves against the storm's relentless violence. Holding onto sturdy pipes, railings, or any piece of equipment securely bolted down, the men below cursed and pleaded and prayed for an end to the torture. The motion was more than many stomachs were designed to withstand, and bouts of seasickness exponentially exacerbated the misery of men compelled to endure their unique agony encased in their narrow steel cylinder.

The life-saving tether presented its own hazards. One particular incident not recorded in U-953's war diary involved Helmut Aue, Karl's traveling companion from Kiel. Heavy seas battered the boat and partially hid the horizon from view while soaked Wache members kept a precarious foothold on the exposed bridge. Suddenly, a terrifying sight appeared between the breaking whitecaps in Aue's sector.

---

36.   *KTB*, 16-18 October 1943. The war diary commonly referred to any Kriegsmarine vessel by the name of her commanding officer, as was the case with *Stahl*, but did not make reference to the boat's codename.
37.   Werner, 93.

"I see masts!!" the lookout shouted. The watch officer swung his binoculars toward Aue's sector—zero to ninety degrees on the compass—and quickly confirmed the sighting.

Alaaarrrm!!! The *Offizier* shouted, and a second later the watch party unhooked their tethers and surged toward the main hatch. Third in order to clear the bridge, Aue threw himself into the hatchway, but his downward plunge was stopped an instant later with a violent jerk that left him breathless. To his horror, he had forgotten to unsnap the long tether from the security belt around his waist, and was suspended in mid-air inside the conning tower. Worse, his dangling body blocked his comrades from tumbling through the hatch even as the boat began her plunge below the ocean surface. Miraculously, at the same instant Aue flung himself into the hatch, Petty Officer Albert Bechtel glanced up from belowdeck and saw the man hanging from the tether like a yo-yo. The *Maat* realized a disaster in the making and charged up the tower ladder to lift Aue onto his shoulder, unclip the tether from Aue's belt, and drop the unfortunate lookout onto the conning tower deck below. The rest of the *Wache* then poured through the hatch with barely a second to spare as the sea crashed down atop the conning tower. The watch officer was drenched as he spun the hatch wheel to seal out the cascading water that otherwise would have quickly swamped *Kater* to send her into a death dive. In the next moment a destroyer's bow slashed through the choppy waves directly above the U-boat as the loud whine of spinning turbines rang in the ears of the German crew. Aue's nearly-fatal mistake during his first combat patrol ended his career aboard U-953.[38]

The main hatch posed dangers from inside the U-boat as well. A pressure vacuum built up inside the pressure hull whenever the boat remained submerged for an extended period of time. To correct the imbalance between outside and inside air pressures, the boat's interior was vented from the outside as soon as she rose onto the surface. Like every crucial function conducted aboard the boat, perfect timing was essential to prevent a pressure imbalance. Marbach himself became the unwitting victim of the pressure vacuum once when *Kater* vaulted onto the surface. The imbalance had not yet equalized before the skipper ran up the conning tower ladder and spun the handwheel underneath the main hatch cover. The instant he released the watertight seal the spring-loaded lid flung open with an ear-popping wooooosh, and the U-boat commander was ingloriously sucked

---

38.   Assigned to U-3014., Aue later was promoted to *Maat*. He and Marbach sailed together again when the skipper commanded U-3014 between 17 December 1944 and 3 May 1945. See the Internet websites www.ubootwaffe.net/crews, and www.deutsche-uboote.de/kommandanten/marbach_karl-heinz.html.

out of the open portal. The slapstick sight of the skipper being flung out of the conning tower hatch brought muffled guffaws of laughter from the men nearby, despite the underlying concern that Marbach might have been seriously injured during the mishap.

Oberbootsmann Albert Bechtel saved U-953 and her crew when he rescued a man who helplessly blocked the open main hatch during a crash dive.

The *U-flak* surfaced on the morning of 19 October and headed onto a southern course to the meeting point, where at 11:30 Marbach notified BdU that U-648 had never made their rendezvous.

"How long shall I wait?" the skipper implored. Visibility had worsened by noon and high waves pounded the men standing watch on the bridge. Through the din of the raging tide, each man in soaking misery struggled to keep his eyes on the sky and the watery horizon in his assigned zone. Marbach was handed a message from the radio operator shortly after 13:00, which reported Stahl's U-boat had arrived at the meeting point. Before anyone could make visual contact, however, a *Flieger Alarm* was sounded and the boat slid back into the depths.

Four aircraft had been sighted on a northerly heading between 5,000 and 6,000 meters distant. Marbach wasn't about to take a chance that his boat had been spotted and would have to defend herself under the prevailing weather conditions; the gunners would have been imperiled had they tried to man their exposed weapons platforms. Instead, *Kater* would remain underwater until nightfall and take frequent sound readings to fix U-648's position now that she was inside Marbach's operational area. When U-953 surfaced at 22:22 the weather had turned decidedly worse. Very high waves and a heavy overcast turned the night skies pitch black. Marbach received a message from Stahl sixteen minutes later, which directed U-953 to remain in her present position. The mid-ocean meeting of the two vessels had been called off. The weather-related risk of collision and the threat of attack that attended the planned rendezvous had won the day.[39]

A coded radio message from BdU on the morning of 20 October ordered Stahl to resume his patrol activities and Marbach to obtain the needed replacement parts from another U-boat when calmer seas would allow a brief and successful rendezvous. Despite high waves, increasing overcast and rain showers, U-953 remained on the surface much of the day on patrol in her *U-flak* role. The boat sailed on an easterly course in order that the crashing Atlantic waves would help camouflage *Kater* from enemy aircraft that approached from the stern. The *U-flak's* task was to invite attack if necessary to protect other boats, but the element of surprise had to be maintained wherever possible to maximize the chance of success against marauding planes. An even more important tactical consideration was that the gunners could not possibly bring their weapons fully to bear on targets that disappeared behind approaching high waves. The forward location of the quadruple-mounted 20mm antiaircraft guns that Karl usually manned limited its protective firepower to an arc that surrounded the sides and bow of the boat, but not the stern. The 20mm mount also would sustain greater mechanical damage if *Kater* were to sail directly into the waves. During the day the helmsman in the conning tower fought against the boat's tendency to pitch and yaw sideways while he steered the boat on her intended course. U-953's big diesels roared under full power as the tall swells propelled the boat toward the Bay of Biscay. The skipper determined that as long as the brutal weather held out the boat would submerge and sail west at night, then resume her surface run to the east during the day. The skipper's decision was wholly logical and sound, even if not daring.[40]

---

39. *KTB*, 19 October 1943.

Shortly after 19:30 Marbach received a message from BdU to rendezvous with U-211, a partially-converted *U-flak* commanded by *Oberleutnant* Karl Hause, the following morning inside grid square BE 6728. Assuming favorable weather, U-953 would receive the needed replacement parts for her gun mounts. At 10:35 on 21 October the boat surfaced into sunny skies and greatly diminished tides; good conditions for a meeting between two U-boats, but also good flying weather for the enemy as Marbach noted cautiously in *Kater's* war diary. He undertook to search for U-211 along a north-south line that ran through BE 6728. Even as the sun began its westward trek in the early afternoon, the skipper and his gunners doubtless were relieved that soon the needed parts would be delivered for their weapons. Even in their damaged condition, the deck-mounted guns stood ready while their crews waited below deck for the call to battle stations.

At 13:40 a *Wache* member sprang into action with a spine-chilling warning.

"Flieger Alaaarrrm!!!" the lookout shouted as an aircraft approached between 2,500 and 3,000 meters off the boat's port side. The watch party on the bridge stood aside as the gunners stormed out of the main hatch and ran to the three gun platforms. Baumann charged to the forward *Flakvierling* and took the position of the *Kanoneer* while two ammunition loaders pulled four heavy magazines of 20mm rounds out of waterproof containers on the bridge. While Karl buckled the chinstrap on his steel helmet the loaders shoved the ammo magazines into the gun breeches and pulled back their cocking arms. Baumann hand cranked the four cannon barrels simultaneously onto the horizon toward the plane. The *Flakvierling* gunners on the aft *Wintergarten* and the 37mm crewmen just below them also tracked the aircraft in their crosshairs.

The U-boat gunner strained to focus his eyes on the plane through his large gunsight. Still some distance away, the threat appeared to be an American PBY Catalina patrol bomber, a lumbering and ungainly-looking seaplane whose slow speed and affable nickname Dumbo belied its lethality. Eighteen of 103 U-boats sunk by the U.S. Navy were officially credited to the Catalina, which carried three fifty-caliber machineguns, racks of depth charges, and a Magnetic Airborne Detection system designed to locate German U-boats. Dumbo squadrons flew patrol sorties over the Bay of Biscay from Lands End, England and Pembroke Dock, South Wales. A member of one PBY squadron wrote:

> In the summer of 1943, Hitler ordered his submarines transiting the Bay of Biscay to cruise on the surface and engage enemy aircraft with anti-aircraft

---

40. *KTB*, 20 October 1943. See also Buchheim, 78, for reference to the Type VII U-boat's steering tendency.

fire rather than diving when attacked. His submarine personnel proved worthy fighters with deck guns and they fought their way out of many scraps against Allied aircraft.[41]

Others members of the *Wache* identified the aircraft as a British Sunderland, an equally cumbersome-looking amphibian armed to deliver devastating blows against Axis submarines. Sunderlands bristled with ten to twelve machineguns intended mostly for defensive protection against enemy aircraft, while bombing comprised the plane's main offensive threat. RAF Coastal Command countered the Kriegsmarine's new *U-flak* threat with four additional forward-firing machineguns mounted in the noses of its Sunderlands. For good reason, U-boat men referred to the hulking British plane as *Das Fliegendes Stachelschwein*—the Flying Porcupine—in deference to its numerous protruding guns and a row of projecting antennae that supported its ASV Mk. II radar. The hulking, low-flying Sunderlands would claim at least fifty-three U-boats sunk or damaged by war's end.[42]

The gunners followed their target and awaited orders while the seaplane stalked along its parallel course past U-953 at a height of 500 to 1,000 meters. Finally, the skipper commanded the gunners orders to fire. The gun mounts instantly shuddered with violent recoil as the weapons pumped out murderous volleys of *Flak*. Unprotected ears rang from the sharp bark of the cannon fire and nostrils filled with the acrid smell of burned cordite. Ejected shell casings tumbled out of the guns' hot breeches with each volley, then clattered and clanged onto the platforms and boat deck and into the murk. Luminescent strings of tracers reached toward the aircraft to display the gunners' acumen with their calculations of ranges and trajectories. The strange beauty of the graceful glowing red arcs hardly concealed their deadly intent. As suddenly as the plane took *Flak* from astern, it quickly and unexpectedly turned to starboard and cut across the horizon well beyond *Kater's* bow. The pilot then began to circle the *U-flak* far beyond the range of the German guns in an attempt to locate a soft spot where he could press an attack against the strangely-configured vessel. When next the aircraft lumbered across U-953's bow it suddenly angled hard to starboard and lined up for a headlong assault directly toward the U-boat. Marbach instantly ordered hard right rudder and the helmsman swung the boat perpendicular to the plane's line

41.   Mel Crocker, *Black Cats and Dumbos; WWII's Fighting PBYs* (Blue Ridge Summit, PA: Aero, 1987), 88, 100-101.
42.   Internet: http://uboat.net/allies/aircraft.sunderland.htm. Also Jon Lake, *Sunderland Squadrons of World War 2* (Oxford: Osprey, 2000) 65, 104-105.

of attack. This time Baumann did not wait for the skipper's command to resume fire; he shoved his foot against the trigger pedal and all four 20mm cannon instantly unleashed a wall of fire. The aft gunners followed Karl's lead. The continual firing of the quadruple 20mm cannon mounted just above the heads of the 37mm crew shattered the men's eardrums; blood streaked down their necks even as they laid down a sustained barrage of *Flak*. After the 37mm fired about fifty rounds it overheated and would not automatically eject the spent shell casings from its breech; the gun crew had to pull the searing brass casings out by hand. The aircraft turned sharply away and out of range seconds after the barrage began, then circled the boat ominously three more times. During the thirteen-minute confrontation the *U-flak* gunners had filled the sky with nearly one hundred 37mm shells and fifteen hundred 20mm rounds. The seaplane never fired a shot in return.[43]

The *Flakvierling* quadruple-barrel 20mm anti-aircraft gun was a lethal weapon at close range. Allied pilots quickly learned to remain out of range of *U-flak* guns until multiple aircraft arrived to attack the boat in force.

Adrenaline surged through Baumann's body after his first taste of combat, as did heightened confidence in himself and his ability as a U-boat gunner. He assured himself that if the slow-moving patrol plane attempted another frontal attack he would shoot it down. He also guessed, however, that the pilot already had called in more aircraft to take on the obstinate *Kater*. If his assumption was

---

43. *KTB*, 21 October 1943. The war diary officially listed the attacking aircraft as a Sunderland.

correct, the next attack against the *U-flak* might be too terrible to contemplate. Karl and his ammunition loaders busied themselves to prepare the *Flakvierling* for the enemy's inevitable return.

Marbach was pleased with his gunners' rapid and exacting response to the threatening aircraft, but also was uneasy about their prospects to withstand multiple and continued air attacks. Then and there he determined that after one or two approaches by attacking aircraft, the *U-flak* in her prescribed gunboat role no longer maintained any tactical advantage over the enemy.[44] Despite all the planning at BdU to redesign and deploy U-boats as anti-aircraft decoys, the Ubootwaffe chiefs apparently had neglected a fundamental consideration that all but insured tactical failure: namely, the seemingly limitless number of Allied aircraft that could be brought to bear against the miniscule number of *U-flak* boats. The *U-flak* strategy was fatally flawed from the very beginning when employed against two or more attacking aircraft. BdU knew well that the Allies largely owned the sky above the Bay. The admirals should have realized the enemy simply would deploy multiple aircraft against virtually any *U-flak* that invited a fight. In fact, operational instructions for U.S. Navy PBY Catalinas flying anti-submarine patrols directed pilots to delay their attacks until additional aircraft arrived to join the melee.[45] U-boats and *U-flak*s that remained on the surface to battle enemy aircraft did so at their own peril and with devastating losses.

"*Auf Tiefe gehen!*" Marbach ordered with firm conviction. To fight it out with a swarm of patrol bombers under such circumstances was nothing less than suicidal, and therefore contradictory to the rules of engagement against enemy aircraft that U-boat commanders were expected to follow.[46] The dive alarm blared and the crew instantly flew into the practiced choreography of the dive procedure. Gunners and watch party members abandoned their exposed battle stations and surged through the tower hatch. The watch officer, always the last man down, closed off the encroaching daylight and sea as he swung the heavy steel cover onto the open portal and sealed it tightly with a quick spin of the locking wheel. A minute later the *Ubootfahrer* heard the unmistakable splashes of three small but well-placed airborne depth charges, followed several seconds later by spine-chilling detonations near U-953 that registered no damage.[47]

---

44. *KTB*, 21 October 1943.
45. Crocker, 99.
46. *U-Boat Commander's Handbook* (Gettysburg, PA: Thomas Publications, 1989); 27. This text of this book is the U.S. Navy's direct translation of the actual *U.Kdt.Handbuch* issued to U-boat commanders by *BdU* during 1943.
47. *KTB*, 21 October 1943.

"I would rather be a coward for five minutes than dead forever," Marbach had declared to one of his officers earlier during a discussion about being faced with hopeless odds. His men never questioned their skipper's courage; rather, they recognized he simply was a pragmatist who realized futility when he saw it. Officers and crew alike knew the true measure of their commander and placed total trust and faith in the young *Oberleutnant*. They inherently understood as well that no one was more dedicated to U-953's success and survival than Karl-Heinz Marbach, and that he alone bore the burden of having to make life and death decisions often within the span of thirty seconds of deliberation.[48]

During the rapid succession of mechanical functions that attended the emergency dive procedure, a faulty diesel clutch caused the big engines not to power down immediately when electrical power was engaged to propel the boat while submerged. Black engine exhaust suddenly poured into the boat and hung momentarily in an ominous cloud. The diesel mechanics frantically cut off the engines by hand, but not before the interior of the boat was filled with noxious fumes. With enemy aircraft circling overhead waiting for the kill, Marbach could not order the boat to the surface to be vented out. He instead ordered all hands to don their charcoal-filtered breathing masks and limit all unnecessary movement to preserve the precious air that remained inside the boat.

The scene inside the boat soon resembled some otherworldly existence out of a nightmare: the life-sustaining but homely breathing apparatus hid every man's facial features behind an inhuman, impersonal and mechanical countenance. Men variously stood, sat or lay motionless throughout the cramped pipe-and-dial infested cylinder as if they were in suspended animation. Those who walked around did so in the slow and deliberate manner akin to the primitive automatons of the old German films that mocked post World War modernity and warned of a dreaded future.

The uncomfortable breathing gear blocked only some of the noxious air from reaching the lungs. Soon the entire crew suffered terrible pounding headaches and nausea from the foul air. Finally, after an eternal six hours inside the poisoned chamber, Marbach ordered the boat to periscope depth. There he scanned sea and sky for any sight of enemy ships and aircraft, and determined the area was clear in all directions to the far horizon. Grateful for the good fortune, even if it were momentary, he ordered *Kater* to the surface. The watch party soon stum-

---

48. Hans Stemmler, telephone conversation with Karl Baumann, 5 June 2000. Both Stemmler and Baumann recalled Marbach's outlook, which formed numerous life and death decisions aboard U-953.

bled out of the hatch onto the conning tower bridge, thankful for the chance to breathe in the limitless ocean air. The boat's ventilators quickly roared to life to force out the poisoned atmosphere inside and draw in clean air to the oxygen-starved men below. The fresh air was so inebriating that Karl Baumann nearly passed out when it filled his anguished lungs. Marbach tallied his casualties: fifteen crewmen had suffered significant carbon monoxide poisoning before being revived. At 21:02 he ordered the boat underwater and all crewmembers to stand down to the greatest extent possible, to rest and restore themselves to good health.[49]

U-953 again surfaced at 03:34 on 22 October and pumped in additional fresh air to help the crew recover from the nearly-fatal poisoning. The effects of the sickness already had begun to abate, but Marbach consulted with a BdU physician about the incident and decided to extend the recuperation period an additional day. The boat thus continued to plod along slowly underwater in relative safety and by noon had covered only seventy-nine nautical miles for the twenty-four hour period just ended. During the stand-down the skipper contemplated the often-frustrating series of events of the past few days. Several attempts to link up with other boats for replacement gun parts had cost much time, effort and energy that could have been spent searching for convoy targets. U-953 had battled indecisively with the British seaplane; the skipper observed that the only positive result obtained from the confrontation was the knowledge that his crew had worked and fought splendidly, and the guns had functioned well despite their earlier damage. He still had not been able to rendezvous with U-211, but also had concluded that the planned rendezvous posed too many hazards for both boats, and repair parts for the guns no longer were necessary. The broken diesel clutch posed its own serious problems, however, and Marbach reported the malfunction to BdU.[50]

By noon on 23 October U-953 had crept only sixty nautical miles in twenty-four hours while the crew took advantage of their brief hiatus from war. The boat finally surfaced at 14:00 inside her operational area, again in her *U-flak* role. Once she leveled out and the inside air pressure was balanced with the pressure outside, the gunners rushed out of the conning tower to their mounts. The men carefully checked their weapons for seaborne debris and double-checked the readiness of the ammunition stowed in nearby watertight containers. When they were satisfied the weapons were ready to fire on a moment's notice, the gun crew-

49. *KTB*, 21 October 1943.
50. *KTB*, 22 October 1943.

men retreated back down the main hatch to the deck beneath the conning tower to wait out the surface run. An hour later, inside grid square BE 8355, a four engine bomber emerged from the cloud cover, 4,000 to 6,000 meters from the boat, then just as quickly disappeared. The watch officer declared a *Flieger Alarm* anyway, Baumann and his fellow gunners charged out of the main hatch in a matter of seconds. Mounting the deck guns, the cannoneers and the watch party scanned the broken overcast in every direction for tell-tale signs of the bomber.[51]

Enemy pilots preferred to fly unseen above the clouds to track unsuspecting U-boats. Once the boat's location was fixed by radar, a patrol bomber would approach its target as quickly as possible, then punch through the overcast virtually overhead at the last moment to unleash a devastating attack. Prevailing winds and the rumble from a boat's diesels sometimes drowned out the sound of deadly anti-submarine aircraft until an attack already was underway. Combat pilots also were taught to line up on targets with the sun behind their planes if possible, then drop through a break in the clouds to launch their attacks. The defenders would have to strain their eyes in the blinding sun to locate the onrushing aircraft, which sometimes became nearly invisible in their gunsights.

The skipper felt uneasy about the plane's intentions, especially since the weather was advantageous for a surprise attack. After ten minutes he ordered *Kater* below the blue-green Atlantic waves. U-953 much more often played a defensive role instead of the offensive role for which she was designed, a fact that was neither lost on the men nor good for their morale. Twelve minutes later, however, BdU transmitted electrifying orders to the five U-boats and three *U-flaks* in their operational area. The boats were to proceed south onto the northerly course of a convoy plotted 1,700 miles away along the African coast, and engage the massed cargo and transport ships on the evening of 27 October. Luftwaffe Condor long-range bombers would track the convoy beginning a day earlier, according to BdU. The U-boats were to remain unseen, which inferred they were to travel underwater during the day. The *U-flaks* were to make daylight surface runs north and northeast of the area where the U-boats were concentrated. No need to endanger the safety of the U-boats if the *U-flaks* should be attacked, headquarters probably had concluded. *Kater* surfaced at 22:00 and, despite high waves, plowed south for the next three hours while the electric batteries were recharged and carbon dioxide-laden air inside was expelled. Moderate weather on 24 October allowed U-953 to run on the surface during daylight hours and again

---

51. *KTB*, 23 October 1943.

operate in her *U-flak* role. The 90 percent cloud cover kept the bridge watch on special alert for enemy aircraft.[52]

U-boat warfare usually involved many days or weeks while boats moved into position, followed by an interminable wait for the enemy to approach and lock horns in combat. Actual fighting, when it finally erupted, often lasted only several seconds or minutes unless Allied destroyers, destroyer escorts, or sub chasers launched an extended depth charge attack. Fighter planes and patrol bombers usually dealt the quickest and most painless forms of death because of the relative suddenness of their attacks, which undoubtedly most *Ubootfahrer* preferred over the slower, anticipatory forms of death delivered by warships that bore down upon them with depth charges. Amid such harsh realities and thoughts of life and death, Karl Baumann quietly celebrated his nineteenth birthday in the Atlantic Ocean's lonely reaches. Home and family had been replaced by the cramped, putrid, spherical world of U-953 and the brotherhood that wartime had forged among *Ubootfahrer*.

The reality of fewer offensive victories frustrated every man in the U-boat force as well as the Kriegsmarine chiefs at OKW, Germany's Joint Chiefs of Staff.[53] Admiral Dönitz had reported in June 1943 that his U-boats often required six to eight weeks to reach their assigned positions, only to find no convoys to attack.[54] He was wholly unaware of the magnitude of success that British Intelligence and their cryptanalysts had achieved to decipher Germany's most secret U-boat operations codes and systems. With German grid square maps and Enigma machines in British hands by mid-1941, convoys were routinely rerouted around known locations where U-boat wolfpacks lay poised for attack.[55]

The daylong run toward the Allied convoy was invigorating for crewmen who had grown increasingly morose over the almost unbroken routine of daily life aboard the U-boat. The prospect for action and the dangers combat imposed

---

52. *KTB*, 23-24 October 1943. For an overview of the problems of reliance on Luftwaffe aircraft serving as aerial observers for U-boat operations, see Buchheim, 56: "'[S]ystematic air reconnaissance' never emerged from the realm of wishful thinking. Certainly, some Condors [Focke-Wulf Fw 200] would occasionally happen to catch sight of a solitary steamer or a convoy, but the position they transmitted was usually so much a product of guesswork that it was useless for finding the target."
53. *OKW* was the synonym for Oberkommando der Wehrmacht, the joint chiefs of staff of the German armed forces, over whom Adolf Hitler as *Führer* maintained absolute control in the conduct of the war.
54. *Conferences*, 332.
55. Gannon, 50-51.

quickened pulses and sharpened the awareness that life and youth were but fleeting commodities in war, and that death was profoundly and forever more present than one could even contemplate in times of peace. If *Kater* could engage the convoy and score one or more victories against the enemy, the men reasoned, all the hardships of U-boat service would be rewarded with the satisfaction of having done their duty for the *Vaterland*. As an added benefit, if all torpedoes were launched during their attacks, the men who lived in the bow compartment finally would have more room to sit, stand, lounge, eat, and sleep; and most likely they would sail for La Pallice earlier than scheduled. An attack on the convoy would be a winning proposition all around, so long as they survived the confrontation.

The U-bunker at La Pallice is shown under construction by *Organization Todt* in 1942.

While U-953 ran at full speed toward the convoy blockade one of the huge diesel engines suddenly seized up and ground to a stop. Despite the best efforts of the diesel mechanics, who had babied their charge around the clock and labored to maintain its throbbing rhythm as if it were a heartbeat, the engine could not be restarted. Though the boat's underwater speed was considerably slower than that of a surface run on one diesel, at 17:45 Marbach ordered U-953 to submerge so repairs on the frozen engine could be carried out in greater safety. The boat continued her trek southward throughout 25 and 26 October. In the meantime, BdU transmitted orders to all U-boats sailing toward the convoy. Skippers KL [*Kapitänleutnant*] Gerhard Thäter (U-466), Marbach, KL Claus von Trotha (U-306), KL Karl Hause (U-211), KL Heinz Franke (U-262), KL Götz von Hartmann (U-441), Oblt. z. S. [*Oberleutnant zur See*] Günter Gretschel (U-707), and KL Peter-Erich Cremer (U-333) were to form into a *U-Gruppe*, or wolfpack, codenamed Schill. The commanders were ordered to set speed and course adjustments to line up their boats, in the order by which they were named, by 19:00 on 28 October.[56]

Marbach set U-953's course due west at midnight and proceeded underwater until nearly 20:00 on 27 October, when the boat surfaced into high waves and a solid umbrella of cloud cover. Mercifully for the men on watch atop the bridge, the weather began to moderate and by midnight the wakes had become less threatening, the cloud cover began to break, and visibility began to improve. *Kater* continued westward until 16:00 on 28 October, when the skipper ordered an abrupt tack to the southeast. Shortly after 21:30 BdU transmitted another message to *Gruppe* Schill. The lineup of boats was to stretch between grid squares BE 8721 and BE 8823 to form a nearly sixty-mile rake, as the intercept line was called, and was to be in place by 08:00 the following morning. A second part of the message reported Luftwaffe reconnaissance had plotted the convoy in CF 9179 at 13:00 on 27 October and at CF 5386 at 11:00 on 28 October, about 270 nautical miles south of the rake, bearing north-northwest at a speed of about ten knots. Fifty-four ships, guarded by one cruiser, two destroyers, and three other escorts comprised the large convoy.[57]

The assembly of Allied ships that sailed toward the wolfpack actually was a convergence of two smaller convoys designated MKS 28 and SL 138. MKS 28 had sailed out of Alexandria, Egypt on 14 October and SL 138 originated in Freetown, Sierra Leone, on 13 October. Both convoys were bound for Liverpool, England. The two groups merged off the coast of Gibraltar on 24 October. The large convoy probably could never have escaped German detection, either from aircraft, U-boats, or Axis spies that hid among the scrub bushes along the African coast. The gaggle of transports was due to dock in Liverpool on 5 November; BdU was determined the convoy would not make port unbloodied.[58]

U-boats in a rake often were spread much farther apart than sixty miles to maximize the observation and interception potential of the attack group. Variable factors determined the length of a rake, including the number of boats assigned to it and the prevailing weather conditions that either helped or hindered visibil-

---

56. *KTB*, 24-26 October 1943. The attack line of U-boats was called a *rake* because the alignment of boats along the width of the imaginary patrol line resembled the business end of the common garden implement.

57. *KTB*, 27-28 October 1943.

58. Internet website: www.warsailors/com/singleships/hallfried.html.

ity. Tacticians at BdU early in the war had calculated that the top of the main mast on an Allied steamer typically soared 130 feet above sea level, which like other tell-tale skyborne signs of an enemy ship was visible up to fifteen miles in clear weather. Headquarters planners determined that boats in a rake should not be spread more than thirty miles apart. Others in the High Command, however, argued that the chances were slim that an enemy ship would ever intersect a rake exactly at the midpoint between two U-boats, but would be closer to one boat or the other. As a result, BdU sometimes ordered boats to spread apart as much as fifty miles during periods of good weather and high visibility. Notwithstanding the strength of their theory, advantageous weather and visibility rarely coincided in deep Atlantic waters. During summer months visibility usually was no more than ten to twenty nautical miles to all points of the compass; during winter it most often was much less.[59]

Only seven or eight miles would separate the boats of *Gruppe* Schill, the inference being that under almost any conditions even a small convoy sailing into the rake would be virtually impossible to miss. The rake's observation area would extend as far as eighty miles, which in the middle of the vast Atlantic presented a very small danger zone for a convoy—especially if the Allies had somehow discovered its location. BdU relied upon the certain integrity of the supposedly indecipherable Enigma Code to safeguard messages transmitted between Headquarters and its U-boats. Thus, it was reasoned, the rake would be secretly and strategically deployed; the northbound convoy most likely would plow directly into the rake and straight to its destruction.

BdU's coded message ordered all *Gruppe* Schill boats to remain submerged during the daylight hours of 29 October to avoid Allied warships or aircraft, but to remain at suitable depth to receive further Luftwaffe reconnaissance reports. All boats then were to surface at 18:00 to employ maximum visual observation and surface speed to respond to any reported convoy sighting, which was to be expected no earlier than 17:00. The final segment of the message ordered U-953 and the other two *U-flaks* to engage the enemy convoy fully as attack boats. As the U-boats sailed toward their rake positions every sound technician strained to make out any distant resonance that signaled the approach of the enemy merchant vessels and warships.[60]

Kater submerged at 02:41 on 29 October leaving completely overcast skies, increasing winds and waves, and diminished visibility above for the calm depths

---

59. Buchheim, 77.
60. *KTB*, 28 October 1943.

of the eastern Atlantic. Excitement grew among the officers and men—those who had a reason to know and all others who had tapped into the rumor mill—over the expected encounter that grew more likely with each passing hour. Torpedo mixers methodically inspected their missiles and reset mechanical guidance and gyro controls on the ordnance that had become disabled during the long *Feind-fahrt*. Anticipation and tinges of apprehension for the looming fight displaced the listlessness and monotony Karl Baumann and his crewmates usually felt. In lieu of any official announcement to the crew at large, rumors continually ran in high gear to provide general information about the looming battle.[61]

At 17:59 U-953 broke through the surface at BE 8722, and was positioned toward the western boundary of the rake. Heavy swells rocked the boat as the *Wache* members rushed through the conning tower hatch and tethered themselves to the armored bridge wall. Completely overcast skies and rain squalls enshrouded the area over the next two hours and reduced visibility at times to no more than 300 feet. Marbach ordered the boat onto an east-west course to be certain no enemy vessels had begun to slip through his sector. *Kater* returned to BE 8722 at 20:00 without sighting the convoy, and over the next three hours dived twice to take panoramic sound readings of the area in case the convoy's leading escorts lurked in the gloom just out of visual range. Franke's U-262 reported several sounds at the same time from BE 8812 on the eastern end of the rake. Squalls again blew across the Atlantic at midnight as the wolfpack, on orders from BdU, rushed toward the sound signals. Just before 01:00 on 30 October, Headquarters again radioed the *Gruppe*; the convoy was suspected to be heading north—but where? By dawn Franke had lost all contact with the Allied ships. Frustrated U-boat commanders and crews awaited further orders from BdU, undoubtedly tormented by fears that more than fifty ships somehow had slipped past their rake to safety. Finally at 06:30, *Gruppe* Schill was ordered to chase the invisible convoy at full diesel speed on a northwest heading until dawn, then dive and tack west. Obviously, the admirals at BdU also keenly felt the frustration of having lost track of the large lumbering assembly of fat targets. At 18:07 BdU notified the *Gruppe* that at 10:40 air reconnaissance had located the Allied convoy—fifty merchant ships, one cruiser and five small escorts—at BE 8442, then only seventeen miles from U-953. Headquarters ordered all boats to proceed at full speed to that location immediately after surfacing. The last part of BdU's message undoubtedly was predicated more on hopeful conjecture than probability.

---

61. *KTB*, 29 October 1943.

U-boat Gunner   113

"Tonight something has to fall out of this convoy," the message proclaimed, and, "Attack; give honor" to the Kriegsmarine.[62]

The skies registered 40 percent cloud cover and high waves pounded against the conning tower as *Kater* broke onto the surface at 20:00. Some evidence of the convoy should have been visible on the horizon, but not a trace was observed. Marbach ordered his boat onto a northeasterly course in hopes that he could intercept any ships that somehow had gotten through *Gruppe* Schill. Again, nothing was observed. The boat again submerged just before midnight to take new sound readings, but after twenty-two minutes of silence the sound operator reported his vain efforts to locate the enemy ships with hydrophone readings. U-953 repeatedly submerged for sound readings during the night, then surfaced to run at full speed throughout the early morning hours of 31 October to search in grid coordinates beyond the rake. Just before daybreak, BdU notified the wolfpack:

> At dawn remain on the surface and continue operation in case a boat reports sound contact. In case no boat has a sound contact, dive and head west underwater. *Use available attack opportunities.*[63]

The *Wache* observed four flares astern at 07:13 while U-953 sailed due north. The officers on the bridge concluded the illumination probably indicated another U-boat was under attack from aircraft. The Watch Officer declared a *Flieger Alarm* from the bridge. Gunners boiled out of the main hatch and ran to their weapons as *Kater* tacked sharply off her zero-degree course. The deck-mounted guns quickly were made ready to fire and were aimed over the southern horizon. Stressed gun crews waited with tightened shoulder and neck muscles and clenched teeth as they anticipated the instantaneous roar of cannon that would follow a *Wache* member's warning that an enemy plane was spotted on its deadly approach. After six minutes, however, neither the expected warning nor sight or sound announced the location of any aircraft rushing toward the boat. Since partly cloudy skies again might shield attacking planes, the skipper broke the palpable tension when he ordered everyone off the bridge. A minute later the boat was submerged and hydrophone detection attempts resumed. Noises from the south-southwest almost immediately cascaded into the sound operator's ears and quickly increased in intensity. Among the cacophony another U-boat very close

---

62.   *KTB*, 29-30 October 1943.
63.   *KTB*, 30-31 October 1943. Italics were added by the author to emphasize the attack order.

by to the north was heard to submerge, followed by unmistakable splashes, the gurgling descent and detonation of depth charges.

The sound operator had just overheard the death knell of U-306, the boat next in line to U-953 in the rake formed by the *U-Gruppe*. [64] Commanded by KL Claus von Trotha, U-306 had sailed out of Brest on 14 October on her fifth war patrol. Trotha and his crew had scored several successes on earlier patrols, sinking one ship and damaging two others, and also had survived several air attacks unscathed. But luck—always a most precious and finite commodity for U-boats and the men who took them to war—now had run out for the forsaken boat in the open ocean northeast of the Azores. Somehow the British destroyer *Whitehall* and corvette *Geranium* of the Escort Group B1, escorting the sought-after convoy, apparently had surprised the U-boat on the surface and attacked her with hedgehogs, weapons that propelled heavy depth charge canisters fifty yards or more to create a wide kill zone. The escorts had fixed U-306's position by HF/DF, the Allies' radio transmission detection system known as Huff-Duff, to corner the boat and send her to the bottom with all hands. Gigantic surface eruptions from the terrific underwater explosions marked only temporarily the common grave of fifty-one men. [65]

The Atlantic—and any ocean—was a mysterious and lonely place to die; nothing on the surface ever would indicate the location where the light of young and hopeful lives had flickered out. Unlike dry land battlefields, the ocean quickly repaired itself to hide all battle scars and leave no visible reminders of the horrors visited there. The detritus of war alone would identify the final resting place on the ocean floor for U-306 and her entire crew. Probably rendered asunder by the blast, large sections of the mangled vessel would be surrounded by the flotsam and jetsam of men and materiel scattered across a wide area. In a matter of days the sea and its mysterious inhabitants would conspire to strip away all human tissue, leaving bared skulls and bones to dissolve much later into invisible particles to be swept away by the ocean's undercurrents. Over the following decades chunks of rent leather alone from shoes, boots and clothing will mark where men once had gone to rest on the ocean bed. After many more years the

---

64. *KTB*, 31 October 1943. The exact position where U-306 was destroyed is 46.19 North-20.44 West, in BdU Grid Square BE 4935. See Internet website: www.u-boote-online.de/dieboote/u0306.html. This German website also indicates the U-boat was sunk by hedgehogs.

65. Internet websites: www.ubootwaffe.net/ops/boat.cgi, www.naval-history.net/WW2194306-2.htm, www.angelraybooks.com/diewehrmacht/Kriegsmarine/uwp2.htm.

boat herself finally will yield her derelict form to the elements and rust almost entirely into oblivion. Shifting sands at long last will cover the last small pieces of insoluble debris. Thus time will erase the once fearsome and menacing U-boat, which in her day had seemed almost a living being in her own right—once nearly as alive as the men who took her to sea. In BE 4935, where U-306 lies, and in many other locations, hundreds of boats and the ghosts of thirty thousand *Ubootfahrer* inhabit the deep. Their spirits, like fleeting memories, reappear mostly in the occasional thoughts and dreams of the few U-boat survivors and the passing generations who once knew and loved the young men.

> *There are no roses on a sailor's grave,*
> *No lilies on an ocean wave,*
> *The only tribute is the seagull's sweeps,*
> *And the teardrops that a sweetheart weeps.*

> *—Unknown*

Why Huff-Duff had not fingered U-953 for destruction can only be speculated; the randomness of life and death in war at sea is little different from that of air or ground combat. Luck, in its limited supply, whether measured in terms of inches, meters, or nautical miles, sometimes simply runs out for certain unfortunate warriors chosen for sacrifice by the Marsian gods, which spare others seemingly without rational justification or explanation.

Less than three *Seemeilen* from the sunken U-boat, the crew of U-953 maintained strict silence as their submerged boat slowly skulked away; dawn and the prospect of death had arrived together, and for the moment *Kater's* skipper wanted nothing more to do with either. As *Obersteuermann* Eduard Hartmann plotted their southerly course, the boat's hydrophone picked up the sound signature of a surface vessel. Marbach took the boat to periscope depth and swept the low horizon with his scope; at 08:12 he spotted an Allied destroyer—a one-stacker—amble astern of U-953, heading north-northeast. The skipper maintained visual contact with the destroyer, and at 09:00 ordered the crew to battle stations. The destroyer suddenly tacked to the northeast at 09:18 and disappeared over the horizon, where for a time oily smoke clouds continued to mark her position. Marbach had pondered his options before he let the sub-killer sail out of sight. He believed *Kater* was in position to strike better convoy targets than the destroyer, and determined that other boats in closer proximity to the escort would have a better opportunity to attack her successfully at close range. The convoy escorts were just as determined to protect their assembly of merchantmen from the U-boat threat, however. Marbach earlier had noted distant depth charge detonations; then, at 10:00 three Allied warships converged near U-953 and began to walk hedgehogs toward the boat. For the next six hours the three escorts lobbed the exploding canisters on both sides of the U-boat and astern, but never closer than 1,000 to 2,000 meters. Running silently on electric power, crewmen limited all movement and spoke in whispers lest their voices betray their precarious position. Rather than dive for the greatest possible depth below the escorts' fast-turning screws, the skipper kept *Kater* dangerously near the surface at periscope depth to better monitor the enemy's movement. Presumably he felt exceedingly confident in his men's ability to quickly take the boat farther below if any of the escorts suddenly presented a more serious threat. As the U-boat plodded along a southerly course, the radio operator received a message at noon from BdU: Franke's U-262 had attacked the convoy; and Cremer aboard U-333 claimed he had sunk the leading convoy escort at 09:42. Marbach concluded Cremer's victim was the destroyer U-953 had observed and tracked less than two hours earlier.[66]

In the wake of Cremer's attack three convoy escorts stormed after U-333 and U-707 to catapult a phalanx of depth charges after the deep-diving boats. Marbach and his crew listened intently to the sustained counterattack off *Kater's* stern. With each attack series three surface detonations announced the coordinated launch of hedgehogs; seconds later the 250-pound drums splashed heavily into the water, then nerve-rattling explosions reverberated through U-953's steel skin. Marbach considered options to help his *Kameraden* but, as he later explained to his war diary, he felt it useless to attack the three small slow-moving vessels because each displaced 500-tons at most. Though such life and death decisions were the skipper's prerogative, the skipper may not have convinced himself—at least in retrospect—that his inaction was the proper course to take during the confrontation. U-953 tacked eastward at noon, even while the renewed sounds of the depth charge attack echoed through the boat and continued for almost six hours. *Kater* again surfaced at 18:19 in the evening at BE 5746, where Marbach hoped to place his boat behind some of the convoy escorts. The watch party swarmed onto the bridge and trained their binoculars on the horizon in all directions. Two destroyers soon appeared on the northwest horizon, unseen earlier by Marbach through his periscope, and unheard by the sound operator.[67]

---

66. *KTB*, 31 October 1943. The author could not substantiate, from postwar sources, that any Allied vessel was sunk in the Atlantic Ocean on 31 October 1943.
67. *KTB*, 31 October 1943.

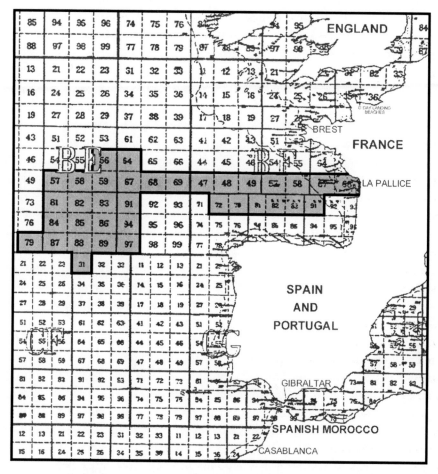

Karl Baumann's first war patrol aboard U-953 spanned 47 days and approximately 4,005 nautical miles, 1,500 of which were logged underwater; 2 October to 17 November 1943. Each numbered grid square measured 54 nautical miles per side. Shaded grid squares indicate U-953's area of operations.

Alaaarrrm!!! the skipper declared, which sent the crew to battle stations in a frenzy of deliberate, well-rehearsed motion. Moments later faint engine noises hummed into the sound operator's headset, then disappeared altogether along with visual contact by the *Wache* on the bridge above.[68] Marbach knew his only chance to tangle with the destroyers would necessitate a perilous pursuit at full

---

68. *KTB*, 31 October 1943.

surface speed in the waning daylight. Instead, he chose to remain at his present location and await further orders from BdU. At 20:50 the anticipated directives crackled into the radio room and were decoded. U-boats closest to the convoy again were implored to take advantage of any attack opportunities that presented themselves. Other *Gruppe* Schill boats, including U-953, on the opposite end of the rake were to head west to BE 80 and remain underwater during the day; there they would wait for the trailing edge of the convoy to zigzag into their lair. Headquarters also ordered skippers Cremer, Franke, and Trotha to report their positions—wholly unaware that Trotha's U-306 already lay in jumbled wreckage on the ocean floor. For all the men and machines that plied the Atlantic and jockeyed for position to seek each other's destruction above and below the surface, the day ended with scant success for the Kriegsmarine and the irreplaceable loss of one U-boat and her experienced crew. Meanwhile, the largely unmolested Allied convoy steamed ever closer to Liverpool.[69]

U-953 spent most of 1 November quietly, wandering submerged about grid square BE 81 and waiting for any hint of convoy traffic to relieve the burden of monotonous inactivity and frustration. The men so far had nothing to show for their contribution to the war effort. A destroyer steamed into view through Marbach's periscope at 18:46, running at high speed at a distance of 3,500 to 4,000 meters. The skipper again calculated his chances for success should he launch a salvo of torpedoes but concluded the warship presented no opportunity for an attack. Marbach and his officers probably concluded as well that the destroyer was a screen to protect the flank of the convoy located somewhere nearby. Dusk had settled across the Atlantic by 20:04 when ships' smokestacks, masts, and bridge platforms suddenly rose into view just beyond the horizon. The tall sections of the superstructures gave every indication that the ships were passenger steamers—most likely troop transports—capable of running many knots faster than the slow, plodding cargo vessels that often steamed no more than ten knots. A PBY Catalina also lumbered into view through the sky periscope. Sound signals at 20:30 picked up two other destroyers speeding along a northwesterly course. The security screen of aircraft and fast escorts underscored the convoy's importance and again heightened tension aboard U-953, as anticipation for a rare chance to score one or more big victories against crucial targets pulled officers and men alike out of their common lethargy. Rather than take up the chase, however, the U-boat held her position for reasons Marbach chose not to share with his war diary. With all hopes to win laurels for sinking a troopship gone, the *Ubootfahrer*

---

69. *KTB*, 31 October 1943.

settled back into their routine of endless waiting for new targets or threats to present themselves. The boat surfaced at nightfall into skies that had become fully overcast and moderate waves that slapped against the windward side of the bridge.[70]

At twenty-one minutes after midnight on 2 November BdU notified *Gruppe* Schill that a troop transport was reported in the convoy bound for Britain. Boats in the rake that could reach the convoy should do so, Headquarters announced. Five minutes later U-953 submerged to take sound readings. Hearing sounds of the convoy at a distance of more than twelve miles, Marbach determined not to take up the pursuit. Instead, he ordered his boat to the surface at 04:00 and onto a southerly course. If any crewman wondered why *Kater* had not given chase, they dared not ask. The rationale was simple: commander's prerogative, crew's orders. Fog enshrouded the watch party on the bridge when the U-boat dived at 07:30 to leave the daylight skies and ocean to the Allies and their mysterious technologies. Some new and unknown scientific breakthrough or intelligence now allowed them to locate hidden U-boats above and below the surface and reroute convoys away from unseen wolfpacks. Late in the evening a radio telegram from BdU ordered U-953 and seven other boats to form a rake between BE 7647 and 8557 before 20:00 on 3 November. Ubootwaffe Headquarters seemed perturbed at the wolfpack's lack of success against the convoy when it admonished the eight skippers not to report a late arrival at their new picket posts. Marbach did not have far to travel to his new location, and reached his position in the rake at 01:04 on 3 November. The weather was calm as any U-953 had encountered during the *Feindfahrt*, with only four-foot swells and 20 percent cloud cover; the night, however, was pitch dark with limited visibility. *Kater* submerged and remained silent for the remainder of the night, then surfaced at 07:37 into the heavy morning fog only long enough to vent out and replace the foul air for the daylong wait underwater, to which BdU had ordered all boats. Twelve hours later the boat again surfaced into fog even thicker than that encountered during the morning, which limited visibility to five hundred meters—a dangerously low distance for any warship at sea, whether hunting for prey or being hunted. Before midnight orders arrived from BdU; the latest air reconnaissance could find no trace of convoy traffic. As a result all *Gruppe* Schill boats were to take up new positions between BE 7813 and 8722, shifting the rake about thirty miles to the southwest by 10:00 the next morning. U-953 arrived at BE 8479 at 04:00 and took up her new position, remaining submerged until 07:25. Mist glistened on

---

70. *KTB*, 1 November 1943.

the superstructure and on the rubberized canvas slickers worn by watch party members while the boat rode the calm morning sea in solid overcast. The boat remained on the surface only long enough to vent out the offensive air, again to prepare for another long day underwater. *Kater* then slid quickly below the waves as rain settled over the area.[71]

After a month on war patrol in oppressively close quarters, crewmen tended to turn their thoughts inwardly to find solace and some sense of serenity. Karl Baumann and his crewmates struggled to find new topics of conversation. Discussions were redundant, songs were monotonous in their frequency, and minor irritations with comrades proliferated and festered. Karl-Heinz Patzer spoke so incessantly about his girlfriend by name that his crewmates retaliated by regularly calling the *Matrosenobergefreiter* himself Natalia. The air stank, the food stank, the war stank, and best friends stank as badly as anyone else. With adequate provisions and ordnance, the *Feindfahrt* might last another four, five, or six weeks—a dreadful thought if, at the end of the long patrol, no enemy ships or aircraft could be claimed destroyed in return for all the time and effort the men had expended.

In all probability, only two personalities aboard the U-boat never complained about their situation in life, their living conditions on the boat, or the length of their war patrols. Rather remarkably, Marbach permitted the crew's mascots, a Doberman pup and a black tomcat, to accompany them on each mission. The pup had been bought for a bottle of rum before U-953 first sailed for La Pallice, and took on the name Rin Tin Tin before an astute observer discovered their mascot was a female and renamed her Rin Tin Tina. The entire crew adored and loved the pup, though she tended to spend most of her time with the petty officers—purely for practical reasons of better quality food and lodging, Marbach theorized. When on one occasion the dog fell out of the conning tower into the *Zentrale* and nearly died, the men worked virtual miracles to treat her wounds and nurse her back to health. Just as her human comrades received the coveted *Ubootkriegsabzeichen* badge that recognized ninety days of combat service, Rin Tin Tina received the award in the form of a collar badge designed by several mechanics. Peter the tomcat appeared after U-953 was assigned the radio callsign *Kater*, and like all cats was more selective of those with whom he chose to associate himself. His feline arrogance irritated *Obersteuermann* Hartmann, for one, and probably a few other crew members as well. Peter thoroughly disliked Rin Tin Tina and considered the dog an interloper upon his territory, which comprised the entire boat from bow to stern. Both mascots raised morale wher-

---

71. *KTB*, 2-4 November 1943.

ever they showed up, and hardened men became boys again when they showered attention upon the animals.[72]

The fourth day of November passed slowly and restlessly, as had so many previous days on patrol, with no sight or sound of the Allies' expected appearance. Surfacing at 08:00, heavy fog and mist enveloped the conning tower and bridge watch, and lent an air of mystery—if not anxiety—to the invisible surroundings, much as if the legendary abyss at the end of the world lay just 200 meters beyond U-953's bow. The boat submerged at 09:42 to scan the surrounding area for sound signatures of unseen enemy traffic shielded by the fog. A twenty-minute hydrophone search by the sound operator revealed nothing whatsoever, which BdU confirmed an hour later when it notified *Gruppe* Schill that reconnaissance by the Luftwaffe for the second day had not been able to locate MKS 28 and SL 138, or any other Allied convoy. The *Gruppe* was then ordered yet again to new positions farther west, between BE 7797 and 7998. Marbach immediately ordered the navigator to set the course; momentarily, new compass headings were called to the helmsman, and *Kater's* huge diesels surged to life to propel the boat through the fog and mist. Diving twice during the early morning hours of 5 November to take sound readings that showed no sign of enemy vessels in the area, U-953 reached her new position at 07:30. The old *Ubootfahrer* song, *So klein ist das Boot und so groß ist das Meer* would have been entirely appropriate to strike up for the occasion.[73] *Wache* members scanned the seemingly empty ocean as far as the eye could see, and easily could have felt as if they alone inhabited the world. Allied warships and planes by the hundreds and thousands were somewhere over the endless horizon as were *Kameraden* in other U-boats. Hidden either behind earth's graceful curvature or deep beneath the waves, unseen legions stood ready, able and willing to rend nature's complete solitude with man's destructive power.

Though tensed for action, the day passed without incident or interruption of any sort until 20:10, when BdU reported that no further convoy traffic was expected in the wolfpack's operational area. The message ordered U-953 to maneuver at will until fuel ran low, then return to La Pallice. The skipper wasted no time; checking his charts and grid map, he ordered the boat onto a northerly

---

72. Uwe Eduard Hartmann, e-mail letter to author, 7 March 2006. Hartmann explained that Marbach had related the stories about the boat's mascots in his book, *Von Kolberg überLa Rochelle nach Berlin* (From Kolberg via La Rochelle to Berlin (Haag+Herchen Verlag, 1994).

73. Translation of song title: *So Small is the Boat and so Large is the Sea.*

heading through BE 84 and 81, ultimately to change course due east for the Biscay coast and home.[74]

There followed eight straight days of inactivity, boredom, and restlessness; eased only by the fact that the U-boat was homeward bound. The Allies seemed to have disappeared, and nothing so much as a smoke cloud on the far horizon was observed during the period. Gunner Karl Baumann and his *Kameraden* stood down from their duty stations each day without ever manning their weapons except to routinely prepare them for surface combat and later secure them for diving. Recording only routine daily activity, the *KTB* regularly tallied the boat's mileage totals from noon to noon each day. The eight-day journey spanned only 573 *Seemeilen*, of which the U-boat logged nearly half the distance, 267.5 miles, underwater.[75]

At 05:30 on the morning of 14 November *Kater's* shark-like prow broke onto the surface amid a cascade of white foam that the high waves quickly swept away. A full moon shone brightly through broken clouds above the eastern Biscay to create a silhouette of the U-boat against the dim night sky. Fortunately, the boat's dark gray skin blended well with the dark pre-dawn waters when observed from above. Thirty-five minutes later at grid square BF 4974, a lone Vickers Wellington suddenly emerged from the cloudbank off the boat's port side and passed overhead, 1,500 meters from the bow at seven hundred meters altitude. The gunners charged toward their deck-mounted weapons, but the British patrol bomber disappeared into the low clouds as quickly as it had appeared and never challenged the boat.[76]

The plane's crew either had not been scanning the Bay with anti-submarine radar or the aircraft was not so equipped; otherwise, *Kater* easily would have been discovered. The plane then would have held the decided advantage in the firefight that ensued. British airmen would rake the boat's superstructure with machineguns to suppress return fire and kill or trap men helplessly on the bridge and gun mounts. The boat could not have dived safely without sacrificing those still alive atop the tower, and most likely could not have submerged at all. An open main hatch would have caused the diving boat to swamp with seawater and sink with all hands lost. With precious seconds ticking away and U-953 still riding the surface, the Wellington would have banked into a wide turn toward the boat for a second attack, probably with both bombs and machineguns. As

74.   *KTB*, 4-5 November 1943.
75.   *KTB*, 6-13 November 1943.
76.   *KTB*, 14 November 1943.

with any U-boat that remained on the surface under such circumstances, *Kater's* chances for survival would diminish in a prolonged fight. The gods of war continued to smile upon the U-boat, however; at 06:23 she quickly and quietly slid beneath the waves into the otherworldly realm of the fishes and other sea creatures as the dawn sun rose magnificently over the Bay of Biscay.[77]

Intermittent rains fell across the Bay on 15 and 16 November, which helped shield U-953 from surface and air attacks as she slowly plowed toward La Pallice. Contact with BdU established the location and time Marbach and crew were to meet an escort ship and make the dangerous final leg of the *Feindfahrt* into the port. By noon the next day the boat had sailed 142 *Seemeilen* during the previous twenty-four hours to reach BF 6858, where an escort vessel steamed up to *Kater* precisely as planned. With guns fully manned and pointed into the grey overcast, U-953 followed the escort the final fifty miles through the perilous submarine kill zone in front of La Pallice, above the Bay floor thick with boats and the skeletons of lost *Ubootkameraden*. The escort kept watch over its charge until 14:30, when U-953 prepared to enter the La Pallice lock and artificial harbor. Gunners remained at their battle stations as huge steel gates on each end of the lock slowly closed and trapped the U-boat inside for an interminable few minutes. Boats were especially vulnerable to attack inside the harbor locks, and became favorite targets of Allied fighters and bombers that exploited their advantage with devastating results. Seawater finally was pumped out of the lock to gently lower the boat to the consistent water level inside the harbor. The inside gate then slowly swung open to release the boat into the harbor.[78]

Inside the harbor the helmsman sharply heeled U-953 180 degrees around until the bow again faced the Biscay. An anxious delay then passed with agonizing slowness as the exposed U-boat awaited further orders from the harbor master. Marbach ordered the boat's anchor dropped until permission was granted to proceed into a vacated bunker *Boxe*. The giant camouflage-painted concrete bunker was a welcome sight to everyone who basked in its shadow. Its massive size dwarfed the U-boat, and the unparalleled protection it offered mitigated its foreboding appearance. Enemy bombs had yet to damage a single U-boat that had found refuge inside the cavernous shelter. U-953, under electrical power driving her screws in reverse, eventually edged into the gaping entrance of her assigned

---

77. *KTB*, 14 November 1943.
78. *KTB*, 17 November 1943; and Buchheim, 11. La Pallice and St.-Nazaire were artificial harbors that required the cumbersome locks to maintain a constant water level inside the anchorage. The U-boat bases at Bordeaux, Brest, and Lorient were situated in natural harbors where locks were not needed.

Boxe. Gunners and watch party members kept their tense vigil until the last rays of the sun could not reach the boat. Officers converged on the conning tower bridge as petty officers and enlisted men lined up on deck to await their official homecoming reception. After forty-seven days on patrol the men were filthy, bearded, and bedraggled; young men all, the *Ubootfahrer* looked many years older. U-953 heaved anchor at 16:30.[79] Crewmen tossed lines up to sailors who stood along the dock to lash them around mooring posts. A boarding plank finally was laid down to the boat to the blaring accompaniment of a brass band.

The strains of martial music echoed loudly off the concrete walls as a delegation from 3rd Flotilla headquarters stood dockside to welcome home U-953. The skipper and each officer saluted the delegation and received a return salute and handshake as they stepped across the gangway onto dry land. Several German women from the base offices were on hand to present flowers to the skipper, who warmly accepted them with the wry grin of satisfaction that was his trademark. He would have preferred much more the satisfaction of reporting one or more enemy ships sunk, but the confluence of fortunes that delivered victory in battle had not attended his boat and crew to the fullest. Had mere sightings of enemy warships and aircraft been a valid measure, it then could be said that U-953 frequently was on the cusp of victory—or disaster.

Marbach turned to the crew standing at attention on the boat deck and dismissed them. The men piled onto the dock, relieved at being back on dry land and eager for several weeks of shore duty and leave time. Willi Schmall, the errant lookout who had fallen asleep on watch, was promptly released from five-weeks of confinement in his hammock. Schmall disembarked from U-953 with great trepidation; he would now be subject to whatever punishment lay in store for him. He soon would learn, however, that the skipper had filed no report against the young crewman, and would say nothing more of the matter. The fitting but unconventional punishment positively cured the grateful *Ubootfahrer* from ever again sleeping on watch. Schmall would remain a loyal and enthusiastic member of U-953's crew.

---

79. *KTB*, 17 November 1943.

Crewmembers crowd onto U-953's aft quadruple 20mm gun deck, 17 November 1943.

The men formed up at the storage bunker and collected their seabags, relieved at least for the time being that BdU would not have to ship their personal belongings home to grieving families as the last vestiges of war-shortened lives. Officers and crewmen alike lugged their bags to the train stop near the bunker; a short time later they boarded the little Kriegsmarine train for the short trip back to the *Kaserne* in La Rochelle.

Back in his quarters, Karl Baumann and his comrades reveled in long showers that washed away the grime of six weeks at sea. Luxuriously warm and soapy water cleaned out pores clogged with sweat and cologne. The putrid odors that permeated the interior of the U-boat would linger in their nostrils long after the end of the patrol. Men scraped off or trimmed scraggly beards and mustaches to restore youthful appearances. Replete with fresh uniforms they later converged at the *Ubootheim*, a club on base for both U-boat officers and enlisted men, where they were feted with food and drink to revive and renew their spirits. Karl chose to celebrate passing the crucible of his first patrol and his first combat by having his portrait taken in a photo booth. The rendered images portrayed a confident young man, with pipe in hand, who clearly enjoyed the distinction of membership in the elite U-boat arm of the Kriegsmarine.

To top off their good fortune, the U-boat men received their back pay, which soon greased the local economy of occupied La Rochelle and vicinity and guaranteed good times aplenty for those who sought them. Had anyone concluded that the U-boat war was a lost cause, no one spoke his mind. The men of U-953 simply were happy to be alive, and rightly so with more reason than they could know.

Karl was a veteran *Ubootfahrer* by the age of nineteen; La Rochelle, 1943.

There was no homecoming in Brest for U-211 or in St. Nazaire for U-648, both of which had attempted to rendezvous with U-953 to deliver replacement gun parts. U-211 was sunk northeast of the Azores on 19 November by a depth charge from a Vickers Wellington, and U-648 was fated to be sent to the bottom four days later by three British frigates near the same location. More than one hundred officers and crewmen joined the fifty-one lost from U-306, also out of Brest, which was sunk during the convoy pursuit on 31 October. Of the remaining U-boats from *Gruppe* Schill, U-707 out of La Pallice went down with all hands on 9 November. U-441 later would be lost on 8 June 1944 during her attempt to attack the Normandy invasion fleet, along with U-333 on 31 July during a similar mission. U-262 would be bombed at Gotenhafen before being fatally stricken at Kiel on 1 April 1945. The bodies of more than 350 U-boat men who had sailed in *Gruppe* Schill would lie on the ocean floor by war's end. Only two boats from the *U-Gruppe* would survive the war to be surrendered to the Allies: U-466 and U-953.[80]

---

80.   Internet: http://uboat.net/boats.htm.

5

Casualty

Beginning 18 November *Kater* spent a full month in the shipyard, where she was completely overhauled and repainted again to be made seaworthy. After her first and only *U-flak* patrol, BdU wisely scrapped the ill-fated strategy. The *U-flak* superstructure had seriously altered the boat's hydrodynamic streamlining, which made her top-heavy and produced significantly greater drag that reduced both diving and underwater cruising speed. Extra weight from additional ammunition and gunners also had hindered performance and reduced living space inside the boat. Diving time during combat emergencies was lengthened as well because a greater number of gunners had to enter the boat through the single hatch in the conning tower. Perhaps of greatest consternation, American and British pilots quickly learned not to take on a *U-flak* without calling other aircraft to the boat's location.[1] The gunboats stood little chance either to win the fight or dive to safety while under concentrated attack by two or more aircraft. Marbach and his crew were relieved when U-953 was reconverted nearly to her original configuration. Navy engineers removed her forward gun platform along with the forward and aft *Flakvierling* cannon. They then mounted two *Flakzweilling*—twin-barreled 20mm cannon—onto her *Wintergarten* port and starboard.

Several days after the boat went into drydock, Karl Baumann traveled to Brambauer on a fourteen-day furlough. He had looked forward to taking along a sizable collection of scarce canned foods he had accumulated to share with his family and with Anneliese, but when he retrieved the seabag where he had stored his sizable food stash in his billet he found it completely empty. Peremptory investigation revealed that his best friends had stolen the hoarded canned food and sold it to several local Frenchmen just to watch the fiery reaction Baumann would unleash when he discovered their prank. Though Karl was exceedingly disappointed to arrive home empty handed, the lost food was not enough to

---

1. David Miller, *U-boats; The Illustrated History of the Raiders of the Deep* (Washington DC: Brassey's, 2000) 34.

dampen his newfound enthusiasm for Brambauer. He and Anneliese spent considerable time together and grew closer in thought and spirit with the passing days. Strict orders forbade any discussion about the U-boat or the Battle of the Atlantic; so the young seaman was careful divulge nothing, even to his closest loved ones. Still, the war was pre-eminent in every aspect of daily life, from rationed food and all the basic elements of survival to the limitations and difficulties of travel. And always, the sad goodbyes and longing for loved ones in harm's way wore heavily on hearts and minds.

This illustrates the typical conning tower and gun platforms on a Type VIIC U-boat. Aft of the bridge is the *Wintergarten* with two twin-20mm cannon and the lower platform where a 37mm gun was mounted.

Karl returned to La Rochelle in early December, where he remained during the Christmas holiday. He collected a mound of assorted chocolates, cookies, and other foods that he wrapped up and shipped to Anneliese. Some days later, young Miss Samhuber was thrilled to receive the package. Not only had he remembered her with the gift, she was glad to share the rare and treasured commodities with her family. The package was a wonderful reminder of the mutual fondness that had developed between the young couple. The stresses of war had made their longing for each other more deeply felt. She viewed his assignment to the U-boat force with great trepidation, as the inherent dangers of undersea warfare were quite obvious even to the uninitiated. She realized she could do nothing more to help maintain Karl's spirits than to write to him almost daily.

Matrosenobergefreiter Karl Baumann, U-953 gunner; 1943.

From 19 December through Christmas Day the boat was fully equipped and provisioned for her third patrol, and Karl Baumann's second mission into contested waters. Like Baumannl, a number of other crewmembers took the opportunity to return home on leave. Having survived the Battle of the Atlantic thus far, hearts ached to celebrate the 1943 Christmas season with loved ones lest it be their last. Melancholy and trepidation tempered anticipation and expectation for the holidays. Under the dark skies of approaching winter, sometimes amid the ruins of their neighborhoods and homes, young *Ubootfahrer* gathered families near and plied them with little gifts from France. With inescapable sadness they intently watched grateful parents, siblings, wives, children and sweethearts enjoy spare Kriegsmarine rations of foodstuffs that had begun to disappear from grocers' shelves on the home front. Muted voices sang *Vom Himmel Hoch* and *Stille Nacht, Heilige Nacht* while men remembered and dreamed about their lives before the war. Some silently confronted profound guilt born of conflicting desires to stay home to help struggling families, but also to return to the war and their *Ubootkameraden*. The inevitable last day and last moments of leave arrived, and with tearful farewells crewmen made their way west to the Atlantic coast and the unknown but frightful future they would share with all those entangled in the perilous sea battles that lay ahead.

Oberleutnant Marbach's relaxed attitude usually bade well for the men aboard U-953 while they sweated out difficult days and weeks during combat patrols. Misconduct on his own part in December 1943, however, soon would imperil his entire crew and nearly his naval career; only the exigencies of war would intervene to retrieve it. While U-953 lay in drydock, Marbach and First Officer Bischoff decided to visit Paris on their return trip to La Rochelle from holiday leaves in Germany. The two spent a wild night of raising hell in the City of Light with far too much injudicious abandon to suit the German field police. Cornered in their third nightclub by a military police major, Marbach unsteadily issued his informal spread-fingered salute and was promptly arrested along with Bischoff for public drunkenness.

"Don't you have anything better to do than chase a couple of U-boat guys around?" Marbach protested as they were hauled to a stockade full of offenders who represented the multifarious branches of the Wehrmacht.[2]

The officers' untenable predicament clearly required decisive action. U-953 was scheduled to sail out of La Pallice on 26 December to patrol off the coast of Spain. Marbach and Bischoff knew that if they were not present to take command of their boat at the scheduled departure time they would be arrested for being absent without leave, if not desertion. In desperation, the pair hatched a daring and devious plan. When the two officers appeared before the provost in command of the stockade they implored their host to allow them to retrieve their baggage from the train station. The provost looked momentarily into the eyes of the young naval officers to gauge their veracity; then he spoke.

"Upon your honor as officers of the *Reich*, will you collect your gear and return to the stockade?" the provost inquired.

"*Ja wohl*," Marbach and Bischoff solemnly declared, whereupon the provost ordered the men released temporarily on their own recognizance.

The prisoners immediately made their way to *Gare du Nord* and grabbed up their belongings from the luggage storage room like they had promised—then jumped aboard the next Wehrmacht train bound for La Rochelle. The two fugitives held their breath and looked over their shoulders at every stop as the train traversed the flat terrain southwest of Paris, and prayed the military police had

---

2.   Uwe Eduard Hartmann, interview by author, 16 November 2000. The son of U-953's Navigator, Hartmann related his father's often-told recollection of Marbach's and Bischoff's arrest in Paris.

not relayed bulletins across occupied France to intercept them. Their invocations to the Almighty were answered when the train finally chugged into the station at La Rochelle. In a few short hours U-953 and her full complement of officers and men sailed out of La Pallice en route to the African coast. Marbach's and Bischoff's furtive flight from their Paris jail cell was not over, however; their misadventure haunted them during the war patrol and ultimately endangered *Kater* and her crew.

Christmas Day 1943 was a muted affair. All *Ubootfahrer* scheduled to sail out of La Pallice the next day were sequestered inside the flotilla's compound, surrounded by the hostile streets of La Rochelle. The men were forbidden to imbibe any form of alcohol as dulled senses or responses might prove fatal during any dive sequence or an enemy attack. A traditional feast of roast goose with all the trimmings was served in the large mess hall, but the celebratory mood itself underscored a sense of urgency and the realization that all pleasures at the war front were fleeting. Time had begun to draw to a close for many young men there who unknowingly celebrated their last Christmas; the coming battles of 1944 would decimate the German U-boat fleet.

After midday on 26 December U-953 slowly emerged from *Boxe* 3 at La Pallice with Karl Baumann crammed into the bow torpedo room. Seven boats waded into the Bay behind a minelayer that would shadow them throughout the following day. Marbach spent more than ten hours conducting a test dive that discovered several mechanical problems, but the repairs he ordered did not jeopardize the boat's mission. As for the mission itself, scuttlebutt declared the boat was to test a new radar system for its effectiveness and was not supposed to engage the enemy except in self-defense.[3] With La Pallice nearly one hundred *Seemeilen* astern when the escort broke away and *Kater* submerged into the Bay the next evening. Two hours later the skipper received a radio telegram that ordered the seven boats onto a southerly course toward the northern coast of Spain. The coded message warned the U-boat commanders to expect to be overtaken by two German destroyers on a southward heading as well. The waters of the Bay glistened brightly when U-953 surfaced two hours after midnight to run on diesel power. The approaching dawn drove *Kater* underwater again near the Spanish coast, where Marbach ordered the boat onto a slow westerly course parallel to the shoreline. U-953 surfaced and recharged her big electric batteries the

---

3.   Rumors of the mission's ultimate purpose were wrong. U-953 would not have been sent on a 56-day mission only to test radar equipment; moreover, the boat was assigned to an attack group during part of the mission.

next night under a shroud of heavy darkness.[4] Though officially a non-belligerent nation that had declared its neutrality, Spain was infested with Allied and Axis spies. German vessels observed from the shore would be reported to Supreme Headquarters in London through an organized network of Allied agents scattered throughout the country.

Marbach received a radio telegram on the afternoon of 29 December, warning him to expect a German destroyer heading eastward. An hour later the sound technician notified the skipper that he had picked up the strong sound signature of a destroyer some distance astern of *Kater*. Marbach then ordered the boat to periscope depth to scan the horizon. He observed nothing, but determined the sound reading must have come from the German vessel. U-953 continued on her westward heading along the coast until the evening of 30 December when a coded message ordered Marbach and *Kapitänleutnant* Wolfgang Wenzel of U-231 to adjust their courses beyond the northwest corner of Spain. The dark nights also had provided cover for the boat to run along the surface again to recharge the critical batteries. On *Silvestertag*—New Year's Eve—the skipper ordered several bottles of a watered-down alcoholic concoction distributed to the men, which allowed each member of the crew a single swallow. With little further fanfare the officers and crew of U-953 greeted the New Year of 1944 at BF 7584, fifty miles off the northwest tip of the Spanish coast. There, Marbach relayed a message to the crew from the high commands of the U-boat force and the Wehrmacht:

> U-boat men: For the New Year we remember the challenges, the difficult circumstances of the U-boat war of the past year to which you dedicated your lives for the *Führer* and the Fatherland. Your sacrifice is a commitment and an incentive for us to continue the struggle of our beloved force, which in the coming year will hit our enemy hard with new methods and new tactics.[5]

The next ten days on patrol were typical of most the *Ubootfahrer* encountered: endless hours of weariness followed by brief events of abject terror. Daily orders from BdU repositioned the U-boats in further fruitless attempts to locate and attack American and British convoys that had been rerouted away from the known U-boat concentrations, thanks to the British mathematicians who had broken the top secret Enigma codes. The new dynamic of the sea war was akin to

4.   *KTB*, 26-28 December 1943.
5.   *KTB*, 29-31 December 1943.

a chess player unable to watch and match his opponent's every move, but whose very life was dependent upon winning the match.

U-953 stalked the Spanish coast throughout New Years Day. That evening Marbach was ordered by radio telegram to join an attack group code-named Borkum, which was to form a cordon of ten U-boats stretched across a 350 mile east-west line from northern Spain to the eastern Atlantic. German naval intelligence had learned that an Allied convoy was scheduled to pass through the area the next day and *Gruppe* Borkum was ordered to take up their assigned positions by 10:00. Complete radio silence was ordered, other than to transmit crucial tactical information or confirm successful attacks. The silence order was intended to prevent convoy escorts from intercepting even innocuous messages that would give away the presence of the attack force lying in wait for the kill.[6]

Air reconnaissance was unavailable to shadow the convoy's progress. Each boat also was on her own to plan individual attacks whenever the enemy was sighted. Thus began a seemingly endless waiting game: a dreary existence U-boat men endured mostly in silence, entombed inside their humid, submerged chambers until—mostly by chance—an enemy target sailed into the line of attack. *Kater* logged 191 nautical miles for the twenty-four hour period that began at noon on New Year's Day. After surfacing in the late evening of 2 January, Marbach held his boat in position amid the low hanging night fog that shrouded her from direct enemy observation, though not from radar. Except for the sound of the big diesels that recharged the batteries, the U-boat waited silently for her prey to appear first as an electrical signature on the sound operator's optical screen.[7]

U-953 traversed a small area the following day. Little movement, no action, radio silence, and the putrid environment left Karl and the other men listless and craving the hours of darkness when the boat would surface for fresh air to rejuvenate their senses. The conning tower broke onto the surface at 20:00. Fresh sea air poured into the boat as the stench of perspiration, fuel, grease, and foul breaths was pushed out. Restless youthful spirits that had given in to endless boredom were quickly restored. Yet *Gruppe* Borkum had produced no results; the convoy had not arrived to present its fat targets. At 10:30 Marbach received a message from BdU that ordered the *Gruppe* to split into three smaller groups to reposition themselves farther south and west into the Atlantic in the belief that the Allied ships had altered their course. The young *Kapitän* needed only to shift *Kater's* location only a short distance farther southwest, but his mission had

6.   *KTB*, 1 January 1944.
7.   *KTB*, 2 January 1944.

changed. The new orders called for the small groups to exploit any chance for attacks—if or when the convoy finally was spotted—rather than wait for unsuspecting ships to run headlong into concentrated line of attack. Henceforth, the boats were permitted to run on the surface during the day unless they ran into enemy aircraft or adverse weather. The maneuver was fraught with danger, but BdU seemed almost desperate for its boats to locate and engage the elusive convoy.[8]

Running submerged, Marbach shifted his boat's position another fifty miles to the southwest during the early morning hours of 4 January, then surfaced into the evening fog that protected the boat from visual observation until bright moonlight illuminated the sky at midnight. On 5 January BdU again ordered the three small groups into new positions to intercept a convoy scheduled to move north out of Gibraltar on the seventh or eighth. *Kater* moved about forty miles due north from her previously established position. Marbach and his officers again felt a surge of anticipation about their prospects for a successful attack. This time, BdU promised, Luftwaffe aircraft would shadow the convoy and report its northward approach. All U-boats were ordered to remain submerged during the daylight hours.[9]

Tedium and frustration again ruled as the men plodded through endless hours and days crowded into stinking living quarters where bunk spaces remained the domain of unspent torpedoes. Crewmen on long patrols needed diversions to reduce stress and boredom. When not in danger from enemy contact, Marbach sometimes ordered music broadcast over the intercom system from the boat's portable record player and a small collection of 78-rpm disks. The men were left mostly to their own devices to entertain themselves. Since very few details about the U-boat's mission or her destination and present location were officially announced, the enlisted ranks spread and analyzed an unending supply of rumors, which played vital roles in stress management, psychological wellbeing, and entertainment. In small groups they also took up impromptu rounds of singing or lively discussions of topics that ranged from bawdy to serious. The most popular song among the crew was *Denn Wir Fahren Gegen England*, the unoffi-

---

8. *KTB*, 3 January 1944.
9. *KTB*, 4-5 January 1944. The *Enigma*-coded messages from BdU to Group Borkum almost certainly were intercepted by the Allies and the convoy rerouted as a result to avoid the U-boat line of attack. The British broke the first Enigma code in May 1941, and by December 1942 routinely decoded messages transmitted in the latest variant within 26 hours of reception. See Robert C. Stern, *Type VII U-boats* (London: Brockhampton Press, 1998), 115-116.

cial anthem of the Kriegsmarine.[10] U-953's men updated the song's rallying cry to take the fight to England and America as well.

Unsere Flagge und die wehet auf dem Maste,
Sie verkündet unseres Reiches Macht,
Denn wir wollen es nicht länger leiden,
Daß der Englischmann darüber lacht.

Gib mir deine Hand, deine weiße Hand,
:/: Leb wohl, mein Schatz, :/: leb wohl!
Lebe wohl, denn wir fahren, denn wir fahren,
Denn wir fahren gegen Engelland,
Engelland.

This pre-war postcard displays the words to the popular *Kriegsmarine* song, *Denn Wir Fahren Gegen England.*

Such nationalistic songs were safe diversions for U-boat men. On the other hand, to express either youthful defiance or the thrill of getting away with a forbidden act, Baumann and several *Kameraden* joined voices on one occasion to sing the world wide communist anthem, the *Internationale.* The ad hoc boy choir sang in a low, low whisper for fear they might be overheard by someone who misunderstood their intentions. They imagined themselves reported, arrested, tried for treason, and marched in front of a firing squad for their indiscretion.

The Sixth of January passed slowly, mechanically, and methodically for the *Ubootfahrer* aboard U-953, which submerged at the break of dawn and slowly plied the general area throughout the day. The boat surfaced into the crisp clear night after a fruitless search for enemy vessels turned up nothing. *Gruppe* Borkum's skippers later received orders to move ninety miles south of their present positions, and on 7 January *Kater* sailed toward her new sector in the relocated line.[11] Marbach first shifted his position twenty-five miles southeast, where he

---

10. Translation: We Sail Against England. The song actually was written during the First World War.

11. The new grid positions either were incorrectly transmitted by BdU received by *Kater*, or erroneously recorded in the *KTB*, because the locations recorded in the war diary did not exist on BdU's Atlantic grid maps.

scouted the general area on 8 January. The evening message from BdU reported that Luftwaffe aircraft had not been able to locate any Allied vessels that day, but that two JU 290 reconnaissance bombers would renew their search for the enemy ships the following afternoon. BdU then issued orders for the groups again to reposition themselves approximately fifty miles southeast of their present locations by 18:00 the next evening, 9 January. In the meantime, Marbach ordered U-953 on a westerly course of nearly one hundred miles, then sharply southeast on a surface run at top speed. The skipper had disobeyed the BdU directive, but apparently had a hunch he would run into the Allied convoy or escorts during his frenetic nighttime dash away from the new line of attack. His efforts again proved fruitless, however, as the enemy was nowhere in sight. The boat submerged at dawn on 9 January and plodded the remaining distance toward her assigned position, where she finally arrived at 22:00.[12]

BdU notified *Gruppe* Borkum while en route to its new staging point that air reconnaissance had spotted an Allied escort vessel about 270 nautical miles south of the wolfpack's sector. The ten U-boat commanders were ordered to maintain their positions in sequence; then, at 04:00 on 10 January, form a stepped line of attack in an east-northeast to west-southwest zone across a 200 mile stretch of ocean perpendicular to the enemy's projected line of approach. Luftwaffe aircraft would patrol south of the U-boat positions during the early evening hours. U-953, assigned to the farthest northeast group, proceeded about twenty miles to her new position as light rain gently pelted the watch party on the conning tower. By midnight the rain had passed and a beautifully moonlit and cloudless sky cast a glimmer of light onto the smooth ocean surface. Just before dawn on 11 January, Marbach ordered his boat to submerge, but remained on the lookout for the Gibraltar convoy. By noon the boat had sailed 188 *Seemeilen* over the previous twenty-four hours.[13]

While U-953 patrolled inside CF 2375, a section of ocean approximately 435 miles off the Spanish coast, the sound technician suddenly detected distant propeller noises at 16:30. Marbach peered into the periscope of the submerged *Kater* to scan the area for enemy traffic. The sea was calm and flat as a duck pond, without a trace of enemy activity; neither distant smoke trails nor smokestacks or masts were visible anywhere on the horizon. The skipper ordered the boat to the surface to gain a better view of his surroundings, though it was highly dangerous to expose it to daylight observation. The water level soon dropped in the

12.   *KTB*, 6-9 January 1944.
13.   *KTB*, 9-11 January 1944.

conning tower's depth gauge until it indicated the ocean surface was below the main hatch. Marbach raced to the top of the conning tower ladder and, as soon as the air pressures were equalized, spun the handwheel to open the main hatch cover.[14] He climbed onto the bridge while the watch party followed close on his heels. When the skipper peered over the bridge wall he gasped with astonishment. A sleek, fast destroyer steamed directly across the near horizon at full speed. Marbach quickly glanced toward the stern for signs of danger and discovered to his horror that a cordon of warships surrounded U-953. Wide eyed, he lunged for the main hatch and met the watch party as they clambered up the tower ladder.

"*Alaaarrrm!!!*" the skipper shouted down the hatchway into the conning tower. The watch party and Marbach tumbled back down the ladder in a solid mass of bodies as the emergency dive bell clanged.

"*Auf Gefechtstation!!!*" Marbach barked. The boat responded immediately to the precise mechanics of the dive procedure and shortly sank beneath the placid surface. The skipper ordered torpedo tube II in the bow and V in the stern armed and readied to launch their missiles.[15]

Karl ran to the stern compartment when the crew manned their battle stations and remained there to help the torpedo technicians during the emergency. Torpedo *Mixer* Karl Kühn already stood by tube V's control panel. A moment later the skipper ordered *Kater* back up to periscope depth. The chief engineer monitored critical gauges as compressed air was pumped into the ballast tanks. The boat rose gently and in perfect trim to a shallow depth that allowed the attack periscope alone to break the ocean surface, hopefully unseen by enemy eyes. Down in the *Zentrale,* an electric motor whirred as it extended the length of the attack periscope until Marbach could observe the low horizon from his seat in the

---

14. *KTB*, 11 January 1944.
15. Translation: "Man Battle Stations!!!" The *KTB* reports that the U-boat submerged at CF 2384; then, more than an hour later, while at CF 2375 propeller noises were detected; forty minutes later the alarm for battle stations was sounded. Karl Baumann recalled that U-953 had surfaced, and Marbach immediately had spotted a cordon of five warships from the bridge. The boat would have had to surface during the forty-minute period, if Baumann's memory is correct; and if so, one may only speculate why the action was not recorded. The *KTB* probably was subject to the skipper's editorial review. It is apparent from Baumann's clear memory of the 11 January action and numerous other events aboard U-953 that certain details and incidents were not recorded in the *KTB*, which BdU scrutinized after each war patrol. U-953's *KTB* entries tended to be terse, and did not reveal the full picture of events recorded other than to detail critical technical and mechanical information.

conning tower above. The skipper quickly scanned the visible area in several 360-degree sweeps. Bischoff took up his position in the *Zentrale*; as first officer, he was responsible for the torpedoes and their launch systems. The sound operator detected multiple hydrophone readings and reported each heading and bearing to the control room. In response, the skipper swung the periscope viewfinder toward the indicated sound sources. A British destroyer loomed into the viewfinder, then a second and a third, and finally a corvette—the warships of an anti-submarine hunter-killer group.[16]

Tension mounted as Marbach sighted each enemy ship. The destroyers were fearsome adversaries; heavily armed and with speeds that often exceeded thirty knots, they could outrun any U-boat and some Axis torpedoes as well.[17] Marbach determined from their converging courses that the ships were looking for U-953 and intent on closing in for the kill. Somehow his boat had given away her position or had been detected by some electronic means employed by the Allies. Regardless, the hunt was on as the hunter-killer force tightened its noose around *Kater*. Twenty minutes after he ordered the crew to battle stations Marbach observed the corvette cross the boat's bow at high speed, then tack hard to port. The maneuver churned up an artificial wake that stood in stark contrast to the calm tide. U-953 likewise responded with a hard turn of her own to line up her bow for a broadside shot from torpedo tube II, but was unable to fire before the corvette charged well past *Kater's* line of attack.[18]

Karl stood by the speaking tube, a rudimentary communication system that ran from the control room to the bridge, to both the bow and stern of the boat, and to crucial locations in between. There he took on the task to pass along any commands from the conning tower and the *Zentrale* to the technicians in the stern compartment. While he monitored the tube, Karl overheard Marbach discuss the developing attack with Bischoff and the action they should take to counter the threat. Amid the life and death choreography of warships, the two officers' flight from arrest in Paris again entered their thoughts.

"You think we ought to sink a couple?" one asked the other in a low voice.

"I don't know," replied the other, "but we better do something to help ourselves when we get back to port and find the military police waiting there for us."

---

16. Translation: A torpedo technician was known as a *Mixer*.

17. Dan van der Vat, *The Atlantic Campaign; World War II's Great Struggle at Sea* (New York: Harper & Row, 1988), 307.

18. The British Admiralty probably knew, by decryption of the Kriegsmarine's Enigma codes, the general location of U-953, the purpose of her patrol mission, and other details of her voyage as well.

Marbach continued to ponder the matter with Bischoff while he executed another 360-degree periscope sweep of the area. At 17:52 he swung the periscope 180 degrees to scan the horizon aft of the boat. Suddenly a terrifying sight filled the periscope viewfinder: the corvette was bearing down on the U-boat dead astern and no more than one hundred meters away. The ship seemed to have appeared from nowhere while the skipper and First Officer were distracted by their discussion. The corvette apparently had spotted the periscope's wake and was determined to ram U-953 under full steam.[19]

"*Rohr Funf fertig! Rohr Funf los!!!*" Marbach yelled into the speaking tube in a single breath. The command rang into Karl's ear. Though startled by the sudden, tense bark of the skipper, Baumann immediately relayed the desperate command.

"*Rohr Funf fertig! Rohr Funf los!!!*" Baumann shouted frantically at the top of his lungs.[20]

Torpedoman Kühn lunged for his control panel and jammed the armed launch button home with the palm of his hand. The next few seconds were a nightmare of intertwined crises. The long T-V acoustic torpedo streamed out of the stern launch tube, where its propulsion system immediately engaged. In what seemed a heartbeat later it slammed against the hull of the corvette, which was so close that the tremendous explosion rocked U-953. A violent shock wave from the blast surged through the boat and slammed into Karl and his crewmates as if each had been hit with a board full-force in the chest. Lights throughout the boat flickered off for a second and then returned to everyone's relief, while a medley of groans emanated from stressed pipe fittings, bolts and steel rivets. Men grabbed onto anything solidly bolted down to stop their bodies from being flung help-lessly about by the passing wave. At the same time, the sudden torpedo launch instantly made the U-boat bow-heavy because the stern tube had not been prop-erly flooded prior to the launch sequence. Before the *Leitender* could order four or five men from the bow to run at top speed to the trailing edge of the boat to act as counterweights, U-953's stern broke through the ocean surface and for a few terrible seconds stood out of the water, bow heavy.

---

19. Ramming was an acceptable practice in anti-submarine warfare, though conven-tional means of combat were preferred. "A weapon of last resort was ramming and, though this action usually brought damage to the [attacking ships'] bows, requiring seven to eight weeks to repair, by May 1943 about twenty-four [U-boats] had been dispatched by this means." See Gannon, 62.

20. Translation: "Tube Five ready! Tube Five launch!!!" All commands had to be relayed exactly as stated by a superior officer or non-commissioned officer, with words nei-ther deleted nor added.

"Auf Tiefe gehen!!" Marbach ordered abruptly. The urgent command set the men's automatic responses into motion. The exposed stern soon slid below the surface as the boat descended toward the dark regions. With water now pouring into the stern ballast tank U-953 regained her proper balance. Then, unexpectedly, she became stern-heavy as she plunged into the high-pressure depths. Excessive heat from a driveshaft bearing had caused a crucial watertight seal to loosen and admit excess water into the boat. The *Leitender* ordered one crewman from the stern compartment to the bow—fast—to restore critical trim. Karl immediately charged to the stern bulkhead without a word and plunged his large frame through each of the small bulkhead hatches as he ran through the length of the boat.

The men worked frantically to restore control to the U-boat amid the amplified cacophony of grating and desperate sounds that issued from the dying corvette. The *Ubootfahrer* gathered their senses after they finally regained the boat's trim, and only then fully took stock of the spine-chilling incident.[21] By all indications, they had destroyed the enemy vessel almost directly atop their own position as it charged headlong to ram their U-boat. Seconds before meeting grisly death themselves, they had spared their lives by killing their enemy. To an outsider, the men would have appeared uncharacteristically reserved in the wake of victory and their own salvation, but throughout U-953 each sailor was happy simply to be alive. Any round of cheers also would ring loudly through the destroyers' sound detectors and betray the U-boat's position. Another thought crossed the minds of some crewman as well: a number of young sailors like themselves had died when the corvette disintegrated. Either fate or good luck, measured in mere seconds, now separated the living participants from the dead. Victory celebrations would wait until *Kater* returned home—if she returned home.

The violent concussion had rendered the boat's sensitive sound detection system and periscope temporarily inoperable. Not only was Marbach unable to visually confirm the sinking corvette, the sustained damage immediately imperiled the boat, the men, and their mission. The torpedo's powerful detonation brought

---

21. *KTB*, 11 January 1944, reported twelve to thirty seconds elapsed between the time the torpedo was fired and when the detonation wave slammed against the U-boat. The *KTB* description of the attack, "I decide on a shot from tube V and turn into position," implies the launch was a product of Marbach's careful, calculated decision rather than a desperate, split-second command to save the boat from immediate peril.

the remaining hunter-killer force charging full steam toward U-953, which presently had neither mechanical eyes nor electronic ears.[22]

The depth gauge in the control room measured the progress of the boat's descent: fifty meters, then seventy-five. Anxious eyes alternately watched the depth gauge and studied Marbach's every move and facial expression to anticipate and respond instantly to his next order.

The skipper was relieved to learn the hydrophone had been quickly repaired.

One hundred meters depth.

The sound operator reported the approach of fast-turning screws.

"They're coming, they're coming!" he whispered into his speaking tube.

One hundred twenty meters.

The silent electric motors drove the U-boat's propellers barely enough to maintain forward momentum and prevent an uncontrollable plunge fifteen thousand feet to the ocean floor. Marbach watched the depth gauge and held to his dive order.

One hundred thirty-five meters.

No one dared speak above a whisper for fear he would give more sound detection readings to the destroyers. The seawater magnified every sound emitted by the ships on the surface as well as the submerged U-boat. The *Ubootfahrer* limited all movement; those required to move around could don specially made submariners' socks instead of shoes, the soles of which were thickly stuffed with human or horse hair to deaden the sound of footsteps.

One hundred fifty-five meters.

The Asdic detection systems aboard the Royal Navy destroyers sent out a familiar and distinctive PING-ping-PING signal that reverberated through the boat and strained the taut nerves of the encased crew.[23] A series of sonar signals then rapidly tapped against the hull of the boat with an unsettling click-click-

---

22. *KTB*, 11-12 January 1944. Marbach could make no visual confirmation to conclusively report whether its torpedo had damaged or sunk the corvette, or struck a decoy or a hard wave. At his first sighting Marbach indicated the corvette bore the designation "*K 151.*" That designation belonged to HMCS *Lunenburg*, an American-built Canadian vessel of the Flower Class, which survived the war to be decommissioned on 23 July 1945. Records from U.S., British, and Canadian sources located by the author do not indicate any ships sunk on 11 January 1944. In his post-mission summary Marbach reported "strike on corvette '*K 151*' possible," but the actual identification of the corvette U-953 engaged remains a mystery.

23. Gannon, 62. Asdic was so named after the Anti-submarine Division of the Royal Navy, which developed the sound-ranging device similar to the U.S. Navy's Sonar.

click-click-click that reminded the men of handfuls of pebbles being thrown against the steel skin. The destroyers' twin propeller screws constantly whined, and increased in dynamic intensity to a loud rumble whenever one of the warships passed directly above the U-boat.

One hundred seventy-five meters.

The water pressure against the U-boat magnified with each additional meter of depth; the pressure hull groaned and strained against the tremendous force. Men tightened down bolted fastenings throughout the descent to preserve watertight seals that threatened to burst. Marbach watched the depth gauge as it edged to one hundred eighty-five meters, then one hundred ninety. Finally, the skipper ordered the *Leitender* to level out the boat.

Two hundred meters.

U-953 silently lay below nearly 657 feet of ocean, while the destroyers converged overhead and prepared to wreak vengeance on the German boat and crew. The warships above continued to create a nerve-wracking commotion as their propeller screws chewed into waves, sailors ran with feet pounding across their decks, Asdic pings sought out their elusive target, and countless muffled sounds echoed through the sea. Meanwhile, the U-boat crew awaited the coming terror in total silence, in part to preserve the limited amount of oxygen that remained.

"*Licht, Luft, und Nerven sparen!*" was the standing order for the U-boat crew in such desperate times.[24] Men stood or sat by their duty stations and control panels while others lay in bunks or in the walkways of the sealed compartments. No one dared move a muscle. Karl lay on the floor below the four bow torpedo tubes and the spare missiles that hung suspended in chains. Deep below the surface, the lethal *Aale* were completely useless in the present life-and-death struggle.[25]

Suddenly, a new sound echoed through the U-boat; two heavy splashes were followed by a gurgling hum that grew nearer with every second. A moment later the sea was rent with two deafening explosions of depth charges. Shock waves slammed into U-953, which shuddered and rocked amid the violent, manmade tempest. The helpless crewmen absorbed each blast with limbs tightened against their tensed bodies, squinted eyes and clinched teeth—natural survival responses inherited from their earliest ancestors—as if to present smaller targets. The radio operator recorded the exact time each steel drum packed with 250 pounds of

---

24. Translation: "Save light, air, and your nerves!"
25. Translation: *Ubootfahrer* referred to their torpedoes as *Aale*—eels.

explosives detonated, and scrawled a mark for the blast on a sheet of paper for later entry into the *Kriegstagebuch*.

U-953 sailed a frequently altered evasive course at approximately two knots, the lowest speed to maintain buoyancy. The continual movement also prevented leaking oil or other fluids from rising to the surface to mark the boat's location like a bull's-eye. The destroyers, in turn, constantly adjusted their locations to maintain contact with their target. They swarmed about the area in crisscross patterns that roiled the surface with competing wakes. Seven more depth charges followed the first two. Hour after hour throughout the night the destroyers surged overhead and released salvoes of charges preset to detonate at varying depths. The ocean surface erupted with giant geysers from the upward force of each explosive canister that detonated. The U-boat crew suffered an interminable twelve hours under attack in thin, stale air that became more putrid with each shallow breath taken. Ten minutes or more might pass between explosions while the destroyers took new sound readings. The men could not move around or use the hand-pumped toilets for fear that any sound might direct the depth charges ever closer to the battered boat.[26]

The depth charges that detonated nearby shattered electric light bulbs and chipped paint off the interior wall of the pressure hull. Loose steel floor plates levitated several inches before they clattered back into their slots. Pipes and valves burst from the concussive forces and saturated officers and crewmen who scrambled to stem streams of water, oil, hydraulic and other fluids. Other men stared blankly as they waited for the special, manmade hell to end one way or another. Frayed nerves and exhausted oxygen-starved bodies neared the point of crisis, but never broke. Some crewmen accepted their fate with stoicism, while others fervently prayed and prayed—and prayed.

No one wanted to use the bucket that substituted for the inoperable bow toilet during the depth charge attack, but one man's strained constitution could no longer withstand his utmost desire to hold back the urge to relieve himself. No sooner had he lowered his trousers and crouched onto the metal container than another round of depth charges plunged toward the boat. Before the hapless sailor could interrupt his efforts the charges exploded with soul-jarring concussions that ripped through *Kater* and sent the bare-bottomed crewman sprawling off his precarious seat and onto the walkway. The bucket noisily tumbled across

---

26. Due to an inability for the toilets aboard the Type VII U-boats to compensate for the outside water pressure, they usually were inoperable at depths below twenty-five meters. See Stern, 76.

the deck planks and scattered its vile contents, which worsened the already putrid air that permeated the bow compartment. Had the seemingly endless attack not consumed the men with unbridled fear they could not have contained the outburst of laughter that would have pursued their poor humiliated *Ubootkamerad* while he fumbled to restore his trousers and his pride.

Karl Baumann had never experienced such terror. In the close confines of the bow compartment he waited for the next detonation to stagger his boat and crewmates with its startling ferocity. For the first time since he went to sea at age fourteen, Karl thought seriously about death; survival now did not seem even a remote or viable option. Wild and terrible nightmare scenes played in his imagination. The very next depth charge might rip through the pressure hull and rend the U-boat asunder. The very next moment—or second—might be his last. To be sunk 200 meters below the surface meant no crewmen could possibly survive; death at least would be instantaneous. A worse possibility was that the boat's control systems were damaged beyond their ability to raise the boat to the surface; with no oxygen left to breathe the crew would slowly suffocate inside their iron coffin. If, on the other hand, Marbach ordered the boat to the surface for lifesaving air the lone U-boat would have to fight it out with the destroyers; U-953 stood no chance to attack before being blown apart by the enemy's massed deck guns. In any case, the South Atlantic most likely would become an unmarked grave for fifty-six more young *Ubootfahrer*. In hometowns like Brambauer, or Hamburg, or Essen, worried loved ones would never exactly know their sailor's fate—how, when, or where he died. Anneliese Samhuber simply would never again receive another letter from Karl. At some point the families would receive the personal belongings the men had deposited at the storage bunker in La Pallice. Official records would list each member of the crew, beside which would be the terse notation: missing at sea; presumed dead.

"Don't let me die! I don't want to die!" Karl Baumann pleaded over and over in silent prayer, fervently and for the first time truly from the heart. The little prayers *Oma* had taught him to recite when he was a child simply were not up to his present need. The brash young man who with rugged self-reliance had learned to persevere against life's adversity now prayed to God in Heaven to deliver him and his comrades from their abject hell; to deliver them, that all might live to return safely to their homes, families, and friends. Whether he then and there would live or die was a matter entirely out of his hands; his fate would be determined altogether by external forces.

Twelve hours after the depth charge attack began, Karl waited with eyes closed and teeth clenched for the next explosion to tear into his consciousness. He had been unable to keep conscious count amid his terror; how many more detonations his battered U-boat could absorb he did not know.[27] Then, to his surprise he realized no sound echoes emanating from above—no propeller screws, no Asdic pings, no sonar clicks—and no depth charges gurgling downward to trigger their horrifying detonations. The destroyers had disappeared!

At 05:30 on 12 January, twenty-one hours after U-953 had last submerged with a fresh air supply, battery power and oxygen both were nearly expended. Marbach ordered the battle-scarred boat to the surface at cautious ten-meter intervals. All of the bolted fastenings that had been tightened down during the descent now were gradually loosened to allow the fastenings to expand against the reduced water pressure outside the boat. Crewmen stood ready at their battle stations as air compressors forced seawater out of the ballast tanks and the U-boat slowly rose from the deep ocean sanctuary. Sound checks were made at each interval; hearing nothing, the boat continued toward the surface until she reached periscope depth. Marbach then raised the periscope and peered into the viewfinder. The destroyers had fled the area to catch up with the convoy, which German reconnaissance had last spotted at 23:00 the previous night. *Wache* members felt renewed by the rain that soaked them when finally the main hatch flung open and they scrambled onto the bridge.[28] Sweet, life-sustaining air poured into the boat through the hatch and the intake vents. The bodies and spirits of every crewman soon were revived, and each man in his own way was thankful for his deliverance from seemingly certain death. U-953 plowed through the rain and swells for several hours as the big diesel engines recharged the electric motor batteries. To mislead enemy electronic observation Marbach directed crewmen to release Aphrodite, special balloons with metal strips attached that provided a defensive countermeasure against Allied radar. At almost 09:00 the skipper ordered the refreshed U-boat again into the depths, there to undergo repairs to her damaged equipment. The young U-boat commander was exceedingly proud of his crew; his men had stood up well under the terrific onslaught of destructive force that had been launched against them.[29]

---

27. U-953's sound operator recorded 57 detonations in the *KTB*, 11-12 January 1944. Marbach related years later that he had counted 135. Either man could have miscounted the actual number. Also, single detonations might have reverberated through the boat in such a manner that Marbach and others counted them as multiple detonations.
28. Karl remembered the weather being a raging storm, whereas the *KTB* on 12 January reported the weather as "cloud cover with thin rain" accompanied by high waves.
29. *KTB*, 12 January 1944.

U-953 was repaired and restored to fighting trim by 19:30, when she surfaced and charged on a northerly course at full speed toward a convoy reported by BdU. An attack in the rapidly fading dusk and light rain still was slightly possible, but before the boat could intercept her quarry the blacked-out convoy disappeared into the dark night. BdU dissolved *Gruppe* Borkum on the morning of 13 January and suspended its convoy attack operations. U-953 was ordered to patrol an area off the North African coast, inside DJ 21, approximately 785 miles southeast of her present location. For all its time and effort, BdU and *Gruppe* Borkum had failed to sink a single Allied troop transport or freighter. The Germans were confounded by the enemy's continued luck and its own lack of success, but not once did BdU suspect that the Allies now routinely rerouted their convoys after they decrypted Enigma messages transmitted between the U-boats and their headquarters.[30]

U-953's stern barely rides the waves during a combat patrol. A surface run during daylight hours was an extremely hazardous undertaking.

Kater sailed for eight days to reach the more temperate climes of North Africa. In the early morning hours of 16 January the sound operator had picked up a strong sonar signature. As the hydrophone contact grew stronger, Marbach suspected they were tracking a single fast moving ship. A little less than an hour later

---

30. *KTB*, 12-13 January 1944; Stern, 116.

the skipper peered into his periscope viewfinder and framed a smoke cloud and ship's silhouette on the horizon at 5000 meters. Within the next hour the silhouette materialized into an Allied destroyer, which shortly was joined by three others. Clearly, Marbach concluded, the ships were a hunter-killer force on the prowl for U-boats. He weighed his chances for success in a bold surface attack and determined that the bright moonlight and calm seas would marginalize the element of stealth and surprise *Kater* would require. The skipper reluctantly ordered his boat to continue on a southerly course away from the line of enemy warships. With the horrific depth charge attack still fresh in their thoughts, the officers and crewmen who were aware of the present threat were content to avoid a confrontation that entailed so much risk with so little chance for success.[31]

U-953 received two radio messages from BdU on 19 January that assigned the boat to an attack zone directly off the Moroccan coast at Casablanca. Marbach was to slip into the coastal area unseen, and there launch surprise attacks against unsuspecting targets that for some time had not been threatened by U-boats. Already there was plenty of activity along the coast; another boat had reported sighting a destroyer and a large number of native fishing boats in the attack zone. The second message reported numerous sightings of large and small enemy convoys hugging the coast to better protect their landward flanks from U-boats. Opportunities for success appeared very great for any U-boat commander who could take advantage of the massed targets and press home an aggressive attack. Despite BdU's optimistic reports, by the evening of 21 January the only vessel U-953 had encountered was a fishing steamer and three smaller fishing boats forty nautical miles from land.[32]

Darkness and high visibility allowed *Kater* to run on a course parallel to the coast at Casablanca during the waning hours of 21 January. The *Erste Wache* was crowded onto the bridge, with Karl Baumann at his lookout station. The men basked in the luxury of warm night breezes and calm seas, and marveled at the warm glow from a million city lights that illuminated the southeastern horizon.[33] The U-boat sailed silently through a group of twenty fishing boats at 10:48. Native men and boys, silhouetted against the glowing lights on their gently bob-

---

31. *KTB*, 16 January 1944.
32. *KTB*, 19-21 January 1944.
33. The stunning glow from Casablanca at night impressed Allied sailors as well. In November 1942, an American submarine captain "likened surfacing seven miles from the city to coming up 'in the center of Times Square.'" See Rick Atkinson, *An Army at Dawn; The War in North Africa, 1942-1943* (New York: Henry Holt, 2002), 108.

bing boats, peacefully worked their fishnets wholly unaware that a giant killing machine prowled in their midst. Through their powerful binoculars the watch party members observed the natives' every move with curiosity if not some small amount of envy. Amid the peaceful night's silence the men atop the conning tower could breathe a sigh of contentment, however fleeting.[34]

U-953 kept secret company with numerous fishing boats off Casablanca and along a 150-mile stretch of coastline for more than a week, where not a sign of Allied convoys was detected despite urgent radio messages from BdU. Headquarters had signaled on 22 January that heavy Allied shipping activity had been reported off the North African coast—not at all surprising since Operation Torch had landed a large Anglo-American invasion force in Morocco and Algeria the previous November. A convoy of eight freighters with a destroyer escort had been seen steaming out of Gibraltar the previous day; another from the United States was due to arrive in the area on 22 January, and a third was expected to set sail from Gibraltar on 27 January. The boat's Naxos radar system occasionally detected distant seaborne activity, but no enemy vessels presented themselves inside the killing zone assigned to *Kater*. Unbeknownst to the *Ubootfahrer*, on 22 January a large American attack force of 36,000 troops was pulled from the fighting around Salerno, Italy and landed farther up the Italian coast at the towns of Anzio and Nettuno. Six troop transports, four navy cruisers, and twenty-four destroyers transported and supported the landing force.[35] U-953 and the other boats of *Gruppe* Borkum could have disrupted the invasion plans and resupply lines to the Allies' widening Mediterranean Campaign had they been able to intercept the inbound convoys that sailed through the narrow Strait of Gibraltar. However, the Germans' technical expertise in U-boat warfare no longer could match the Allies' superior countermeasures; January's heavy convoy traffic reached its destinations largely unmolested.

---

34. *KTB*, 21 January 1944. Also, see Michael Beschloss, *The Conquerors; Roosevelt, Truman and the Destruction of Hitler's Germany 1941-1945* (New York: Simon & Schuster, 2002), 12-14. Ironically, probably no one aboard U-953 recalled or knew that exactly one year before, President Franklin D. Roosevelt and Prime Minister Winston Churchill had led a secret conference at Casablanca to set fundamental strategies for the Allies' conduct of the war in Western Europe. There, on 24 January 1943, they had drafted the declaration that demanded the unconditional surrender of Germany and its Axis partners.

35. *KTB*, 22-23 January 1944; and Cesare Salmaggi & Alfredo Pallavisini, *2194 Days of War* (New York: Gallery Books, 1979), 477.

Enemy activity throughout the U-boat's patrol area was sporadic but pervasive, reminder of the cat-and-mouse duel of death that attended the men engaged in war at sea. Throughout the daylight hours of 24 January, as *Kater* remained submerged at periscope depth, Marbach sighted a number of Allied bombers flying on an easterly course toward Gibraltar. Distant radar signatures occasionally punctuated *Kater's* mundane existence for the next six days, but no targets were sighted either in the air or on the ocean surface. Then, on 30 January at 12:05, a plume of steam was sighted at a distance of at least 7,000 meters; shortly thereafter, a mast and red-capped smokestack rose above the horizon. Marbach identified the ship as belonging to neutral Spain, sailing probably out of the Azores, so he did not sound the alarm to send the crew to battle stations. The amount of air and sea traffic along the North African coast always kept nerves taught until an approaching plane or ship was identified as a neutral. On the night of 1 February the watch party spotted an aircraft 3,000 meters astern as it approached the surfaced U-boat. The watch officer immediately signaled a *Flieger Alarm*, which sent a swarm of gun crewmen out of the main hatch to man their armed and waiting weapons. By the time Karl and his fellow gunners swung their 20mm and 37mm cannons around to draw beads on the oncoming plane it was almost directly overhead. The gunners placed their feet against the trigger pedals and awaited the order to commence firing. Just as the aircraft roared overhead, the men at their battle stations noticed interior lights that indicated it belonged to a neutral country, probably Spain or Portugal. The gunners held their fire, but barely.[36] The plane droned on unharmed into the black night; its passengers never knew they had been mere seconds from fiery death and a plunge into the dark Atlantic inside a twisted aluminum funeral pyre. The gun crews aboard the unseen U-boat only 500 meters below could not have missed a target so close, so visible, in the crisp, clear night sky.

As the moon dipped below the horizon in the early morning hours of 3 February, *Kater's* radar picked up an aircraft bearing a hard right angle off the boat's starboard side. Marbach signaled the *Flieger Alarm* and ordered U-953 immediately into the depths, but not before the plane's radar operator fixed the boat's location and distance. As the U-boat sank into the safe environs of the Atlantic the Allied warplane passed overhead and a single *Fliebo* plummeted into the black ocean with a splash and then a detonation that slammed against the U-boat.[37] With rattled teeth and nerves in the wake of the air attack, the *Ubootfahrer* counted their blessings for having been spared destruction yet again.

---

36. *KTB*, 24 January–2 February 1944.

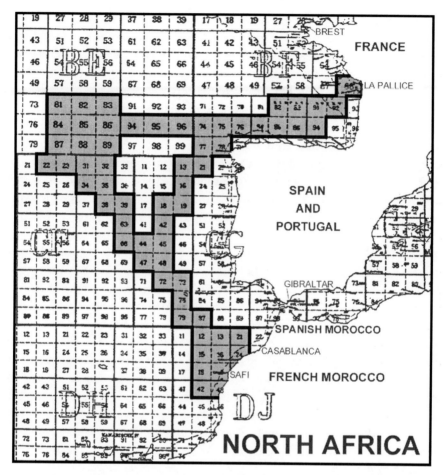

Baumann's second war patrol covered 57 days and 6,068 nautical miles, with 1,588 *Seemeilen* logged underwater; 26 December 1943 to 20 February 1944. Shaded grid squares indicate U-953's area of operations.

U-953 remained underwater during the daylight hours. Through his periscope Marbach later sighted a steamer at 6,500 meters, above which a twin-engined aircraft flew in wide circles on the lookout for U-boats. The skipper at first believed the steamer would sail through his patrol area; instead, the ship

---

37. *KTB*, 3 February 1944. The war diary reported, "the plane doesn't appear to have located us very well and dropped a bomb out of frustration." The aircraft pilot and crew probably would have argued that their attack against the perpendicular, unseen target was very nearly a complete success.

changed course and disappeared over the horizon. The boat re-emerged from the deep after sunset to recharge her batteries while she patrolled the area just off Cap Mazagan on the Moroccan coast, and remained there on 4 February. The *Wache* spotted a group of mysterious lights in the early morning hours that turned out to be the flickering lanterns of native fishing boats.[38]

For reasons the *KTB*, with its unique vernacular, did not reveal, U-953 submerged at 01:01 on the morning of 5 February 1944. Marbach obviously took a pragmatic approach to deal both with his crew and BdU, and probably exercised great editorial control over his boat's war diary to save himself and his subordinates undue difficulties with superiors ashore. Karl was directly involved in at least one incident that was not reported in the *KTB*. One pitch-dark night—perhaps 5 February—while the *I. Wache* manned the conning tower, Marbach ordered *Obermaat* Poldi Kabert to secure the 20mm cannon on the port *Wintergarten*. As Karl stood watch at his post he heard the petty officer lower the double-barreled weapon to a nearly horizontal angle and lock it into place, then remove the ammunition canisters from the twin breeches. After he locked the canisters inside their watertight compartments on the bridge wall, Kabert returned to the weapon and began to eject the live rounds from the breeches. Karl noticed, however, that the procedure did not create the familiar sounds of the big 20mm rounds being cleanly ejected. When he diverted his eyes momentarily to the cannon he observed a 20mm round projected sideways from one of the receiver mechanisms. Kabert also saw the obstruction and yanked it out of the weapon with his free hand, then closed the breech as the shell fell onto the deck.

"*Herr Obermaat*," Karl warned, "*doppelte Patronen zufuhr!!*" The veteran petty officer didn't take well to being told by the young seaman that a second round remained in the breech.

"You keep your attention on your post," Kabert growled.

"*Jawohl, Herr Obermaat*," Karl replied, and returned to his lookout duties while Kabert secured the gun.

After four hours duty on the bridge, bone-tired *Wache* members untethered their safety harnesses and removed the heavy binoculars from around their necks. Happy finally to be relieved by the next watch party, Karl had turned toward the main hatch to go below when Marbach ordered him to clear the port 20mm cannon. The young gunner trod over to the gun and shoved his foot onto the pedal trigger to send the firing pin into the supposedly empty chamber. Instead of the harmless clack he expected to hear, a stunning blast from the 20mm cannon

---

38. *KTB*, 3-4 February 1944.

nearly deafened him. A tracer round instantly erupted from the barrel and zinged just inches over the top of the conning tower where officers and men stood in dumbfounded shock. The illuminating round streaked across the ocean surface on a long, low glowing red arc that would reveal the U-boat's location to every enemy plane or ship in the vicinity.

"*Alaaarrrm!!!*" Marbach shouted for the men to clear the bridge, which signaled their mad rush to the main hatch. On the *Wintergarten*, Karl had regained his wits and charged for the portal. His assigned position on the *Wache* dictated he always was second in the group to enter the hatch to avoid a confusing and dangerous pileup at the hatch entrance. By the time the last man—Marbach—jumped onto the ladder inside the conning tower and pulled the hatch cover closed, the errant tracer had long since disappeared to return the night sky to pitch black.

"*Auf Tiefe gehen!*" the skipper commanded, and crewmen raced to send the U-boat below the surface. Kabert's simple mistake could have cost the lives of everyone aboard U-953; either Providence or mere luck had again smiled upon the men. Marbach had no desire to blame anyone involved in the mishap, serious as it was. He certainly found no fault with the tall, brawny gunner he jokingly called "*Baumannchen*;" Karl simply had followed orders to clear the weapon.[39]

U-953 surfaced a few minutes after 04:00, thirty nautical miles from the North African coast. At 06:09 the *Wache* spotted an approaching aircraft in the clear night sky just before dawn and signaled the *Flieger Alarm* to dispatch the anti-aircraft gunners to their posts. The three gun crews rushed to their battle stations and awaited orders to open fire on the plane. Again, as on 3 February, at the last moment lights were spotted inside the plane's cabin and, being possibly a neutral aircraft, the German gunners allowed it to pass overhead unhindered. Though the *Ubootfahrer* hoped they would never mistakenly identify a neutral or friendly plane as an enemy, the aircraft would have been blown out of the sky if it had even inadvertently projected any form of overt threat against the U-boat. In the wake of the alert, the *Wache* remained on duty another half-hour before the rising sun forced U-953 back underwater for yet another fruitless day of hunting and waiting for enemy ships that would not pass through her killing zone. The vast ocean seemed vacant of any other vessel but U-953 on 6 February; neither was the sound of distant engines heard nor any trace of smoke or steam spotted on the horizon.[40]

---

39. *KTB*, 5 February 1944. Also, translation: Marbach referred to Karl as "Little Baumann."

Listless men sat or lay wherever they could find space and passed the time warily in their cramped confines. Unless an enemy vessel or aircraft were sighted and engaged, the next minutes, hours, and days would tick away at a plodding pace without relief. As days on patrol turned to weeks, the free flow of conversations—like their foodstuffs and water supply—became less plentiful between crewmates in their dank, stifling quarters. The quality, freshness, and taste of the discussions that were convened likewise suffered approximately the same rate of spoilage.

Inactivity tends to breed mischief among young males, and *Kater's* crewmen were immune neither to the compulsion to perpetrate devilment upon one another, nor to sometimes become unwitting victims. Machinist Theo Lischewski's ability to sleep even through bomb detonations amazed and irritated his crewmates, who continually had to prod and cajole him to wake up so he could report for duty in the engine room or with his assigned *Wache*. Lischewski inevitably awakened at the very last moment to sleepily jump down from his hammock, which hung from the ceiling of the bow compartment, and run to his duty station just in time to avoid being late. The opportunity for mischief finally proved too much for his friends to pass up, so two men first lowered the hammock containing the comatose Lischewski to the floor. One man blew a handful of talcum powder onto the machinist's face while others cut an Aphrodite balloon into small squares. The men then blew up the squares to make small balloons, which they tied tightly into Lischewski's hair. At precisely two minutes before he was to go on duty, a chorus of shouts bombarded the sleeping crewman.

"Get up! You're always late for duty! Wake up! Get up!

The machinist awoke with a start and began to lunge out of the hammock, but sprawled onto the deck on all fours after falling one foot. As the bow compartment exploded with laughter, Lischewski gathered his wits and began a mad dash to the *Zentrale,* the conning tower and the bridge above, where he reported to the *Wache Offizier* with a ghostly white mask covering his face and his hair full of balloons. The pranksters regretted only that they could not watch Lischewski frantically explain his bizarre appearance to the watch officer.

Food most consistently broke the monotony of long days and weeks on patrol, though the communal ritual was specially adapted for the peculiarities of U-boat service. Meals were devoured quickly so that men on duty could be relieved in order to share the prepared food.[41] The variety, quantity, and quality of meals

40. *KTB*, 5-6 February 1944.

varied widely with the passing days and weeks on patrol. Food naturally was a frequent subject of conversation, debate, argument—and occasional intrigue.

Throughout the combat patrol a large carton of Camembert cheese stored in the bow compartment had been raided piecemeal by the men. Karl loved the little cans of cheese and often took one along on watch duty to stave off hunger. Being the best-fed members of the German armed forces, hunger was never a consideration; the young men who lived in the forward compartment coveted the purloined snacks for the simple fact that they tasted great. When they had completely emptied the carton of its contents the guilty parties realized the seriousness of their action and hoped their wanton thievery would remain undetected.

Shortly before the end of the *Feindfahrt*, Marbach called to Hartmann, who stood over the navigator's table in the control room.

"What do we have left to eat?" the skipper inquired.

"We have a box of cheese," the *Obersteuermann* reported as he studied the supply list, which was a secondary responsibility for the U-boat's navigator.

A moment later the cheese thieves were horrified to hear the skipper call on the bow speaking tube for the crate of Camembert to be delivered to the galley at once.

"What are we going to do now?" frantic crewmen implored as the minutes raced by. Each man in the forward compartment knew big trouble lay ahead if the food theft was discovered; even the affable Marbach would demand some form of retribution for the breakdown of supply discipline. Finally, two brave souls devised a daring plan to deliver the big crate *sans du fromage*. Their brethren held their breaths and prayed while the actors picked up the empty carton and lugged it through the boat as if they were burdened by the full weight of the missing contents. They strained and panted and bumped their way down the narrow walkway through the bulkheads into the officers' quarters and past the skipper in the control room.

"Delivering the cheese!" the men called out, following the navy's protocol for enlisted men to announce the purpose for their presence, as they labored toward the galley. The feint was so well executed that no one detected the clever subterfuge. When the enraged cook later reported to the skipper that the crate was completely empty, the deliverymen were neither suspected nor questioned about their role in the affair. The thieves never were identified, even after the banner headline in the boat's small newspaper demanded to know, "Who Stole the

41. Barrie Pitt, *The Battle of the Atlantic*, World War II (Alexandria, Virginia: Time-Life Books, 1977), 74.

Cheese?" A follow up investigation ended with accusatory glares directed toward the wholly innocent crewmen in the boat's stern, which pleased the guilty parties in the bow to no end. After all, this was war; and desperate times called for desperate measures.

The boat's hydrophone detected Asdic signals at 09:00 on 7 February, which indicated an Allied ship might be on course to enter *Kater's* kill zone. Before noon, a steamer was sighted near DJ 1689, but close investigation of her profile and other identifying factors left Marbach to conclude the ship was a Spanish vessel sailing to Cap Mazagan; another stroke of misfortune for the skipper to record in the war diary. Later that afternoon a small escort vessel sporting a single 40mm Bofors cannon was sighted at a distance of 2000 meters; with certainty she was the source of the Asdic submarine-detection signals reported earlier. Marbach considered his response; he could launch a T5 acoustic torpedo and sink the small craft without doubt, but decided the small victory would not be worth the expenditure of the missile. Perhaps a convoy was just out of view below the horizon; if so, the unseen fat targets probably would divert their courses or call for air support to take on U-953 if Marbach were to press an ill-advised attack against the escort. The skipper allowed the escort to pass unscathed, but the convoy he hoped would sail into view never appeared. *Kater* began a surface run back to the Casablanca coast at nightfall, and by midnight arrived without detection, despite the appearance of a bomber that flew close to starboard past the undetected boat.[42]

Asdic pulses repeatedly pinged into the headset of *Kater's* hydrophone operator at 08:00 on 8 February, and continued for two hours as Allied warships hunted the submerged U-953 and other U-boats that patrolled the Casablanca coast. Then, at 10:00 the unmistakable reverberations of distant depth charge explosions rumbled through the boat. The detonations gave the *Ubootfahrer* pause to wonder which of their fellow submariners might at that moment be dying or experiencing the horror they had endured a month earlier. Marbach was unable to observe anything at periscope depth when he swept the horizon, but as a safety measure he deployed Aphrodite to camouflage *Kater's* position. Before dawn the skipper had set the boat onto a course that would zigzag alternatively farther north and northwest into the Atlantic. In the U-boat's wake lay Casablanca and any hopes of success against the enemy's seemingly invisible coastal convoys. The boat and her crew settled into a dreary routine for the next two days as they sailed underwater during daylight and ran on the surface as soon as

42. *KTB*, 7 February 1944.

twilight afforded them the relative safety of dark seas and skies. Marbach changed course during the morning darkness of 11 February to make a long northward run approximately 150 miles off the Portuguese coast. The day's mundane activity was broken only at 23:00 by an Azores-bound Portuguese steamer that sailed into view with lights blazing to announce her neutrality to all combatants.[43]

U-953 maintained her northward course the next day with no sightings of Allied ships or aircraft. The skipper received a radio message from BdU on the night of 13 February, which ordered the boat to return to La Pallice. The order almost immediately restored the men's enthusiasm, at least in part; they could realistically anticipate the return soon to their home port—unless, of course, their luck ran out in the meantime. On St. Valentine's day *Kater* again began to zigzag both as an offensive and defensive measure when she approached the northwest corner of the Iberian Peninsula. The boat re-entered the Bay of Biscay at midnight, and by nightfall of the following day the high ocean waves had become shallow Bay currents. A thin veil of mist enshrouded the surfaced U-boat and coated her rusted steel skin with a glistening sheen. The sound operator picked up a steady stream of Asdic pings on the afternoon of 16 February, no doubt from an Allied search and destroy group at work somewhere off U-953's starboard side, between the boat and the Spanish coast off El Ferrol. Interspersed with the chattering Asdic pings, a stream of depth charge explosions resounded. That night a series of aerial bombs also was heard detonating somewhere in distant waters.[44]

The unsettling reminders of war's powerful death machinery had one positive but very troubling aspect for the men of U-953: the ordnance that exploded on their *Ubootkameraden* elsewhere at least was not killing them. Combat veterans acknowledge that men who experience the deaths of comrades in battle confront a common dilemma born of self-preservation. First and foremost they are thankful they have not shared the savage end with those to whom they may have felt closer than brothers. Then, in the next moment and for the rest of their lives, they are burdened by guilt for their very human reaction to the inhumanity of their thoughts.

Kater sailed an easterly course along the northern Spanish coast on 17 February, and the next day while headed north and then due east toward the French coast. Marbach received an order from BdU to proceed toward a pre-assigned meeting point where U-953 was to await the arrival of an escort ship that would

---

43.   *KTB*, 8-11 February 1944.
44.   *KTB*, 12-16 February 1944.

accompany her into La Pallice on 20 February. An evening message specified the exact location and time the U-boat would meet her escort. Under the cover of darkness, rain gusts greeted the *Wache* that stood guard on the bridge while the boat's batteries were recharged. The squall turned to gusting hail during the morning hours of 19 February while the boat remained 150 nautical miles from port. Varying air temperatures alternately caused rain and hail that accompanied *Kater* to her meeting point on the morning of 20 February; there the *Wache* sighted the escort ship that arrived precisely at 08:00 as scheduled.[45]

U-953 drew into the fortress bunker of La Pallice for repairs and a complete overhaul. Her officers and crew were overjoyed to return to dry land, clean beds, and plentiful fresh food. They needed and had earned time to rest, to be alone, to contemplate, and enjoy some modicum of privacy in their quarters. Karl Baumann and his *Kameraden* would always remember the fifty-seven day patrol for the desperate engagement with the enemy corvette and their redemption from a concentrated depth charge attack. For all the terror and hardship they had endured, they had failed to locate and engage a single convoy target. Back in their billets at the *Kaserne*, the exhausted men shaved off their accumulated growth of beards and washed away eight weeks of sweat and grime, but could not cleanse their minds of the horrid memories of the hunter-killer group that had unleashed its vengeance upon the U-boat on 10 and 11 January. Many credited *Gott der Allmächtige* for the miracle of their deliverance.[46]

Military policemen were awaiting U-953's arrival in La Pallice, and soon after the boat was belayed dockside Marbach and Bischoff were arrested for their December flight from justice. *Kater's* two most senior officers were downcast and humiliated by the legal process that ensued. An investigation was launched to learn the details of the fugitives' escape from Paris; and a detailed report later was issued to the Third Flotilla commander, *Korvettenkapitän* Richard Zapp. Upon consideration of their courageous service and the exemplary leadership they had displayed during their latest combat patrol, Zapp ordered Marbach and Bischoff to serve two weeks of detention in their quarters in La Rochelle. The irreplaceable loss of so many veteran U-boat officers dictated their lenient treatment; the Ubootwaffe could ill afford to lose two more because of foolish misbehavior in Paris, of all places. To be sure, Marbach endured his punishment rather well; every day while on detention he ordered two different crewmen to report to his

---

45. *KTB*, 17-20 February 1944.
46. Translation: Almighty God.

quarters after duty hours, where he feted them with strong drinks and casual conversation.

Crewmen and mascot Peter disembark from U-953 at the end of a long patrol.

Despite Bischoff's arrest with Marbach and their furtive flight from justice, the young *Leutnant* soon received the coveted orders to report to Pillau in March 1944 to attend training school for new submarine commanders.[47] Good-natured, high-strung Bischoff was to undergo months of rigorous work to develop the necessary skills and proficiency to command his own boat. Before his last day with U-953, he approached Karl with a splendid offer.

"Baumann, how would you like to go to Paris with me to carry my bags?"

"*Jawohl, Herr Leutnant,*" Karl beamed, very pleased to be invited on the trip. He truly liked Bischoff, his *I.W.O.* Before the war Bischoff had captained a fishing trawler, so he and Karl felt a kinship born of shared experiences with the North Sea fishing fleet. Karl had seen Paris only briefly when his BdU train passed through *Gare* du Nord the previous July, so he readily agreed to serve as Bischoff's orderly.[48] As he prepared to leave La Rochelle, Bischoff made the rounds among his former crewmen to bid them farewell and good luck. Ambitious young junior officers like Bischoff frequently sought higher rank or skill lev-

---

47. Horst Bredow, Founder and Director of the U-boot-Archiv, Cuxhaven-Altenbruch, Germany, 14 July 2000, letter to author, with accompanying data relative to U-953.
48. Translation: The *I.W.O.* was the *I. Wachoffizier*, or First Watch Officer.

els after completing several patrols on their first boat. After they attended special training or technical schools they usually were transferred to other U-boat crews.[49] Few men from U-953 had ever applied for such transfers, however, so the original crew of Marbach devotees had remained largely intact. As a result, the loss of Bischoff was keenly felt.

Ubootkameraden were pleased the *I.W.O.* had been selected by BdU for higher command, but Bischoff had often displayed nervous tendencies that caused crewmembers not to want to sail with him as skipper of his own boat. For example, as Karl's watch party on one occasion stood lookout duty on *Kater's* bridge, a flight of five bombers appeared over the horizon. Startled by their approach, Bischoff jammed his binoculars into his eyes and grew noticeably more anxious as he counted the aircraft, which began as a whisper but ended with a bellow.

"*Eins, zwei, drei, vier,*" Bischoff called out as his voice wound to an excited crescendo, "*funnnnnf!!!*"

Karl followed a respectable distance behind Bischoff while he lugged the lieutenant's heavy bags through the La Rochelle *Gare* to the train's passenger car, and deferred to his rank during the trip to Paris. After they checked Bischoff's luggage at *Gare* du Nord, however, privileges of rank gave way to the brotherhood of two former civilian sailors and fishermen. The pair unleashed a whirlwind celebration in the city's bars, bistros, and cabarets—most memorably *Les Folies Bergere*.[50] Bischoff happily funded Karl's entry into the notoriously famous and popular *Folies*, and throughout the night of sleepless merriment Karl in turn ably helped Bischoff celebrate his achievements and career advancement in the ranks of the Ubootwaffe.

The next morning Karl loaded Bischoff's luggage aboard a BdU train destined for Pillau on the Baltic coast. The young men shook hands and offered sincere best wishes and good luck to each other; then Karl headed for his train to return to La Rochelle and U-953. Shortly, the steam whistle on the northern-bound engine shrieked a long, mournful blast. The cars of the BdU train clanked to a start and slowly rumbled into motion. *Leutnant zur See* Gustav Bischoff departed Paris and France for his own U-boat command, and in the end a gruesome death with his entire crew five days before the end of the war in Europe.[51]

---

49. Gannon, 10.
50. The *Folies Bergere* and its scantily-clad can-can girls were made famous by artist Henri Toulouse Lautrec, who inspired visits by the likes of Ernest Hemingway and countless American doughboys during and after the First World War.
51. Internet website: http://uboat.net/boats/u2359.htm

Leutnant Gustav Bischoff, right, First Officer of U-953. Bischoff later commanded U-2359 and was killed with his entire crew when his U-boat was sunk five days before the end of the war in Europe.

U-953 lay in drydock at La Pallice for five weeks while again she was completely refurbished, repaired, repainted, refitted and made ready for battle on her next *Feindfahrt* in the Bay or the open Atlantic. Several days before the mission, while the boat rested inside its bunker *Boxe,* the crew stocked her ordnance storage holds with four torpedoes—two each of the G7e compressed-air type and the G7a electric-driven version. A full load of 20mm and 37mm ammunition also was stowed aboard. The men laid in enough fuel, water and food for only seven days at sea, however. The re-supply effort indicated the upcoming patrol would be short in duration but potentially as hazardous as any longer mission.[52]

The best-trained crews risked death at every turn, and inadequately trained crews did not stand a chance to survive the Allies' concentrated offensive against the U-boats. It was therefore essential for every man to hone his skills continually through training exercises. While U-953 was being provisioned, *Obermaat* Leopold Kabert ordered the watch parties to practice the *Flieger Alarm* drill. Karl took up his regular position on the bridge while the Viennese petty officer assumed the role of the watch party leader. With all the realism he could muster, Kabert tested the men on the emergency procedures they would undertake dur-

---

52. *KTB,* 30 March 1944.

ing an aircraft attack. He repeatedly challenged them on aircraft recognition, compass headings and bearings, and their reaction speed to his commands. During one drill the *Obermaat* ordered closed the main hatch on the bridge deck. Baumann acknowledged the order and ran to the hatch. As he reached for the wheel of the hinged hatch cover he noticed the preoccupied petty officer was standing with the points of his shoes extended over the hatch opening. With gleeful malice, Karl grasped the heavy hatch cover and heaved it closed. The steel lid met Kabert's shoe leather with a sickening thud, and instantly launched the unsuspecting *Obermaat* into a wild high-stepping dance across the bridge.

"What did you do that for?" the outraged Kabert roared as he inspected his throbbing feet to see if any toes had been broken.

"The Watch Officer ordered the hatch closed," Karl shrugged with a matter-of-fact reply and a straight face while he fought the monumental urge to erupt with a bout of uncontrollable laughter. News of his devious act spread like wildfire among the crew to the delight of all those who enjoyed black humor at someone else's expense, especially brash or disagreeable superiors.

The main advantage U-boats provided over surface vessels naturally was their stealth—their ability to submerge and travel virtually unseen underwater. Stealth was compromised more and more frequently as the war progressed, however, with new technologies the Allies employed to eliminate the U-boat threat. A seemingly limitless arsenal of improved detection systems, long-range aircraft, and small escort carriers kept constant vigil over individual ships and convoys of every size, which spelled ultimate defeat for the Ubootwaffe.[53]

Before the advent of specialized underwater breathing systems, U-boats often violated crucial stealth by necessity when they were forced to surface to recharge their essential electric motor batteries. During such periods of maximum vulnerability a number of boats were attacked, damaged, or sunk. Those caught on the surface with uncharged batteries could not escape their attackers by submerging, but had to remain on the surface and fight, a battle scenario that virtually always proved fatal for the U-boat. Then, in late 1943, three U-boats were fitted with an innovative underwater breathing and exhaust device called the *Schnorchel.* The device restored the advantage of stealth to the boats, albeit only temporarily, since it eliminated the need to recharge batteries on the surface. The equipped U-boats could sail underwater for many days or weeks at a time, as necessity demanded.

---

53. Clive Ponting, *Armageddon; The Reality Behind the Distortions, Myths, Lies, and Illusions of World War II* (New York: Random House, 1995), 183.

During her overhaul in February and March 1944, U-953 became one of nine boats fitted with the *Schnorchel.*

The snort, as the British called the *Schnorchel,* worked like the snorkels worn by shallow-depth recreational divers. The device consisted of an air pipe that protruded above the ocean surface to allow a U-boat to proceed underwater on diesel power as it sucked in fresh air and expelled foul air and diesel exhaust. Not only did *Schnorchel*-equipped U-boats sail faster underwater than when they used electric propulsion, their batteries were recharged with greater safety. The system also was intended to provide a continuous supply of fresh air for the interior of the submerged boat.[54]

Despite its significant advantages, the snort never achieved operational perfection because it presented special hazards for men and boats alike. Worst of all, the length of the breathing pipe relegated U-boats to a depth of four meters for *Schnorchel* operation, far too near the surface to evade attack if spotted by the enemy, especially from the sky. In addition, the flotation bulb—the *Schwimmer*—at the top of the pipe through which both fresh air and exhaust passed sometimes became clogged with flotsam or inundated by seawater if the device malfunctioned. The air intake would shut off as a result, and the breathing system inadvertently would then suck the men's fresh air out of the pressure hull and into the diesel engines. If the exhaust pipe became blocked, the system then expelled lethal carbon monoxide into the crew compartments. Ultimately, the marginal advantage gained from the installation of *Schnorchels* on U-boats was entirely mitigated when the Allies introduced new, more powerful radar that detected the snorts' flotation bulbs that bobbed on the surface above the submerged boats.[55]

U-953 emerged from the La Pallice bunker at dusk on 30 March to test her new *Schnorchel* on an operational patrol, Karl Baumann's third. The boat and her escort soon passed through the harbor lock cloaked by 80 percent overcast skies. The Biscay greeted the German vessels with calm winds and low waves, so they quickly sailed toward an assigned point beyond the locations of numerous enemy air attacks and known minefields sown by Allied aircraft. Farther out in the Bay, *Kater* reached the location code-named *Pumpe,* just before 23:30. The night sky was completely blocked by low hanging clouds and misty haze reached down to obliterate the visual horizon.

---

54. Gannon, 474.
55. Gannon, 386-387. The British referred to the *Schwimmer* as a snort. Lake, 64. The nickname "snort" may have originated from the sound of splashing seawater being sucked into a malfunctioning *Schnorchel's* intake valve.

The *I. Wache* stood silent vigil and hoped the black overcast would prevent the enemy from shattering the tranquility of the dark night that surrounded them in *Marinequadrat* BF 6881. Karl Baumann peered through his binoculars into the pitch darkness in search of the smallest flicker of light to announce the approach of an aircraft or another seagoing vessel. The crucial duty fully occupied his consciousness when at exactly midnight an antisubmarine patrol bomber burst out of the low hanging overcast no more than seventy meters above the surface. The boat was caught completely without warning; neither her *Naxos* nor *Wanze* radar detection systems had registered warning blips from the incoming bomber. A *Flieger Alarm* sent the gunners out of the main hatch and to their waiting weapons. Only 300 meters distant, the bomber suddenly threw a powerful searchlight beam onto U-953 and dropped four bright light buoys that lit up the surface surrounding the boat. Harsh beams of light reflected off startled faces as the men on the bridge braced themselves for a hail of bullets or a rack of bombs. In the meantime, Marbach barked orders to the helmsman, who immediately turned U-953 hard to port at full speed. In so doing the bomber passed parallel to the boat. *Kater's* gunners opened up on the aircraft as it thundered by, low and almost directly overhead. A responding hail of bullets from the bomber churned up geysers of water nearby, but caused no damage to the boat or her crew. The frightening confusion of searchlight beams, buoy lights, arcing tracers, automatic gunfire, blasts of cannon fire and the loud rumble of aircraft engines so distracted the gunners and *Wache* members that no one noticed whether the bomber had been damaged during the attack. All the while, Baumann kept watch over his 180-degree zone of responsibility. He looked out of the corner of his eye to see tracers streaming down from the bomber's tail guns, and then saw the other *Wache* members crouched behind the armored bridge wall while he alone remained at his post. The aircraft disappeared into the overcast as quickly as it had come, and an uneasy silence resumed. The four buoys still bobbed nearby, their lights undulating with the waves. The gunners girded themselves for the bomber's next move while U-953's big diesels strained at full speed to propel the boat quickly away from the buoys. When the bomber did not return to press the attack, Marbach concluded it had been on a minelaying mission when its radar detected the U-boat. Though it had launched an initial attack after using its Leigh Light and buoy markers, the bomber was not prepared to commit itself to a sustained gun battle. U-953 had been only a target of opportunity rather than a mission target for the U-boat hunter-killer.[56]

Inside grid square BF 9137, another bomber emerged from the nearly solid overcast at 04:00 and flew past *Kater's* stern at a height of only 150 meters. The boat's 37mm gunners unleashed a salvo of anti-aircraft fire against the intruder's dim outline, apparently without effect. The bomber disappeared into the night without returning fire or pressing a follow-up attack. Marbach recorded in his *Schußmeldung*—the *KTB* entry required each time a torpedo was launched or any of the boat's guns was fired—his suspicions that both bombers were laying mines and were not in pursuit of U-boats. Suspicions and reality being of unequal weight, however, the skipper sought the safety of deep waters and ordered U-953 below the surface at 04:07 where she remained for the next fifteen hours. The boat surfaced at 19:17 into bright evening skies that afforded great potential to observe enemy activity as well as to be easily observed. After fourteen minutes Marbach ordered the boat to submerge to resume her underwater course until 01:18 on 1 April.[57]

While U-953 ran on the surface in the early morning hours, a malfunctioning aircraft warning radar detector was reported to Marbach, who was told that reliable readings were no longer possible. In view of the enemy activity he already had encountered, the skipper thought it foolish to conduct any snorkel tests or invite further air attacks. With no enemy in sight, he ordered *Kater* back to La Pallice for equipment repairs. Though by necessity the *Feindfahrt* had been cut short, BdU protocol apparently held that Marbach and his crew would be credited with an active combat patrol, which official records later would confirm. At 08:10 the watch party on duty spotted the escort ship that was assigned to accompany the boat back into the harbor. When U-953 slipped into a bunker *Boxe* at 10:45, Marbach logged the mission's results in his *Kriegstagebuch*. The boat had sailed 302.5 nautical miles, of which only 50.5 percent were logged underwater. She had been compelled to defend herself twice from enemy bombers; she had developed radar detection malfunctions that shortened the *Schnorchel* test mission, and had been unable to actually test the breathing device. At least the U-boat and her crew had survived, which alone was no small victory in the waning months of the Battle of the Atlantic.[58]

U-953 underwent twenty-two days of repairs and restocking before Marbach and crew took their charge back into the Bay of Biscay at 20:00 on 23 April, en

---

56. *KTB*, 30-31 March 1944. The British had perfected the use of nighttime radar detection combined with the tactic of illuminating U-boats with the Leigh Light—a very powerful, narrow-beam searchlight attached to the underside of the aircraft—only seconds before launching a sudden attack. At least one RAF squadron (No. 172) of Vickers Wellingtons was equipped with the Leigh Light. See Gannon, 96-100.

57. *KTB*, 31 March–1April 1944.

58. *KTB*, 1 April 1944.

route for the First U-boat Flotilla at the great U-boat base of Brest. Absent the usual complement of foodstuffs for a long patrol, the boat was laden with sea-bags, which all members had again deftly packed with all their belongings, not intending to return to La Pallice and their quarters in La Rochelle anytime in the near future. Neither was the mission to be credited to the men as a combat patrol; BdU had transferred *Kater* and a small number of remaining Biscay-based U-boats to the base nearest the western entrance to the English Channel. The boat ran on the surface all night in perfect sailing conditions: low waves, only 10 percent cloud cover, and clear starry skies that maximized visibility against aircraft.[59]

Marbach dismissed the escort ship that trailed U-953 only at 08:35 on 24 April. The boat slipped beneath the waves at 09:03 and continued to cut a short zigzag course into the Bay rather than making a beeline directly into Brest. The skipper again intended to put the new *Schnorchel* to the test to satisfy his own and BdU's curiosity about the feasibility of the underwater breathing system. U-953 had plowed only five nautical miles beneath the surface by noon, all without engaging the snort; but the boat would remain underwater for another thirty hours as Marbach ordered the device engaged. The new system proved itself fully able to replace noxious fumes and odors with fresh air for the crew, recharge the big electric batteries and provide submerged diesel operation for faster underwater speed. The skipper would later detail the success of the *Schnorchel* with his endorsement of its capabilities in a *KTB* summary report for the mission.[60] In spite of its obvious advantages toward crew survival and comfort, the snort presented a unique problem for the submerged men. The engaged system created an uncomfortable vacuum inside the pressure hull when the diesel engines sucked in the breathing air. Baumann sometimes covered his face with his hands to lessen the thoroughly disagreeable sensation that his eyes were being pulled out of their sockets.

---

59. *KTB*, 23-24 April 1944. The First U-boat Flotilla (Erste U-Flotille) was commanded by *Korvettenkapitän* Werner Winter from July 1942 until September 1944.
60. *KTB*, 24-25 April 1944.

Karl Baumann, Portrait, 1943.

U-953 and U-275, a boat out of Brest, received a radio message at 22:00. The boats were to proceed along a pre-designated route called *Eisbär*—Polar Bear—to meet up with U-963 on 26 April at 04:45. At a rendezvous point identified as map coordinate 344, the three boats were to proceed together into the port of Brest. *Kater's* sound operator swept the area in all directions with the hydrophone from 23:30 until shortly after midnight, and reported no signs of sea or air traffic, either enemy or friendly. By noon on 25 April U-953 had trekked sixty-four *Seemeilen* underwater, and continued submerged toward Brest until 22:23. Marbach then ordered the boat to the surface, which sent the watch party scrambling onto the bridge. The skipper also ordered the gun crews to their battle stations aft of the bridge on the *Wintergarten* and the gun deck below. *Kater's* diesels propelled the boat at full speed toward the meeting point without incident until 02:09 on 26 April. As the boat passed through BF 5512 two flares suddenly illuminated the sky over the low horizon and flickered brightly until the fiery projectiles slowly dropped into the Bay. Marbach presumed some sort of confrontation was underway in the distance. At 03:00 the sound operator's Naxos system picked up an aircraft radar signature that he reported to the skipper. Then at 05:00 a four-engine aircraft flew over the U-boat but did not fire a shot; likewise, *Kater's* gunners let the plane pass unhindered. The dark night prevented positive identification of the aircraft, though most likely it was a British patrol bomber. The gunners maintained their wary vigil, and at 05:20 an escort vessel steamed into view to lead the lone U-boat into the bunker at Brest. U-275 and U-963 had not arrived at the appointed place and time, so at 05:45 U-953 alone followed the escort toward the French coast. The gigantic U-boat bunker with twenty *Boxen* finally rose into view on the horizon, and at 08:30 *Kater* slid into *Boxe* B2.[61]

Elektriker Obermachinist Gotthilf Buck (left) and the Diesel *Obermachinist* celebrate U-953's return from a combat patrol.

The gathering of U-boats at Brest formed the vanguard of an attack force set to strike the gigantic Allied invasion armada that already was building up to

---

61. *KTB*, 25-26 April 1944.

assault the western French coast. The German high command knew the cross-channel attack was coming and had monitored the buildup of the massive invasion fleet, but could not ascertain where or when the Allies would strike. Stepped-up Allied attacks on U-boats during the first four months of 1944—in the Atlantic and the Bay of Biscay, and at the sub bases on the Biscay coast—had taken a devastating toll. At least fifty-five boats and their crews, 80 percent of the U-boats dispatched from Brest during the period, had never returned from their missions. The total tonnage in enemy ships sunk by U-boats during the same period was negligible. By spring of 1944 the Ubootwaffe had become an anachronism of the fearsome predator that had savagely and relentlessly preyed upon Allied ships and sailors during the early days of World War II. The U-boat now was no longer the scourge of the Atlantic.

The most forward element for the seaborne defense of the *Reich*, a paltry fifteen operational U-boats, waited at Brest for the inevitable orders to strike the invasion fleet. Two of the fifteen were the only survivors of twenty boats recently dispatched from Norway to bolster the Brest U-boat fleet. Seven of the fifteen boats were equipped with the *Schnorchel;* these alone stood the only realistic chance to confront the invasion force; the rest could count on being blown out of the water long before they reached the Channel. Only forty-three additional U-boats—twenty-one in other Biscay ports and twenty-two in Norway—remained operational.[62]

Though defeat was as unthinkable as death, no one in the Ubootwaffe honestly could have felt optimistic for the future. The Allies had assembled overwhelming numbers of ships and aircraft to fend off the Kriegsmarine in submarine and surface attacks against the invasion fleet. The snort would have to work perfectly for any U-boat to have a fair chance to slip into the Channel between throngs of enemy vessels in strong defensive lines. As such, after her arrival at Brest, U-953 would be laid up in drydock until 22 May. Naval engineers had ordered additional modifications to her *Schnorchel* system to improve its functionality and operational capabilities.[63]

By 22 May 1944, spring's long daylight hours threatened every U-boat that ventured out of her protective bunker *Boxe*. U-953 eased out of her pen at 22:10 into extremely dangerous conditions for stealth movement: calm Biscay waves that barely disturbed the almost flat surface, and dark but mostly clear skies that provided good visibility to the horizon. The outbound boat and her escort scur-

---

62. Werner, 211, 217.
63. *KTB*, 26 April–22 May 1944.

ried toward *Punkt* 342, a designated point about twenty-eight nautical miles southeast of Brest, where at 01:14 the next morning Marbach dismissed the escort and began the lonely trek across the Bay. The fear of early detection by anti-submarine aircraft had determined the escort would remain with *Kater* only a short distance before she would break off to leave the U-boat to her own devices to survive. The boat arrived at BF 5212, the one hundred-meter depth line, where she submerged at 01:46 and immediately set upon a westerly course. U-953's latest mission was designed to test the improved *Schnorchel* for its seaworthiness and tactical capability. A long-distance *Feindfahrt* was not intended, nor was there a planned contingency for one, so minimal provisions—except for ammunition and ordnance—had been taken aboard the boat before departure. By noon the boat had churned only sixteen miles underwater as the men again acclimated themselves to the peculiarities of living and working in the snort's precarious atmosphere. During the afternoon the skipper put the *Schnorchel* through its paces as fresh air was replenished, electric batteries were recharged and diesel engines powered the submerged U-boat. Between tests the sound operator engaged the hydrophone but detected no signals from enemy air or surface traffic. The late evening hours passed without the need to surface, for which *Kater's* officers and crew were delighted; the deep now seemed more than ever a blessed sanctuary. If necessary, U-953 now could remain underwater for days on end, to surface at Marbach's discretion rather than at the insistence of the boat's limitations. By noon on 24 May the boat had logged 47.5 *Seemeilen* entirely underwater during the previous twenty-fours hours. The only reportable activity that occurred during the afternoon hours was the *Schnorchel's* sixteen-minute procedure to vent fresh air into the boat and push the stale submarine air outside.[64]

Kater's crew had settled into a routine of satisfied boredom by nightfall. Being relatively close to Brest on a short mission, the men did not apprehend the imminent drudgery of a long *Feindfahrt*; the snort also was still new enough to generate interest and conversation that competed with the news and rumors about the invasion everyone knew was soon to come. The sound operator took an underwater reading at 23:10 and was jarred out of whatever lethargy he may have fought earlier in the evening. Distant surface sounds were detected in three locations and growing louder. The operator notified the skipper; together they monitored the sound signatures as U-953 tacked onto a nondescript, tightly winding course into BF 2828 that interrupted the navigator's clean geometric deliberation and his carefully plotted course.

---

64. *KTB*, 22-24 May 1944.

Auf Gefechtsstation! Marbach commanded calmly at 11:48. Men ran to their underwater battle stations and waited for the skipper's next orders. The skipper weighed the scant information to determine how or whether to do battle. He then ordered torpedoes readied in tubes II, III and V. The Torpedo Officer in the *Zentrale* ordered the fore and aft tubes' outside doors opened, and listened intently for launch orders as he poised his palm several inches from the firing switches. Several minutes later, however, the skipper terminated the torpedo pre-launch sequence. At fourteen minutes after midnight he ordered *Kater* to the surface, his intention being to attack the still unseen sources of the sound signatures. U-953 bounded onto the waves and into 90 percent cloud cover, then began to sail toward the sound readings. Forty-five minutes later, the sound operator warned the skipper that he had detected airborne radar contacts along with the surface sound readings. The latest news compelled the commander to forego his hunt for enemy targets and take on a defensive posture. Marbach ordered the sound operator to deploy Aphrodite to deflect the radar contacts, then immediately ordered *Kater* to submerge. Only two minutes after the waves closed forty meters over the boat's conning tower, six *Fliebos* crashed into the Biscay after the U-boat. The bombs' near-miss detonations damaged some of the sensitive electrical systems on board and jarred the men to their core. Marbach, in his *KTB* notation, speculated that the enemy aircraft probably had dropped the aerial depth charges randomly. In reality, the plane most likely was equipped with the Allies' new, stronger radar system that could detect a surface target as small as the flotation bulb that bounded along the waves atop the *Schnorchel's* big and ungainly intake-exhaust pipe. In any case, the *Ubootfahrer* of U-953 again had barely survived violent death under the Bay of Biscay.[65]

In the wake of the attack, Marbach reported the incident to FdU West, which responded with orders to discontinue further sound detection attempts—doubtless in the mistaken belief that the attacking aircraft had fixed *Kater's* position by triangulating the boat's hydrophone signals.[66] Headquarters also ordered U-953 back to Brest on a direct course to the east. The boat had sailed fifty-six nautical miles at midday on 25 October, of which only 6.5 miles was logged on the forty-five minute surface run prior to the bombing attack. The boat remained underwater the remainder of the day and in doing so proved the value of the snort. The

---

65. *KTB*, 24-25 May 1944. Translation: *Fliebos* were aerial bombs, or *Fliegerbomben*. The H25 radar system carried by RAF aircraft by mid-1944 use a 9.7cm wavelength that could detect a surface object as small as the snorkel's flotation bulb. The Germans later developed an anti-radar coating specifically to counter the 9.7cm wavelength detection. See Stern, 131.

breathing system continued to perform admirably its functions to recharge the electric motor batteries, replenish breathing air, feed air to the diesel engines and vent out the diesel exhaust during the *Unterwassermarsch*. U-953 logged an entire day underwater or the first time during her short operational life when, at noon on 26 May, forty-eight nautical miles was recorded in the war diary. The U-boat logged a seven mile surface run of only fifty-five minutes in the clear moonlight, after which Marbach ordered *Kater* below the surface to avoid detection and utilize the snort to its full potential. The noon report to the *KTB* on 27 May noted a further forty-eight nautical miles underwater after twenty-four hours on her eastward course. U-953 arrived at the pre-designated point at 22:52 and surfaced to meet an escort vessel for the fifty-six mile run into Brest, but the escort was nowhere to be seen. Watch party members manned their bridge stations to scan the bright night sky and shimmering waters that undulated with graceful swells. With their large binoculars, visibility was nearly perfect to the clear horizon. The escort finally arrived after midnight, at 01:20, and both vessels soon gunned their diesel engines as they pointed their prows toward the French coast and home. Gliding between minefields and other unseen obstacles, *Kater* passed through the harbor barrier at 04:30 and eased into *Boxe* A of the U-boat bunker an hour later. Marbach and crew had sailed only 326.5 nautical miles during the mission, which nonetheless would count as a war patrol. For their efforts they had survived another enemy air attack and confirmed the tactical value of the *Schnorchel* within certain operational limitations.[67]

---

66. Translation: FdU West was the acronym for Führer der Unterseeboote West, who commanded all U-boats in the Western area of operations whenever they were in the French ports or the Bay of Biscay. *Kapitän-zur-See* Hans-Rudolf Rösing served as FdU West. His headquarters were located at Chateau de Pignerolles at Saint Barthelemy d'Anjou, a suburb of Angers, France, until after the Normandy invasion, when FdU West transferred to Norway.
67. *KTB*, 25-28 May 1944. Marbach concluded that the prescribed time for optimal use of the snorkel (23:00 to 06:00) did not provide enough time to fully charge the electric batteries, which contradicted early snorkel tests that determined recharging could be completed in three hours. The prescribed time for optimum snorkel use doubtless was based upon the fact that U-boats easily could be seen from the air when submerged only four meters to employ the snort. Translation: *Unterwassermarsch* literally means an underwater march.

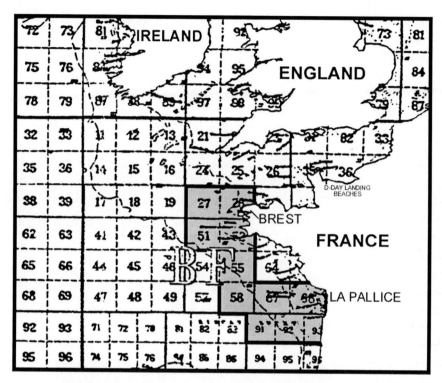

The third, fourth and fifth war patrols credited to Karl Baumann covered
806 nautical miles and fourteen days at sea; 30 March to 1 April 1944,
23 April to 26 April 1944, and 22 May to 28 May 1944. Shaded grid
squares indicate U-953's area of operations.

Many among Marbach's crew became uncharacteristically ambivalent about
their early return to dry land. In response to the imminent invasion threat, First
Flotilla Headquarters initially had placed all U-boat officers and crews on a six-
hour alert. The curfew effectively relegated the men to spend their off duty hours
either on base or in the near vicinity of downtown Brest, where diverse and tawdry
enticements still invited them to spend their money unwisely. In the final days
before the invasion, FdU West shortened the curfew to one hour, which for all
intents and purposes prohibited U-boat men from venturing even downtown.
The looming battle, the alarming loss of many U-boats and crews during the past
months, and the restrictions imposed on the men conspired to create a melancholy atmosphere that penetrated the psyche and depressed the soul. Ever
resourceful, Marbach was determined to maintain the *esprit* of his crew and
occupy their time productively while they waited for the Allied invasion force to

present itself. At his insistence, U-953's officers bounced uneasily on horseback in full dress uniforms, complete with sabres, as they trod behind their grinning commander through the French countryside.

The already gloomy mood was dealt a further blow by the sudden death of the crew's beloved mascot, Rin Tin Tina. So protective was she of her crewmates that she rushed into the path of an approaching truck to protect some of the men, according to witnesses. The *Ubootfahrer* buried their loyal comrade beside the Naval College at a spot that overlooked the Bay of Biscay and the Atlantic beyond, where together they had gone to war.

"*Jede Ubootfahrer muß ein Tennisspieler sein!*" the skipper commanded every member of his crew.[68] So it was that the men of U-953 marked off a plot of ground to construct a tennis court on the hill above the U-boat bunker. With hand tools they scraped away the sod and leveled out a flat surface, then rolled a smooth hard clay surface onto the court. The hard work exercised bodies and minds and somewhat eased the stress of war. Although the men anticipated many hours of diversion and perhaps a few heated matches on their new court, they were destined never to use it.

The somber mood among U-boat officers and men at Brest turned dreadfully downcast in the early morning hours of 6 June 1944. Around 02:00 orderlies pounded frantically on the doors of the U-boat commanders' quarters and shouted that the Allied invasion was underway on the Normandy coast two hundred miles to the north. Meanwhile, enlisted crewmen were startled awake by loudspeakers that suddenly blared into their sleeping quarters.

"*Alarmstufe Zwei! Alarmstufe Zwei!*"[69]

Karl awoke abruptly but did not immediately leap out of bed, because he and most others assumed the alarm was yet another drill that shortly would be terminated. The alert had been sounded a week earlier and startled the men out of their sleep, but almost immediately was declared a practice alarm. Grumbling crewmen then collapsed back into their bunks and tried to resume their rudely-interrupted slumber, not wanting to be fooled again. Now, after the real alarm sounded, nearly fifteen minutes elapsed before the men realized unmistakably that the signal was not an exercise. Men bolted from their bunks and exhorted their *Kameraden* to move fast and get to their boat. The U-boat gunner finalized

---

68.   Translation: "Every U-boat crewman must be a tennis player!"
69.   Translation: "Alarm code two!!! Alarm code two!!!" The announcement was meant to order all men to man their boats, though apparently not necessarily that the invasion had begun. Otherwise, Karl Baumann and his crewmates would have reacted more seriously when the announcement first was issued.

his mad rush to get dressed when he stuffed a blue French beret onto his head and charged for the doorway with the rest of his crew. Outside, a wave of officers and men already stormed down the steep hillside path to their boats. The one-hour alert that essentially had confined the men to the naval base assured that full crews were on hand to sail toward the invasion area on short notice. Every corridor of the U-bunker soon echoed with running footsteps and shouted orders as hundreds of *Ubootfahrer* manned their boats and furiously set to work on last minute preparations to sail for the battlefront.

U-953 was ready to sail fifteen minutes after her crew arrived dockside. Amid the flurry of activity that swirled around and inside the boat, Karl noted with considerable misgiving that Marbach nervously paced *Kater's* deck, uncharacteristically preoccupied, lost in deep thought. As crewmen frantically prepared their boat for one of the most crucial days of combat in the twentieth century, *Obersteuermann* Hartmann shouted a most incongruous order to Karl as the gunner hurried toward the bow compartment inside the boat.

"You get a haircut as soon as we get back into the harbor," the rankled chief petty officer demanded as he pointed to the long hair that curled from beneath Karl's beret.

Fully manned, fueled, provisioned and armed, the U-boats silently sat inside their reinforced concrete sanctuary as their wary commanders awaited final orders from flotilla headquarters to sail for the invasion front. Minutes passed, then hours; while to the north, American, British, Canadian and other Allied forces swarmed ashore from thousands of transport vessels protected by hundreds of warships and legions of aircraft. More than five thousand Allied ships had formed the world's largest invasion fleet. While the U-boats waited, a nearly solid phalanx of destroyers, destroyer escorts, cruisers, carrier escorts, frigates, torpedo boats, and other vessels established a defensive perimeter across the entrances to the English Channel to prevent encroachment by the Kriegsmarine's few remaining undersea and surface warships.

At noon Marbach received orders to sail. The scheduled afternoon departure time allowed U-953's crew to eat lunch on the dock next to their boat. The mooring lines finally were cast off at 15:30 and U-953 sailed out of the bunker to join six minesweepers to traverse the minefields at the harbor entrance. The skippers who had not yet received their orders to sail looked on with anxious frustration. The U-boat passed beyond the harbor entrance at 16:00 and into the Bay, where her Metox radar immediately detected the constant presence of aircraft above the 90 percent overcast. An RAF Halifax droned high overhead, which warned the crew that the very low but changing cloud cover also might conceal an air attack until the last fatal seconds. On that crucial day in the war, the gunners and the watch party anxiously scanned the sky and the Biscay horizon with an expectation of being attacked. U-953 slowly edged due west into the Bay to where Hartmann, the navigator, had plotted to nose her toward the Channel.[70]

Back at Brest, the boats that remained inside the bunker received a confounding succession of attack orders, each of which superseded previous directives. Several times wary crews cast off their mooring lines, only to be notified afterward that their orders had been rescinded. Leadership seemed to have faltered at the moment of ultimate crisis, and the men grew more confused, annoyed and angry at U-boat headquarters as the afternoon wore on. U-boat commanders next were ordered to a meeting at Flotilla headquarters. In the skippers' absence rampant rumors passed between the boats and heightened the incomprehension many crewmen expressed over the loss of crucial hours that had been allowed to elapse. *Ubootfahrer* emerged from their boats throughout the day to sit on the decks or pace up and down the quays to console their thoughts and fears. They chain-smoked and checked their watches, and listened to shipboard radios that had been hooked up to broadcast German martial music and reports from Joseph Goebbels' Propaganda Ministry in Berlin. Excited voices announced that the Wehrmacht continued to hold its beachhead defenses and even claimed—erroneously—that some of the invaders had been thrown back into the sea.

The men cheered every hopeful news report, which bolstered their spirits if but momentarily. The skippers finally returned to their boats in the evening with firm attack orders from Ubootwaffe chief Dönitz. The sound of eight hundred loudly singing crewmen echoed through the concrete corridors as the commanders strode toward their boats inside the massive bunker. The officers were gratified their men exuded such *esprit* and youthful enthusiasm for the mission that lay ahead, but they knew well that too much time had been squandered during that fateful day—time the U-boat fleet could ill afford to lose. By nightfall the Allied invasion fleet and assault forces already were firmly established in the Channel and on the Normandy beaches. Any hopes that the Ubootwaffe would constitute a serious threat to the Allied invasion were utterly and completely dashed. Nonetheless, at 21:00 that evening the rest of the pitiable German U-boat force sailed into the darkness to attack the Allied fleet. At 21:30 six *Schnorchel*-equipped boats at ten-minute intervals submerged into the Bay of Brest. Following the lead of U-953, they first sailed west into the Biscay. Eight

70. *KTB*, 6 June 1944.

boats without snorts were ordered to attack transports and warships in the English Channel, a desperate directive that was tantamount to suicide.[71]

Kater's radio operator received a message from FdU West at 16:41 that cancelled the initial operations orders for U-953. New orders called for all *Schnorchel*

---

71. *KTB*, 6 June 1944; and Werner, 217-219. Werner wrote that during a meeting in May between the Senior Officer of U-boats West and his U-boat commanders, *Kapitän zur See* Hans-Rudolf Rösing read a headquarters directive that ordered the U-boat skippers to attack and sink the invasion fleet by ramming. See Werner, 213. Werner and Marbach were two of the fifteen commanders who attended the meeting, which may explain why Marbach uncharacteristically appeared so nervous and preoccupied on June sixth. However, Horst Bredow, the director of the *U-Boot-Archiv* in Cuxhaven, Germany—who also was a former U-boat officer and in later years a friend of Admiral Dönitz—asserts no suicide order ever was issued. Bredow, however, was not present at the May conference as was Werner. Harry Cooper of Sharkhunters, Inc.—who claims close friendship with both Werner and Bredow—stated during a telephone conversation with this writer on 28 February 2000, that the two have never reconciled their adverse claims regarding the alleged order. For decades the two have harbored an abiding dislike for each other as a result. To further confuse the issue, the official minutes of a conference between Dönitz and Hitler on 13 June includes the statement that the submarines of Group *Landwirt* stationed in the Bay of Biscay were to be withdrawn from the area because, "...they risk serious losses in that area..." See *Conferences*, 397. The statement appears somewhat in stark contrast to a suicide order purportedly issued several weeks earlier to the U-boat commanders in Brest. In view of Germany's desperate situation in 1944, however, it is not wholly inconceivable that the Naval High Command may have felt compelled to issue a suicide order to impede the invasion. Nonetheless, Dönitz never would have ordered such drastic measures to destroy a significant portion of the remaining U-boat fleet without express permission from the *Führer*. No discussions of suicide attacks were recorded in the minutes of any conferences between Dönitz and Hitler in the months leading up to the invasion, nor in the minutes of the conference held on 13 June. In a 1993 letter to Karl Baumann, Herbert Raschewski broached the issue when he wrote that he personally overheard Marbach discuss the ramming order with the *I.W.O.* once while the two officers sat in the captain's nook of U-953. After the war, Marbach refused to discuss the alleged ramming order. "Let it go," he implored in response to inquiries by former crewmen. Such an admonition, rather than a simple "no" response to the question, tends to imply that Marbach indeed received the order. This, along with Werner's assertions, increases the likelihood that the U-boat commanders in Brest were ordered to fatally ram enemy ships. If Admiral Dönitz truthfully never ordered the suicide assault, then one must conclude that it originated with Rösing, who, according to his friend Harry Cooper, denies that he ever issued such a drastic order.

boats to proceed to BF 2730, northwest of Brest, then tack to BF 3184. The new operations area would place U-953 roughly midpoint in the Channel between England's Isle of Wight and the northeast corner of France's Cotentin Peninsula. In his newly assigned area of operations, Marbach would position his boat to strike the right flank of the invasion fleet. The radio telegram also warned the *Schnorchel* boats to avoid nearby BF 3186 and 3194 because German S-boats had heavily mined the area. A follow-up radio message at 17:24 warned U-boats to avoid the English coast at BF 2357, 2358, 2359 and 2377 as well, due to heavy mining in the Channel west of the Isle of Wight. If U-953 could reach her objective, her torpedoes could wreak untold damage on the invasion force, but simply getting through the British and Canadian naval blockade, the Allied air cordon and the German minefields would be fraught with danger. The minesweepers scoured the path ahead of *Kater* until 19:10, when they reached their break-off point in the Bay. Before Marbach could dismiss the escorts, however, an Allied reconnaissance plane flew overhead. The skipper ordered the bridge watch and gunners belowdeck and, while the six escorts provided a curtain of covering fire to divert the aircraft, U-953 charged beneath the waves at BF 5213. The boat proceeded slowly toward the Channel as the final hours of the Longest Day—as the sixth of June became known—settled uneasily into history and the Nazi era entered the final eleven months of its horrific existence.[72]

Fourteen U-boats from St. Nazaire, four from La Pallice, and one from Lorient eventually joined the seventeen that sailed from Brest toward the invasion fleet. The combined force included all the *Schnorchel*-equipped boats assigned to the Biscay bases. As with those from Brest, the additional boats with *Schnorchels* were ordered to attack the invasion forces in the Channel. Allied intelligence sources had read masses of decrypted German radio and Enigma signals, and had developed considerable knowledge about the U-boat force and its intentions. To counter their underwater threat the British and U.S. navies had deployed three destroyer groups, seven frigate escort groups, and three escort aircraft carriers to the U-boat lanes between the Bay of Biscay and the English Channel. RAF Coastal Command aircraft constantly patrolled the sky over the Bay and the Channel.[73]

---

72. *KTB*, 6 June 1944. Karl's memory had U-953 diving shortly after reaching the outer boundary of the harbor at Brest, at approximately 15:30 rather than the 19:17 time recorded in the *KTB*. Either his memory is not correct or the boat in fact submerged when a Halifax bomber was spotted and the dive information was not recorded in the *KTB*, as other events also were not recorded. The *KTB* is an invaluable but imperfect record.

With her *Schnorchel* engaged, U-953 sailed due west through the darkness of early morning on 7 June accompanied by the terrifying sounds of constant air attacks on other U-boats that reverberated loudly through *Kater's* hull. The *Ubootfahrer* were assailed by crashing bombs that hit the water nearby with unmistakable splashes and large caliber machine gun rounds that reached deeply into the murk with rapid swishing sounds before all their momentum was spent and they floated lazily and harmlessly to the bottom of the Bay. Neither Karl Baumann nor his enlisted crewmates yet had received any specific details about U-953's objective from their officers, though most presumed their boat was sailing directly toward the Normandy coast. Baumann felt the twang of nervousness in his gut that always appeared at the beginning of each war patrol, but had no special misgivings about the upcoming mission. Few if any realized that the pandemonium above them heralded the desperate beginning of the end of the war in Europe. As if to underscore the point, later that morning U-953 received two radio messages from Admiral Dönitz at Ubootwaffe headquarters:

> All Commanders at Sea: The enemy has begun the invasion in Europe. The war has now entered the decisive phase. If the landing of the Anglo-Americans is successful it will mean for us the loss of large areas necessary to the life of the war effort and constitute an immediate threat to our most important industrial areas, without which the war could not be continued. The enemy is weakest at the moment of the landing itself. Everything must be done to beat him back at this time point and bring about losses that discourage him from further attempts at landing. That will also provide the Eastern front with strength to carry on.

> U-boat Men: The future of our German people depends on you more than at any other time. Therefore, I am requesting from you a ruthless commitment without regard to normally applicable measures of caution. Every enemy vehicle that serves the landing is to be attacked with a maximum effort, even if there is a danger of the loss of your own boat. Every man and every weapon that can be destroyed before the landing reduces the enemy's chances of success. I know that I can depend on you, my U-boat men who have proven themselves in difficult battles.

---

73. David G. Chandler & James Lawton Collins, Jr., eds., *The D-Day Encyclopedia* (New York: Simon & Schuster, 1994), 577-578. Altogether, fifteen snorkel boats and twenty-seven non-snorkel boats participated in the largely unsuccessful U-boat counteroffensive against the Allied invasion fleet during June 1944.

By the time the messages clacked into *Kater's* radio room the Normandy landings already had entered their second day. Allied troops had established themselves—if tenuously at isolated hotspots—on all beachheads and were moving inland. American, British and Commonwealth land forces would continue to pour onto the French coast for many days to come, all the while strengthening the foothold from which they could not be forced off the continent. The U-boat force might inflict minor damage against the invasion fleet, but even its maximum effort could in no respect now reverse the reeling fortunes of war for Germany and its Axis partners.[74]

U-953 tacked due north at 09:00 onto a new course to align herself more closely with the western entrance to the Channel. Marbach quickly determined his boat would remain constantly underwater with the snort engaged throughout the crucial mission. He saw the tactic as his only hope to slip beneath the solid air cordon the Allies had deployed to keep the U-boat force from the invasion fleet. Under diesel power the U-boat could make her underwater run at a pace equal to or better than her surface speed, and with a degree of stealth that would not have existed on the surface even on the darkest night. Still, by noon on 7 June, *Kater* had put only sixty nautical miles between herself and Brest, of which only half were logged underwater. Soon afterward, a radio message from headquarters warned that BF 3156 was contaminated with mines. The original attack orders, *Kanal Nr. 1*, thus were altered for U-953 to avoid the newly identified minefields. Hiding from the sunshine and clear visibility that reached to the horizon, the boat remained underwater and slowly trekked north throughout the afternoon. With the *Schnorchel* engaged during the early evening, the boat's rancid air was vented out and batteries recharged in relative safety.

The battles of 7 June in the Biscay and at the Channel entrance usually matched U-boats against the Royal Air Force. By day's end U-970 lay on the bottom of the Bay, destroyed by a Sunderland of 228 Squadron; while U-212, U-256, U-415, U-963 and U-989 were damaged by aircraft and forced to return to Brest for repairs. A Vickers Wellington and two RAF Liberator patrol bombers were shot down by U-boats during the attacks.[75]

A U-boat targeted HMCS *Saskatchewan* on the evening of 7 June and launched two GNATs—as German Naval Acoustic Torpedoes were known to the Allies—against the warship at 21:01 and 21:38 from a distance of about one

---

74.   *KTB*, 7 June 1944, and *KTB* recapitulation section for radio messages received and transmitted.
75.   Chandler and Collins, 578

thousand yards.[76] From his battle station on HMCS *Skeena's* open bridge, navigation officer Lieutenant Peter Chance was startled by a gigantic explosion about a mile away that ripped the Channel surface into a geyser so large that *Saskatchewan* momentarily disappeared from view.

"My God, she's gone," navigator Chance exclaimed, certain that the stern had been blown off *Skeena's* sister ship. Chance soon was relieved to see *Saskatchewan* reappear through the settling mist. The acoustic torpedo had obliterated the recently developed CAT gear decoy that was streamed 150 yards off the destroyer's stern, and left the destroyer entirely undamaged. The simple, dirt cheap decoy had proven its worth many times greater than its weight in gold.[77]

Surprisingly, U-953 encountered no enemy presence until 23:08, when an RAF Halifax bomber appeared out of the north one thousand meters above and two to three thousand meters off the port side of the submerged boat. Had the boat not been fitted with the snorkel, the bomber might have caught her on the surface and sent her to the bottom of the Biscay. The crewmen were grateful for their renewed stealth and the protection the snort provided, however tenuous or temporary. The final minutes before midnight ticked off the clock when the U-boat's sound operator swept the area and noted the nearby presence of two other *Schnorchel* boats. The company of fellow *Ubootkameraden* in BF 2768 probably manifested some degree of comfort among those aboard U-953, as if somehow their mutual safety now was more assured. Such thoughts were wholly irrational and illogical by June 1944, but helped bolster the men's morale and determination to take on the Allies' vastly superior numbers. Meanwhile, as the second day of the Normandy invasion drew to a close, a seemingly endless stream of Allied troops swarmed toward the French coast.[78]

Marbach ordered round-the-clock, half-hour sound readings at 00:32 on 8 June, while U-953 slowly aligned herself with the Channel entrance. The hydrophone operator reported only routine sound traffic until 02:13, when he detected a distant, entirely new and mysterious timbre that resembled a circular saw or a high-pressure steam turbine. A strange sound varied in volume, and when again detected at 06:50 its pitch had modulated. Karl Baumann and other crewmen

76. "Report of Attack on a U-Boat, 8th June, 1944." CAT was the acronym for Canadian Anti-Acoustic Torpedo gear.
77. Peter Chance, Commander, RCN (Ret.), Sidney, British Columbia, telephone interviews by Author, 21-26 April 2006. The incident also is recounted in CDR Chance's autobiography, *Before It's Too Late; A Sailor's Life, 1920–2001* (Sidney, BC: Self-Published, 2001), 98.
78. *KTB*, 7 June 1944.

learned that Marbach first believed the noises emanated from an unknown mechanical failure on the boat, but the sound operator soon disproved the presumption when signatures showed up on his sound detection screen. The skipper ordered *Kater* deeper below to engage the periscope. While he swept the area in the direction of the sound, an Allied destroyer steamed into view six to seven thousand meters distant, bearing north. The strange grating tone emitted by the destroyer was so loud it drowned out the familiar sound of the powerful screws that drove such small warships at high speed through heavy seas and combat maneuvers. Marbach ordered U-953 to proceed north behind the destroyer despite the mystifying sounds, hoping to determine their exact origin and purpose while he attempted somehow to close to attack range.

Unbeknownst to the skipper and his crew, *Kater* had encountered one of four Canadian destroyers of the 12th Escort Group, part of the large force of Allied warships deployed across the Channel entrance and into the Biscay to intercept German surface ships and U-boats before they could ambush the invasion force. At the moment the destroyers HMCS *Qu'Appelle, Saskatchewan, Skeena,* and *Restigouche* steamed toward a rendezvous point along a picket line drawn between Wolf Rock Island, off Lands End, England; and Ushant Island, France, just northwest from Brest. The destroyers were to form up by 08:00, then conduct box searches for U-boats inside rectangular perimeters around which each would sail. When contacts with the enemy were made, one or more destroyers would converge at the sites of the contacts to dig out the detected U-boats. The warships operated under general orders to execute Operation Observant, a tactic intended to drive U-boats below effective torpedo launch depth, then destroy each boat or inflict as much damage as possible.[79]

"*Auf Gefechtsstation,*" Marbach commanded at 07:35, in case the destroyer should alter course and present her flank as a target. A moment later the outer doors of the torpedo tubes opened and seawater flooded into the chambers around the huge missiles that sat poised for launch. Karl watched intently while the torpedo *Mixers* readied the bow tubes with mechanical precision. Every *Ubootfahrer* not on duty was expected to lend a hand when the crew was called to battle stations, so Baumann stood nearby to help the *Mixers* during the looming attack. Tubes I and IV were armed with *LuTs*—electrically driven torpedoes programmed to run in zigzag patterns—and tubes II and V each held Type V acous-

---

79. "Report of Attack on a U-Boat, 8th June, 1944," HMCS *Skeena,* 12th June, 1944. Record Group 24, Series D-1-C, Volume 6904, File NSS 8910-353/28. Library and Archives Canada, Toronto, Ontario; and Chance interview.

tic torpedoes designed to home-in on the source of the loudest sound emitted within a given attack zone. At 07:47 an aircraft flew into view in *Kater's* air periscope, a signal to Marbach that the enemy soon would make its presence most profoundly known. The skipper was certain the plane and destroyer were part of a coordinated, combined air and surface anti-submarine strike force, which confirmed his determination to remain submerged throughout the invasion counterattack mission.[80]

By 08:00 the four destroyers had lined up 2,000 yards abreast to sail on courses due south at a speed of twelve knots. Each of the fast ships towed CAT gear in their wakes. The CAT gear consisted of two heavy steel bars, loosely attached side-by-side and one inch apart, connected to steel cables that could be reeled astern 150 yards or more. When deployed—streamed, in Royal Canadian Navy parlance—a destroyer's constant forward motion conspired with underwater currents to vibrate the bars against one another and generate a grating sound much like the rasp of a table saw, and louder than the her fast-turning screws.[81]

Skeena steamed hard onto a southerly course while *Restigouche* and *Qu'Appelle* tacked due west at 08:05, then due south at 08:30.[82] The three destroyers by their tandem maneuvers unsuspectingly had placed themselves along with *Saskatchewan* into U-953's attack zone. Snorkel-equipped U-621 and U-984 also lurked somewhere inside the 12th Escort Group's sector.[83] *Kater* silently had trailed one of the destroyers north for two hours, but her lower speed caused her to lose her target bearing whenever the warship altered its course or increased its speed. Now, at 08:50, Marbach ordered a course change to obtain flank attack bearings on the multiple targets that soon would steam across his bow. The skipper doubtless believed sudden good fortune had placed U-953 on the threshold of victory unlike any opportunity his boat previously had been accorded.

80. *KTB*, 8 June 1944. Translation: *LuT* was the abbreviation for the *Lagenunabhängiger Torpedo*, meaning bearing-independent torpedo.
81. Leighton H. Steinhoff, Kitchener, Ontario, telephone interview by Author, 14 April 2006. Torpedoman Steinhoff witnessed the events of 8 June 1944 from the deck of HMCS *Skeena*, where he also serviced *Skeena's* depth charges. One wonders if the acronym CAT also referred to the unnerving shriek of a combative feline, a seemingly appropriate comparison to the sound of the decoy.
82. Ship's Log: HMCS *Skeena*; Record Group 24, Series D-2, Volume 7861. Ship's Log: HMCS *Restigouche*; Record Group 24, Series D-2, Volume 7795. Ship's Log: HMCS *Qu'Appelle*; Record Group 24, Series D-2, Volume 7762. Library and Archives Canada, Toronto, Ontario.
83. Chandler and Collins, 578.

The bewildering sawing sounds resumed at 09:00 and increased in intensity. Minutes later a destroyer sailed slowly across the horizon in front of U-953 at four thousand meters. Marbach sat upon the commander's steel bicycle seat with his knees straddling the attack periscope. While he peered into the viewfinder he quickly decided the target was worth the expenditure of two torpedoes. Rather than zigzag in a common defensive maneuver, the destroyer headed straight and true on a steady course at seven knots, as if she were inviting an attack. *Kater* slowly continued on her course as well to close the distance to the target. The skipper announced his intention to fire the two *LuTs*, after which the firing switches for tubes I and IV were engaged on the fire control panel in the *Zentrale*. Since he presumed the prominent sawing sounds would misdirect acoustic torpedoes away from their intended targets, the skipper chose not to waste them needlessly. He carefully lined up the distant ship in his viewfinder and called out the destroyer's range, speed and heading, and *Kater's* rate of turn. *Obersteuermann* Hartmann then manually entered the data into the boat's analog attack computer. Mechanical connections to the attack periscope and gyrocompass already had automatically transmitted the U-boat's current position and speed as well as the target's bearing into the attack computer. In seconds, the computer calculated a firing solution, which it then automatically fed into the waiting torpedoes' guidance systems.[84]

Despite two more enemy aircraft sightings that might jeopardize *Kater's* survival after the attack, at 09:32 Marbach barked the torpedo launch order into the speaking tube that ran between the conning tower and the *Zentrale* below. A palmed hand immediately pushed against the master launch switch on the fire control panel, where red lights identified the armed torpedo tubes. Firing switches I and IV instantly sent electrical signals to the tubes to trigger a blast of highly compressed air against a heavy piston behind each torpedo. The compressed air blasts pushed the 1,600 kilogram monsters out of their tubes. Once outside the boat, the *LuTs'* electric motors engaged automatically and propelled the deadly warheads toward their targets. Forty-five seconds later all hands aboard the U-boat heard the unmistakable detonation of a torpedo, followed by cracking, breaking and sinking noises that continued for three minutes. Shortly afterward the boat rose to periscope depth. Marbach scanned the horizon in all directions for the destroyer but saw nothing. Momentarily, only the clear sound of the still-running second *LuT* disturbed the otherwise eerie silence. With the target now nowhere in sight and almost silent hydrophone readings, *Kater's* skip-

---

84.   *KTB*, 8 June 1944; and Stern, 86, 92-93.

per and crew concluded they had sent the destroyer to the bottom of the Channel at BF 2739.[85] Karl quietly cheered his boat's successful attack, and knew the Canadians would have celebrated sinking U-953 had the fortunes of war momentarily favored the destroyer instead of the U-boat.

Renewed sawing sounds suddenly broke the relative calm six minutes after the first torpedo detonated. Two minutes later *Kater's* second *LuT* exploded somewhere in the distance, to what effect no one knew. Marbach again made a panoramic sweep of the surface and sighted a second destroyer approach from the east-northeastern horizon, and a third out of the north-northwest. He had restricted his use of the periscope because the scope's trailing wake during daylight was certain to attract the attention of RAF Coastal Command ASW aircraft that swarmed over the Bay and the Channels. The powerful whines of the destroyers' fast-turning screws were again drowned out by the mysterious sawing sounds. The Allied warships closed the distance between themselves and U-953 before Marbach realized the present danger. While the skipper pondered his attack options, the irritating noises that emanated from both destroyers ceased and immediately were replaced by the familiar and dreadful resonance of spinning propellers on their deadly approach. The acoustic torpedoes in tubes II and V suddenly provided the best hope for the U-boat to defend herself. At 09:44 the third destroyer turned sharply to starboard and steamed at high speed on a westward course only eight hundred meters from *Kater's* stern. In seconds Marbach called his coordinates to Hartmann, who then engaged the attack computer to feed the target data into the torpedo that waited in tube V.

"*Rohr funf fertig! Rohr funf los!*" Marbach commanded at 09:45. The *Zaunkönig* launched from the stern tube and charged toward the third destroyer. Meanwhile, the second destroyer closed to within eight hundred meters of U-953 before she tacked hard onto a northerly course. The warship's bridge watch probably had detected a disturbance above the U-boat that gave away the boat's position.

Through his scope, Marbach suddenly watched twenty to thirty objects fly skyward and toward the U-boat. The projectiles splashed into the surface and detonated with depth charge force, but caused no damage. *Skeena* had fired a barrage of twenty-four hedgehogs from a distance of 220 yards, but came up short of her target.

"*Rohr zwei fertig! Rohr zwei los!*" Marbach again ordered, and the second *Zaunkönig* boiled out of Tube II and started for the destroyer at a fifty-three

85.   *KTB*, 8 June 1944; and Stern, 86.

degree angle from its broadside target. The skipper quickly scanned the area through the attack periscope; several more destroyers steamed into view dead ahead at four to five thousand meters.[86]

Skeena's bridge watch suddenly shouted a warning that a torpedo was headed directly toward the ship's bow. Commanding officer (Lieutenant Commander) P.F.X. Russell instantly ordered the ship steered hard to starboard. The helmsman spun the pilot wheel with all the energy he could muster, and in seconds *Skeena* began a violent right turn in response. Down on the main deck, torpedoman Lee Steinhoff leaned over the starboard railing just seconds after the end of the maneuver to see the torpedo race by on a parallel course five feet from the destroyer's steel plated broadside. The missile then struck *Skeena's* CAT gear being towed well astern and exploded with startling ferocity and a shock wave that surged through the U-boat.[87]

"Auf Tiefe gehen!" Marbach ordered. U-953 plunged from periscope depth and was steered hard, bearing south, as the hydrophone operator detected sonar signals searching for the submerged boat. After 128 seconds and a 1600-meter run, the first *Zaunkönig* detonated. The loud explosion reverberated through *Kater's* hull, and immediately was attended by thirty seconds of sounds the *Ubootfahrer* attributed to a foundering warship breaking apart and sinking. The second *Zaunkönig* had run thirty-five seconds and a distance of only 440 meters before its 274 kilogram warhead plowed into *Skeena's* CAT gear. U-953 quickly drifted sixty meters below the surface and waited for the anticipated depth charge response to the torpedo attack. From the near distance the men heard distinct shaking, cracking and hissing sounds for three or four minutes that unquestionably confirmed to them that the fourth torpedo had struck its target. The short intervals between the torpedo launches and the necessity to protect his boat and crew from an expected counterattack did not allow Marbach to visually confirm that any of the targets had been sunk before he ordered U-953 to the bottom of the Channel.

Karl Baumann and all others aboard U-953 were convinced beyond question that they had heard the death knell of three enemy destroyers during a single engagement—an impressive feat of arms few had experienced even during the heady early days of the U-boat war. The men would remember this day for the rest of their lives, but they now listened and waited apprehensively for retribution from Allied ships and aircraft above. Instead, a strange silence took hold, if only

---

86.   *KTB*, 8 June 1944; and "Report of Attack on a U-Boat, 8th June, 1944."
87.   Chance and Steinhoff interviews; and *KTB*, 8 June 1944.

briefly. Two enemy destroyers soon steamed toward the U-boat from beyond the horizon. At 09:53 *Kater* released a number of *Bold* decoys, chemical containers that unleashed dense clouds of hydrogen bubbles to create false sonar readings. While the bubble clouds distracted the attention of the sub-killers, U-953 silently skulked away and three minutes later settled softly onto the Channel floor, sixty-two fathoms below the surface.[88]

The distinct sounds of the two destroyers at 10:00 indicated their fast approach from the west-northwest. For the next eighty minutes the destroyers sailed slowly and deliberately, like a stalking hunter, back and forth directly above the U-boat. All the while, the warships deployed their CAT gear decoys, which vigorously grated on the fraying nerves of the *Ubootfahrer.* The mysterious

---

88.   *KTB,* 8 June 1944; and Miller, 111. Marbach noted in the *KTB* that the three destroyers were of the H-Class, one of which bore the marking H90. He actually may have mistaken hull number H00 on the Canadian destroyer *Restigouche* for H90, the hull number for the destroyer HMS *Broadway,* which at the time was in service off Rosyth, Scotland and did not participate in the D-Day invasion or its defense. See Chandler and Collins, 578. According to *The D-Day Encyclopedia,* all four torpedoes from U-953 exploded prematurely in the hard wakes from the destroyers HMCS *Restigouche* (H00, C-Class), *Qu'Appelle* (H69, F-Class), *Saskatchewan* (H70, F-Class), and *Skeena* (D159, A-Class), as did four that were launched on 7 June from U-984, and two from U-621. According to the *Encyclopedia* entry, none hit the destroyers during the confrontation. Marbach reported the attack in detail in the *KTB* entry of 8 June, but duly indicated he could not observe the ships sinking. In his post-mission report *KTB* entry on 18 June, Marbach reported three destroyers sunk, based upon evaluation of the sound and visual evidence that was available. Herbert Werner wrote that during the sea battle Marbach's U-953 "sank three destroyers." See Werner, 235. On 22 July 1944 Admiral Dönitz awarded Germany's highest decoration for bravery, the *Ritterkreuz*—the Knight's Cross of the Iron Cross—to Marbach for his reported sinkings during several missions against the Allied invasion fleet. See Werner, 238-239. Karl Baumann recalls that Marbach was promoted to *Kapitänleutnant* specifically for having sunk the three destroyers on 8 June. The confusion of after-action reports also attended the ships' log entries aboard the Canadian destroyers, where times recorded for German torpedo attacks and detonations varied, though not significantly, or were not recorded at all. *Skeena's* commanding officer also incorrectly reported that its attack on a U-boat on the morning of 8 June destroyed the boat. Amid all the conflicting war diary entries for 8 June, it can be said conclusively that U-953 launched all of the four torpedoes fired against Escort Group 12 on 8 June; and for all the ordnance expended that day, none of the U-boats in EG12's sector—U-621, U-953 and U-984—or any of the four destroyers was sunk.

sounds had to be some sort of new defense against acoustic torpedoes, the skipper reasoned; he also noted that the sawing noises alternated with sonar signals and other submarine location devices. The U-boat crewmen held their breaths and barely moved their muscles to avoid giving away their position. Despite *Kater's* nearly perfect silence, at 11:25 a destroyer steamed hard overhead, and immediately afterward six heavy splashes sounded through the U-boat hull. The Germans braced themselves for the horror they knew was coming as depth charges gurgled toward the Channel floor. Seconds later the explosive-laden canisters erupted with tremendous explosions that narrowly missed U-953. The now-familiar deafening detonations were quickly followed by shock waves that rattled through the boat and the gut-wrenched men trapped inside. Had the charges detonated beneath the boat, the upward force of the blasts easily could have ripped the boat in two. Mercy again had prevailed to spare *Kater* and all hands, but the Normandy invasion had taken the war into a new and more deadly phase. Escort Group 12 replied to every sonar contact with high explosives, even when maps indicated an attack location was the known site of a sunken ship; the Canadians intended to deprive any U-boat from attempting to hide next to the wreckage.[89]

Marbach spoke for all the men when he described in the *KTB* their first encounter with the strange sawing sounds and the as yet unknown source that produced them:

> It could be confirmed without a doubt that the "circular saw" sound drowned out the screw noises and they [the spinning propeller screws] were only audible directly over our boat. One heard the "saw" the loudest when the screw noises had already passed. The source of the sound is dragged behind the ship and can be turned off and on—as later observed through the periscope and sound detector. When the sound source is turned on, the destroyer runs no faster than 7 sm [*Seemeilen*] or has stopped. If the ship runs for a short time at higher revolutions...the "saw" is turned off. The "saw" will never be forgotten as a "nerve in the jaw" when it passes overhead.[90]

The Royal Canadian Navy continued to pound U-953. A destroyer charged above the U-boat at 11:50 and bounced sonar signals off her submerged hull. Five more depth charges soon plunged beneath the surface and sank toward *Kater* to explode with bone-jarring force. Then, at noon, the hunter-killers

89.   Chance, 98.
90.   *KTB*, 8 June 1944.

suddenly shifted their attention away from U-953 to one or more U-boats in another location. Marbach and crew listened to the distant resurgence of the sawing sounds interspersed by depth charge explosions, and hoped their fellow *Ubootkameraden* would live to fight another day. From a purely practical standpoint, however, the attacks on other boats presented an opportunity for U-953 to slink out of BF 2739 and continue her slow trek toward the invasion fleet. At 14:50, while the concerted attacks continued in the distance, the skipper ordered the boat to periscope depth. Slowly and deliberately, U-953 quietly came to life and momentarily lifted stern first off the sandy floor. Twenty-two minutes later Marbach took his seat at the attack periscope in the conning tower and scanned the surface. Two destroyers loomed off *Kater's* stern at 2,500 meters.

"Auf Gefechtsstation!" the worried skipper ordered. Only one torpedo, a *LuT* in tube III, could be launched immediately if either destroyer threatened the U-boat. The clatter and clank of chains and pulleys lifting the greased missiles into position behind their launch tubes was sure to attract warships to the area like wild beasts to a kill. The boat could only maintain stealth and run silently until the torpedo tubes were rearmed. Attempts to elude the destroyers during the remainder of the afternoon resulted in a deadly cat and mouse game that sent both hunters and hunted on a roundabout course through BF 2739 as each tried to outmaneuver the other. Uncharacteristically, the destroyers gave up the chase promptly at 16:00, but stood in sight of U-953 and again engaged the towed decoys. The maneuver taunted and challenged the U-boat to attack. The 12th Escort Group commanders were exceedingly confident their CAT gear would disrupt the ship-bound path of acoustic torpedoes. An Allied patrol plane appeared overhead and circled time and again above the destroyers, probably to attempt to detect *Kater* from the air by tracking the paths of any launched torpedoes back to the boat. By 17:55, however, the warships and aircraft disappeared. Marbach knew he needed to make the best use of any time that was devoid of enemy contact. He quickly ordered the boat to *Schnorchel* depth and directed the stern torpedo *Mixer* to reload Tube V. Crewmen quickly pulled up the steel floor plates in the stern compartment to gain access to the spare torpedo, then winched the one-ton monster out of its stowage rack. With the missile suspended by chains and positioned in front of the opened tube hatch, the men maneuvered the torpedo into the launch tube and tightly sealed the steel hatch. Not unexpectedly, two destroyers soon steamed toward *Kater's* position. Charging at high speed, the warships at a distance of three thousand meters slowed down and streamed their sound decoys. For nearly two hours the destroyers alternately stopped, disengaged their decoys and switched on their sonar as they tried to fix

the U-boat's position. Marbach ordered tube II reloaded with a *LuT* when the CATs resumed their dreadful howl, in order to cover the noise the reloading procedure would generate. With three torpedoes ready to fire, the skipper waited for the destroyers to steam to within a more favorable distance inside U-953's attack zone, but the warships stood well off from the boat. The Canadians again sailed out of sight at 22:30, and Marbach cancelled battle stations even as low, distant sawing sounds ground through the underwater currents to assault the ears of the weary *Ubootfahrer*. Crewmen in the bow reloaded a *LuT* into Tube IV, then stood down after the forty-five minute procedure was completed. Midnight finally brought an end to a long and arduous day of underwater combat, which many crewmen forever would regard as one of the most dramatic and memorable aboard U-953.[91]

The new day was ushered in by the sounds of war that chattered into the hydrophone operator's headset; continuous, changing sounds that warned of danger perhaps just beyond the horizon. The warning was enough to convince Marbach it would be suicide to engage the *Schnorchel* anywhere near the submarine hunter-killers. Instead, he ordered U-953 again to the Channel floor to sit out the Allies' strident attempts to prevent any U-boat from breaching the defensive cordon that stretched across the western entrance. "*Licht, Luft und Nerven sparen*" again became the watchword for all hands since the snort had not been engaged long enough to refresh the atmosphere or recharge the boat's electric batteries. Only time would tell how long *Kater* would remain effectively trapped on the bottom by the Royal Canadian Navy. When at 03:25 no nearby sounds were detected, Marbach risked rising to *Schnorchel* depth to replenish the dwindling electric power supply. He engaged the snort at 03:48 while the U-boat slowly ran just beneath the surface. Much to the skipper's consternation, the sound operator reported two sources that became louder before they eventually trailed off. More saw-sounders and depth charges were detected in the vicinity at 05:00. Allied surface activity simply was too dangerous for snort operations, so U-953 again submerged to the Channel floor; Marbach had determined the boat would stand down for the day at thirty-three meters depth. All hands remained as quiet as humanly possible throughout the day; no one wanted to be guilty of creating noise that could bring deadly consequences to his boat and his *Kameraden*. The rasping sounds were *Nervenklauen* to Karl Baumann—things that steal away one's nerves. Every man knew he was part of a life and death struggle that could end suddenly and at any moment. Reality itself was enough to cause introspec-

---

91. *KTB*, 8 June 1944.

tion and quiet contemplation that consumed many minutes and hours at the bottom of the Channel. At 20:30 another *LuT* was loaded into Tube I as carefully and quietly as the muscle straining task would allow. With all five tubes loaded, *Kater* was ready for either offensive or defensive combat operations. Only three Type V *Zaunkönige* remained for the mission, which actually had not yet begun since U-953 still had not entered the Channel to attack the Anglo-American invasion fleet. The boat again slowly lifted off the floor at 21:30. At the *Schnorchel's* operational depth the system began to vent out the miserable stinking air to relieve the crew. Several minutes later a large four-engine bomber flew into view four thousand meters from the sky periscope. Since the plane's altitude was only fifteen hundred meters, it probably was an RAF Coastal Command aircraft in search of U-boats. Marbach declared a *Flieger Alarm* and the snort immediately was disengaged. While *Kater* reached for the shallow depths the motor that powered a forward hydroplane rudder malfunctioned when seawater leaked through a broken seal around its housing. Worse, since the *Schnorchel* had not been engaged long enough to recharge the boat's batteries the remaining charge of electrical power was extremely low, which prohibited hiding again on the Channel floor. Marbach had no alternative but to resume *Schnorchel* depth to fully recharge the batteries while U-953 sailed into the eastern darkness. Meanwhile, the grating sawing sounds began anew and announced to the Germans that enemy warships had steamed back into the vicinity.[92]

The early morning hours of 10 June found the U-boat's *Schnorchel* fully engaged with the diesel motors providing underwater propulsion. To minimize the threat of detection Marbach ordered nearly constant sound readings and reduced the battery charging time to three hours, during which time the electric batteries could never be fully recharged. Nonetheless, the procedure would provide enough electrical power to maintain the boat sufficiently and safely during most underwater emergencies. All U-boat commanders received a radio telegram at 04:28 that warned of a minefield discovered at BF 3569, off the coast of France's Cotentin Peninsula. U-953 still was nowhere near the peninsula and the Normandy beachheads that lay farther east beyond the landmark. The boat had logged an average of just over thirty nautical miles each day since 6 June virtually every mile of which she was engaged in defensive maneuvers that effectively prevented her entry into the Channel. The Allied air and sea cordon so far had worked exceedingly well. An inexplicable absence of the enemy, however, finally opened a window of opportunity for Marbach to order U-953 onto an east-

---

92. *KTB*, 9 June 1944.

northeasterly course throughout the day toward the Channel entrance, though frequently at a plodding underwater speed of five knots. The boat made her first enemy contact of the day at 20:21 when the skipper, through the sky periscope, spotted a four-engine bomber and shortly thereafter four RAF Coastal Command aircraft on anti-submarine patrol. The hydrophone operator also reported destroyers on the move within their phalanx of steel, through which the passage of any U-boats seemed more unlikely each day. After Marbach recorded in the *KTB* that enemy destroyers had appeared on his starboard side and aircraft had swarmed across the sky, he concluded the war diary entry with classic understatement: "Without the snorkel [the mission] would be difficult to manage." At 22:00 four destroyers churned up hard wakes in *Kater's* immediate vicinity. In their role of U-boat killers, the Allies had amassed an unbelievable number of ships and aircraft to cover every square mile of the northern Biscay and the English Channel. The day ended as *Kater* and another *Schnorchel* boat nearby slowly and tentatively eased their way farther into the Channel entrance.[93]

U-953's commander had realized early into the crucial mission that the U-boats without *Schnorchels* that were ordered into the Channel stood no realistic chance to attack and survive the defensive elements arrayed over and around the gigantic Allied invasion force. That BdU had committed the boats to battle against such hopeless odds was emblematic of the desperate condition to which the Wehrmacht at large and the Kriegsmarine in particular had been reduced by 1944.

Beginning five minutes after midnight on 11 June, U-953 engaged her snort and partially recharged her batteries for three hours and ten minutes; all the while, the sound operator took careful readings every fifteen to twenty minutes to help prevent surprise attacks during the crucial procedure. By noon the boat had traveled fifty-six *Seemeilen* toward her objective over the previous twenty-four hours, and at BF 2826 was positioned near the northwestern Brittany coast. A radio message received by *Kater* at 15:27 warned that Allied destroyers had placed themselves to block any German warships—especially the fast, torpedo-firing *S-boote*—that might try to set out from the Cotentin port of Cherbourg. The U-boat touched the Channel floor at 16:06, where mechanics tore apart and repaired the forward depth rudder motor and fixed other minor equipment problems they found among the complex maze of mechanical components. The following day was attended by almost exactly the same routine. Repairs continued on the rudder motor and other systems while the boat remained on the bottom.

---

93. *KTB*, 10 June 1944.

In addition, torpedoes were pulled out from launch tubes for the *Mixers* to service and reset. The missiles' sensitive guidance systems frequently needed to be reset and realigned so that the jostling ride in their launch tubes would not render them entirely useless—or worse yet, dangerous to the safety of the U-boat herself. Under the best of conditions the procedure was arduous and painstaking; on the floor of the English Channel and under the noses of massed enemy U-boat killers, the chore was a nightmare. The full day of concentrated repair work limited U-953's advance to only thirteen *Seemeilen* farther north by midday on 12 June. No enemy contact was recorded in the *KTB* on either day, which doubtless was a welcome respite for the *Ubootfahrer* who had taken *Kater* into enemy infested waters. The temporary lull allowed the skipper to attend to several administrative details: at 20:36 he sent a terse message to BdU: "Have sunk 3 destroyers at BF 2739."[94]

Marbach ordered his boat to *Schnorchel* depth at five minutes before midnight, and for the third consecutive night cruised into the Channel while the electric batteries were recharged according to his newly established routine. The sound operator, as usual, took frequent readings to confirm the absence of any direct threats to the boat. At 02:16 a blinding light suddenly appeared out of the black sky at BF 2596 and disrupted the recharging procedure. A Coastal Command bomber with its Leigh Light beaming rumbled above the Biscay waves in search of unsuspecting U-boats riding on the surface. The plane's surprise and destroy tactic could have doomed U-953 had not the snort allowed the boat to remain underwater during the critical procedure. Despite the successful adaptation of the *Schnorchel* to combat operations, after one week of nearly constant contact with the enemy, *Kater* began to exhibit more extensive signs of mechanical fatigue.

At 08:20 the hydrophone operator detected several sounds Marbach thought necessary to investigate, but when the attack periscope in the conning tower was raised to eye level, the skipper was unable to see anything. The glass lens in the periscope head had become clouded and the drive mechanism that powered the scope no longer worked properly. An extended periscope was extremely vulnerable to the vibration forces of breaking waves and the momentum of the U-boat at periscope depth; breakdowns of the system were not uncommon and were a constant frustration and worry both for *Ubootfahrer* and design engineers alike. The skipper was blind to the unknown source of the external sounds that continued to approach U-953, so he ordered the boat toward the bottom of the Bay for a

---

94. *KTB*, 11-12 June 1944.

third day of mechanical repairs. The periscope had to be dried for several hours before it was taken apart to determine why it had malfunctioned and the extent of repairs required before normal combat operations could be resumed. Unknown but potentially threatening sounds recurred at 14:28; since the periscope still was being repaired Marbach's only course of action was to order the boat onto the Bay floor.

The massive bunker complex at Brest, the largest U-boat base on the French coast, was nearly impervious to damage until the RAF introduced the 12,000 lb. Tallboy bomb.

Kater touched down with a low, muffled crunch while the sounds of depth charges both far and near coursed through the U-boat. Repairs to the periscope finally were completed and the intricate mechanism was rebuilt by 19:15, when the grateful skipper ordered U-953 to periscope depth. He again sat in the commander's seat in the conning tower and peered into the scope to scan the horizon. After several moments the viewing mechanism malfunctioned as it had earlier in the day. Marbach noted that the problem originally had occurred at La Pallice and was repaired there. *Kater's* crucial mission to attack the massed ships of the Normandy invasion fleet now hung in the balance, and depended upon whether the periscope could be made functional long enough to take the boat farther into the Channel to launch her remaining torpedoes. The boat was raised to *Schnorchel* depth at 21:40 and vented out, but during the process an oil leak was discovered that apparently involved the invaluable snort. Officers gathered to discuss the problem and concluded the leak might leave a visible oil track on the surface that would lead directly to the boat. The skipper contemplated the seriousness of the situation and its likely manifestations, and decided his only proper course of action was to return to Brest for repairs. U-953 had been thwarted from her mission against the invasion force, not only by the Allies' strong defensive cordon, but by the U-boat herself. *Kater* reached BF 2648 at midnight, her farthest advance inside the Channel and toward the Anglo-American fleet. Marbach's only concern now was to safely return his damaged boat to Brest.[95]

Sailing back to port would be a slow process. The threat of detection by air and sea anti-submarine forces was extremely high. The unreliability of the periscope and the probable oil slick trailing behind the U-boat gave all advantages to the Allies. Still, the *Schnorchel* had been a lifesaver and would be relied upon to fulfill that role on the perilous underwater return to Brest. The snort was engaged at eighteen minutes after midnight on 14 June for three hours to prepare for *Kater's* homebound journey. Already concerned with a growing list of malfunctions, Marbach was notified at 02:45 that the forward depth rudder motor again had failed when the starter was tested. Since the hydrophone had not detected any present enemy threats, the skipper decided to continue a southwesterly course until 05:38, when he ordered the boat to the bottom of the Biscay. Frustrated mechanics labored there to repair the rudder motor yet again. The boat eased off the shallow Channel floor at 12:35 and soon reached periscope depth, where bright sunshine met Marbach's eyes when he peered into the sky scope's viewfinder. Under such perfect weather conditions the boat's outline at *Schnorchel* depth was clearly visible from the air, so the skipper ordered U-953 to the greater safety of the depths and a homeward run on electric power. The hydrophone remained silent throughout the day, so the slow plodding trek away from the Channel offered the crew some semblance of relaxation, though their vigilance had to remain high to react immediately to any emergency. Amid the tumult that took place in every corner of the battle area that comprised the Allies' Second Front in Europe, the U-boat sailed peacefully and without incident for the duration of the day. The calm evening was interrupted at 23:27 only by the powerful sucking action of the snort when it pulled air out of the U-boat's atmosphere and into the diesel engines while the batteries were recharged.[96]

The silhouette of a fast-moving warship crossed the dim horizon at 00:35 on 15 June, and prompted the *Zweiter Wachoffizier* to declare a *Schnorchel Alarm* on

95. *KTB*, 13 June 1944. See also Miller, 107, for a discussion of the frequent problems encountered with U-boat periscopes.
96. *KTB*, 14 June 1944.

the presumption that the Allied vessel had spotted U-953. The boat immediately dove for the bottom of the Bay to wait out any depth charge barrage that might follow. Mercifully for the *Ubootfahrer*, the expected attack never materialized, but the very possibility stranded the boat on the Biscay floor until 14:20. The hydrophone operator reported distant depth charge detonations and ships' screws chewing through the waves far astern as *Kater* rose to the surface. Marbach ordered a slight course change to sweep beyond the attack zone, but otherwise continued on his planned west-southwest track. The maddening sawing sounds that first taunted the men on 8 June again reverberated through the boat's hull at 15:42 and continued throughout the afternoon. As a result, *Kater* remained fully submerged until 19:37, when she rose to *Schnorchel* depth to recharge batteries and vent the air. After only five minutes, however, two de Havilland Mosquito fighter-bombers stormed out of the low horizon directly toward the U-boat. A *Flieger Alarm* was declared, which seconds later plunged the U-boat to relative safety of the Bay floor while the fast, wooden British aircraft blazed overhead. Once again the survival of the boat and her crew depended upon the severely diminished power supply that remained in the electric batteries. U-953 could not remain underwater for an extended period of time, but at 22:00, while worried officers and crewmen watched the needles on their ampere gauges drop precipitously, the raw rasping sounds of destroyers' CAT gear grew louder and louder. The submarine killers were coming.[97]

The *Ubootfahrer* ushered in 16 June with complete silence. Ten minutes after midnight two destroyers passed directly above U-953 and their saw sounders roared loudly past several seconds later. Marbach at last determined with finality that the sound producing devices were towed decoys designed only to deflect the paths of acoustic torpedoes, and posed no offensive threat. The nerve-grating buzz-saw sounds thus became merely irritating rather than terrifying. The Germans maintained strict silence in case the sounders suddenly went silent for sonar and other listening devices to locate U-boats in the vicinity. For nearly two hours the warships crisscrossed paths and churned up angry waves in a fruitless search for *Kater*, while their sound decoys loudly sawed almost without interruption. When the decoy sounds steadily lessened in volume, Marbach and crew realized the destroyers had given up their search for the U-boat and had sailed on to find more tempting targets elsewhere. After the hydrophone operator located the war-

---

97. *KTB*, 15 June 1944. Translation: *Zweiter Wachoffizier* was the Second Watch Officer, who when on watch duty commanded the boat in the skipper's absence from the conning tower or bridge.

ships about twelve nautical miles off *Kater's* beam, the skipper ordered U-953 off the sandy bottom of the Bay. The boat again resumed her south-southwest *Schnorchel* run to Brest at 02:17, though by that time the port was only twenty-eight *Seemeilen* to the southeast. RAF Coastal Command aircraft had long controlled the daylight skies over the Bay, which limited U-boats to the darkest hours of night to pass through the Allies' kill zones en route to and from the Biscay ports. For that reason the skipper chose to extend his course away from Brest to better prevent detection and wait out the daylight hours. As if it were part of a maddening conspiracy of machines against men, the faulty forward rudder motor again seized and ground to an abrupt stop at 05:00. Significant overhaul or motor replacement obviously was needed before the boat could again be committed to combat operations. In the meantime, mechanics once more disassembled and temporarily repaired the crucial dive component, which they hoped would remain operational until the boat sailed into port for permanent repairs. After an otherwise uneventful day U-953 picked up a radio message at 23:10 from an escort vessel twenty-seven hours out of Brest. With that news Marbach decided to rendezvous with the escort to maximize defensive firepower for the final leg of their return voyage. Together the concentration of anti-aircraft weapons would better protect both vessels.[98]

With her snort engaged during the early morning hours of 17 June, U-953 began her tenth day fully underwater. The skipper received a radio message from the First U-boat Flotilla at 00:47 that directed him to meet the escort at 03:00 on 18 June at a location near Brest known as *Punkt* 344. With the rendezvous time slightly more than a full day away, a faulty rudder motor that compromised the safety of any emergency dive procedure, and enemy air activity near the French coast, *Kater* set on a daylong roundabout course to the meeting point. Bright daylight and good visibility cast even greater danger upon the boat because her shallow cruising depth scarcely disguised her long slender silhouette beneath the waves. Remarkably though, Canadian destroyers and RAF Coastal Command aircraft so far had allowed the U-boat to slip back through the Allies' heavy defensive cordon deployed across the Biscay and the Channel entrance. U-953 reached the outer perimeter of the defensive zone in front of fortified Brest by late evening, which was visibly confirmed at 22:00 when the unmistakable and increasingly rare form of a Luftwaffe Ju88 patrol bomber appeared in the sky periscope. *Kater*, battered and damaged, had returned her men from an almost impossible mission. Dry land and a little relaxation beckoned the young sailors

---

98. *KTB*, 16 June 1944.

who had set out in the vain hope that somehow they might seriously damage the Normandy invasion force. Repairs would take at least several days, so *Ubootfahrer* began to plan and plot a few brief diversions.[99]

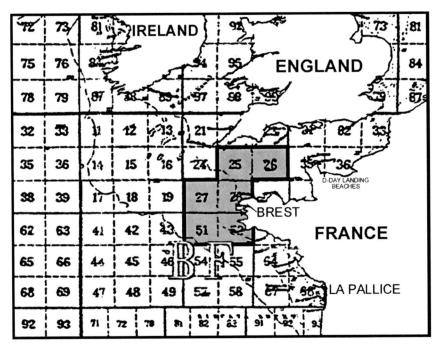

U-953's abortive mission to attack the Normandy invasion forces in the English Channel included torpedo attacks against three destroyers of the Royal Canadian Navy's 12th Escort Group; 6 June to 18 June 1944. Virtually the entire mission was conducted underwater by employment of the boat's *Schnorchel* breathing system. Shaded grid squares indicate U-953's area of operations.

U-953 rose to *Schnorchel* depth a few minutes after midnight on Sunday, 18 June, to pull luxurious fresh air into her interior for sixteen minutes. At 00:45 the snort was disengaged while Marbach scanned for enemy aircraft through the sky periscope. A blazing white light suddenly illuminated the east-northeastern horizon in cold artificial daylight, and flared for fifteen minutes before complete darkness recaptured the night. The U-boat commander worried that the eerie blinding light revealed a devastating attack against a German ship or another sub-

---

99. *KTB*, 17 June 1944.

marine, and decided to contact FdU West for any information headquarters might be able to relay. He then ordered the boat to eleven meters depth to give his radio operator the prescribed underwater environment to transmit his signal. For more than one hour, until 02:00, the radio operator attempted to raise FdU West without success. Then, with an hour remaining before the scheduled rendezvous with the escort vessel, *Kater* pushed ahead on diesel power with air supplied by the snort as she closed the final *Seemeilen* to her assigned meeting point.[100]

Marbach ordered U-953 to the surface for the first time since the sixth of June. At 02:32 the leading edge of the bow erupted from beneath the surface like a shark lunging for floating chum. Down in the *Zentrale* the skipper, watch party and gunners wore red-tinted goggles to help their eyes adjust immediately to the darkness outside. Karl Baumann and the others assigned to the 37mm *Flak* gun anticipated an extended period at battle stations that night, and had agreed to take a snack with them to enjoy on deck in the fresh sea air. On their way to the *Zentrale* one of the gunners snatched a loaf of bread out of a hammock and another lifted a block of butter out of its refrigerated container. When Marbach ordered the lights dimmed in the control room, Karl took advantage of the half-darkness to pull down a stick of salami that swung from a nearby pipe. As he stuffed the salami inside his gray leather jacket the main hatch cover sprang open and the *Ubootfahrer* tore through the portal to their weapons and lookout positions. The watch party raised their binoculars to their eyes without hesitation, wary that enemy air and sea traffic might pose an immediate threat to the boat. Marbach also scanned the horizon in all directions for the German escort vessel that was due at 03:00, and quickly discovered the escort was nowhere in sight. The frustrated skipper had hoped to reach Brest and the safety of the U-boat bunker before dawn.[101]

Each 37mm gunner swung himself beneath the *Wintergarten* railing and planted his feet onto the lower gun deck as U-953 sailed into grid square BF 5224, twenty-eight nautical miles west-northwest of Brest. Karl was revived by the fresh air and openness of the Biscay after having been sequestered nearly two weeks inside *Kater's* steel chamber. Despite the *Schnorchel* that vented the foul air out of the boat's interior each day, the inhospitable artificial environment had incubated a thoroughly unwholesome odor that assaulted the senses. Myriad dangers attended gunner Baumann at his battle station, but he was grateful to be a

100. *KTB*, 18 June 1944.
101. *KTB*, 18 June 1944.

member of the gun crew and watch parties for the opportunities they presented to ride on the deck of the surfaced U-boat.

Both 20mm cannon crews worked feverishly on the *Wintergarten* to ready their anti-aircraft weapons. If enemy aircraft attacked while U-953 followed the escort into port, the gun crews would have to stand and fight. While the 37mm crew gathered on the lower deck the 20mm teams above them loaded large metal canisters of high-explosive rounds onto the twin-barreled cannons. Seconds later the starboard 20mm crew pivoted their weapon toward the sea to test-fire it according to standard procedure. No one in Karl's crew noticed that the twin 20mm gun barrels were aimed at a shallow angle from U-953 and not fully ninety degrees from the boat as prescribed. Nor did they give second thought to the inherent warning sound the weapon issued when Poldi Kabert pulled the lever to load the first round into both chambers of the 20mm *Flakzweilling*.

An explosion of startling ferocity jarred everyone on deck when *Obermaat* Kabert pressed the trigger. A millisecond later, hundreds of red-hot steel shards sprayed across *Kater's* starboard side and splashed into the water. One of the heavy barrels of a 20mm cannon had been obliterated, blown apart probably from some seaborne obstruction. The 20mm crew stood shocked and confused; below them, the 37mm gunners on the *Wintergarten* had no time to react to the unexpected blast, and stood by their weapon while the lethal shrapnel zinged past them. A second too late, the men instinctively crouched down and shielded their faces from the explosion. Regaining their wits, shaken crewmen stared at the demolished, smoldering 20mm cannon. Miraculously, no one lay dead on the deck from the mishap.

"What happened?" the men on deck asked rhetorically. No answer was necessary as the reality of the moment immediately asserted itself. Marbach leaned over the conning tower railing and gravely observed the scene. Though the crewmen had been spared, there now was one fewer gun to protect the boat precisely at the time that mechanical problems prevented *Kater* from diving quickly if an attack materialized out of the night.

Still dazed by the fury of the explosion, Karl suddenly was startled by a sharp stinging pain in his left side. In the darkness he quickly ran his hand across his life vest above the site of the irritation and found a large section had been torn to shreds. Beneath his vest, his thick leather coat also had been ripped open. A bewildering unreality swirled around him as he stood on deck; he could not understand how or why his vest and coat suddenly had jagged tears in them. He ignored the animated crewmates around him who spoke excitedly about the blast and the destroyed gun.

"Do I have a hole in my jacket?" Baumann asked as he fumbled with the shreds of canvas and leather.

A gunner bent down to focus his vision in the dim light of the clear night sky. "You're bleeding!" the man exclaimed.

Unable to comprehend his situation and without another word, Karl slowly walked away from his gun and climbed onto the *Wintergarten.* When he finally made his way to the bridge the gunner, obviously in distress, presented himself to the skipper according to navy protocol.

"*Obergefreiter Baumann. Bietet abwärts gehen zu dürfen?*"[102]

Without hesitation Marbach granted permission to return belowdeck. Karl stepped onto the ladder inside the main hatch and clumsily slid through the portal, down into the *Zentrale.* The Second Officer stood nearby loading 20mm rounds into a large ammo magazine. *Leitender Ingenieur* Hans Stemmler, U-953's Chief Engineering Officer, looked up from his work, irritated that his concentration had been interrupted by the young seaman standing before him.

"What are you doing back down here?" the *L.I.* demanded to know.

"I—I have a hole in my jacket," Karl muttered in reply to the chief engineer—unsure why he explained his presence so illogically.

"You don't come back down here just because you have a hole in your jacket," Stemmler snarled.

The young gunner did not respond to the upbraiding, but looked down at his side as he slowly pulled up his life vest, leather jacket, and tattered sweater. The first sight of his wound horrified him: a large section of his left side had been slashed open by shrapnel from the explosion. The *L.I.* stared with disbelief at the exposed tissue and intestine, blood-smeared skin and saturated clothing. Luckily, the searing-hot shrapnel had cauterized the major vessels inside the gaping wound to stop most bleeding, but the ragged incision was very deep. The physical shock that began to set in almost instantly after the explosion now overwhelmed the grievously wounded young gunner. Karl's knees grew weak, his world went dark, and he sank into Stemmler's arms.

A brief entry in U-953's war diary reported the accident in a few spare words: *Beim Anschießen Üb. 2cm-Zwilling Rohrkrepiarer, dabei Mtr. Ob. Gfr. Baumann durch Rohrsplitter verletst.*[103]

---

102. Translation: "*Obergefreiter* Baumann. May I please go down?" In the Wehrmacht, subordinates always were required to state their names when they made a request to a superior officer.

103. *KTB,* 18 June 1944. Translation: While firing 2 cm twin, tube burst, resulting in wounding *Matrosen Obergefreiter* Baumann by tube fragments.

6

Witness to a Siege

Karl Baumann desperately needed immediate attention for his savage wound. He was carried to the U-boat commander's bunk, but little more could be done to help him. Suffering from shock, he risked life-threatening infection in the unsanitary environment of the boat. Like most U-boats, U-953 normally carried no doctor on her missions.[1] Along with a shortage of available physicians, there simply was no room to carry an additional officer and adequate medical supplies. Doctors who earlier in the war had sailed on combat patrols died with alarming frequency when their boats were destroyed. BdU could not afford to further deplete the critically low number of Kriegsmarine doctors, and therefore had discontinued their assignment to U-boat patrols.[2] As a result, men seriously wounded or ill in the most distant expanses of the Atlantic sometimes suffered grievously and died for want of skilled medical help. By contrast, Karl was most fortunate; the large Wehrmacht *Lazarett* in Brest would be reached after sailing a few hours rather than days or weeks.[3]

Shortly after the blast, Marbach ordered a message transmitted to FdU West with an urgent request for permission to join the escort, which still had not arrived in the rendezvous area. The radio operator soon reported he was unable to send the request. Unbeknownst to Marbach and the radio operator at the time, the boat's antenna had sunk into the Bay, probably sheared off by shrapnel from the destroyed gun barrel. By the time another antenna was installed the boat's clock stood at 04:00. The escort ship still had not arrived and the last hours of darkness rapidly loomed. The skipper faced a difficult decision: U-953 either would have to sail unescorted through the German minefields, or wait for the

---

1. A Kriegsmarine doctor named Mulkau had briefly sailed on U-953, but had been transferred to shore duty by the time of the Normandy Invasion. Mulkau is included in the U-953 officer's register provided by the *U-boot-Archiv*.
2. Werner, 158.
3. Translation: *Lazarett* was a military hospital.

escort—which might never arrive—and risk air attacks that were almost certain to come with the morning light.[4] Concerned also about the seriousness of Karl's wound, as well as the greater safety of *Kater* and her entire crew, the skipper finally decided he could wait no longer for the escort ship.

"We'll go in on our own," Marbach declared. He ordered the entire crew topside except Karl, the radio operator, and the diesel mechanics. *Ubootfahrer* poured out of the main hatch and donned life vests as they swarmed about the main deck. Lookouts maintained their positions while the rest of the crew inflated several large rubber life rafts that would be their only salvation if the boat hit one of the floating underwater German mines or those that British aircraft frequently dropped into the Bay. *Kater's* huge diesels thundered to full power after the skipper, from the crowded bridge, ordered U-953 to proceed through the treacherous minefields. At the same time, the radio operator notified Marbach that he had overheard a message from the missing escort ship: "Being attacked by aircraft."[5]

Danger lurked silently under the waves as the boat navigated the narrow lane between hundreds of German-sown mines that lay unseen before the harbor entrance. If the boat detonated a mine, Karl thought, he would never make it out alive. Death likely would come with slow agony with an unstoppable wave of seawater pouring through the ripped hull to engulf him where he lay. Better to die instantly 200 meters underwater, he concluded, by a depth charge imploding the pressure hull.

The watch party sighted a *Vorpostenboot* on picket duty sometime before 05:00. In view of the severity of Baumann's injury, Marbach ordered an urgent signal sent to the boat to request the immediate assistance of the ship's doctor, should one be aboard.[6] A short time later the vessel dropped anchor next to U-953 and dispatched her doctor with a small boat that bobbed unsteadily toward the boat. The middle-aged navy doctor who clambered onto the deck probably never had descended into the bowels of a U-boat. Amid mysterious and claustrophobic mazes of pipes and valves belowdeck he nervously examined the wounded man. Harsh mechanical noises emanated from the boat's interior and accentuated the doctor's trepidation. He administered a powerful dose of morphine to counter the severe pain that had begun to wrack Karl's body, and asked if there was anything else that could be done to make the patient more comfortable. Karl

---

4.   *KTB*, 18 June 1944.
5.   *KTB*, 18 June 1944.
6.   *KTB*, 18 June 1944. Translation: Literally, "outpost boat;" in U.S. Navy parlance, a "picket boat."

asked for a cup of juice to quench his parched throat, which the doctor quickly prescribed. Then, without another word he fled the commander's cabin and scrambled up the ladder into the fresh air, grateful to return to his own ship. The radio operator, who was trained in first aid, waited anxiously for the doctor to leave, then immediately admonished Karl.

"Baumann, *trinken Sie nicht!!!*" he warned, fearful that serious or fatal peritonitis might set in as a result of the apparent internal injuries.[7] Karl realized the wisdom of his trusted crewmate above that of the doctor, who probably would have agreed to any request simply to hasten his own departure from the U-boat. He refused the juice, despite his raging thirst that would intensify terribly as *Kater* sailed toward Brest and the Wehrmacht hospital.

While the ship's doctor looked over Karl's wound a second German escort vessel arrived, and at 05:00 skillfully guided the *Vorpostenboot* and U-953 through the remainder of the minefields and into the fortified harbor that guarded the port city. The *Ubootfahrer* expected to be attacked any moment as dawn gave way to the bright sunshine of early morning. Officers and men, crowded about the deck and the conning tower, finally breathed sighs of relief as the helmsman slowly maneuvered *Kater* toward the gaping entrance of the giant U-boat bunker. Before the boat sidled stern-first into *Boxe* B1 at 08:20, however, Marbach ordered the boat to a nearby pier.[8] There crewmen tossed several mooring lines to sailors on the pier as stretcher bearers stood by to remove the wounded gunner from the boat.

Karl's body surged with pain when he was lifted out of the skipper's bunk and lashed onto the stretcher. The next minutes were even more excruciating as Karl was hefted up the vertical conning tower ladder and through the boat's main hatch. Gravity became his greatest foe as the weight of his lower body stretched and pulled open the gaping wound without mercy. The young sailor had resolved never to cry out, no matter how terrible the pain; in such moments of torment he wondered if he could keep his promise. The torturous journey finally ended with his arrival by ambulance at the large, main Wehrmacht *Lazarett* in Brest, more than a mile from the Kriegsmarine base. Six endless hours had passed since he had been severely wounded by the nearly lethal mass of molten steel. Though he did not know it at the time, his career as a U-boat crewman was over. He had sailed more than 11,100 nautical miles aboard U-953. He had defended his boat against air attack and had endured more depth charge attacks than he cared to

---

7. Translation: "Baumann, drink nothing!!!"
8. *KTB*, 18 June 1944.

remember. Now, he wished for nothing more than to be able to recover fully from his wound and return to the boat he loved and his *Kameraden* with whom he had formed an indelible brotherhood.

Baumann was carried into an x-ray room, where an orderly knelt down and untied the cords that bound him to the stretcher. The attendant then told him to climb onto the x-ray table. The wounded gunner was incredulous, and complained that he was unable to stand up because of his injury, much less climb unassisted onto the examination table. Finally, several aides arrived and lifted the stretcher parallel to the x-ray table, onto which Baumann painfully inched himself. X-ray photographs clearly showed a large jagged chunk of shrapnel lodged inside Karl's intestine. The stark image of malignant steel and rent tissue prompted the medical staff into fast action. He was wheeled into an operating room, placed on the operating table on his right side, and tied down until he was entirely immobilized. Anesthesia was administered directly into his spine. In seconds Karl's body felt the dead weight of temporary paralysis, though he remained fully awake and coherent during the long operation.

"How much longer?" Karl asked the surgeon after what seemed like hours.

"We're not at a carnival," the doctor barked, "we're in an operating room! Keep your mouth shut!"

The patient's thoughts replayed *Kater's* desperate mission to Normandy, and the events that led up to his incapacitating wound. Perhaps to allay his own fears and uncertainty for the future, and to put his life into perspective, the young seaman issued a bold statement to the surgeon and his assistants.

"We sank three destroyers—so if I die, it's worthwhile."

While Karl suffered through surgery and the first hours of recovery, U-953's commander evaluated his thwarted *Feindfahrt* to the English Channel. From the beginning of the mission, he wrote, his only chance for success clearly lay with the *Schnorchel*-equipped boat's ability to remain continually submerged to avoid detection during the voyage to and from *Kater's* objective. Had the boat infiltrated into the Channel, night operations alone would have been possible, but only because of the inherent confusion that would attend the massive buildup of Allied ships in the narrow strait. Marbach then recorded his observations regarding the technical capabilities U-953 had exhibited while she remained underwater entirely for thirteen days. In spite of numerous enemy contacts and mechanical difficulties, he concluded with obvious pride, "the crew held up well as always."[9]

---

9.   *KTB*, 18 June 1944.

The crew had performed with skill and courage against the concentrated Allied naval and air forces that had been deployed to stop the U-boats in the Bay of Biscay and the western entrance to the Channel. The Allies had determined that as many as one hundred U-boats in the Bay would be ordered to attack the Normandy invasion forces. In response to the threat, the British had established a constant air cordon over the northern Biscay. Nineteen squadrons of maritime patrol bombers had been committed to the operation, supported by four squadrons of fighter-bombers and five squadrons of torpedo bombers. Between 6 June and 10 June a total of thirty-six Biscay U-boats were spotted; twenty-three were attacked, of which four were damaged and six were sunk. During June alone, the Allies would fly 4,724 combat sorties over the Bay in search of U-boats and would launch seventy-five attacks. By the end of the Normandy campaign Allied aircraft would destroy twenty-eight U-boats, with another five sunk by combined aircraft and surface vessel attacks, and damage twenty-nine others. U-boats would shoot down thirty-eight aircraft, while another twenty-two planes would be lost over the Bay due to accidents and other causes. In concert with the air cordon, three destroyer groups, seven frigate escort groups and three escort aircraft carriers had formed a massive surface fleet in front of the Channel entrance. Against a loss of seven Allied escorts, three landing ships and thirteen transports with damage to one escort and six transports, eighteen *Schnorchel*-equipped boats would be sunk. Had mechanical problems not cut short her desperate mission to Normandy, U-953 may have succumbed to the overwhelming superiority of Allied might as well. Enemy aircraft and warships had dogged the U-boat during much of her 475-mile underwater sortie.[10]

Quick death would have been less traumatic for Karl, whose recovery was to be exceedingly slow and painful. He eventually came to suspect his own culpability in his lingering agony, but never informed the medical staff of his suspicions. For what seemed an eternity after surgery, by necessity he was denied anything to eat and drink. Unrelenting thirst seemed to make time stand still; nothing but a wet swab could be given to slake his dry mouth, throat, and parched lips. The doctors went so far as to post a guard at the door to his intensive care room to prevent visiting *Kameraden* from secreting liquid or edible contraband to him.

The day following surgery again was marked by the complete absence of food and liquids. A nurse briefly interrupted the endless monotony when she delivered

---

10.   Chandler and Collins, 157-159, 577-578. The air campaign was directed by RAF Coastal Command, which formed the numerous squadrons into No. 19 Group, based in Plymouth, England.

a vase of carnations from Karl's crewmates. Rather than lift his depleted spirits the inviting, cool water in vase that sat on his bedside table taunted the perished youth more than he could bear. When at last a distraction outside the doorway caught the guard's attention, he grabbed the vase, pulled out the carnations, and gulped down the water to the last drop. He stuffed the flowers back into the empty vase and sank back onto his pillow, his thirst momentarily quenched.

The bitter-tasting fluid that helped relieve Karl's insatiable thirst and flagging spirits also may have poisoned his system. In a matter of hours his fragile condition worsened significantly. He would suffer terribly for more than three months while the trauma to his intestines resisted healing and the doctors kept open the wound in his side to apply direct topical treatment. He dreaded the daily medical procedure, where a Wehrmacht doctor or orderly pulled long strands of soiled and blood-dried cotton out of the raw wound, which he then cleaned and repacked with fresh sterilized lengths. A course, flax-like substitute was used when the antiseptic material no longer was available, which turned the painful procedure into a purely excruciating ordeal. The doctors and nurses constantly feared deadly peritonitis would set in through the wound, which by its very nature offended the senses and upset visitors' squeamish stomachs. More extensive treatment was unavailable because of the alarmingly limited medical supplies on hand.

Leitender Ingenieur Stemmler visited Baumann the day after surgery, and openly carried a foil-wrapped package past the guard without being challenged.

"You forgot your salami," the *L.I.* declared as he handed over the large sausage link that the 37mm gunners had not had an opportunity to eat. The young gunner was profoundly moved by Stemmler's compassion for an enlisted crewman and his gesture of forgiveness over the obvious theft from the boat's food supply.

The guard at the doorway stared wistfully at the sausage stick after the *L.I.* left the ward. Karl rightly concluded that army troops in the desperate year of 1944 probably had not seen, much less eaten, a fraction of the food that well-fed *Ubootfahrer* took for granted. Unable to eat presently anyway, Karl held out the salami to the young soldier. The gray-uniformed young *Landser* gratefully accepted the package and rejoiced in the unexpected windfall as if it were manna from Heaven.[11]

For six days while U-953 was laid up for critical repairs, visits from Karl's crewmates helped him pass endless painful hours. Then, late on 24 June, Mar-

---

11. *Landser* was a nickname given to members of the German Army, who fought the war on land rather than on the sea or in the air.

bach and crew quietly slipped the boat out to sea under the veil of darkness.[12] Their absence from Karl's bedside the next day revealed that his good friends had sailed out of the relative safety of *Festung* Brest and returned to the perilous unforgiving sea and the hazards of combat.[13] By virtue of his own patrol experience he logically concluded that U-953 could have been dispatched far into the Atlantic, but most likely had sailed again toward the Channel. Despite all the hardships and conceivable ways to die horribly on or beneath the sea, he longed to sail again with his trusted comrades and *Kapitän*. All at once a pall of loneliness and anxiety enshrouded him while he lay helplessly in his hospital bed, fully aware that he would not see their familiar faces again for days, weeks, or months—if ever. No one but fellow combat veterans could ever appreciate Karl's painful longing to return to the U-boat and his *Kameraden*.

The unrelenting danger of submarine warfare dogged U-953 throughout what was to be a twenty-eight day patrol. Marbach's mission was to reconnoiter with ten other U-boats to set up an offensive line along the English coast and intercept the post-invasion traffic that sailed across the Channel to the Normandy beaches. *Kater* was forced to run a gauntlet of minefields, motor torpedo boats, destroyers, anti-submarine aircraft with airborne searchlights, and illumination flares that transformed the coveted darkness into moments of terrifying, flickering daylight. While Baumann languished in the *Lazarett*, hundreds of U-boat crewmen in their attack boats sweated out mind-numbing hours on the Channel floor. There they waited silently for unseen but ever-present threats to pass before they cautiously resumed their long *Unterwassermarsch* toward a forty-mile battle line between Portland and St. Catherine's Point on the Isle of Wight. Sound technicians constantly monitored the dissonance of war overhead as *Wabos* and *Fliebos* sought out illusive underwater targets with detonations and shock waves that rumbled through the murky waters. Though U-953 finally breached the Channel's western boundary on 29 June, Marbach had to wait nearly two days for orders via radio to establish a *Schwerpunkt* with two other boats farther north toward Portland.[14] The boats lay on the southern edge of a traffic lane jammed with ships that formed a supply lifeline for the Allied invasion forces. Amid the seemingly unbroken double line of freighters, destroyers, and gunboats, troopships ferried fresh combat units and support personnel to the Second Front. Through their periscopes, U-boat skippers spied silver barrage balloons that

---

12. *KTB*, 24 June 1944.
13. Translation: Fortress Brest.
14. *KTB*, 24 June–5 July 1944. Translation: The *Schwerpunkt* was the boat's zone of responsibility, or strongpoint.

floated passively overhead to protect larger ships from German aircraft that by then rarely pierced the sky. "*Diese sind unser Ziel!*" Marbach exclaimed as he scanned the panorama of tempting targets.[15] The now familiar routine of attack, pursuit, and evasion soon commenced with the launch of torpedoes and the sounds of detonations and ships in peril.

Karl was elated and relieved on 22 July when haggard crewmates finally returned to Brest. They had sought him out first at the big Wehrmacht hospital, but learned that their wounded gunner had been moved to a *Revier* at the Navy base operated by the First U-boat Flotilla.[16] The visitors realized at first glance that Karl's condition had deteriorated significantly since they had last seen him. They tried to cheer their gravely ill crewmate as they recounted the Channel mission and their latest battles. U-953 most assuredly had sunk a fourth destroyer and three cargo ships to increase the skipper's total score by twenty thousand tons, though BdU had not yet confirmed the skipper's reports. As usual, the victories were discussed in terms of cold, inanimate tonnage rather than the number of enemy lives lost.[17]

Crewmates visited frequently whenever *Kater* was in port, which boosted Karl's spirits immeasurably. They plied their friend Kuddel with the latest news and rumors about the state of the U-boat war and the Normandy invasion, and treated him with lavish accounts of their latest exploits on land and at sea. The men retrieved his seabag from the storage bunker before one visit and delivered it to him. Their thoughtful act was stark but unintentional evidence that their *Kamerad* would not return to U-953. Resigned to his uncertain fate and future, Karl sighed and placed his newest souvenir—several inches of 20mm gun barrel shrapnel removed from his gut—into the seabag along with his few other possessions.

In addition to Karl's critical condition, his *Ubootkameraden* soon were troubled by other unsettling incidents that marked the hot summer days of 1944. A bomb planted in Adolf Hitler's conference room at the Wolf's Lair near Rastenburg, East Prussia on 20 July exploded and nearly killed the dictator. The

---

15. *KTB*, 5 July 1944. Translation: "These are our destination!"
16. Translation: A *Revier* was a small first aid clinic.
17. According to the *U-boot Archiv* in Cuxhaven, Germany, U-953 was officially credited with sinking on 7 July 1944 the 1,927 ton British steamer *Glendinning* while she escorted convoy ETC-27 in BF 3196 en route from the Arromanches landing beaches to London. Four of the crew of thirty-three were killed during the sinking. For the first time aboard U-953, the skipper observed and visually confirmed the sinking. See also Internet website www.ubootwaffe.net/ops/boat.cgi?boat=953.

Führer's immediate response to the assassination attempt by high-ranking members of the Wehrmacht had been swift and certain. He immediately tightened his stranglehold on the armed forces as he sought to root out every vestige of disloyalty among the ranks. While hundreds of guilty and entirely guiltless Germans alike were to suffer Hitler's vengeance with their lives, every member of the Wehrmacht would be required to render the straight-armed Hitler salute—an expression of renewed loyalty and absolute obedience—rather than the traditional hand salute.[18] Closer to Brest, the Allies soon would break through the stiff German defensive perimeter in Normandy and roll across the Brittany Peninsula toward the Biscay ports and the submarine bases. Though the Battle for the Atlantic already was irretrievably lost, the capture of the U-boat bases would sound the death-knell for the Ubootwaffe in France.

Baumann's physical deterioration was suggestive of the condition and plight of the entire Wehrmacht as the dark days of July surrendered to the even more depressing days of August. The Americans launched a bold armored assault into the Brittany peninsula on the first day of the new month, with Brest their ultimate objective. Karl realized that unless he recovered significantly from his debilitating wound, he would be left behind whenever U-953 and her crew set sail out of the fortress city for the last time. Minor wounds surely would not prevent his evacuation aboard the U-boat, but in his serious and worsened condition the unsanitary and dangerous undersea journey probably would prove fatal. He rationalized that the uncomfortable vacuum created by the *Schnorchel* might actually pull out his intestines through the wound in his side. With great apprehension, Karl accepted the fact that he had no choice but to remain at the *Revier* to endure whatever fate lay in the wake of the imminent battle for the city—quite possibly to die among the ruins of Brest.

In the early morning hours of 1 August, Lieutenant General George S. Patton, Jr. ordered his Third U.S. Army's 6th Armored Division of to launch an attack into the Brittany peninsula. Patton informed the Major General Robert W. Grow, the division commander, that he had wagered British Field Marshal Bernard Montgomery five pounds that American armor could capture Brest, "by Saturday night," five days hence. Old Blood and Guts smiled as he placed his hand on his subaltern's shoulder.

"Take Brest," the old cavalryman ordered.[19]

---

18. Werner, 237.
19. Martin Blumenson, *Breakout and Pursuit*, United States Army in World War II; The European Theater of Operations (Washington, DC: U.S. Government Printing Office, 1961), 370.

Patton predicated his attack order upon the belief that Brest would be defended by only two or three thousand troops. He did not reckon that the city had been reinforced by the elite 2nd Parachute Division, or that some fifty thousand German troops would be pushed into Brest, Lorient, and St. Nazaire by the American assault. Worse for the Allies, OKW had ordered each new fortress city to be defended to the last man.

The RAF attacked the Brest U-boat bunker on 5 August, about a ten-minute walk down a steep hill from the *Revier*. While air raid alarms wailed, medical aidmen hurriedly carried Karl on a stretcher into a nearby bunker. The sky soon rumbled with the throaty crescendo of sixty Merlin engines as a formation of fifteen Lancaster bombers of 617 Squadron approached the U-boat pens. Anti-aircraft gunners in *Flak* towers atop the bunker's high rooftop sent up a wall of steel from rapid-firing 40mm Bofors cannon. The barrage brought down one of the bombers, but the other Lancs and two accompanying Mosquito fighter-bombers maintained their course as if some invisible shield made them impervious to the exploding shrapnel. The planes pressed on through the *Flak* while the bomb-aimers lined up the target in their bombsight crosshairs.[20] The Lancs' cavernous bomb bays were so heavily laden that the great doors beneath their fuselages bulged open, unable to be fully closed during the flight from England.

Germans on the bunker roof and on the ground below watched in horror as a single gigantic bomb slowly fell from each Lancaster's gaping belly—twenty-one foot Tallboys that weighed over twelve thousand pounds and packed more than two tons of explosives. The Tallboys had been specially designed to tear through the twenty-foot-thick reinforced concrete roof of a U-boat bunker.[21]

Time stood still as the Tallboys shrieked directly toward the U-bunker's roof. Men who were not petrified by fright dove into any depression or beneath any cover they could find. The Bofors gunners crouched beside their weapons in a hopeless effort to save themselves. The giant missiles slammed onto the top of the bunker or around its base and disintegrated with deafening, earth-shaking explosions that reverberated across the city. Mangled bodies and body parts instantly spiraled off the *Flak* towers by the massive blasts and shock waves that roiled out from the impact points. Each of the concussions rumbled through Karl's bunker

---

20. The British referred to their aircrew bombardiers as bomb-aimers.
21. Schmeelke, 8. See also Mike Garbett and Brian Goulding, *Avro Lancaster in Unit Service* (New York: Arco Publishing Co, 1970), 5. The Lancs were flown by 617 Squadron of the RAF, whose men became known as "The Dam Busters" after their May 1943 attacks on the Mohne, Eder, and Sorpe River dams made them heroes and their exploits legendary. Such hazardous missions were their stock in trade.

seconds later with passing waves that slapped against loose objects and the people inside like a great invisible hand. The stretcher upon which he lay skidded several inches along the floor as each shock wave ripped through his concrete sanctuary.

The British 12,000 pound Tallboy bomb was developed to penetrate the thick concrete roofs of U-boat bunkers; Brest, 1944.

The 5 August bombing raid would be followed by more attacks; sixty-eight Lancs and Mosquito fighter-bombers attacked the U-boat pens at Brest, La Pallice and Bordeaux on 12 August. Twenty-eight Lancasters and a Mosquito fighter-bomber returned a day later to pound the Brest *U-bunker* and nearby warships. From all of the bombing missions a total of nine Tallboys struck the bunker roof, five of which penetrated the thick reinforced concrete.[22] An armada of 155 Lancasters and four Mosquitoes made two attacks on ships in Brest harbor on 14 August. The old French battleship *Clemenceau* and the cruiser *Gueydon* were left in shambles before the Germans could move them to positions where they would hinder Allied ship traffic after *Festung* Brest was captured. On the

---

22. Schmeelke, 8.

night of 25-26 August the RAF returned with fury as 334 bombers battered artillery positions near the city. Another twenty-four Lancs and a Mosquito launched a raid the next day on two ships in the harbor.[23] U.S. Eighth and Ninth Army Air Force bombers and fighters punctuated the skies over besieged Brest with even greater ferocity. Karl knew well that when the U-boat pens no longer were able to fairly guarantee the protection for which they were built, the scant number of surviving U-boats would be ordered to escape the siege. He acknowledged to himself that U-953 was destined to retreat soon from her former sanctuary, never to return.

Across the city, groups of soldiers, sailors and a large contingent of combat engineers feverishly worked to bolster the defenses of *Festung* Brest. The initial attack on the city began on 7 August and locked American troops against a determined force of 35,000 Germans.[24] U-boat crewmen without assigned boats were ordered into the front lines as infantrymen.[25] Gen. Patton's anticipated skirmish to take the city soon evolved into a major battle. Karl Baumann, immobile and unable to defend himself, lay trapped inside a fortress about to be taken under siege. He harbored no illusions about a miraculous, impossible salvation; and with the recent bombing raids he already had experienced a portent of the terror that was to come. His future seemed almost too dreadful to contemplate.

Ninety-nine authorized crewmen, high-ranking civilians, and military officials who had won passage out of the looming firestorm rushed aboard U-953 on 19 August as she prepared to sail out of Brest for the last time. Other desperate souls who somehow had learned of the boat's secret departure also gathered at the battered U-boat bunker. The uninvited had to be held back from the boat at gunpoint, for fear they would storm aboard and inundate the cramped interior.

The appointed time of departure arrived and passed. *Kater* remained dockside to the consternation of those aboard who actually knew the sailing schedule. The skipper had received late word that four technicians had been ordered out of Brest to avoid capture. After three days and numerous interminable delays, U-953's final departure out of Brest was cleared by *Korvettenkapitän* Werner Winter in one of his final acts as commander of the First U-boat Flotilla. Where the *U-Flotte* once numbered several hundred U-boats, U-953 now was virtually the only seaworthy vessel that remained in service.[26]

23. Royal Air Force Bomber Command 60th Anniversary; Internet website: www.raf.mod.uk/bombercommand/diary/aug44.html.
24. Geoffrey Perret, *There's a War to be Won; The United States Army in World War II* (New York: Random House, 1991), 342-343.
25. Werner; 239, 242.

On 22 August Karl's comrades dropped by the *Revier* one last time before they embarked upon their final patrol out of Brest. During their solemn visit Karl asked a special favor of helmsman Herbert Raschewski, his closest friend. When they made it safely back to the *Vaterland*, Karl implored, would Raschewski write to Anneliese Samhuber in Brambauer to inform her that her lifelong friend had been badly wounded and that his fate was uncertain? The forlorn helmsman readily agreed to Karl's wish. He would at least perform this last favor for his *Kamerad*; he could do nothing more.

Final farewells weighed heavily upon young men's hearts as Karl Baumann's crewmates reluctantly left his bedside. The timbre of the American assault that thundered outside underscored the urgency of their departure. An American armored task force had launched a preliminary attack a day earlier in the outskirts of Brest to close off a possible German escape route across the harbor from the U-boat base. With no friends now left to console him and share his burden, the fallen U-boat gunner prepared to face the full fury from the tempest of steel that was about to descend upon the center of Brest and Recouvrance, the western section of the city where the giant Kriegsmarine base was located. The sprawling naval base was the ultimate objective—and the ultimate target—of the American juggernaut.

In addition to Baumann, not all of U-953's crew manned the boat when she sailed for the last time out of Brest. Some had gone home on leave and were unable to return because the American stampede through France had cut off all routes between the Atlantic coast and Germany. Peter the tomcat had traveled home with one of *Kater's* crewmen, but the sailor gave the cat to some acquaintances at the Hotel Westminster in Paris after he and Peter were unable to continue their return trip to Brest.

The most conspicuously missing member of U-953's crew was *Oberleutnant* Karl-Heinz Marbach, *Kater's* affable commander. He had traveled to Berlin under express orders from Admiral Dönitz, who on 22 July awarded the *Ritterkreuz*, the highest award for valor conferred by the *Reich,* to the young skipper.[27]

Before his departure for Berlin and the award ceremony, Marbach had paid a pleasant visit to Karl. The skipper appeared in the advanced stages of the three-day alcohol binge he had staged for the crew to celebrate his Knight's Cross com-

---

26.   Werner, 242-247. Werner wrote that U-953 was the last to leave the doomed fortress; however, other sources report U-256 departed Brest more than a week later, on 3 September 1944.

27.   Werner, 238-239. The *Ritterkreuz* was the coveted Knight's Cross of the Iron Cross.

mendation and his upcoming promotion to *Kapitänleutnant* on 1 September. He usually managed to enjoy life even in the midst of the deadly firestorm of war. Marbach had fully intended to resume command of U-953, but advancing American troops thwarted his return to Brest. Reluctantly, *Kapitän* Winter realized he had lost another experienced U-boat commander as surely as if the skipper had succumbed to the sea. Winter named *Oberleutnant zur See* Herbert Werner to take over Marbach's boat and crew. Marbach would have wanted it that way; he knew Werner was a superb U-boat commander who had seen more than his share of combat. For several weeks Werner had busied himself for his first mission aboard U-953. He filled out *Kater's* incomplete crew with survivors from U-415, his former command. Several weeks earlier Werner had watched helplessly from the hillside above the port as his boat exploded in a huge geyser of water and flotsam from an underwater mine a British bomber had secretly dropped in front of the U-bunker.[28]

Profound loneliness swept over Karl as he contemplated the final departure of U-953. Most likely he never would see his *Kameraden* again, whatever the future might hold for them and for himself. Without their essential support and friendship, he would lie helplessly in his hospital bunk while the next uncertain chapter was played out in his war-shattered life. As for the progress of the war, he realized the Battle of the Atlantic was waged almost invariably with an advantage in ships, aircraft, and technical resources that belonged to the Allies. The Ubootwaffe would continue the fight with little more than courage alone. Karl Baumann continued to believe Germany was destined to win the war regardless of whether he survived to celebrate the ultimate victory. He would have been incredulous to know that the course of events that ultimately would determine his fate and future—and that of tens of thousands of fellow Germans trapped inside Brest—had been set into motion with Patton's wager of five pounds British currency.

The siege of Brest began at noon on 25 August by the U.S. Army's entire VIII Corps, commanded by Major General Troy H. Middleton, which replaced the 6th Armored Division. The massed Corps was composed of the 2nd, 8th, and 29th Infantry Divisions along with an armored task force.[29] Thirty-four battalions of artillery supported the assault troops with an astounding number of heavy weapons assembled to pour high explosive howitzer and cannon fire onto the city and its entrenched defenders. Eight thousand tons of artillery rounds were allot-

---

28. Werner, 239.
29. *Report of Operations*, 42.

ted to the siege, an ammunition allocation considered adequate for a six-day battle. However, only a portion of the American ordnance had arrived before the opening salvoes rained down on Brest. The ammo supply ultimately proved insufficient, and soon the siege was curtailed or suspended in various sectors until more artillery rounds could be committed to the battle.[30]

The *Revier* where Karl was sheltered was evacuated during the temporary lull in the American attack. The patients were moved by ambulance a few blocks to a giant *Lazarett,* an imposing concrete hospital bunker with large Red Cross symbols painted on the sides and roof. It was hoped that the red crosses would ward off enemy aircraft and artillery spotters, which otherwise were certain to concentrate their firepower on the huge concrete facility.

The battle resumed full intensity on 8 September and continued almost unabated for ten days. More than thirty-five thousand Americans fought aggressively for every building, concrete pillbox, and natural defensive position with a complete inventory of small arms and personal weapons, tanks, and artillery. Equally determined Germans, with the Second Parachute Division leading the defense of Brest, stubbornly defended their ground with their own array of infantry weapons and scores of anti-aircraft artillery pieces. They gave up territory only reluctantly when they were overwhelmed, wounded, captured, or killed.

A terrifying, incessant symphony of death resounded throughout the city. Artillery rounds fell into Brest with nerve-shattering whines that ended with dull thuds or sharp reports. Mortar rounds left their firing tubes with an innocuous, hollow thud, only to slam into targets with devastating explosive power. The slow, plodding rhythm of American machineguns contrasted sharply with the ripping sound of rapid-firing German MG-34s and 42s. Offshore, the British battleship HMS *Warspite* hurled fifteen-inch shells weighing one ton each into targets with an air-splitting, heart stopping rattle.[31] Hundreds of light, medium, and heavy bombers from the U.S. Eighth and Ninth Air Forces darkened the sky over Brest during the siege. Five hundred-pound and one thousand-pound bombs slammed into the ground during eleven bombing raids that saturated the city. Fighter planes in close aerial support of the infantry flew in fast and furiously to strafe German strongpoints with countless rounds of fifty-caliber machinegun fire.[32]

---

30. Blumenson, 636.
31. Blumenson, 643.
32. Carter and Mueller; 419, 422, 433, 434, 439-443, 446, 448, 450, 453-455.

The thick reinforced concrete *Lazarett* absorbed considerable punishment, but protected the medical personnel and patients who were housed inside. The inhabitants were not immune, however, from horrifying scenes inside the bunker that rendered Brest a vision of hell. Scores, then hundreds, then thousands of wounded Germans soon overwhelmed wards, treatment stations, and operating rooms across *Festung* Brest. Dying and dead *Landser, Seemanner,* and *Fallschirmjäger* lay everywhere. For many, terribly wounded and maimed, a quick death would have been merciful.[33] German and French nurses worked around the clock to help Wehrmacht doctors revive and restore those who could be saved.

The windowless *Lazarett* seemed as stifling as the submerged U-953 after an extended period without natural light or fresh air. A French nurse assisted Karl one day as he walked slowly and painfully out of his ward and into the long hall-way that led to the bunker's steel entrance door. The exercise boosted his spirits considerably and provided a brief respite from the endless hours that dragged by while he was confined to the bottom level of a hospital bunk. While the nurse and her patient stood by the entrance door a soldier warily strode up behind them from the long hallway. The *Landser* carried a large bucket laden with human flesh, bone, and tissue forfeited by the defenders of Brest in the *Lazarett's* carnage-swamped operating rooms. The heavy bunker door vibrated against the pounding shock waves of artillery rounds that whined and moaned on their downward trajectories to shatter into red-hot chunks and shards of steel. The sol-dier instinctively backed away from the doorway with fear in his eyes, certain he would be cut down by flying shrapnel the instant he stepped outside to empty the bucket. The French woman stared for a long moment at the petrified young sol-dier; then, consumed with contempt, she yanked the heavy bucket from his hands. The sounds of battle streamed into the hospital corridor when the woman pushed open the heavy door and charged into the daylight outside. The concrete exterior of the *Lazarett* bunker had been pulverized by shellfire; the huge red crosses that had been painted on the walls were nearly obliterated. The nurse heaved the bucket forward and a ghastly collection of bloody hands, bone frag-ments, and offal sloshed and tumbled across the rubble. Back inside the *Lazarett,* the nurse shoved the slimy, dripping bucket back into the shaken *Landser's* hands and sneered, *"Du Feigling!"*[34]

---

33. Translation: Soldiers, sailors, and paratroopers.
34. Translation: You coward!

By his debilitated condition and the appearance of his wound, Karl's recovery seemed highly questionable if not doubtful. The wound had affected his digestive system and by August he had wasted away nearly to skin and bones. Perhaps because they could do little else for him and thought he might die anyway, medical personnel eventually allowed Karl to venture wherever he wished during the long days of the siege. He sometimes asked orderlies to carry him on a stretcher outside the *Lazarett* walls so he could observe the battles that raged around the city and in the sky overhead. In the shadow of the huge bunker, with cigarette in hand or tightly wedged in his mouth, he lay in the No Man's Land of Brest as if he were oblivious to its danger. He often felt a strange detachment from the vicious battles that surrounded him, even as explosions shook the ground and waves of Allied bombers and marauding fighter planes stormed across the sky above him. American P-38 Lightnings and Luftwaffe fighter planes once engaged in a twisting, turning dogfight directly overhead. Karl merely noted the action with the half-hearted interest of one who already had seen it all, whose senses no longer summoned the adrenaline or emotions to react to the surreal life and death aerial ballet being performed above him.

Time seemed to lose all meaning in Brest. Karl kept no diary to record the events of his life in the midst of the siege. Why bother; most entries would have mirrored those of each previous day: unrelenting pain, sickness, loneliness, hopelessness, waiting for the end to come.

Rumors invariably ran rampant through the *Lazarett* wards, as suppositions came to life and soon were mysteriously transformed into hard fact wherever two or more soldiers or sailors congregated. Such "latrine news" was especially painful when it dealt with the hopes and fears of desperate people, which may not have contained a grain of truth, but heightened the anxiety of the emotionally distressed. One particular rumor exclaimed that a Red Cross ship had entered the harbor to evacuate the wounded to Germany, but had been deliberately bombed and sunk by the Allies.[35]

One day the fortress commander, General Bernhard Hermann Ramcke of the Second Parachute Division, visited the hospital. Ramcke was a tough, skilled commander, a diehard Nazi, and the essential motivator for the defense of Brest. OKW had ordered him to hold Brest to the last man and he intended to carry out those orders. The General and his staff walked from bed to bed with the

---

35. The author was unable to locate any information to substantiate the rumor that a Red Cross or German hospital ship had been sunk any time during the siege of Brest. The rumor probably began when the RAF bombed two old French warships in Brest harbor on 14 August and two other ships on 27 August.

ward's doctors and talked to the wounded men quietly and with apparent sincerity. Ramcke soon stood over Karl's bed while muffled sounds of explosions could be heard through the thick concrete walls. The old warhorse turned to the doctors.

"Is this man going to be well again?" Ramcke asked in reaction to Karl's emaciated condition. Karl watched the attending physician and waited apprehensively for him to respond to Ramcke's inquiry. The Kriegsmarine doctor assured the General that Baumann would recover. Without another word, Ramcke moved on to the next patient. After a time, the General stepped into the alcove that separated Karl's large ward from another, and spoke loudly to address the men in each ward. He encouraged the men to persevere in spite of their wounds, and explained the necessity for the protracted, seemingly senseless defense of the doomed city.

"We have to defend Brest as long as we can hold out. The longer we defend Brest, the fewer bombs they will be able to send over Germany!" he declared.

As if to accentuate Ramcke's salient rationale for his audience, at that very instant a large-caliber shell or bomb struck the *Lazarett* roof with an ear-splitting explosion and a rumbling shock wave. Light bulbs shattered in their sockets and left the interior of the hospital suddenly in pitch darkness. When the lights finally flickered back on, Ramcke was long gone; the random explosion had quite convincingly underscored the General's point for the continued suffering the wounded would have to endure.

Countless acts of courage and sacrifice attended the savage fighting on both sides of the battle lines. A badly wounded *Landser* in Karl's ward was visited one day by his commanding officers. While they stood over the soldier's bed, the officers quietly praised him for his defense of Brest and the *Reich*, and explained that they had awarded the Iron Cross Second Class to him for his valor. Unfortunately, one officer confessed, they were unable to obtain the commendation medal anywhere in the besieged city. Baumann watched the impromptu ceremony with interest and was moved by the plight of the officers and especially the grave condition of the soldier. He then reached for the seabag that sat beside his bunk and searched among the contents inside for a small rectangular box. He and four crewmates earlier had received the Iron Cross Second Class after they had completed several combat patrols aboard U-953. Though he greatly appreciated the honor, he knew his medal would serve a greater purpose for the fallen soldier in the nearby bed. One of the officers shortly moved his sympathetic gaze from the *Landser* and saw the young sailor hold out the small black box and motion to him. The man quickly went to Karl's bedside and took the box, opened it, and thanked the *Ubootfahrer* with a grateful smile and handshake. A moment later, the officers solemnly presented the Iron Cross to the dying soldier and pinned it onto his pillow. For the first time in days Karl felt a sense of renewed humanity as he sank back onto his bed and stared at the underside of the bunk above him.

Almost ceaseless bombing and artillery fire finally became so intense that the battered concrete *Lazarett* bunker was evacuated. Ambulances shuttled the legion of badly wounded men to a giant, labyrinthine tunnel complex that engineers had carved out of the solid rock hillside during the months leading up to the Normandy invasion. The deep manmade cavern was impervious to any artillery round or the largest bomb. Only the sound and shock of the heaviest rounds that landed on the hillside directly above were detected deep inside the sanctuary. The mad chaos that accompanied the treatment and handling of huge numbers of patients, the newly wounded, the dying, and the dead, permeated the tunnel complex and made the new sanctuary a place of foreboding.

Captured *Kriegsmarine* personnel await evacuation from the ruins of Brest.

The siege of Brest continued for ten harrowing days until American troops battered their way into the city center and surrounded the last two strongpoints that remained in German hands: an old French fortress and the U-boat bunker itself. Both holdouts surrendered on 18 September. Nearly ten thousand Germans in Recouvrance and at the Kriegsmarine base surrendered to troops of the 29th Infantry Division—National Guardsmen from Pennsylvania, Maryland,

and Virginia. Many among the large number of German headquarters personnel prepared for the day's dramatic events with their usual morning rituals. They washed, shaved and donned clean dress uniforms, then packed suitcases for their journey out of the totally devastated city and into American captivity. Their appearance contrasted sharply with the filthy, exhausted and unkempt dogfaces who had won the brutal victory at Brest.[36]

The campaign that had been launched with a five-pound wager culminated in the total destruction of Brest, its port, and its harbor facilities. The artillery rounds and bombs—fragmentation, jellied gasoline, and white phosphorus—that rained down from above burned, gutted, or pulverized nearly every building in the city center and in the Recouvrance district. Streets were filled with rubble and left impassable. The city had been wrested from the Wehrmacht at the cost of more than three million rounds of small arms ammunition, nearly 500,000 heavy artillery rounds, hundreds of U.S. Army Air Forces and Royal Air Force bombing and strafing missions, and 9,831 American casualties. German forces suffered 12,000 killed and 38,000 taken prisoner. In a mad irony of wartime rationale the port of Brest, which Allied planners initially believed was desperately needed to supply American forces in France, was by the end of the prolonged siege deemed unnecessary to support the fighting in western Europe. The port was never reopened during the war.[37] Brest served only as a killing ground for thousands. And Patton lost his wager to Monty.

Matrosenobergefreiter Karl Baumann became a prisoner of the U.S. Army without trepidation. Some Germans had been especially terrified that they would be turned over to the French Resistance, which would have been only too glad to take them off the Americans' hands. But, Karl reasoned, the American army would never allow those who had honorably surrendered to face wholesale retribution. As a result, his first sight of an American soldier was anticlimactic and utterly without fear. A GI with terrible blisters on his feet limped into Karl's ward to find a German doctor to treat his condition. The dogface's uniform was filthy, his shirtsleeves were rolled up, and his steel helmet was tilted informally on his head. The manner and bearing of the weary young sergeant somehow reassured Karl that his well-being as a prisoner of the Americans was not in doubt. Difficult as captivity might be in some respects, he was certain he would survive to return home—after Germany won the war.

36.　Blumenson, 651-652. Gen. Ramcke and a small group of diehards escaped the city, but surrendered to the U.S. 8th Infantry Division the following day.

37.　Blumenson; 653, 655.

7

Prisoner of War

American troops took scant time to celebrate their hard-won victory over the defenders of Brest. Exhausted and spent GIs gathered up survivors and re-formed their battered units in staging areas outside of the city on 19 September. There they rested, repaired weapons and equipment, and received new uniforms and gear for the battles that remained to be fought. Fresh replacement units arrived the same day to take over the daunting tasks to secure the vanquished fortress city and manage nearly forty thousand German prisoners.[1]

Most of the prisoners—those without incapacitating wounds—milled about the rubble inside hastily established holding areas, while their American captors struggled to provide sustainable food and shelter for them. Within two weeks the majority of prisoners were processed through a bureaucratic maze that established them officially as prisoners of the U.S. Army. Officers and enlisted men were sorted out and confined in separate compounds, where each was identified and photographed. Army intelligence teams gathered up some Germans for interrogation depending upon their rank, military unit, or the work to which they had been assigned.

The Allies had been confronted with the issues of containing, housing, clothing, and feeding for tens of thousands of prisoners since May 1943. The logistics of war prisoner management dictated that prisoners of war (PWs) could be confined most efficiently away from the battle zones. American combat troops seldom had adequate food, clothing, and shelter to maintain more than minimal levels of comfort. Provisions funneled to prisoners of war would have further deprived large numbers of GIs of the supplies they should have received.[2] Equally

---

1.   Blumenson, 653. The VIII Corps turned over the city and the prisoners on the evening of 19 September to occupation troops under command of the Brittany Base Section of the Communications Zone.
2.   Judith M. Gansberg, *Stalag: U.S.A. The Remarkable Story of German POWs in America* (New York: Crowell, 1977), 4.

important, the number of troops needed to guard large contingents of prisoners in combat zones would have depleted the already-slim ranks of fighting units.[3] Prisoners held in compounds near their own forces presented greater security risks for escape or possible liberation by enemy counterattacks as well. Finally, transports that delivered thousands of troops from the United States to the war theaters otherwise sailed home largely empty.[4] Allied planners concluded, therefore, that offensive operations were best served when prisoners of war were far removed from combat zones and placed near the source of adequate supplies and manpower to sustain and supervise them: namely, the United States.[5] Beyond the tactical military advantages, large numbers of German prisoners would provide a readily available source of labor for American farmers and businesses whose manpower supply had been seriously drained by the armed forces through recruitment and conscription.

Several days after the end of the siege, huge U.S. Navy troop transports that had delivered troops from the United States to French ports in Normandy began to steam into the battered harbor of Brest. Prisoner compounds were emptied as long columns of Germans marched under guard to the docks and to waiting U.S. Navy landing craft. Throughout the day U. S. Navy and Coast Guard helmsmen maneuvered their prisoner-laden boats around waterborne hazards and debris over to the troopships. The ungainly-looking flat-bottomed landing craft sloshed back and forth through the waves between the port and the transports until each ship was filled with prisoners and their guard details. With permission to set sail granted by the American port commander, each transport slowly turned seaward and sailed on a westerly heading, their human cargoes destined for prisoner of war (PW) camps in the United States.

The large number of wounded prisoners from the underground hospital presented more of a problem for the U.S. Army medical personnel who entered the cavern shortly after the Germans surrendered the city. Assisted by German doctors and medics, GI doctors evaluated each patient to determine his overall condition and the urgency of treatment needed, then directed their attention to the most seriously wounded.

Karl Baumann was carried on a stretcher out of the hospital tunnel to a waiting ambulance. Along the way, the sight of heavily armed men wearing white

---

3.   Perret, 374-376.
4.   Gansberg, 4.
5.   LTC George G. Lewis, USA, and CPT John Mewha, USA, *History of Prisoner of War Utilization by the United States Army 1776-1945* (Washington: Center of Military History, U.S. Army, 1988), 83.

armbands and civilian clothes suddenly unnerved him. The French Resistance! For a moment he feared he might be turned over to the guerilla fighters who had waged a ceaseless campaign that had terrorized German occupation troops since 1940. He did not realize that the French had been placed under the command of the U.S. Army, which would not allow the civilian force to exact the revenge it coveted. Karl breathed a sigh of relief when the door of the Army ambulance was slammed shut behind him and an American soldier jumped into the driver's seat.

The ambulance sped away from the bunker and a few minutes later arrived at the port, where the stretcher cases were shuttled aboard a landing craft and placed in rows. The small craft soon churned her way to a gleaming white hospital ship emblazoned with large red crosses. Redeemed at last from the dust, rubble and filth of war-torn Brest, Karl was carried aboard the ship and soon was settled into a clean bed in a spotless hospital ward. When all the wounded prisoners were accounted for, the ship set on a direct course for Southampton, England.

Karl left behind the city of Brest with only one deeply unsettling concern. In the first moments or hours after he became a prisoner, his seabag had vanished—stolen by American soldiers, whose quest for enemy souvenirs was legendary.[6] The canvas bag contained all his possessions from La Rochelle: uniforms, personal gear, his prized *Ubootfahrer* boots and a number of trinkets he had not shipped home earlier. A special loss was his cherished golden *Ubootkriegsabzeichen*—the U-boat war badge attached to his dress uniform jacket that recognized service of at least ninety days on combat patrols. The brooding *Ubootfahrer* was left with nothing but his *Soldbuch*, a toilet kit, and the hospital pajamas he wore.[7] His lone consolation, he recalled with relief, was that at least he had mailed a small number of photographs home some months earlier.

The hospital ship steamed on her four-hundred-mile Samaritan's journey to Southampton through the very waters where U-953 and the few other surviving U-boats lurked in search of targets after the Normandy invasion. At night the entire vessel was flooded in brilliant light to clearly identify her as a hospital ship

---

6.   A popular saying during the war was that Germans fight for territory, British fight for Empire, French fight for glory, and Americans fight for souvenirs. The 14 January 1945 issue of *Yank, The Army Weekly*—the unofficial magazine for American troops—carried a detailed article entitled, "Souvenir Savvy; You Can't Take It With You if It's Loaded or Looted." The article described how to ship war trophies home safely and properly.

7.   The *Soldbuch* was the official identity document issued to each member of the Wehrmacht, and contained detailed and updated individual, medical, and service information.

to U-boat commanders. She arrived safely and without incident at the port of Southampton the following day. Karl and hundreds of other wounded Germans were carried onto a waiting hospital train that sat on a siding near the dock. The train was destined for the 82nd General Hospital in Liverpool, one of many U.S. Army hospitals located in England.

General hospitals ranked at the top of the Army's medical treatment hierarchy in the European Theater of Operations. The severity of a wound largely determined how far up the ladder of progressive care a GI traveled from his combat or service unit. Serious, debilitating or life-threatening wounds were treated at general hospitals with state-of-the-art facilities, equipment and medical staffs that rivaled the most progressive civilian hospitals in the United States or anywhere in the world.[8]

Baumann arrived at the American hospital without medical records, so Army doctors and medics busily worked up a thorough examination. A short while later an Army major strode into the hospital ward. The German-speaking major explained that a minor operation was necessary to repair the intestinal wound, if the prisoner-patient would permit it, and assured him the surgery would be entirely successful. Karl readily agreed to put an end to his agony and underwent the procedure soon thereafter. The doctors also successfully treated and closed the entrance wound in his side. By January 1945 he had fully recovered from the debilitating shrapnel wound, fully seven agonizing months after the exploding gun barrel nearly killed him.

The absence of any correspondence from Karl since June greatly distressed his family and friends in Brambauer. The ominous silence weighed especially heavily upon Anneliese Samhuber. She and Karl had grown considerably fond of each other even as the vortex of war threatened to destroy all future hopes and dreams. Both had cherished their infrequent times together, especially his last visit home in November 1943. Each day that now passed without a letter or postcard from the war front seemed to confirm something terrible had happened to him. The Kriegsmarine had not notified Karl's family that he was missing in action or had been killed, so loved ones held onto the slim hope that a long patrol at sea had prevented him from writing. Otherwise, they could only speculate about what had happened to Karl and his U-boat.

With *Oberleutnant zur See* Herbert Werner in command, U-953 had left Brest on 23 August to embark upon a perilous course to La Rochelle and her former

---

8.   Albert E. Cowdrey, *Fighting for Life; American Military Medicine in World War II* (New York: The Free Press, 1994), 162.

homeport at La Pallice. *Kater* was the only U-boat dispatched from La Pallice in May that ever would return there—the old flotilla's lone survivor of the desperate patrols launched against the invasion fleet after the D-Day landings. On 7 September she became the last U-boat to sail out of any Biscay base, where the Ubootwaffe once thrived and waged brutal war during the Happy Time before May 1943. At least 90 percent of the operational U-boat fleet assigned to combat duty had been destroyed by the autumn of 1944. The Battle of the Atlantic was over; all that remained was for the men trapped inside the port cities to survive the sieges that were sure to come. As darkness fell on their last night in La Rochelle, Karl's crewmates raced to their heavily guarded quarters. Two Kriegsmarine officers had been found dead in a side street gutter that morning, their throats cut and bodies mutilated, compliments of the French Resistance.[9]

An hour after midnight on 7 September U-953 slipped out of La Pallice to begin a harrowing, circuitous journey to Norway. Werner and crew were forced to run a gauntlet of enemy aircraft, destroyers, and hunter-killer warship groups deployed along much of their two thousand-mile course. The Allied air and naval phalanx forced Werner to route U-953 around the western coast of Britain, through the Outer Hebrides and the Shetland Islands to the Norwegian Sea. *Kater* remained underwater during the entire six-week journey to Bergenfjord, Norway, and arrived a battered, beaten vestige of her former being. Somehow the boat then was patched up enough over the next several weeks in drydock to withstand a two-day voyage to Kiel.[10] Werner finally led U-953 into the sprawling Kriegsmarine base on the Baltic coast on 7 November. The following day, helmsman Herbert Raschewski kept the promise he had made to Karl months before in Brest and mailed a letter to Anneliese through the Wehrmacht *Feldpost* at Lübeck. Anneliese was surprised to receive the letter in mid-November bearing the return address of a sailor she did not know. She quickly opened the letter, and tears welled up and clouded her eyes as she finally learned Karl's fate.

On Board, 7 November 1944
Dear Miss Anneliese!
It is always my greatest pleasure when I can fulfill a wish for a good comrade with whom I've gotten along very well. Perhaps you will be amazed to suddenly receive a letter from a sailor who is a total stranger, or maybe not. I am writing

---

9.   Werner; 249, 254, 256, 259.
10. Werner; 259-268, 270-271.

this letter on behalf of and at the request of my best comrade and your dear friend Karl Baumann and would like to explain to some extent his long silence. You very probably heard from Karl himself that he was wounded in June. At the time, we were at port in Brest (France). Karl was taken immediately to a field hospital where I visited him every day for a week until we had to return to duty; Karl remained in the field hospital. Then when we returned after four weeks on duty, Karl was still laid up in Brest, but at a different field hospital. Once again I visited him every day and did whatever he wanted. However his situation was worse than it had been four weeks earlier. Instead of healing, his wound got worse and worse. They could not send him to Germany any more because on the one hand he was in no condition to travel, and on the other hand no transportation could make it through since we were already almost entirely surrounded. Then after ten days we left Brest again and knew that we would not return. Unfortunately, we could not take along our good comrade Karl Baumann—because you know what military branch we are with. We also knew that we were going to Germany. As I said goodbye to Karl, the tears rolled down my face although I am certainly a tough soldier. I had never had such a good comrade as Karl before. There was nothing anyone could do; he had to stay there. We still have Karl with us in spirit on board. After a while we heard that Brest was taken by the enemy—and with that Karl B, too. Now neither I nor our group knows if Karl is still alive. In any case, if he is still alive, then he is a prisoner of the English. We also assume that he is still alive—and then, dear Miss Anneliese, you will see your Karl once again. The war will not last forever, and all of the prisoners will be released. I hope and wish for you and Karl that he is still alive and that you will see each other again. I do not know if perhaps you have in the meantime already received news from Karl from wherever they are holding him. If so, then I would be very happy and grateful to you if you would send me his address.

We just arrived a couple of days ago here in Germany and have been released for a few weeks from the front lines. I would like to end my letter now. In case you would like to know more, I am ready to answer your questions any time. Please write soon and let me know if you received this letter.

So once again, Karl Baumann remained in Brest in the field hospital.

Yours Truly,
Herbert Raschewski![11]

---

11. Herbert Raschewski, Lübeck, to Anneliese Samhuber, Brambauer, 7 November 1944, original handwritten letter in the possession of Anneliese Baumann, Stuarts Draft, Virginia.

As a prisoner of war in the custody of the U.S. Army, Karl Baumann entered the massive and costly logistical undertaking that transported nearly four hundred thousand German captives to the continental United States during World War II. American citizens in forty-four states witnessed the presence of enemy soldiers, sailors, airmen, and a small number of diplomats in their home communities between 1942 and 1946. A total of 425,871 prisoners of war—371,683 German, 50,273 Italian, and 3,915 Japanese—were confined on American soil in May 1945, the high water mark for the PW program.[12] Nearly all captured enemy personnel were transported to PW camps within the United States until overwhelming numbers of Germans who surrendered during the final weeks of the war in Europe rendered further transports impracticable.

From the moment he was captured until the Americans released him to an English prisoner of war camp in January 1945, Karl considered himself a first-class prisoner by virtue of the treatment he and the other German prisoners received. Though he was confined in a guarded section of the hospital he received superb treatment and food that was good and plentiful: orange juice, grapefruit juice, chocolate candy, and two hundred cigarettes each month. During his recovery a medical orderly named Valentine frequently invited him to play checkers. Neither man understood the other's native language, but each learned to communicate with simple sentences and gestures. International diplomacy won the day over a simple game board whenever the young black soldier from Pennsylvania challenged the young sailor from Westphalia.

Karl experienced democracy in practice on other occasions as well. After he had recovered well enough from his final surgery he was able to walk to the prisoners' mess hall for meals. Another prisoner on one occasion tried to push his way in front of others who stood in the long mess line. An American soldier observed the incident with disgust.

"Hey you, come back here," the GI growled. "What are you doing there?"

"I'm Austrian," the obstinate prisoner declared as he looked down his nose at the young American. The GI was not the least impressed; the prisoner was one of many Austrians who had joined the Wehrmacht after his country melded into Greater Germany in the wake of fellow Austrian Adolf Hitler's unseemly 1938 *Anschluß*.

"Okay, you Austrian; you go to the back of the line!" the American bellowed as he jabbed his finger toward the end of the mess line. The amused Germans looked on with delight at the man's public comeuppance.

---

12. Lewis and Mewha, 91.

Karl surely began to feel like a prisoner of war in January 1945, when he was released into temporary custody of the British Army at a camp outside Liverpool. First, he was compelled to hand over his *Soldbuch*, which he had zealously guarded since his enlistment into the Kriegsmarine. Also, unlike his American captors who at the time usually harbored no deep-seated hostility toward German prisoners, British guards and camp personnel frequently displayed abject hatred toward their enemy. Commands and remarks to the prisoners often were punctuated with the epithet, "sons of bitches." The British people no doubt felt justified to inflict such acts of psychological violence upon their captive cousins. The Germans had fought them savagely for more than five years, had humiliated them at Dunkirk, and had nearly invaded Britain itself. The Ubootwaffe had severely damaged their navy and merchant fleet, and the Luftwaffe had blitzed their cities. Now, terrifying V-1 and V-2 rockets randomly slammed onto English towns and cities. Though Karl at first did not understand the meaning of the epithet, he clearly understood the intensity of hatred that powered the words angry-faced Tommies spat out at the German prisoners.

For the first time since he was captured, Karl was interrogated at the British camp. A German-speaking intelligence officer sought specific military information, but also wanted to gauge overall morale when he inquired about Baumann's hometown. Since Karl did not wish to be more specific, he replied he was from Dortmund.

"Dortmund! We bombed your coal mines!" the Englishman declared.

"No!" Baumann angrily shot back. Since the Royal Air Force had carpet-bombed Germany night after night, he was certain many residential areas probably had been destroyed as well. "You bombed our houses!" the young prisoner shouted. The brief interrogation abruptly ended.

After more than a month in British custody, Karl realized the prisoners soon would to be transported by ship to another location. He dared not contemplate the final destination of his next ocean voyage. Russia, perhaps? He feared even the thought of life in a Soviet prison. The Tommies never informed the uneasy prisoners, even as they were marched en masse from the camp one evening to a nearby harbor, then returned to the camp later that night. Karl suspected the British needed to know how quickly the entire group of prisoners could be moved to the harbor, obviously for no other reason than to meet a ship.

The following morning, on or about 28 February, after roll call and breakfast the Brits again formed the Germans into marching columns. This time each prisoner carried a small bag that contained all of his meager possessions; clearly, they would not return to the camp. As they passed through the side streets of a small town that bordered the harbor, Karl felt the uneasy gazes of the English women—mostly weary and sad-looking, with aprons tied around their waists—who stood in their doorways to watch the silent procession. So many husbands and sons must have gone away to fight the Germans, he thought, and so many wives and mothers in Germany were equally anxious over the absence or loss of their loved ones. The sight of the forlorn women with fearful eyes and disrupted lives spoke more profoundly about the futility of war than all of the horrific battle scenes he had witnessed in Brest.

"How can we do this to each other," he asked himself rhetorically as tears momentarily welled up in his eyes.

The sight of a giant troopship moored in the harbor refocused Karl's thoughts toward his immediate circumstances and confirmed that his imminent journey was to be a significant endeavor. To his disbelief, the top decks of the ship were jammed with American soldiers; men going home, Karl concluded as he glanced up at the happy and relaxed GIs who leaned over the rails to watch the forlorn prisoners. Suddenly he was disturbed by the realization that the troopship probably was bound for the United States, and soon would carry him toward a prison camp in that mysterious and unfamiliar land thousands of miles from home. He was particularly distressed that his own fate so clearly was beyond his ability to control.

Karl could barely comprehend that German prisoners would be transported to America, but when he reached the water's edge several GIs pointed to the small bags the prisoners carried.

"Throw away! America! Everything new!" the soldiers shouted and gestured animatedly toward a pile of discarded bags that lay dockside. While some prisoners held onto their personal belongings as if their utmost personal security depended on them, Karl tossed his bag onto the growing mound. British guards eagerly retrieved many of the meager cast-offs.

The prisoners were directed onto the gangplank that angled up to a hatchway near the water line of the cavernous troopship. Machinegun-toting guards inside then motioned them down a passageway that led into a large wardroom in the bottom hold. Several hundred prisoners eventually milled about the wardroom; then claimed floor space against walls, bulkheads, and stanchions where they settled in for what they hoped would be a safe Atlantic crossing. The potential for disaster was especially unsettling for *Ubootfahrer* like Baumann, who knew from first-hand experience that troop-ships were coveted prizes for U-boat skippers. Karl resented that his captors had placed German prisoners in harm's way, possibly to be killed by his own crewmates aboard U-953. His trepidation soon appeared well-founded.

Submarine alert! Midway into the otherwise uneventful crossing, the alarm signal abruptly barked through the ship's loudspeakers. The eventuality Karl feared above all others had come to pass. Fright and anxiety quickly mounted among the human cargo locked inside the deepest recesses of the troopship. Every man knew he would be utterly trapped in the hold below the water line if a torpedo slammed into the ship. Fear and anger soon overwhelmed some prisoners, who charged desperately for the door that led to the passageway. The men shouted pleas and curses while they pounded and pulled on the locked door that blocked their only exit to safety. At the same time a cordon of GIs stormed down the passageway to reinforce the guards outside the hold. With angry shouts and machineguns poised and ready to fire, the guards ordered the Germans to move away from the door. Subdued by the threat of gunfire, the prisoners apprehensively settled back down to await whatever outcome the immediate future held for them. A frightened young prisoner sat down and nervously asked what they should do.

"When a torpedo looks through the hull, then we'll go. Calm down; forget about it," Baumann declared with bitter resignation.

Karl hoped that for once the normally reliable German torpedoes would run wild if any were fired at their fat target, and that some otherwise determined U-boat skipper would give up the chase and break off his pursuit. Unarmed and unescorted Allied troopships, some of which were fast passenger liners converted to military use, countered the U-boat threat with speed. To Karl's and every other passenger's great relief, the ship must have outrun her U-boat threat. The frightening prospect of more submarine alerts was enough to unnerve many prisoners during the remainder of the voyage.

The Germans were allowed twenty minutes of fresh air each day when they were taken under guard to an upper deck. While the U-boat gunner looked over the railing across the vast ocean horizon he frequently thought about U-953 and his crewmates, the camaraderie they shared, and the missions they had sweated out inside their cramped steel cylinder. He hoped his fellow *Ubootkameraden*—Raschewski, Kühn, and other good friends—were not already entombed inside a crushed submarine hull somewhere on the bottom of the Bay of Biscay, the English Channel, or the open Atlantic.

Prisoners also left the bottom hold twice daily to eat their meals. Small groups of prisoners were escorted to an upper deck mess room, where they ate in shifts standing at long tables. An adjacent mess room served American troops. A dumbwaiter located in an alcove between the two mess rooms connected the dining areas to the ship's galley one deck below. Large quantities of prepared food in big stainless steel pans were sent up the lift to an attendant who then delivered them to either mess. The prisoners were amused to watch the seemingly endless procession of pans appear on the lift whenever the mess attendant leaned into the shaft and yelled "Okay!" to the galley crew below. Before one meal, Karl watched as another German yielded to the temptation to mimic the mess attendant. While the attendant carried several pans of food to the American mess, the prisoner leaned into the dumbwaiter shaft and with his best American impersonation shouted, "Okay!" Just like clockwork, a moment later the lift arrived under the strain of giant pans of meatloaf. The prisoners lunged for the pans and had grabbed handfuls of the hot ground beef and oatmeal concoction when the mess attendant suddenly reappeared.

"You hungry?" the American sailor asked the startled crowd of Germans caught meatloaf-handed.

"Yeah, we all are," one responded in English.

"Well, eat it up then," said the smiling American, whose countenance suddenly turned sour; "all of it!" he thundered. The brawny sailor's stern gaze confirmed he was not kidding. For the next few interminable minutes, the prisoners nervously gorged themselves on all the meatloaf their stomachs could handle—and more. At long last the ultimately noxious meat mixture was choked down. The bloated and groaning captives, faces and hands covered with grease, stumbled back to their hold having learned a valuable lesson: never run afoul of a U.S. Navy mess attendant and his meatloaf.

The weeklong transatlantic passage ended on 6 March in the port of New York. Jubilant American troops cheered with unfettered elation as the big transport sailed past the Statue of Liberty, and rejoiced at their redemption from the terrible battlefields of Europe. Some might have been destined for the killing grounds of the Pacific Theater, but for the moment the men who crowded the upper decks exulted simply to be home. No one cheered inside the windowless hold at the bottom of the ship. Now in the homeland of their country's sworn enemy, the prisoners of war were glad simply to have survived the voyage without German torpedoes tearing through the hull to send them to a certain, watery grave.

The transport eased into a quay at the huge port and dropped anchor; after mooring lines were belayed the upper decks quickly emptied as grateful GIs ambled down the gangplanks to a raucous outcry of cheers, shouts, loud greetings and not-too-sad farewells. The wild dockside commotion finally subsided after the swarm of troops dispersed individually or with their units. The guard detail then unlocked the door to the prisoners' hold. The Germans unceremoniously filed out of the troopship and formed up dockside, then were led into a large building nearby. Inside, the prisoners were deloused while their official personnel folders were handed over to the provost officer with the U.S. Army's Military Police Corps. The in-processing procedures worked smoothly, since by early 1945 more than 300,000 German prisoners had arrived at either the port of New York or the port of Hampton Roads, Virginia.[13]

The personnel folders were updated with entries that recorded the PWs' arrival from England. In the meantime, the Germans were issued food rations and packs of cigarettes. Those without adequately warm clothing to ward off the cold New England winter temperatures of March 1945 were issued standard U.S. Army gear. The letters P and W were boldly emblazoned on the front and back of each new army jacket. Some Germans continued to wear their Wehrmacht uniforms complete with Nazi regalia, a privilege allowed by the Geneva Convention of 1929. Karl wore the herringbone army fatigues issued to him at the American hospital in England after his Kriegsmarine uniforms had been stolen with his seabag.

Several hours after the new arrivals were medicated, processed, fed and provisioned, they were escorted out of the building to a long passenger train that waited on a rail siding. At the signal of the MP guards, 950 prisoners swarmed onto the train cars.[14] The Germans, to their complete astonishment, then settled into comfortable cushioned seats as if they were tourists about to embark on a pleasure trip. Three men were directed to each four-passenger seat section, which left room for one man at a time to stretch out and sleep. Only the MPs armed with machineguns mitigated the scene of unexpected and almost dizzying comfort; their forbidding presence at the back of each car clearly reminded the Germans that they were prisoners of war. Still, Karl could not fathom the degree of luxury he already had been provided in America.

---

13.   Forest Burnett Wall, Jr., "German Prisoner of War Camps in Virginia During World War II" (Ph.D. diss., Carnegie-Mellon University, 1987, 59.

14.   Prisoner of War Camp, Camp Pickett, Virginia (Inspection Report), Enemy POW Information Bureau, Subject File, 1942-1946, Box 2669, Inspection & Field Reports—Camp Pickett, Record Group 389, United States National Archives and Records Administration, College Park, Maryland. Karl Baumann almost certainly was among the 950 who arrived at Camp Pickett on 7 March 1945. No other PW groups appear to have arrived from New York during the period when Karl Baumann would have arrived there.

A steam whistle shrieked and clanging couplers jarred the heavy passenger cars into motion to announce the train's departure for a destination wholly unknown to the prisoners. From the time Baumann became a prisoner of war, he often had no idea of the time of day or even the day of the week through which he passed in captivity. Naturally, his captors never discussed matters that involved the times, dates, or future plans to which he inextricably was bound. He inhabited a strange world almost entirely devoid of personal control or the ability to make decisions regarding his very existence.

He keenly observed the narrow swath of American landscape that rushed past his eyes as the train rolled through the new and strange country. In many ways he was not impressed by what he saw when he compared the views with mental images of his native land. He was struck by the amount of litter and debris that lined the tracks and roadbeds, especially when the train passed through towns and cities. He marveled at the young women who waited along the railway platforms or strode down nearby sidewalks. Wearing makeup and smoking cigarettes, they appealed to the teenaged sailor in the throes of culture shock more as prostitutes than gatekeepers of virtue.

One of the most impressive and disturbing sights Karl observed was a large field of gasoline storage tanks on the outskirts of New York City. The big storage tanks covered the ground as far as the eye could see. While the train rolled along its southerly course through the Arsenal of Democracy, he suddenly was struck by a stark and undeniable reality.

"Germany is going to lose this war," he muttered quietly to himself. For the first time he realized that the United States had the ability to positively overwhelm her enemies with unimaginably vast resources committed toward the total destruction of the Axis powers. All Nazi propaganda suddenly seemed pale and hollow.

American guards began to walk among the prisoners while the train sped into the dim twilight and then into night. Though armed, most clearly revealed a relaxed and friendly attitude. The military policemen probably would never leave U.S. soil to see combat, but were curious and as interested in war souvenirs as their front-line brethren.

"I want that!" a guard would declare while he pointed to a Wehrmacht tunic or an American-supplied jacket with the large letters PW painted on both sides. Prisoners already had grown wise through their early experiences in captivity and were prepared to barter and bargain with the MPs. The going rate for prisoners' uniforms soon stood at between twenty and eighty cigarettes. Karl observed with amusement that some Germans sold their PW jackets, then simply asked for replacements at the next PW staging point. There seemed to be no shortage or want for anything in the United States.

The train pulled into Richmond, Virginia the next morning—7 March—and was switched onto a feeder line that set a southwesterly course for the final fifty miles of the long and uneventful journey. An hour later the engineer reduced the speed of the big steam engine nearly to a crawl when he approached a built-up area near the rural Virginia community of Blackstone. Moments later the brakes beneath the passenger cars issued lazy squeals as they eased the wheels to a stop in front of a rail depot at Camp Pickett, a sprawling U.S. Army infantry training center.

The rolling wooded landscape in the remote northeast corner of Camp Pickett had been converted into a prisoner of war base camp, one of a number situated across the country that had been hurriedly constructed to accommodate the con- quered masses of Wehrmacht troops. The 1,900-foot by 550-foot prisoner com- pound was ringed with barbed wire and watchtowers.[15] The Germans soon traded their comfortable passenger cars seats for slatted wooden benches on the back of army trucks that carried them to the PW compound. Along the way Karl noticed prisoners at work outside the main fence. Some wore shorts in the cool Virginia climate, which seemed downright balmy to men acclimated to harsh European winters. The trucks deposited their latest batch of Germans at the com- pound gate, where a head count was taken and file folders again were updated to satisfy the bureaucratic exigencies of the Provost Marshal General's Office. Dur- ing its sixteen months of operation, Camp Pickett's prisoner of war base camp housed as many as 2,436 Germans at one time, not including those assigned to a number of branch camps located throughout Virginia.[16]

Young Baumann could barely comprehend the treatment he already had received at the hands of his American captors. Basic necessities of food, clothing, shelter, Chesterfield and Lucky Strike cigarettes, and other essential luxuries had been so generously provided that by 1945 the prisoners' standard of living exceeded that of the average German inside the *Reich*. En route to the prison compound he contemplated his immediate future behind barbed wire and won- dered whether in a few moments he still would consider himself a first-class pris- oner. All apprehension soon was relieved, however, when he and the other new arrivals were taken to the prisoners' mess hall for their first meal. He was aston-

15. Wall, 85.
16. John Hammond Moore, "Hitler's Wehrmacht in Virginia, 1943-1946," *The Vir- ginia Magazine of History and Biography*, July 1977, 263-264.

ished to find long tables set with dinner plates and coffee cups, placed upside down to keep them clean. A fresh orange, the first he had seen since the war began, sat atop each plate. "You'll be in paradise," he chuckled and reassured himself.

Paradise itself came not without cost to the unwary. One of Pickett's resident PWs had given a small stack of work payment coupons to Karl as a gesture of camaraderie. He was heartened to discover during his first visit to the prisoners' canteen that his sudden windfall would buy an entire box of Peter-Paul Mounds candy bars. He purchased the box to soothe his constant hunger, and by the end of the day had emptied it of its full contents. Before the next morning's dawn two dozen candy bars unleashed a powerful laxative effect that brought Karl to his knees and sentenced him to a full day of penance in the prisoners' latrine.

The prisoners were wholly unaware that the charitable treatment they received, down to the fresh oranges, had been officially mandated and calculated to achieve specific wartime goals. The United States government had determined at the outset of World War II to maintain a policy toward humane treatment of prisoners of war. Such charity reflected the highest ideals of a democratic society and adhered to the letter of the Geneva Convention of 1929. The humane treatment of prisoners had been designed to serve pragmatic purposes that benefited the United States as well; namely, to encourage reciprocal treatment toward American prisoners held by the Wehrmacht. The welfare of American PWs was the paramount concern and driving force behind American prisoner of war policies from which the United States would not be dissuaded, despite often-angry charges from newspaper editors and radio commentators that Germans in American camps were being coddled.[17] The official policy also recognized that the most effective means to re-educate and encourage prisoners to cast off the yoke of Nazi ideology was to practice humane treatment and the democratic principles that free peoples are supposed to enjoy. This approach successfully served as the basis for treatment of German prisoners of war—at least until the end of the war in Europe.

Baumann remained at Camp Pickett only one week, during which time he was put to work alongside other enlisted prisoners. He collected litter and debris from the grounds and walkways of the main camp and the prison compound. German prisoners performed a wide range of jobs on military posts that were not expressly forbidden by the Geneva Convention; such as unskilled laborers, skilled craftsmen, and office personnel. Large numbers of American combat veterans

---

17. Krammer, *Nazi Prisoners*, 258-259.

who just weeks earlier had fought the Wehrmacht in a vicious and brutal war of personal survival were incredulous to find their furlough papers, travel orders, and other official paperwork processed and handled by German office personnel.[18]

The new arrivals soon came to feel icy glares and not-too-veiled hostility toward their presence. The unexpected animosity arose not from Americans, but from fellow Germans, many of whom were hardened veterans of Field Marshal Erwin Rommel's once-vaunted Afrika Korps. The old prisoners had been captured during the desert battles of North Africa in 1942 and 1943, before the tide of war had irreversibly turned against the *Reich*. When pressed for news about the war and Germany's progress toward victory, recently captured prisoners often exclaimed that Germany was going to lose the war. To the old desert fighters such defeatist attitudes were tantamount to treason. As a result, fights erupted out of sight of American guards as members of the Afrika Korps punched and pummeled prisoners who bore such unfathomable news. Karl was relieved the old prisoners did not ask his opinion.

One morning a week after his arrival at Camp Pickett, Karl Baumann and a small number of other prisoners were ordered to collect their gear and report to the front of their barracks. The men hurriedly returned to their quarters, stuffed their meager belongings into their duffel bags, and formed up outside. Two 2 ½-ton trucks soon rolled up to the building, where on command the PWs threw their bags into the canvas-covered beds and then clambered aboard. With no opportunities to say goodbye to comrades and acquaintances, the truck-borne prisoners watched the PW compound and then Camp Pickett itself disappear shortly after the trucks rolled through the main gate, their destination unknown. With a military police escort following behind, the deuce-and-a-halfs soon swung onto the state highway and began a 120-mile southwest trek to Pittsylvania County on the Virginia-North Carolina border. The young prisoners rocked and swayed back and forth as their wooden benches absorbed every bump, gravel, and pothole along the roads that wound through small towns, villages, verdant farmlands and scrub forests. The convoy and its human cargo finally arrived at a small fenced compound hidden in a pine forest near the town of Gretna and the community of Sandy Level.

Camp Sandy Level was a branch of the main prisoner of war compound at Camp Pickett. The camp consisted of one-story CCC-type buildings and a small athletic field surrounded by a high perimeter fence and guard towers.[19] Inside the

---

18. Krammer, *Nazi Prisoners*, 82-83.

camp, three American officers and thirty-six enlisted men watched over as many as 175 prisoners. The PWs, all Kriegsmarine personnel, plied the grounds between their barracks and a dispensary, a canteen, a chapel, a mess hall, and a day room. Permanent prisoner compounds and base camps such as Camp Pickett contained most of the amenities American troops enjoyed. In contrast, Camp Sandy Level was a temporary and more Spartan affair that offered little beyond basic accommodations for prisoners—though in April 1945 visiting Swiss representatives from the International Red Cross would find the condition of the camp and its prisoners entirely satisfactory. Hundreds of temporary branch camps like Sandy Level were located throughout the United States. Their sole purpose was to provide essential and readily obtainable prisoner of war labor for communities that suffered severe manpower shortages in their local work forces. The prisoners at Sandy Level were contracted mostly by local foresters to cut pulpwood in the surrounding area.[20]

The United States government was a signatory to the Geneva Convention of 1929, which asserted that prisoners of war were to be confined not for punishment, but simply to deprive the enemy of manpower resources and to convert those resources to its own use. It therefore adopted a rigid policy that was administered by the Prisoner of War Division of the Office of the Provost Marshal General of the U.S. Army, whereby prisoners could perform any type of work that was neither directly related to the war effort nor dangerous.[21] German PWs almost exclusively bolstered the American labor force that had been dramatically depleted by the war effort. Prisoner of war labor became essential as the armed forces swelled their ranks more than threefold between January 1942 and July 1943 alone to nearly seven million.[22] More than 300,000 Virginians had turned

19. CCC refers to the Civilian Conservation Corps, arguably the most successful, productive, and respected Depression-era federal program created by President Franklin Delano Roosevelt. CCC camps were constructed in close proximity to large-scale forestry projects to maximize the efficiency of the work force and—one suspects—to remove erstwhile unemployed young boys and men from unwholesome or destitute homes and neighborhoods.

20. Prisoner of War Camp, Camp Pickett, Virginia (Inspection Report), Enemy POW Information Bureau, Subject File, 1942-1946, Box 2669, Inspection & Field Reports—Camp Pickett, Record Group 389, United States National Archives and Records Administration, College Park, Maryland.

21. Lewis and Mewha, 78.

22. U.S. Army. *Biennial Report of the Chief of Staff of the United States Army, July 1, 1941 to June 30, 1943, to the Secretary of War*. Washington, DC: Government Printing Office, 1943, Chart 2.

in the tools of their civilian occupations and trades—many of which were in farming, semi-skilled, and unskilled jobs—to shoulder the tools of war.[23]

For several weeks Karl joined fellow prisoners aboard civilian trucks every morning to be transported to one of the sweeping stands of pine and cedar trees that surrounded Sandy Level. With axes and saws the men sweated through long days of hard labor to clear the forest under the supervision of civilian employers and armed guards. Army trucks delivered noontime lunches and water tanks for the prisoners, then carried the Germans back to the camp in the evening. Most PWs preferred the hard work outside of their camp above the monotony they endured inside the prison compound.

Civilians who came into contact with the Germans usually appeared not to resent the presence of prisoners of war in their community. The mostly-young captives were curiosities they occasionally encountered at rural country stores and gas stations when their guards or employers stopped for food supplies or cold drinks. Enemy prisoners symbolized the Allies' battlefield successes in Europe, though Germans on American soil were not universally welcomed. Local citizens—especially those with sons, brothers, or husbands in combat units overseas, or whose loved ones had been wounded or killed—sometimes resented the presence of war prisoners in their communities. One day while Baumann and several other prisoners struggled to cut lumber deep in the woods their water supply ran out. Rather than hike back to the distant roadside where their water supply was stationed, an army guard and a prisoner walked a short distance to a local farmhouse. The GI strode onto the porch and rapped on the farmer's screen door, then asked the man who appeared from inside if his work crew could have some water. The farmer peered over the guard's shoulder and saw the prisoner standing in his yard.

"What does that PW stand for," the man asked as he pointed to the prisoner's jacket.

"Prisoners of war. Germans," replied the guard. The man behind the screen door shook his head.

"No water for *them!*" he growled.

Karl and a dozen other Kriegsmarine prisoners were assembled around 1 April 1945 and told to gather themselves and their gear for immediate transfer to another camp. The PWs had become familiar with the utilitarian nature and routine of prisoner travel. They seldom were told that transfer plans lay in store for them until they were ordered to prepare for departure.

---

23. Wall, 64.

An Army truck soon pulled up to the compound gate. The prisoners threw their duffel bags onto the covered bed, then climbed aboard and settled onto the two wooden benches. Each man was given a one-day supply of canned and boxed Army rations. In short order the truck and an armed escort pulled away from Camp Sandy Level in the direction of the prisoners' next unknown destination. Karl watched the passing landscape through the open back of the canvas-covered truck bed, and noted the route took them north through a town named Lynchburg, and then west. The truck groaned against shifting gears and squeaked over road bumps that he barely noticed as he lost himself to his innermost thoughts. He again pondered his immediate future without fear, but with a measure of fresh anxiety and wondered how well he would adapt to yet another prison home.

8

Camp Lyndhurst Captive

One hundred fifteen miles north of Sandy Level, the olive drab deuce-and-a-half transporting Karl Baumann and other prisoners from Sandy Level pulled onto the first of a succession of narrow country roads that meandered through rural southeastern Augusta County, Virginia. Just south of the farming community of Lyndhurst, the truck turned right onto a dusty gravel incline that ran along a pine-forested hillside at the base of the George Washington National Forest. A permanent encampment there once bore the name Camp Sherando Lake when CCC boys gladly called it home during the Great Depression. The Second World War had consigned the tranquil name, like the CCC and the Depression years themselves, to history. The CCC had been disbanded in 1942 when large numbers of its members went to war. The camp then became home base for a detachment of conscientious objectors when the Brethren Service Committee of the pacifist Church of the Brethren operated it as Civilian Public Service Camp 29. CPS men had performed alternative service on local farms until mid-1944, when the camp was vacated and the group transferred to other encampments across the country.[1]

The exigencies of global warfare required a prisoner of war compound in Augusta County for farmers, loggers, and businessmen to house an inflow of desperately needed rural manpower. With utilitarian practicality, the U.S. Army had claimed the facility and renamed it Camp Lyndhurst, a branch of the large prisoner of war base camp at Camp Pickett. The CCC and CPS facility previously had resembled a Boy Scout camp, being nicely situated along a placid, wooded hillside. Now, with deliberation born of necessity, it had been transformed into a forbidding looking prison compound. Heavy woven barbed wire had been strung onto tall poles that formed a perimeter fence. The top wire strands were angled

---

1. The Church of the Brethren and Mennonite denominations are historically pacifist churches; many members' families have lived for generations in Augusta and Rockingham Counties of Virginia.

inward to entangle PWs who might try to climb their way to out of the camp. Wooden guard towers equipped with spotlights anchored each corner of the camp. Inside the fence, a large new washhouse with latrines awaited the men who would be confined there. A dozen tarpaper-covered barracks and other buildings comprised the prisoners' facilities. Administration buildings and barracks for the American garrison were located outside the fence. The camp stockade, a small wooden building that sat on a concrete base and was surrounded by a perimeter fence of its own, also sat just beyond the main compound. A heavy steel bar hinged horizontally to a post blocked the entrance at the base of the access road to prevent unauthorized vehicles from climbing the hill to the camp.[2] Unlike many temporary branch camps that housed both Germans and Americans alike in large army tents, Camp Lyndhurst was by its provenance more substantial and permanent in appearance. The wooden-framed buildings allowed the camp to operate throughout the year rather than only during the harvest seasons, for which the temporary tent encampments usually were erected.

Barracks street at Camp Lyndhurst, Augusta County, Virginia; 1943, shortly before it was converted into a Prisoner of War camp by the U.S. Army.

The first prisoners had arrived in August 1944 and were transferred into and out of the camp on a continual basis as labor needs arose in the surrounding community and elsewhere. The Germans had been provided by the U.S. Army under

2.   Jack Branch, interview by David Benevitch, 3 January 1991; and Karl Baumann, interview by David Benevitch, 18 April 1991.

the terms of a master labor contract executed with Higgs and Young, a basket and barrel manufacturing concern located in nearby Staunton. In turn, the master contractor sub-let prisoner labor to area farmers, orchardists and businessmen whose manpower needs outpaced the civilian labor market. Camp Lyndhurst housed 272 enlisted and four non-commissioned officer prisoners during the last two weeks of December 1944, the camp's highest population reported to the Prisoner of War Division of the Provost Marshal General's Office. On average, 227 prisoners were confined at the camp between 1 August 1944 and 31 December 1945. The numbers varied with manpower needed to fill contract PW labor demands. During the camp's seventeen months of operation, German prisoners provided 43,000 man-days of mostly agricultural labor—general farm and orchard work—in many rural communities of southeastern Augusta County. To a much lesser extent, they also were engaged in forestry, logging, and food processing. In addition, prisoners performed 25,344 man-days of work at the Lyndhurst compound itself and at the sprawling Woodrow Wilson Army Hospital in nearby Fishersville.[3]

The first group of prisoners confined at Camp Lyndhurst had been members of the Afrika Korps who, like those at Camp Pickett, displayed a brash attitude born of heartfelt belief that Germany still was winning the war. Most observers considered them arrogant and uncooperative in dealings with their American captors. The U.S. Army apparently agreed, and near the end of March transferred the German army prisoners out of Lyndhurst and replaced them with members of the Kriegsmarine.[4] Common knowledge held that, as a group, the German navy was the Wehrmacht branch least infected by the scourge of Nazi ideology; its members the least likely to make troublesome captives. The second influx of prisoners included men captured after the Normandy Invasion who were much more aware than the Afrika Korps prisoners that an unyielding succession of disasters had befallen the Wehrmacht since 1943. Among the disparate latter

---

3.   Prisoner of War Camp Labor Reports, 1 August 1944 through 31 December 1945, Record Group 389, Box 2491, United States National Archives and Records Administration, College Park, Maryland. Each prisoner of war base camp and branch camp was required to submit a biweekly report (W.D., P.M.G Form No. 27, Revised) on labor activities to its headquarters. Statistics were reported on the two-page Form in terms of man-days. Quite interestingly, the tally of 43,000 contract labor man-days is the exact number compiled from all Camp Lyndhurst work reports—not an estimated total.

4.   *"German Naval Personnel Replaces Nazi Army POWs at Lyndhurst,"* Waynesboro (Virginia) News Virginian, 28 March 1945.

group were boys as young as fifteen, middle-aged grandfathers, and nineteen year-old Karl Baumann.[5] His arrival at Camp Lyndhurst early in April 1945 coincided with two significant events that soon established the framework for a confrontational relationship between captors and captives. First, the camp received a new commanding officer in mid-April. Secondly, the long, brutal war in Europe ended on 7 May.

Karl quickly acclimated himself into the daily routine at Camp Lyndhurst, which varied little from day to day and week to week. Every evening in the course of a six-day workweek, the Germans gathered around a rock-and-mortar sign-board at one end of the walkway between the prisoners' barracks. There they scanned a work schedule that listed the names of employers who had entered into contracts with the Army for prisoner labor the following day, and the names of prisoners assigned to each employer. The prisoners who found their names on the list then deduced the type of work they would be required to perform.

The prisoners were awakened in their barracks at 06:00 each weekday and Saturday morning by guards blowing police whistles. With sleepy gazes, men donned work clothes that occasionally consisted of parts of their own Wehrmacht uniforms, but most often were U.S. Army-issue fatigues. They then assembled in front of the camp commander's office for the first roll call of the day. Commanded by German NCOs, the prisoners stood at attention, rank and file in groups of about fifty, while GI guards took a headcount. The count was reported to the American commander or a junior officer while the prisoners remained in formation and waited quietly to be dismissed for the workday that lay ahead. The Germans finally made their way to the washhouse and latrines in the lower corner of the camp, where they jockeyed for position to accomplish the morning's cleansing tasks and rituals. They then headed for the mess hall to receive a small breakfast of bread—the essential prison food—or other staple that was prepared for them by GI cooks at the Woodrow Wilson Army Hospital at Fishersville, ten miles from the camp. On occasion they wolfed down plates of powdered scrambled eggs or bowls of cream of wheat. Prisoners scheduled for work details outside of the compound also were given lunch that had been prepared by the hospital cooks. The usual lunch fare was three apple butter or cheese sandwiches packed in a used bread bag. Strangely, raw bacon occasionally appeared between the sandwich bread slices. The assigned laborers reported to the main gate at

---

5.   Pastor Robert J. Shenck; Mundelein, Illinois, to unknown addressee, July 1969, copy of letter from the collection of Joseph Moyer, Waynesboro, Virginia. Pastor Shenck, a Lutheran minister who spoke German, conducted Sunday services at the Camp Lyndhurst chapel.

07:00, where transportation to their work sites awaited them or soon would arrive.[6]

The sounds of cars and trucks wafted through the trees as a motley collection of civilian vehicles ground their way up the gravel road to the prison camp gate. Each contract employer or his representative checked in with the American Sergeant of the Guard to receive his daily allotment of prisoners. The PWs climbed into the waiting vehicles at 07:30 to ride to their respective work sites. Guards accompanied some, but not all, work crews and were responsible for the prisoners throughout the day. A large container of water was provided for the groups who were assigned to cut wood. The Germans worked about four hours on Augusta County's farms and in her forests, fields, and factories, took a lunch break at noon and water breaks as needed, then returned to work until around 17:00. Their contract employers delivered them back to Camp Lyndhurst at the end of the work day. The PWs usually went directly to the washhouse to scrub the day's accumulated grime off their tired, aching, and frequently sunburned bodies as soon as the Sergeant of the Guard recorded their return.[7]

Germans individually and in small groups made their way to the waiting line at the prisoners' mess hall by 18:00, where at its best a simple meal of potatoes, some vegetables, the ever-present bread, and sometimes meat was served. Their evening repast over, the prisoners usually were relieved from work for the remainder of the evening, but had to be accounted for during the nightly headcount. With lights-out ordered at 21:00, the entire camp settled in for the night; Germans and Americans alike then attempted to rest up to replay the nearly unaltered routine the next day.[8]

Rest and recreation for prisoners after work hours and on Sundays consisted of a diverse range of both informal and formal activities. PWs washed their own clothes, towels, and washcloths with GI soap and a washboard, a chore that might consume an evening's free hours. Wherever two or more gathered there was talk about the war and home, and about when and how they would make it back to the *Vaterland*. Many men chose simply to lie in bed to relax or read from the small library of German books and popular American magazines, while others learned the fundamentals of English grammar from reading the periodicals during their spare time. Some played cards, ping-pong, or volleyball. The musically inclined took advantage of a piano and several guitars, which sometimes they

---

6.   Hans Schages, interview by David Benevitch, 6 May 1991.
7.   Benevitch interview with Schages.
8.   Benevitch interview with Schages.

used to stage concerts. Most weekly schedules included one or more movies on Saturday night—Abbott and Costello, John Wayne, and other standard American fare—which were well attended by prisoners and GIs alike.[9]

Once or twice every week each prisoner could request a correspondence form to write home. Worried PWs anxiously wrote to family and friends they had not seen for many months or years, but some doubtless generated no reply. Tens of thousands of Germans already lay dead beneath the rubble of their cities, towns, and villages—victims of the war that had visited their homeland with unimaginable ferocity. By the time Germany finally surrendered unconditionally to the Allies in May 1945, its devastation was so complete that the USAAF and RAF had run out of strategic military targets to destroy.[10]

Chapel services and a mass for Catholics were held every Sunday, conducted by the prisoners and a prisoner Chaplain.[11] Armin Reda, a PW non-com and interpreter who was a professional musician, played the organ during the several services. Reda was a steadying influence for the other PWs—at least he attempted to be—and constantly found himself positioned squarely between Germans and Americans while he tried to deal with myriad problems and diverse issues of camp administration.

The camp's MP guards usually remained outside the compound, so prisoners were free to talk among themselves—often to complain about their work and living conditions. All the war news provided by the Americans described nothing but unmitigated disaster for Germany and its people. Prisoners longed for freedom from captivity and to be reunited with loved ones. Griping was a natural outgrowth for men imprisoned thousands of miles from home, absent news from and about loved ones, and being compelled to labor for their captors. Complaints were manifold: rides to work often were cold and dangerous, work hours were long and tiring, soccer and other popular activities had been curtailed or eliminated, and the food quality and quantity had turned lousy. An undercurrent of barely suppressed anger surged through the compound and over time gradually increased in intensity.

---

9.   Benevitch interview with Schages.

10. Geoffrey Perret, *Winged Victory; The Army Air Forces in World War II* (New York: Random House, 1993), 372-373. The Eighth USAAF flew its final strategic bombing mission against the Skoda iron works at Pilson, Czechoslovakia on 25 April, 1945, nearly two weeks before the end of the war in Europe. The Eighth's subsequent missions were flown by bombers laden with canned foods that were dropped onto soccer fields across famine-gripped northern Holland.

11. Benevitch interview with Schages.

Even as Karl Baumann settled into his new prison home, a pervasive but unsubstantiated rumor spread among the Lyndhurst prisoners: a large portion of the food intended for the PWs seemed never to reach the camp's dinner tables. Prisoners who had helped transport the meals from the Woodrow Wilson Army Hospital supposedly had sworn that the printed lists that accompanied the food deliveries proved they were not receiving the shares provided for them. Many concluded the stolen goods were being sold on the local black market. Where the missing food actually or allegedly had gone and those responsible for its disappearance remained a mystery, but the PWs found it easy to blame the camp's succession of commanding officers for all their complaints. Within such a climate of mistrust, rumors were combined with facts to feed the captives' growing restiveness and anger. By April the Germans had begun to congregate with increasing frequency to voice their collective grievances, which by mid-month culminated in an ill-advised plan of organized action.

The groundswell of smoldering tension surfaced among the prisoners on the evening of 12 April, and soon was carried from one barrack to another. By the end of the night the men had organized a general strike to protest their conditions. Before the next morning's roll call, every German either willingly agreed to strike or had been cajoled by fellow prisoners to go along with the planned action. No one was certain that a positive outcome would result, but almost every prisoner felt compelled to object to conditions most believed had become commonplace rather than exceptional.

Captain William A. Calafiura, U.S. Army, became the fourth commander of the camp in its nine months of operation.[12] The thirty-one year-old New York City native arrived in nearby Waynesboro on 12 April 1945, depressed and dispirited. During the drive westward from his former duty station at the Hampton Roads Port of Embarkation, Calafiura and his wife Mary Louise were shaken by a flash news report that blared over their car's radio. An announcer urgently reported that President Franklin D. Roosevelt had died suddenly at his retreat in Warm Springs, Georgia. The solemn news magnified the captain's sense of loss, the inescapable feeling that his familiar world had been turned upside down by events beyond his control. At the bottom of his depression lay the fact that he thoroughly hated his assignment to Camp Lyndhurst as its commanding officer, and to oversee the German prisoners of war confined there. All of his previous

---

12. Labor Reports, August 1944 to April 1945. The camp's commanding officer signed each labor report.

experience with PWs, he declared to himself time and again, had been with Italian Internees.[13]

Fascist Italy's 1943 break with Axis partner Germany, as well as its surrender to American and British invasion forces, had created a quagmire of political and logistical ramifications. With Italy now actually an ally, Italian prisoners of war under U.S. control were reclassified as Internees. The dubious status meant Italian captives were not quite prisoners but also not quite free men. Thousands of internees had been organized into aptly named Italian Service Units—ISUs—that performed war-related work under the command of U.S. Army officers and enlisted personnel.[14]

William A. Calafiura, Captain, U.S. Army, (center) accompanied by Mrs. Calafiura, poses with American staff officers, their wives, and members of the 315th Italian Quartermaster Service Battalion at the Port of Hampton Roads, Virginia, circa December 1944. Capt. Calafiura was the fourth and final commander of PW Camp Lyndhurst in Augusta County, Virginia.

Captain Calafiura, a former intelligence officer with the Coast Artillery Corps, had dealt exclusively with Italian PWs and Internees since November 1942.

13.   William A. Calafiura, interview by David Benevitch, 25 June 1991.
14.   Lewis and Mewha, 93-100. Since Italy no longer was an enemy nation, the Geneva Convention did not prohibit Internees from working directly for the Allied war effort. For their efforts the Internees received the same pay as American enlisted men.

Being of Italian stock himself, he spoke Italian fluently. He knew how to manage, interrogate, and screen Italian troops for assignment to ISUs, and had instructed other intelligence officers in the procedures as well. He had commanded the 315th Italian Quartermaster Service Battalion, an 800-man unit at the Port of Hampton Roads, between November 1944 and February 1945. In every respect, the captain had compiled an exemplary record of achievement for his service with Italian troops confined in the United States.

Calafiura was short and slender in stature, but those who mistook his wiry frame for a sign of weakness could find themselves on the losing end of a bitter confrontation. His physical and temperamental attributes were tantamount to a compact tornado in a tight twist.

The captain was thoroughly convinced that his assignment to Lyndhurst was a monumental lapse of military judgement and common sense; that his experience and knowledge could be and should be best utilized elsewhere. In short order he had appealed to his commanding officer at Camp Pickett, then to the commanding general of the Third Service Command, for reassignment to an ISU rather than to German PWs at Lyndhurst. His formal transfer requests had been met with cold silence if not outright rejection. Like it or not, he was going to Lyndhurst.[15] The Army had its reasons, which apparently it chose not to explain to Calafiura, and that was that. The captain didn't want the assignment, didn't like it, didn't understand or truly know the reason for it, and found the Army's lack of logic and reasoning exceedingly galling. Regardless, he was determined to discharge the duties of his new command with all the strength of will that belied his unassuming, slight stature and thin mustache. Multifarious burdens weighed heavily upon the captain as he settled Mary Louise into the boarding house room they had rented in Waynesboro; he would drive out to Camp Lyndhurst the next morning.[16]

The ranking officers of the Prisoner of War Division at Camp Pickett had become dissatisfied with the quality of leadership at Lyndhurst and the overall operation of the camp. Serious complaints from the American cadre and reported incidents both inside and outside the barbed wire enclosure had filtered back to

---

15. William A. Calafiura, letter to the Commanding General, U.S. Army Third Service Command, Baltimore, Maryland, 2 March 1945; and Benevitch interview with Calafiura.

16. Benevitch interview with Calafiura. During his assignment Captain Calafiura lived at Camp Lyndhurst while his wife lived in a boarding house on Wayne Avenue in nearby Waynesboro. Also, Albert Moreman, interview by David Benevitch, May 1991.

PW Division officials, who concluded that Camp Lyndhurst had become a hot potato that needed an even hotter new commander to take firm control of the situation. The officials were convinced one or more troublemakers among the prisoners were working up the others to create some sort of incident. They warned Calafiura that the Germans already had threatened a work strike over grievances that had been presented to the former camp commander. The captain had resolved then and there that if any PWs under his command ever had the unmitigated gall to stage a work stoppage, he would respond headlong to their defiance.[17] To be sure, the Army got its money's worth when it sent William A. Calafiura to Camp Lyndhurst. The timeliness of his arrival at the camp early on the morning of 13 April was nothing short of extraordinary—and quite nearly fateful.

GI guards stood in the barracks doorways and blew police whistles clutched in their teeth to awaken the prisoners out of a night of fitful sleep. The Germans began their morning routine as usual, but all thoughts and conversations were focused upon the showdown that was about to take place. After the first roll call and the usual monotonous breakfast fare was served up in the mess hall, PWs singly and in groups walked back to their barracks instead of the main gate to wait for rides to their work sites. Inside their quarters they waited anxiously and expectantly for the next move that soon would come. None of the prisoners knew or could have contemplated that a new camp commander actually would arrive at the worst possible moment to confront their disobedience.

Captain Calafiura, fresh from Waynesboro and with no forewarning of the strike that already was underway, had just stepped from his car when he was apprised that the prisoners—every one of them—apparently had conspired to refuse to report for work. In short order the captain realized the hot potato he had been warned about had just been thrown to him; he had a general work strike on his hands. Though entirely unaware of the prisoners' complaints, he immediately saw the strike as an act of open defiance and insubordination he did not intend to tolerate. His commands came fast and furiously.

In a matter of moments the entire American cadre stormed into the prisoners' barracks, swinging nightsticks and shouting orders. The GIs forced the Germans outside, formed them up into columns, and marched them through the main gate and onto the soccer field situated next to the motor pool.

Military Police guards were not permitted to carry firearms inside the camp, but outside the fence they faced the PWs with loaded M1 carbines. A team of GIs

---

17. Benevitch interviews with Calafiura and Moreman.

ran atop a raised platform at the edge of the field and mounted a Browning light machinegun onto its tripod, then fed a linked belt of .30 caliber bullets into the weapon. Other soldiers ran to the motor pool and swung open the large doors to the building, then rolled out the camp's several Army trucks to set up a perimeter defense around on the edge of the field. MPs clambered aboard the truck beds to guard the Germans from a higher elevation. In the center of the field the prisoners stood at attention, lined up rank and file an arm's length from each other.

The captain strode out to the soccer field and faced the Germans for the first time. Armin Reda, the Kriegsmarine NCO who served as the prisoners' English speaking interpreter stood nearby.

"Do you understand tough language?" Calafiura demanded to know; the prisoner nodded in the affirmative.

"I want you now to tell these men, 'You stand at attention, and the first son of a bitch that moves will be shot!'"[18] Reda delivered the warning word for word as Calafiura had ordered.

The captain wheeled around and stormed off to his office next to the compound, where he nervously kept watch the rest of the day. Thus began a waiting game that continued through the morning hours while the prisoners stood, silent and motionless. The contract employers who had arrived at the camp to collect their consignments of PWs soon turned their cars and trucks around and drove back down the hill. Karl Baumann took stock of the situation as the spring sunshine fell upon the strange scene at the soccer field. He quickly concluded there was no reason to fear the intentions of the machinegunners or the MP guards. The Americans, he reasoned, would never massacre the prisoners, especially on their home soil. Sound logic, however, is not always met by sensible reality. The palpable tension and strained nerves that attended both groups very nearly got out of hand to create an ugly wartime incident on the nondescript plot of land in Augusta County, Virginia.

The prisoners quietly stood in place until noon when, paradoxically, they were marched into the prisoners' mess hall for a lunch of the quality and nature that had reinforced their determination to strike in the first place. After lunch the bizarre showdown resumed when the prisoners were marched back to the soccer field and ordered into formation, again to stand at attention while the minutes

---

18. Benevitch interview with Calafiura. Nearly five decades later the captain admitted that his threat actually was a bluff, but because he had verbally issued the stern warning in the first place, shooting might have begun if the prisoners had rushed the guns or broken and run. He realized the bluff was a risky proposition, but believed he had to establish absolute authority and deal firmly with the strike.

and hours slowly ticked by.[19] Americans and Germans alike grew weary, tired and irritable under the bright sunshine of mid-afternoon. The strike plodded along uneventfully until an elderly prisoner named Knölle, whose age and jocular personality made him most noticeable, began to bait the guards and make off-hand and sordid remarks about them. A German-speaking MP who stood on a truck bed overheard the breach of silence and ordered the offending prisoner to step to the front of the ranks. Knölle did so, but when the guard turned his back, the old German uttered yet another scurrilous remark. The GI spun around and glared at Knölle.

"Shut up!" the guard yelled.

"You shut up!" Knölle retorted.

The GI suddenly jerked his carbine toward his shoulder and angrily yanked back the cocking bolt. The heavy steel handle slammed forward with a loud metallic *clack* that echoed across the field as it shoved a thirty-caliber round into the chamber. Guards and prisoners alike stiffened at the sound. GIs on the field quickly ran into the ranks of prisoners and pulled them out of the line of fire as the MP leveled his carbine at the obstinate old German who now stood alone. Baumann needed no prodding to flee to the edge of the field and relative safety as the showdown began to take a perilous turn.

"He's going to shoot you!" a frantic German voice exclaimed. Knölle stood his ground and yanked open his jacket.

"Shoot, you coward!" Knölle sneered.

Time stood still for a few interminable seconds while GIs and Germans alike almost feared to breathe. Finally, the guard shook his head in disgust as he lowered his weapon.

"Shoot this old Kraut and *I'll* wind up in prison," the guard most likely reasoned to himself, knowing that momentary humiliation was preferable to the consequences he would face if he squeezed off several rounds into the German.

"Get back into your line," the American bellowed, frustrated with the old man's insolence.

---

19. Memories differ regarding the manner in which the PWs relieved themselves during their daylong strike. Former guard Albert Moreman recalled the Germans were forced to stand in place even to relieve themselves, whereas Hans Schages implied that the PWs could ask permission to use a latrine. See Benevitch interviews with Moreman and Schages. Karl Baumann recalled that a prisoner simply raised his hand to indicate he needed to relieve himself, after which a GI would direct the PW to the woods beside the soccer field.

The prisoners restored their ranks and files. A bloody crisis had been narrowly averted, but for the remainder of the afternoon the prisoners stood uneasily and silently on the soccer field. The results of an outbreak of violence might have fomented dire consequences for other prisoners thousands of miles away at German PW camps in besieged Europe.

Remarkably, at 17:00, the nominal end of the workday, the PWs were marched back inside the camp and dismissed to return to their barracks. The Germans had staged the work strike for an entire day, but as they trod wearily to their barracks and then to the mess hall they asked each other just what they had accomplished. Their action could have precipitated an unintended disaster. Any momentary victory, they realized, was fleeting at best. Food rations would remain painfully lacking, and some civilians would continue to transport PWs with little or no regard for comfort or safety. When the Germans returned from their restored work details the next day they discovered guard-baiting Knölle had been transferred from Camp Lyndhurst without a word. The recalcitrant old PW most certainly had been shipped off to a camp designated for incorrigible prisoners.

Captain Calafiura had determined to deal sternly and immediately with the strike, based upon his perception that the German mindset was to obey orders. He also believed that as a result of his tough response to the work stoppage the prisoners would realize early on that he was a no-nonsense camp commander unlike his predecessors. He asserted the strike occurred in the first place because the prisoners had no respect for—or no fear of—the commanding officer he had replaced, which to him was utterly contemptible.[20]

The prisoners tried to size up the new C.O. who suddenly had stormed onto the scene and now held complete sway over their daily lives. Rumors swept across the prison compound as presumptions were combined with known facts and personal observations, some of which may have been fueled by the American guards themselves. A near-consensus emerged about the man's character and being, which defined the prisoners' stock opinion of Captain Calafiura. The Germans concluded that despite his short stature he was a very tough soldier who said what he meant and meant what he said. He seemed to talk through clenched teeth, with lips barely moving, which to the captives revealed an underlying mean streak. He also exhibited a high-strung, nervous tendency; his hands noticeably shook when prisoners were in close proximity. He obviously was of Italian stock. The PWs also presumed, quite incorrectly, that he was Jewish.[21] In short order the prisoners also concluded that Calafiura hated Germans.

---

20. Benevitch interview with Calafiura.

The captain actually didn't hate Germans, he reasoned; they were prisoners of war, enemy personnel on U.S. soil who had no rights whatsoever other than those specifically conferred by the Geneva Convention. He was determined to treat the prisoners fairly but firmly—very firmly. His resolve was founded upon several additional factors. First, two brothers presently served in combat units overseas, where discomfort, brutality and death were constant companions. Second, the Arsenal of Democracy had produced an extraordinary quantity of war materiel and occasional minor luxuries intended to ease the burden of men in combat. Those products often failed to reach the front line troops, however, when at the very same time PWs confined in the United States were well supplied and cared for; they fared much better than the soldiers, sailors, and airmen who had defeated them in battle. The new camp commander and no small number of Americans—politicians, well-known personalities, and common citizens alike—believed German PWs were being coddled. The prisoners had been having a picnic in America, Calafiura believed, and he would have none of it on his watch.[22]

The morning following the failed strike, a prisoner asked to speak with the captain and was ushered into C.O.'s office. The German stood stiffly at attention while at the doorway in his adjoining quarters the captain stood partially dressed in front of a mirror and shaved. Calafiura ignored the prisoner's presence and slowly continued to scrape the lathered shaving cream off his face with a safety razor. He wanted the German to see that he would conduct himself as he, the C.O., saw fit, without regard to whatever formal protocol a German prisoner might expect or desire.

"What is your problem?" the captain finally demanded to know.

"Captain, sir," the prisoner intoned, "I wish to complain that what you are doing is against the Geneva Convention."

Calafiura interrupted his shaving and stared contemptuously at the prisoner; then carefully placed his razor on the rim of his sink. He then and there concluded, perhaps correctly but without hard evidence, that the spokesman standing before him had been an instigator of the work strike. An instant later the 130-pound captain charged into the office, grabbed the startled prisoner by the scruff of his pants and shirt collar and ran him to the open office door. With the help of

---

21.   Captain Calafiura was Catholic, according to his obituary from *The Journal* (Martinsburg, WV) 9 August 2001.

22.   Benevitch interview with Calafiura.

their forward momentum, the C.O. pitched the German over the flight of six steps onto the ground below.

"I want him on bread and water for ten days," Calafiura shouted to the guard who stood nearby. Then he directed his fury to the hapless prisoner still prostrate on the ground. The captain pointed to the man and unleashed an unambiguous warning:

"Don't you *ever* lecture me again on the Geneva Convention! This nation has bent over backwards being decent to you people and I don't expect you to tell me that! Bread and water! And if you don't behave in ten days, I'm going to let you out for a day and put you back on bread and water for another ten days!"

The guard gathered up the PW and hurried him away from the office and the captain's gaze. The C.O.'s order was not merely a dietary constraint. One of Calafiura's first inquiries about the layout of his camp was whether there were any punishment cells to segregate troublemakers and other PWs who needed to be taught who was in charge. Assured that a stockade indeed was available, Calafiura would not hesitate to order prisoners to solitary confinement inside the forbidding little prison-beside-the-prison as he saw fit, to demonstrate that he and he alone exercised complete control over the German captives under his command.[23]

By the time the captain arrived at Lyndhurst, dissatisfaction ran deep in the ranks of the Army garrison. Complaints by the garrison's enlisted men made the coddling accusations even more intolerable for the C.O. During a well-attended gripe session, the guard cadre vented their frustration that some employers—particularly Mennonite farmers—gave refreshments of milk, cake, and other goodies to PWs working for them but offered nothing to the guards who stood nearby. To make matters worse, some civilians had gone to extreme lengths to show greater compassion for the Germans who labored for them than for the American soldiers.

One PW contractor had for six months paid rent on a piano for the prison compound. He had given a fountain pen to each of the twenty-five PWs who worked at his orchard and later twenty dollars each to twenty-three prisoners. He also gave a watch to the prisoner-foreman and a football for the prisoners at the

---

23. Benevitch interview with Calafiura. The former Camp Commander could not recall in 1991 whether the punishment cells already existed or he ordered them built. Since he ordered at least one PW on bread and water probably on his second day at Lyndhurst, most likely the cells already were available. Bread and water punishment seems unlikely to have been administered unless a PW was segregated in a stockade away from the rest of the prisoner population.

camp. In the wake of such philanthropy, some GIs had written to the local Red Cross chapter to complain about the treatment they had received and conditions under which Americans served at Camp Lyndhurst. Calafiura listened to the volley of complaints and accusations and became more incensed at the state of affairs that existed there. He considered each revelation an indictment against the camp's former commanders, whose lack of military decorum had created the wholly unacceptable conditions at the camp and among civilian employers.[24]

Local users of PW labor who extended kindness to their Germans workers neither set out to intentionally subvert the U.S. Army's prisoner of war program nor the authority of Camp Lyndhurst's commander. Most simply treated the prisoners like their American employees. Mennonite farmers, for their part, treated prisoner workers as they would hope to have been treated if the circumstances were reversed. Naivete perhaps, if one considered the plight of most prisoners of the Wehrmacht, the *SS*, and the *Gestapo;* especially that of prisoners the *Reich* deemed racially inferior. Nonetheless, the Mennonite community was clear upon the matter. To respect their egalitarian and pacifist beliefs, they overlooked the responsibility that devolved to the individual German soldier, sailor, and airman for Germany's vicious aggression against Europe and the world. That some employers chose not to extend their beneficence to the GIs in their midst who watched over the prisoners at farms and in the fields and orchards is less easy to explain or rationalize, if indeed the soldiers' accusations were accurate. Such prejudice may have been attributable to a perception that armed American soldiers held the upper hand over lowly prisoners of war, and that the GIs fed and cared for themselves better than for their captives. In any regard, those who criticized the Mennonites who extended generous hospitality to prisoners of war simply could not ignore the disparity they believed was being practiced by members of the pacifist congregations.

Thirty to forty enlisted men normally were assigned to the camp as guards, administrative personnel, and vehicle mechanics. Though the men lived in barracks outside the compound fence, their duty station in the mountains of western Virginia was very confining to them as well. Most did not view their assignment to the PW camp as choice duty in any respect, even though some enjoyed two or more days off duty between their twelve-hour shifts. Some preferred combat to stateside service, a desire to test their mettle and contribute directly to the Allies' certain victory. Others felt far less martial zeal and simply wished to be anywhere else but in the ranks of the armed forces. Service men's clubs and other comforts

---

24. Benevitch interview with Calafiura.

and amenities that were common fixtures in or near large permanent military installations either were minimal or nonexistent at Lyndhurst and in the surrounding rural community, with two notable exceptions. Lyndhurst community residents usually went out of their way to treat the GIs with kindness, and the men always were offered free drinks and food at weekly parties held for them at the E. I. DuPont de Nemours plant in nearby Waynesboro.

The captain was empathetic to the frustrations his men expressed; but when complaints began to point toward the camp's officers, their abilities and their conduct, he promptly prohibited any further such comments. He determined however, that many of their complaints were well-founded and justified.[25]

Calafiura quickly concluded the former C.O.'s informal command style was wholly the cause for Camp Lyndhurst being "in shambles and improperly administered as a PW camp." He had found the prisoners' canteen amply stocked with a large supply of beer and soft drinks, as well as cigarette brands that local civilians could not buy due to wartime shortages. The canteen also sold hairbrush sets and other fancy items the captain declared unnecessary to any prisoner's survival. The captain immediately ordered his staff to remove all such luxury items from the tiny store, which to the Germans' supreme disappointment included the beer. He vowed to his men and to himself to restore strict military order to the place—fast.

"I'm going to run a tight ship," he told his officers, "and whether you choose to remain or put in for a transfer, I'm going to do things my way; and it's going to be a different way of operating!"[26]

Another of Calafiura's first acts as the camp commander was to inspect the prisoners and their living conditions; in the process he, along with several guards and prisoner representatives, suddenly strode into Karl Baumann's barracks one evening without warning.

"*Achtung!*" someone shouted loudly. The prisoners immediately suspended their various diversions to run to their bunks, where they stood stiffly at attention while the American commander reviewed first the line of men and bunks to his right. Motionless Germans stared straight ahead while the captain critically observed each man and his living space with careful deliberation. At the far end of the long central corridor he swung around to his left and inspected the opposite line of prisoners as he slowly made his way back toward the front of the barracks.

---

25. Benevitch interviews with Calafiura and Branch.
26. Benevitch interviews with Calafiura and Schages.

As he finally made his way silently to the front door he stopped suddenly in his tracks. A portrait of Adolf Hitler hung on the wall next to the door, in keeping with prisoners' rights under the Geneva Convention to display nationalistic symbols during wartime. The Germans still faced ahead but looked out of the corners of their eyes to see just what Calafiura would do. The captain stepped close to the picture and studied Hitler's malevolent glare for several seconds, then launched a heavy salvo of spit squarely onto the dictator's face. Without a word, he pushed the door open and stormed out of the barracks with his small entourage trailing behind.

Audible sighs of relief broke the tense atmosphere of the room as the PWs relaxed after their latest encounter with the camp's new commander. The fiery captain had disparaged the *Führer*, but failed to notice a loose wall panel that hid a homemade Nazi flag and a .22 caliber rifle a prisoner had found while chopping wood. No one dared contemplate the hullabaloo that would have ensued had Calafiura discovered the stash of contraband that served as symbols of their defiant captivity.

Barracks inspections did reveal a variety of weapons the captain relieved from the prisoners posthaste. The confiscated ordnance included a variety of clubs and baseball bats, as well as knives the PWs apparently had been able to buy in their own canteen before Calafiura's no-nonsense takeover at Lyndhurst.[27]

The captain found the prisoners' mess hall not to his liking during his inspection tour. While prisoners watched intently, he pulled a brush and a bar of strong GI soap out of his jacket pocket and ordered a pail of water brought to him. With the cleaning supplies in hand he knelt down and scrubbed a small area of the floor until a gleaming circle of clean wood appeared. Calafiura then stood up and faced the PW first sergeant and his interpreter.

"I want every floor in every building in this compound that color as soon as possible," he commanded while he pointed with emphasis to the circle on the floor. "I want this done; and you're going to do this on your off hours, not when you're supposed to be working."

Having assessed the disarray he apparently had found in some barracks, the captain added, "You are not going to be permitted to hang clothes all over the barracks. They are going to be immaculate, clean, in order, or there will be hell to pay!"

---

27. Benevitch interview with Calafiura.

Row of barracks that housed prisoners at Camp Lyndhurst, Virginia.

The previous day's strike and the threat of further defiance by the Germans still weighed heavily upon the new camp commander, who had dealt immediately with prisoners' discontent through the imposition of strict discipline and order. The prisoners, he demanded, were going to clean up their compound, police it and keep it in immaculate shape. They would be treated sternly but fairly, and would never forget for a moment that they were prisoners of war—the enemy—and not guests.[28] They would not forget that they had been sent to America to work and would fulfill their obligation as prescribed under the Geneva Convention. At the end of the day the Germans would be too tired to conspire to strike. And one more thing, the captain warned the prisoners:

"If you see, or you think you see—or you may think you are going to see—an American officer, and you don't salute him, I don't care if he is ten miles away on the other side of town, you had better salute him. If there is any doubt in your mind, you had better salute him or I will put you on bread and water!"

Captain Calafiura's tough approach to PW camp administration did not spare his American counterparts. All PW camps in the United States were subject to inspection by the Provost Marshal General's office as well as by representatives of the International Red Cross. Some time later, but prior to any of the official visits, several officers advised the captain that in order to receive a favorable inspection report, he should be aware that the Army's inspecting officer liked a particular brand of booze, and liked to fish and tell fish stories.

---

28.   Benevitch interview with Calafiura.

"I don't give a damn what this guy likes!" he thundered to his subordinates. "This camp is going to be in tip top shape twenty-four hours a day. That is how I'm running it. I'm not going to stay awake wondering what this guy likes or doesn't like. He likes fishing; I don't fish. He likes to drink; I don't drink. I am not going to play up to him. This camp is going to be in tip top shape and you guys better keep that in mind!" The captain's brazen command style later caused him to run afoul of his own commanding officer at Camp Pickett, though his efforts were redeemed when an inspecting officer's subsequent field report indicated Calafiura had produced outstanding results since taking command of Camp Lyndhurst.[29]

Nazi Germany's war effort finally was dealt its deathblow in early May 1945. The *Reich's* formal surrender soon affected the treatment German prisoners received in virtually every base camp and branch camp in the United States. The immediate effects were profound and twofold for the prisoners at Lyndhurst. Most importantly for the PWs, the quality and quantity of their food was dramatically reduced from already-questionable levels. Secondly, when the war ended the Germans were forbidden to wear the swastika or any other Nazi insignia; neither could they display Nazi flags, pictures, or symbols. They were forbidden to engage in any Nazi-oriented activities, and all Nazi emblems had to be removed, cut out, or painted over.

The United States had strictly observed its policy to provide the same food and accommodations for German prisoners that American camp personnel received while the war had raged in Europe. When the Allies overran formerly occupied territories in the final weeks of the war, however, they discovered Auschwitz, Bergen-Belsen, and the whole vast network of Nazi concentration camps. Then, when American prisoners of war were freed from the Wehrmacht's *Stalags* and *Oflags*, the newspapers and airwaves were filled with harrowing descriptions of those who had suffered terribly at the hands of their German captors through brutality, lack of food, and inadequate shelter.[30] The sordid reports that came out of Germany prompted outrage from virtually every sector of American society.

American guards one day entered each of the prisoner barracks and the mess hall with a stack of photographs in hand. On the captain's orders, following those he had received from the Third Service Command, the guards tacked up a grisly collection of pictures taken by American and British combat cameramen. The

---

29. Benevitch interview with Calafiura.
30. A *Stalag* was a German prison camp for Allied enlisted personnel and non-commissioned officers; an *Oflag* was a camp that housed only officers.

photos revealed in stark detail the horrendous brutality that ruled the German concentration camp system. In scores and by the hundreds, emaciated corpses with shaven heads and hollow-eyed stares of death were shown stacked in haphazard heaps inside the death camps. Karl Baumann and every other German was required to sign an affidavit to affirm that he had seen the graphic display. The prisoners stared incredulously at the pictures, which remained posted for some time, and forced themselves to come to terms with the most inhumane of legacies their country had fostered during the Hitler era. For most, the truth simply was too horrible or difficult to comprehend and accept. By and large, the PWs dismissed the photos and denied the evidence that had been placed before them as American propaganda. Some continued to believe fantastic rumors that the Luftwaffe had bombed New York City, and elsewhere had returned the tide of victory to the Axis forces. For these reasons, Calafiura wisely allowed prisoners to install radio sets in their compound so English-speaking prisoners could translate the daily news for their barracks mates. In addition to large doses of local hillbilly music, the Germans were free to listen to all American news broadcasts across the AM frequency spectrum and learn the hard facts for themselves.[31]

In the wake of the contemptuous revelations from the death camps, American PW camp commanders on their own volition reduced or abandoned long-standing and officially mandated humanitarian policies. Many prisoners observed that the quality and quantity of food declined most dramatically. The emotional response to German atrocities neglected the fact that the better the PW laborers ate, the better they worked. Within a month of Karl's transfer to Lyndhurst, prisoners' complaints about their food rations began in earnest. Without doubt, his days as a first-class prisoner—as he initially referred to himself—definitely were over.

Employers and prisoners alike were forbidden to fraternize, a rule that was often if not almost universally ignored when civilians learned to know individual PWs and became familiar with their work habits and personality traits. Employers in short order learned which prisoners were the best workers and began to request them by name day after day, ostensibly so they would not constantly have to train other PWs at the cost of time and productivity. Though they never revealed the truth to camp officials, employers frequently became personally attached to certain prisoners; and PWs developed bonds with employers who treated them well. The quality of the work prisoners performed almost always

31. Benevitch interview with Calafiura.

depended upon the quality of treatment they received from their employers and the regular hired help—the classic *quid pro quo* of human relationships.

Karl first was hired out to a logging company to cut pulpwood in the Blue Ridge foothills. He and another prisoner each were expected to fell and trim one cord of pine pulpwood each day; the diameter of trees destined for Virginia's paper mills dictated that between thirty and forty had to be cut to meet their quota. Every tree had to be cut into eight-foot lengths, which then were placed neatly side by side and atop each other to measure a four-by-eight foot stack.[32] The men chopped, sawed, trimmed, and hefted trees on numerous Augusta County hillsides without the aid of power tools. Baumann's partner had been shot in both arms before he was captured, and the damage he suffered to both biceps made him unable to lift heavy tree limbs and trunks. The man's physical limitations compelled Karl to carry out the most tiring work for the pair. To sustain his strength for the backbreaking work he usually received sixteen slices of bread and a strip of raw bacon for lunch.

Captain Calafiura was indignant to discover that some prisoners did not meet their daily pulpwood quota before they were returned to camp at the end of the workday, an affront he was not about to let stand. He ruled that every PW would cut his daily quota even if he had to work into the nighttime hours with the aid of portable spotlights. The decree went into effect and bore extraordinary results that definitely were not to the captain's liking. To his dismay, some prisoners produced their cord of pulpwood by lunchtime and were delivered back at the camp by 13:30 in the afternoon.

"I will not have the Germans hang around this camp from one-thirty onward doing nothing," Calafiura thundered, and ordered the pulpwood quota increased to two cords daily so the prisoners would have to put in an exhausting full day of work.[33]

Karl and his hapless partner so despised the disproportionate wood-to-food ratio that one morning they conspired to avoid the hard work altogether. When they arrived at the work site each quickly swallowed a hearty dose of Bull Durham loose tobacco they had bought at the prisoners' canteen. In no time flat a guard saw both men heave and retch in knee-bending agony before they regurgitated their breakfast onto the forest floor. Bad case of food poisoning, the sympathetic guard concluded; he then told them to take it easy and not to try to work the remainder of the day. Karl and his cohort thanked the guard for his under-

---

32. Benevitch interview with Schages.
33. Benevitch interviews with Calafiura and Schages.

standing as they crawled onto the bed of a utility truck to spend the day peace-fully asleep in the warm sun of early spring.

Except when Baumann worked several days with a prisoner-staffed landscap-ing detail at the Woodrow Wilson Army Hospital, transportation to and from Camp Lyndhurst was provided by civilian employers with contracts for prisoner labor. Some drove ten miles or more to the camp to collect their workers. Com-mutes between the camp and some work sites could be cold, dangerous, and just short of brutal, as was the case when Karl worked for a logging outfit located in rural Nelson County, along Augusta County's eastern border, below a mountain community named Love.

The young man sent by the loggers to pick up their daily allotment of prison-ers exhibited an unnerving and well-known lack of driving skill. While white-faced guards climbed into the truck cab a half-dozen or more Germans hesitantly piled onto the gate-bed. The men then held on for dear life as the driver threw the truck into gear and slammed his foot on the accelerator. The truck jolted to life and generated a dust storm as it tore downhill from the camp. The driver then swung hard right onto narrow County Road 664 in the direction of She-rando Lake and the Blue Ridge Mountains. He barely slowed down as he plowed through intersections and careened around corners almost on two wheels. The weight of the terrified passengers shifted violently with the centrifugal force of each tire-screeching turn. Without a canvas cover over the cargo bed the cold morning air whipped through the prisoners' lightweight jackets and work clothes while the truck roared up the mountain road. At the crest of the mountain the truck hurdled the Blue Ridge Parkway, then plummeted down the treacherous dirt road past Love toward the base of the eastern mountainside. The truck bed creaked and shuddered to protest the countless washboard bumps, potholes, and loose stones that brutalized tires and passengers alike. To add further insult, the driver refused to stop the truck for any reason. When a PW could wait no longer he was compelled to balance precariously over the back of the truck to relieve himself. Embarrassment was complete whenever the hapless prisoner failed to adequately brace himself or shift his weight against the wildly bucking vehicle. The wide-eyed Germans were grateful when the truck finally slid to a stop at a logging site at Crabtree Falls, but positively dreaded their return trip to the camp. The young driver must have taken malicious delight in the torture he inflicted upon his riders. No one innocently could have driven so badly.

"Timber!" PWs assigned to pulpwood cutting and logging teams had been taught a few tools of the trade by a civilian logger who held a brief training course inside the camp. The familiar warning cry was one of the few English words the prisoners learned through official channels. The logging instructor spoke through an interpreter and showed by example the proper use of axes and large crosscut saws, how to notch a tree to coax it to fall in the desired direction, and how to efficiently strip the trunk of limbs and branches. The Germans also learned to properly load and stack the four to five foot lengths of trimmed logs onto trucks to be hauled to the railroad depot in Stuarts Draft.[34]

Camp Lyndhurst's German prisoners became familiar sights on Augusta County's farms and in its forests and orchards, though most residents saw them only from the roadsides when they were transported in trucks and sedans between the PW camp and their work sites. At least one group of eight and nine year-old boys liked to wait by their home stretch of road in Stuarts Draft for the almost daily parade of vehicles that carried prisoners to and from work. The Germans fascinated the boys and personified the vicious Nazi soldiers that Americans once feared and reviled. The boys, third-graders at Stuarts Draft Elementary School, had become fully involved with America's total war effort. They had run an obstacle course set up for students on the school grounds, collected aluminum and scrap metals for war production, helped black-out their homes when the Stuarts Draft air raid warning gong was sounded, and watched some of the young men from their neighborhood go to war and never return. The Germans were the enemy, so the youngsters delighted in yelling curses and epithets at the passing prisoners, or hurling assorted imaginative names at them. During one of the regular roadside confrontations, PWs from nearby Flory's Dairy pitched watermelons to—or at—the boys as their truck ground by on the way to Lyndhurst.[35]

On a much less contentious level, Karl could not help but notice the teenaged girl who sat on the ground at a rural intersection on many a warm summer afternoon. She paid special attention to the young prisoners who passed through the intersection and returned glances and smiles at her. Many young American women sang, "*They're Either Too Young or Too Old*," with a chuckle while they desperately ached for companionship and boyfriends or husbands who had been taken from them.

To Augusta County's orchardists and farmers, the prisoners of Camp Lyndhurst had proven to be their economic salvation during the 1944 bumper crop. The county's 440,000 apple trees hung heavily at harvest time with two million bushels of produce—three times the 1943 yield—that would have

34.   Benevitch interview with Baumann.
35.   Charles W. Blair, PhD; Mt. Solon, Virginia, interview by author, 9 December 2004. Dr. Blair knew the young boys' activities and their reactions to the passing Germans from first-hand experience: he was one of the youngsters.

spoiled on the ground except for the German PWs who were used in large numbers to bring in the fruit crop.[36] Likewise, the farmers who used prisoner labor in
many cases could not have continued production at prewar levels due to severe
local manpower shortages.

On 7 May 1945 German forces surrendered unconditionally to the Allied
armies that had overrun the last vestiges of defended territory within Germany
proper. The Nazi *Reich* died in the rubble of devastated Europe; in the aftermath,
the Allies set about the laborious process to restore order where chaos had reigned
during the last months and weeks of war. Nearly 400,000 German PWs in the
United States were destined to return to their vanquished country, but amid the
turmoil of the Allies' postwar occupation of Germany their planned repatriation
would take months to accomplish. Meanwhile, the daily routine of prison life
continued at Camp Lyndhurst.

One evening soon after the German surrender Armin Reda spotted Baumann
as he walked through the camp's main gate after a hard day cutting pulpwood.

"Karl, hurry and wash up. You have to appear in the kitchen for interrogation," the sergeant implored.

"Interrogation for what?" Karl asked himself as he trudged to the washhouse
to scrub off the day's accumulated sweat and grime. A few minutes later he
arrived at the building that housed the kitchen; a number of prisoners waited to
be called into an adjoining room where an interrogation team conducted the
interviews. He finally was ushered into the room where a U.S. Army captain he
had never seen was seated behind a table.

"Sit down," the captain said gruffly in English. Baumann ignored the order.

"Sit down!!!" the captain shouted. The prisoner continued to stand in front of
the table.

"*Setzen Sie sich!*" the officer bellowed, after which Baumann seated himself on
the lone chair that sat before the table.

"*Danke Schön,*" Karl said, and continued in German, "If you want to speak to
me, you speak German. I'm not going to speak to you in English!" Though he
intended to make an antagonistic point, in truth he could not yet converse well in

36. James M. Gorsline, "Annual Narrative Report and Summary of Extension Work in
Augusta County, Virginia, 1944" (Staunton, VA: Augusta County Extension Service, USDA, 1945), 6. County Agricultural Extension Agent Gorsline praised the
prisoners for their invaluable economic contribution in his 1944 annual report to the
U.S. Department of Agriculture. Gorsline left no doubt that the prisoners had ame-
liorated the local labor shortage more notably than any other groups among the five
thousand seasonal workers hired for the harvest.

English. Unbeknownst to his interrogator, Karl had begun to develop English language skills only after he had become a PW.

"How is the food in camp?" the captain asked, speaking German.

"It is not enough," Baumann said. He explained that he worked for a logging company, where he and another prisoner were expected to cut a cord of wood each day, but was given only a stack of bread and raw bacon to eat. He then proceeded to tell the captain that he alone had to lift the heavy sections of the trees although his own wound also still sometimes caused considerable pain. The captain took notes as the young prisoner spoke.

"That's not enough," the captain said quietly as he looked squarely at Karl. "Alright, go to the next room."

Karl rose from his seat and walked into the adjoining room where an American sergeant sat. Several magazines were spread out on the table in front of him. The sergeant pointed to a copy of Life Magazine with Adolf Hitler's scowling picture on the cover.

"Do you know this pig?" the German-speaking sergeant asked.

"No. In Germany pigs looked different. That's Hitler, not a pig." Karl declared.

"That's a pig!" the GI retorted.

"No," Baumann replied, as his own arrogance mounted. "That's an American propaganda paper!"

"Get out!" the sergeant ordered, and then added, "You're next for Russia! The war is over and you lost!"

"I don't believe you," Karl said as he stormed toward the door. "When I hear the German news, then I'll tell *you!*" His second interrogation was promptly concluded before it began, and his antagonistic demeanor probably was noted and reported to Captain Calafiura. To his American captors *Matrosenobergefreiter* Karl Baumann was not a model prisoner, though from the German perspective he had comported himself properly under the circumstances.

Several days later, while Karl and fellow prisoners busily chopped wood in the nearby forest, the warm temperature and heavy physical exertion weighed down his Army fatigue shirt with perspiration. He removed the herringbone twill garment and laid it aside, relieved that the day's work would be more bearable without it.

The undershirt Karl wore bore a large impromptu Wehrmacht insignia he had stenciled on weeks earlier at Sandy Level. The emblem consisted of an eagle with outstretched wings, standing atop a wreath that encircled a swastika, the dreaded symbol of the Third *Reich*. When the war ended Captain Calafiura had ordered all Nazi symbols removed from wherever they were displayed. Karl had complied with the letter of the order, he reasoned, when he painted over the swastika on his undershirt; the eagle now stood atop a solid black ball. Such reasoning would not stand up to Calafiura's strict standards of compliance, however; the intent of the captain's order was that all symbols of the former *Reich* had to be eradicated—including the familiar form of the Wehrmacht eagle, even if it perched atop a solid black ball.

After the end of the war, the prisoners at Camp Lyndhurst were ordered to remove or paint over all emblems and insignia that bore the swastika, the despised symbol of Nazi Germany. Karl Baumann responded by painting over the German eagle and swastika that had been stenciled onto his shirt.

Later in the day the captain paid a visit to the work site on one of his frequent rounds to enforce the War Department's rules of conduct to which contract employers and prisoners alike were compelled to abide. While he observed the prisoners at work he suddenly noticed the large erstwhile Wehrmacht emblem on Karl's undershirt.

"That man, tell him to come over here," the captain ordered a guard as he pointed in Karl's direction. Momentarily Karl looked up from his work and noticed he was being motioned to approach the captain and the guard. He quickly stopped chopping a length of wood and reported with his ax in hand to the camp commander, entirely unaware why he had been summoned.

"Give me your ax," Calafiura ordered in English while he held out his hand toward the implement. Though Karl understood very little English, the captain's command was quite clearly communicated.

"Take off your shirt," the C.O. ordered and motioned with his hand. Karl removed his shirt and handed it to Calafiura, who then handed it and the ax to the guard. While Karl and other prisoners nearby watched incredulously, the guard dropped the undershirt onto a log. He then swung the heavy ax down onto the shirt with all his might; the blade slashed through the cloth and wedged into the soft wood below. Time and again the guard chopped through the undershirt until it was a mass of tattered fabric and tangled threads. When the guard finished chopping, the captain launched into a roaring tirade that Karl's meager grasp of English could not decipher. With no interpreter present the dismayed German stood uncomprehendingly while Calafiura railed against him. Karl displayed no emotion outwardly, but inwardly he seethed with barely suppressed fury. If somehow he could grab the ax from the guard, he thought, he would split the C.O. in two.

Karl returned to the camp at the end of the workday, exhausted from his hard labor and still angry at the upbraiding he had received. When he walked sullenly through the gate Captain Calafiura and Armin Reda, the PW interpreter, were waiting for him.

"Tell this man, Baumann, fourteen days detention on bread and water," the captain commanded Reda, who then translated the order in German.

Karl was stunned. As he saw it, he had strictly obeyed the captain's order and painted over the swastika on his shirt. And now, he told himself, he was being sent to solitary confinement for no just reason. His anger and bitterness intensified like never before as a PW when a few minutes later he reported to the detention building. The small stockade was located just outside the camp, and was surrounded by a separate high fence that made the place appear stark and forbidding. The building was divided into several cells with concrete walls on all sides. Each cell was about six feet long and four feet wide, with a bunk that covered almost the entire floor. The GIs had nicknamed the stockade The Chicken Coop.[37]

A guard opened the door to a cell and pointed to Baumann to step inside. As he stood in the doorway of his cell he was ordered to hand over his belt and shoelaces to prevent him from cheating punishment by hanging himself. The door then slammed shut and blocked off most of the outside light that had illuminated the cell. Only then did Karl realize that he had not taken time to eat the scant evening meal that had been served up for the prisoners. Too late now, he thought, as he lay down on the bunk in the darkness to wait for the interminable hours to pass until his release. All he could do was sleep or spend the waking hours alone with his thoughts. Sometimes he found it painful to think too long about his life or the people he knew and loved. Streams of questions bombarded

---

37. Benevitch interview with Branch.

his consciousness. Did anyone know he was still alive? Was *Oma* safe, and his uncles, aunts, sisters, and his father? And Anneliese; was she still alive or had she been lost in a bombing raid or an attack on their hometown? Did Herbert Raschewski ever write to her to tell her what had happened to his best friend Karl; or did U-953 and his *Ubootkameraden* vanish somewhere in the Atlantic or the Bay of Biscay? So many people had crossed paths with him since he had gone to sea; how many had the war since taken, and toward what end had they died? The endless unanswerable questions gave rise to overwhelming melancholy and terrible loneliness, uncertainty, and fear that crept into Karl's cramped cell to keep unwelcome company with him in the silent darkness.

In the morning two guards opened the cell door and rousted Karl from his bunk. While he stood in one corner the GIs folded up the metal cot and dragged it out of the cell. Karl then was ordered to stand up throughout the day, and was forbidden to sit or lie on the floor. Without a watch or any other means to determine the time, and surrounded by the oppressive closeness of the four walls, Karl felt almost suspended in a void that defied the reality of his being. Thoughts again crowded into his consciousness and played mad games of contemplation. After he stood several hours and alternately paced several steps back and forth like a caged animal, his limbs began to ache and weigh heavily on his body. Finally, he sat on the concrete floor to rest his muscles.

"Get up," the guard snapped every time he peered into a small observation slot in the door and caught the tired prisoner slumped onto the floor.

The jailer opened the cell door sometime around 10:00 and handed Karl a few slices of bread and a cup that he filled continually with cool, fresh water until the prisoner had taken all he could drink. When the brief repast was finished, the cell door was closed and, with a rattling of keys in the lock, Baumann again was shut off from the rest of the world. In mid-afternoon he again was startled out of weary dullness and daydreams with the sound of his door being unlocked. As subdued sunlight greeted his eyes a guard motioned for him to come out of his cell, and nudged him down a corridor that led to the fenced exercise yard next to the stockade. Once inside the yard he was ordered to walk continuously around the inside perimeter of the twenty-foot by twenty-foot enclosure to stretch his tired muscles. Holding up his trousers with his hands and wearing shoes without laces, Karl slowly plodded around the enclosure with scant satisfaction to be out of his cell. The humiliating procedure fulfilled a dual purpose; while it provided needed physical exercise, it reinforced the notion that every aspect of Karl's imprisonment was entirely out of his control and in the firm grasp of his captors.

As the first full day of solitary confinement came to a close, Karl again was ushered out of his cell, this time for a meeting at the camp commander's office. When he was escorted into the office, Captain Calafiura was seated behind his desk and Armin Reda stood nearby to translate the proceedings. Karl strode up to the captain's desk and saluted. Through the interpreter the captain told Karl that his Nazi emblem was recognizable fifty miles away, the sort of hyperbole the captain was fond of using to drive home a point.

"That is not so!" Karl declared abruptly, taking the ridiculous accusation far too literally, but in any case defending his belief that he had not disobeyed the captain's orders. He need not have bothered.

"Out!" Calafiura commanded. The obstinate prisoner obviously had not learned his lesson, the captain had concluded.

The prisoner was taken back to his dank cell for the second night without dinner, light, and the balm of friendship among fellow captives. Isolated in the clammy darkness of that other world, so near others milling about the compound, yet psychologically so very far from them, Karl pondered how long he could endure the loneliness. He well understood that enforced isolation was perhaps the greatest punishment that could be inflicted upon a young man so far from home and loved ones. He had effectively been rejected from the social construct of Camp Lyndhurst—the only society that mattered in his life at that moment—and presently was considered an outcast from the outcasts.

Several more days passed; Karl Baumann completely lost track of the hours and days he inhabited the cell. The routine of solitary confinement never changed: endless hours standing in place, punctuated only by the daily half-hour exercise period and the bread and water rations. The meager food was never enough to satisfy his hunger, which each day became only more pronounced.

One evening a relief guard approached his duty station—the chair and table that sat in the corridor next to Karl's cell. He peered into the observation door and studied the tired, hungry prisoner inside for a moment. In a sudden rush of anger—at someone or something—the guard slammed his solid oak nightstick full force onto the tabletop. The noise barely echoed through the stockade before the concrete walls deadened it. The unexpected violence startled Karl, who then looked through the observation slot into the angry eyes of the guard.

"For me?" he asked in English, wondering whether he had somehow enraged the guard to earn a striking blow himself.

"No!" the young American replied with disgust in his voice. "For the captain!"

During one night's passage in the stockade, the master sergeant of the guard detail quietly opened Karl's cell door and pressed a full loaf of bread into the inmate's hands. Karl immediately detected a hint of unusual warmth that radiated from between the bread slices, but could see nothing in the darkness of his cell. When he ran his fingers among the slices to trace the source of the faint heat he discovered the sergeant had hidden two warm pancakes there. The American's simple gesture of compassion profoundly impressed the young German and helped relieve the sense of depression the tiny dark cell had engendered. Karl was grateful beyond words, and always would remember the kindness extended to him by the GI on the other side of the cell door.

On his fourth evening in the stockade, Karl once again was ushered to the camp's administration building. Before he entered the captain's office, Armin Reda pulled him aside to whisper a quiet admonition.

"Just say yes, yes, yes, to everything the captain says, Karl; and he will let you out!" the interpreter implored.

"What about the facts," Karl thought to himself, still angry at the unfairness he perceived and the punishment he believed was unjust. He stepped into the camp commander's office and saluted.

Captain Calafiura again leveled the accusation that Karl's shirt emblem was visible from fifty miles. Reda relayed the translation.

"Yes, sir," Karl simply responded to each charge. Calafiura then asked him if he would disobey any order again.

"No, sir," was the reply. The humiliation and indignity of the entire matter was complete; he had yielded principle to distasteful practicality, which was necessary in a confrontation he could not win. He would never forget the injustice of it all.

"Tell this man to wash up and go to the kitchen to get something to eat," the captain ordered Reda, satisfied he had made his point with the now subdued prisoner.

By the time Karl was released from solitary confinement most every man at Camp Lyndhurst—Germans and Americans alike—probably had heard about his confrontation with the captain and his subsequent punishment. Such news would have traveled quickly throughout the small compound, with everyone left to his own devices to decide whether the prisoner had received just treatment or had been wrongly sentenced. After Karl returned from the wash house cleanly shaven, he walked to the prisoners' kitchen in search of something to sate his ravenous hunger. He found plenty of bread, but neither condiments nor anything else to enhance the monotonous flavor. Dejected and depressed, he wearily sat down at a table and wolfed down slice after plain slice until he had dispatched more than fifty.

Prisoners naturally resented their subjugation within the society of the PW camp, the surrounding community where they performed manual labor, and the outside world, after the military defeat of the *Reich*. Despite the captain's rampaging nature and the ill-fated work strike, the relationship between captors and captives at Camp Lyndhurst generally was proper and somewhat distant, which was to be expected of the two disparate groups within the milieu of a prisoner of war camp. Each man quickly determined which men among the American guards and camp administration were likely to cause them the greatest and least trouble. Falling somewhere just short of friendships, guards and prisoners on occasion developed mutual relationships that proved beneficial to all parties involved. Out of sight of officers, one GI allowed prisoners to reach into his pocket to help themselves to cigarettes while he looked on, amused and unconcerned. MP Guard Albert Moreman, a freewheeling twenty year-old West Virginian who thoroughly disdained military formality and decorum, conspired with Karl and Hans Schages to subvert all pretence of protocol when they were detailed together to cut pulpwood. The two PWs agreed to keep watch over the area whenever Moreman crawled behind a large toolbox to catch up on his sleep. When the captain stopped by to inspect the work detail he invariably asked about the guard's whereabouts. Dutifully, Baumann and Schages always indicated that Moreman had gone to the opposite end of the wooded hillside to count the cords of wood. In turn, the grateful guard gave the two prisoners his lunchtime meal. Better yet, Moreman didn't demand they cut the required volume of pulpwood in the course of the day. The American corporal otherwise was a stickler for details of work contracts; he demanded that other prisoners and their civilian employers conduct their work to the letter of the contract terms.[38]

Despite the absolute power Captain Calafiura wielded at Camp Lyndhurst, he was unable to completely control the natural human interaction that evolved between civilian employers and their German laborers. The prisoners realized early on that their greatest opportunities for better treatment rested with the kindness of employers who sometimes disregarded the Army's rigid orders against fraternization. Not all employers relaxed the rules and regulations in their relationship with prisoners, of course, or even liked the Germans who worked for them. The most fortunate PWs almost always worked for pacifist Mennonite and Amish farmers whose lands spread across the rolling hills south of the town of Waynesboro.

---

38. Benevitch interviews with Moreman and Schages.

Karl was one of five prisoners assigned one early summer morning to work on a Stuarts Draft farm. He was thoroughly pleased to be relieved from woodcutting for the logging company that first contracted for his services, not to mention the terrifying ride to and from the work site. While the men stood inside the camp gate a pickup truck eased up the dirt road and came to a stop. The young man who emerged from the driver's seat was twenty-four year-old Galen Heatwole, a well-known Mennonite farmer who recently had signed a contract to obtain five prisoner laborers to work on several farms including his own. He reported to the Sergeant of the Guard, whose duty it was to sign over custody and control of the prisoners during the workday and check them back in at the end of the day.[39] When the two men had completed their paperwork the sergeant directed the farmer to his consignment of PWs. A GI handed a final document to Heatwole, which he read as he walked back to his truck with the Germans. The official notice warned all civilians against fraternization with prisoners of war. Without a guard detail, the prisoner-laden pickup soon turned around in the parking lot and headed downhill, then turned north toward the road intersection at Lyndhurst village. Inexplicably, while prisoners were supervised by armed guards at the camp, at work in the forests and at the Army hospital in Fishersville, they seldom were guarded when they worked for local farmers. The absence of GI guards on valley farms laid the foundation for mutual trust and understanding to develop among prisoners and their employers, sometimes with unexpected consequences. While the pleasant young farmer plied the country roads that led to his home on State Route 340, neither he nor Karl Baumann realized that both had just embarked upon the journey of a lifetime.[40]

Six miles from Camp Lyndhurst the small truck pulled into the driveway of the Paul Wenger farm to deliver one prisoner for the day's work. Galen Heatwole and his four remaining prisoners soon arrived at his own farm. As the truck rolled to a stop behind the farmhouse, Karl watched as the screen door creaked open and Heatwole's wife emerged with a dinner plate in her hands. What appeared to be several golden fried eggs rode on the plate and taunted the hungry Germans. No doubt they were leftovers from breakfast, Karl thought as he recalled his own meager morning meal. He then was mortified to watch Mary Heatwole scrape the plate of food, actually several pancakes, into the family dog's bowl. He wanted the pancakes so badly he considered jumping off the truck to grab them away from the animal, but the dog gulped down the hotcakes before Karl could

---

39. Benevitch interview with Branch.
40. Galen Heatwole, Stuarts Draft, Virginia, interview by author, 1 April 2000.

have cleared the truck bed in a furtive lunge for its bowl. The disconsolate prisoners watched the dog enviously while it happily snorted and snooted the ground for every last crumb that might have fallen into the grass.

The farmer led his four prisoners toward a storage building, where he retrieved mattocks and other tools the men were to use to cut and dig out wild locust trees on the property. When they passed a corncrib on the way to the fields Karl stealthily reached into the bin for an ear and put it in his pocket. The Germans followed the farmer to his apple orchard where the unwanted locust trees waited to be pried out of the ground with brute force. The PWs were left entirely to themselves to pile up cut branches and chop tree roots that only reluctantly yielded their deep grasp in the rich soil. Heatwole returned an hour or two later from other chores to check on the progress the men had made to clear away the scrub trees. When he walked up to the group he noticed Karl chewing on something while he worked.

"What are you eating there?" the young man asked curiously.

Karl could not speak English beyond a few words, but realized the meaning of the question. Somewhat reluctantly, he reached into the large pocket of his Army fatigue pants and pulled out a handful of dried corn kernels. Galen Heatwole was surprised and saddened to discover that the young German, whom he had compelled to work on the farm, had felt it necessary to eat grain that had been harvested for farm animals. He turned on his heels and left the prisoners without a word as they resumed their muscle-straining work. Karl was unsure of the meaning of the incident, and wondered whether he would again find himself in trouble with the captain or other Army authorities. A short while later he looked up from his work to observe the farmer had returned. In his hands were a stack of sandwiches and a large container of milk—enough for all the men to share. With smiles of pure joy, the hungry young Germans devoured the sandwiches and finished off the ice-cold milk. They could hardly believe such kindness had come their way so unexpectedly at the hands of people the *Reich* had declared were the enemy. As they stood together in one of Augusta County's renowned apple orchards, their hunger temporarily abated, the prisoners felt as if they had struck gold. Galen Heatwole, in turn, was greatly pleased to see the men gladly resume the day's work after their short break.

Something about Karl also caught Heatwole's attention: the way the former U-boat gunner seemed to stand out among other prisoners. He was immediately impressed by the manner and bearing of the hard-working and obviously bright young German, and decided then and there to ask the camp authorities to assign Karl whenever possible to his farm. As a result, the two would work together almost continually for seven months, during which time the prisoner's services occasionally would be lent to other Mennonite's farmers as well. He contributed much needed manpower to help harvest large tomato and potato crops, and to fill silos.[41] For his part, Karl always was relieved to find his name beneath Galen Heatwole's when work assignments were posted on the camp's bulletin board. To his great disappointment, he sometimes was assigned to special work details for other employers. Some of the special jobs were not at all unpleasant, such as when he helped a local man sharpen the axes and saw blades the prisoners used to cut pulpwood. On the opposite end of the labor spectrum, one of the most dreaded jobs was loading tree bark and pulpwood into railroad boxcars parked on a sidetrack at the Stuarts Draft railroad depot. The rough bark drove splinters into unprotected hands and arms, and the interiors of the boxcars radiated with heat. The job was painful, filthy, and exhausting; and was despised by all.

Though at first they communicated with each other with the assistance of a German-English dictionary, Karl and the Heatwoles soon developed a bond of cooperation, trust and friendship that far transcended the bounds of the Army's official fraternization policy. Both men carefully concealed their mutually beneficial relationship from the authorities at Camp Lyndhurst. The captain in particular would not have approved of the fact that Heatwole did not consciously regard Baumann first and foremost as a prisoner of war, but merely as another farm helper. Every day Karl worked on the farm, Mary Heatwole provided lunch for him as for a regular farmhand. His lunch ration from the camp normally consisted of a half-loaf of bread and a scrap of meat. He gave the bread to Mary to use for their meals. The Heatwoles discovered on one occasion that PW's meat ration was nothing more than a chunk of solid fat.[42]

Captain Calafiura made impromptu visits to contract employers to see for himself how well the prisoners worked at the various locations. Since he tended to appear around lunchtime, prisoners speculated he wanted to make sure they were not being given any food beyond the lunch ration the Army provided. One day while Karl and another prisoner stood beside a grain bin to eat a bountiful lunch from Mary Heatwole's kitchen, the captain's jeep suddenly sped up the lane to the farmhouse. In a frenzy of motion the PWs opened the lid of the grain bin and shoved their food-laden dinner plates inside. They genuinely feared the consequences they would suffer if the captain ever caught them with contraband food. Someone had started an unfounded rumor among the prisoners that the

---

41.   Heatwole interview.
42.   Heatwole interview.

C.O. had told his troops he would rather give the Germans a beating every morning than feed them breakfast.[43]

Mennonite families throughout the area typically responded in kind to German prisoners as did Galen and Mary Heatwole. The Bible-based pacifism that formed one of the most fundamental elements of the Mennonite faith governed their acceptance of Germans as fellow human beings rather than enemies. With the greatest and most destructive war in history still some weeks from its explosive conclusion, Karl could scarcely accept the fact that anyone or any religious denomination could survive and thrive in daily life under the seemingly unrealistic tenet to love one's neighbors as oneself, including one's enemies.[44]

With a mixture of halting English and German, Galen Heatwole one day asked Karl to tell him about his religious background and his spiritual life.

"Do you like Hitler?" Heatwole asked during the conversation.

"Yeah, he's a friend of mine," Baumann answered obstinately. "Do you like the Japanese?"

"Yes," Galen replied without hesitation. The wholly unexpected response stopped Karl in his tracks.

"How is that possible?" Karl asked as he shook his head in disbelief. The Germans were well aware that the American public in general hated the Japanese for their brutality in China, their dastardly sneak attack on Pearl Harbor, and their conduct during the Bataan Death March. He himself had grown to young adulthood on a steady regimen of vitriolic Nazi propaganda that engendered officially sanctioned hatred for Jews.

"I have no enemies," Galen said with a sincere smile that the PW immediately recognized as a measure of his genuine feelings.

---

43.   The admonition attributed to Calafiura doubtless was only a rumor. See Benevitch interview with Branch. Jack Branch, who earlier had been a prisoner of the Germans after being captured in Italy, served as Sergeant of the Guard at Lyndhurst for two months. He recalled that Calafiura told him, "he didn't want me to go and hurt any of these Germans for nothing."

44.   The Biblical reference being to Matthew 22:37-40.

Prisoners of war Hans Schages and Karl Baumann take a break from farm
work to pose for a photograph while Schages holds Galen Heatwole's
son, Richard; summer, 1945.

Karl realized that he was in the unique presence of a man who quietly and
fully practiced his faith in his everyday life—a faith founded upon unqualified
love for all mankind. The young German had never before encountered such a
person as Galen Heatwole, and at first he could not comprehend the full meaning
of such dedication to one's religious heritage. He had grown to maturity in a
world where an entire race had been demonized and blamed for all the ills Germans had suffered over the centuries. Though he never subscribed to the Nazis'
formalized national policy of hate, neither had he met a group of Christ-centered
believers dedicated to peaceful coexistence with all people as the Mennonites. He
was skeptical about their professed honor and respect for everyone equally, without regard to nationality, race, or religion. But he himself—a German prisoner of
war in the land of his sworn enemies—personally was a frequent beneficiary of
unconditional respect, compassion, and trust. Galen Heatwole and other Believers Karl already encountered proved by their very actions and attitudes that,
indeed, they had no enemies. Many nights while he lay in his bunk, his thoughts

focused upon the incorruptible Godliness his Mennonite employers—his friends—unerringly conveyed to him. He thought, while he struggled to find sleep, how greatly he would miss these good people when he returned to Germany.

Karl became more fascinated with the Mennonite faith over the passing months, but remained distant to his own spiritual foundation and religious education. He never chose to attend regular Sunday morning services at Camp Lyndhurst's little chapel. Armin Reda, the prisoner-interpreter who worked closely with the American authorities, was the organist for the chapel services. The accomplished musician invited his comrade on several occasions to attend the services, but the invitation always was declined.[45] Instead, Karl preferred to play *Faustball* at the camp volleyball court or engage in other diversions on Sundays, the prisoners' only work-free days.

As the cool spring of 1945 yielded to the hot, dry Virginia summer, Karl Baumann became a fixture at the Heatwole's farm as well as at their neighbors. There he enjoyed an element of freedom that helped ameliorate the anxiety of captivity as a war prisoner. One particularly stifling day in late summer, he and several other PWs helped fill several silos with ensilage on a farm near Lyndhurst. The men baked under the blazing sun as they piled the cornstalks onto a conveyer belt that carried them through a chopper and dropped the fine ensilage into the silos. Sweat poured down faces and necks to saturate handkerchiefs and undershirts, and left men parched and drained of energy. At the end of the long day's work the young farmer in charge conjured a splendid idea.

"Let's go down to the river for a swim," the American offered. The prisoners agreeably piled into the farmer's truck and the young Mennonite drove to nearby South River, which was fed by scores of cold mountain springs. The young men whooped happily as they dismounted and ran headlong to the river bank, where they shed all their clothes and plunged into the wonderfully-refreshing water to wash away the day's sweaty grime and irritating ensilage residue. For a fleeting moment the cool water washed away all distinctions of nationality or social condition. The PWs momentarily forgot the war, the terror they had experienced and in some cases had produced, their prison home at Camp Lyndhurst, and its hard-nosed C.O. For an instant some cast off their pervasive fear for loved ones. Just then all were simply young boys again.

---

45. Doris Reda; Diez/Lahn, Germany; letter to author, 28 June 2000. Mrs. Reda described her husband's long professional musical career as a first violinist with several symphony orchestras.

While he labored for his Mennonite friends, Karl imagined himself a free man making a living of his own accord in Augusta County, Virginia. Such thoughts required a very short leap from reality within the pacifist community where, against every rule to avoid fraternization with PWs, Galen Heatwole's brother Alvin had instructed him to help himself to whatever food was in the kitchen refrigerator when the family was away from the farm. The sense of freedom he experienced was nearly intoxicating. However, reality burdened him like a heavy weight and reminded him at every turn that presently he belonged to the U.S. Army's Prisoner of War Division, to Camp Lyndhurst, and to Captain William A. Calafiura. Sometimes Karl simply wished to leave reality and escape to a new life.

Ruel Driver grew a large tomato crop that he usually sold to the Miller Cannery at Bridgewater in neighboring Rockingham County. During the 1945 harvest season, Karl helped the farmer carefully pack crates of tomatoes and stack them inside the farm's panel truck for the seventy-mile roundtrip delivery. He had become quite familiar to the family and was treated like other trustworthy farmhands. He often sat at the Driver's kitchen table to share lunch with the couple and their young son, but always kept a wary ear attuned for the sound of the captain's jeep charging up the driveway. Before each noontime meal, Mr. Driver gave thanks to God for the bounty of his farm, for family and loved ones; and for Karl, the young prisoner they regarded as equal in every respect. With devotions concluded, family members and the German PW eagerly passed heaping bowls of meats, potatoes, and vegetables around the table. Each meal provided grateful sustenance for the body, soul and spirit.

Five year-old Vernon Driver was fascinated with the family's new farmhand, the strange language he spoke, and the man's inability to understand the boy's numerous questions. The youngster was fascinated by the large wound Karl revealed whenever he went shirtless in the hot sun. The PW liked the little boy's innocence and his youthful inquisitiveness. Both enjoyed each other's company.

"You want to go along to Bridgewater?" Driver asked Baumann one day.

"Okay!" he replied without hesitation. He was always curious to see more of Virginia's Shenandoah Valley beyond the now familiar stretches of land between the PW camp and his several work sites. Since the utilitarian panel truck contained a seat only for the driver, he turned a sturdy bushel basket upside down and settled onto it for the long ride to the cannery.

Karl took in the scenery along Route 250 while the little panel truck headed west through the village of Fishersville and into Staunton, the Queen City of the Shenandoah Valley. Driver then turned north onto U.S. Route 11, the Valley

Pike that bisected numerous tiny settlements nestled among some of the most beautiful farmlands in the United States. The men finally drove into the village of Bridgewater, several miles west of Route 11, where they pulled into a gas station. Ruell Driver asked the proprietor if his companion might use the restroom, not wanting to assume beforehand that the German PW would be allowed. The station owner nodded permission, and Karl walked around the corner of the building, where he entered a side door. Once inside the tiny restroom he noticed a small window standing wide open, inviting his escape. For a fleeting moment he considered how easily he could just slip out the window and run away, leaving Camp Lyndhurst, its lousy food, the monotony and humiliation of imprisonment, and Captain Calafiura in his wake.

"Forget it!" he ordered himself and forced his consciousness back into rational thought. There was absolutely no place to run because he would never blend in with the local population, considering his sparse command of English and his Army fatigues with PW painted on the front and back of his shirt. Not only would his flight and certain recapture be potentially dangerous, but afterward he never again would be allowed to return to the Mennonite farms and all the good graces he had come to enjoy. Karl heaved a sign of resignation and a moment later returned to the truck, climbed back onto his bushel basket seat and thought no more about escape. Anyway, he told himself, the war was over; soon he would be repatriated to Germany. With the kindness of his employers he could endure Camp Lyndhurst a while longer.

Among Karl Baumann's several excursions into the heartland of the Shenandoah Valley with local farmers, one venture far surpassed all others. Galen Heatwole belonged to a flying club at the Augusta Airport, a short grass airfield located on the O. C. Powell farm near Waynesboro. He was part owner of a tiny Piper J-3 Cub that was stored inside a converted barn with several other small airplanes.[46] One day while Heatwole talked about his unusual hobby, Karl invoked a brazen request.

"Would you take me flying?" the prisoner implored.

The young farmer considered the unlikely prospect of an airborne PW, and a few days later the men broke off work early to drive to the small airfield. Karl was ecstatic with anticipation of taking to the sky for the first time in his life, but apprehensive about somehow being caught by the authorities.

"Don't say a thing," Heatwole warned as he slowly maneuvered the Ford sedan up to the barn hanger. The men quietly left the car and slid open the wide

---

46. Heatwole interview.

barn doors, then manhandled the small yellow airplane outside and onto the edge of the grassy landing strip. Galen motioned for Karl to climb into the front seat of the two-seater aircraft because the view was much better from the forward position, and he preferred to fly the plane from the back seat anyway. After a few moments of preflight procedures, the flying farmer pressed the starter switch and the little sixty-five-horsepower Lycoming engine coughed and sputtered, then surged to life. The pilot lined up the plane with the runway and slowly revved the engine. The little aircraft rocked its passengers gently while it strained to stand in place with the propeller spinning at maximum revolutions. When the engine ran smoothly with a high-pitched whine, Heatwole released the brakes. The Piper Cub rolled and bounced down the grassy expanse, faster and faster, until finally it lifted from the ground. Karl's first-ever flight was exhilarating for its sense of release from all earthly bounds. The view below was stunningly beautiful as the low-flying aircraft passed over little settlements and seemingly countless farms and apple orchards with their orderly lines of trees. The pilot then set his course for Stuarts Draft and Lyndhurst.

From the air, familiar buildings, roads, and landscapes took on a new and unfamiliar perspective. As the plane approached the Blue Ridge Mountains Karl noticed the unmistakable buildings of Camp Lyndhurst dead ahead. The black tarpaper rooftops created a depressing sight as Karl thought about life there as a prisoner of war. Down below, PWs and GIs alike watched curiously as the little aircraft circled low overhead. Heatwole then eased the plane onto a straight course as his passenger relaxed against the back of his seat and simply enjoyed the exuberant freedom of flight over the valley between Lyndhurst and Waynesboro.

"You want to loop?" Galen shouted over the steady hum of the engine.

"Yeah!" Karl responded.

The horizon suddenly disappeared from view as the Cub accelerated into a steep climb, then reappeared just as suddenly after the plane reached the apex of the loop and began to plummet into a controlled glide toward the ground. The young PW was enveloped by an all-too-rare exhilaration for the blessings of life as Heatwole completed his aerobatic circle in the sky. All too soon the plane touched down on the grass airfield and taxied to the front of the makeshift hanger.

The Piper J-3 Cub in which pilot Galen Heatwole (shown with wife Mary and son Richard) flew PW Karl Baumann above Camp Lyndhurst while Baumann was imprisoned there.

Karl returned to Camp Lyndhurst at the end of the work day determined not to breathe a word to anyone about his most incredible experience as a prisoner of war. Had the captain ever discovered one of *his* PWs actually had contrived to fly in a civilian aircraft over and around *his* camp, the resulting outrage would have verged upon the apoplectic. Probably no form of punishment, regardless of severity, would have satisfied the C.O. for the prisoner's and the farmer's rank indiscretion. Almost certainly Karl Baumann alone—among 425,871 prisoners of war confined on American soil during World War II—could rightfully claim to have taken a pleasure airplane flight over his own PW camp while he was imprisoned there.

The summer sun frequently bore down heavily while the PWs worked each day for thirty-five cents pay, which was issued in coupons to be used like cash in the camp's small canteen. There they bought their own soap and toiletries, but no luxuries after the captain had them summarily removed. Cigarettes also were available, but not in great quantity. To help satisfy the constant craving for tobacco, prisoners bought cigarette butts that were collected by their entrepreneurial *Kameraden* on work details at the Woodrow Wilson Army Hospital. The butts were available in two styles, each of which was sold in reused Bull Durham tobacco bags. Lipstick-smeared butts sold for five cents each, whereas those without lipstick stains sold for three cents.

Karl frequented the prisoners' canteen, but not always to make purchases. Some Sundays, while no one watched, he quickly stole beneath the stilted building where he was completely out of view, but where the sun at a low angle shone for a short while. To secure that rare solitude he sought cover in the domain of the timber rattlesnakes that occasionally slithered into camp to create terror among the Germans. Alone in his private space, he retrieved a razor blade from his jacket pocket and carefully carved sticks of wood into intricate pieces, which he then laboriously connected together to construct tiny ships inside glass bottles he had smuggled into the compound. The U-boat gunner had developed the hobby first as a young *Schiffsjunge* when he sailed out of Hamburg; never in his wildest imagination could he then have contemplated the conditions under which he would one day put his skill to use. He presented one of the completed ship models to Galen and Mary Heatwole and another to Glen Shenk, a young Mennonite farmhand he had befriended.

The summer months of 1945 turned to fall and the harvest season, which kept Karl busily at work on several farms. He had become so much a regular and reliable farm employee that his presence was taken for granted. All the while, however, he was certain he soon would be returned to Germany, and his Mennonite benefactors expected his departure at any time.

"If you go back to the Merchant Marine, would you come back to visit us?" Galen Heatwole asked one cool autumn day.

"Sure I would!" Karl replied with his improved English. He then asked Heatwole a question he had contemplated frequently over recent weeks.

"Would you be willing to help me come back here to live?"

Heatwole said nothing for a moment while he thought of an appropriate response. After a long pause he explained he would need to speak with Mrs. Heatwole on the serious matter. Karl was pleased that his inquiry had not been rejected out of hand, and appeared to be at least within the realm of possibility. Several days later Galen declared that he and Mary would be glad to help him immigrate to the United States as soon as he could receive permission from the occupation authorities in Germany. A wave of excitement coursed through Karl. He was nearly overwhelmed by the Heatwoles' willingness to help him someday return as a free man to the Mennonite community and the people he had come to know and respect above all others. Wisely though, he declared privately that he would never utter a word to anyone inside the camp about his formulating plans for the future.

Prisoners of war in the United States were not immune to American capitalism, even at Camp Lyndhurst. Those at many larger permanent camps were introduced to traveling salesmen who offered commemorative gold rings styled like those for American high school graduates. The rings bore such legends as, "German Prisoner of War, Camp McCoy USA," that encircled a Germanic-styled eagle and most likely sold for ten to twelve dollars, a relatively low cost even for prisoner laborers who received thirty-five cents each workday. While no ring salesmen hawked their jewelry at Camp Lyndhurst, a traveling photographer set up his camera gear at the compound in November 1945. For a few dollars any German prisoner so inclined could have his portrait made.

Portrait of Karl Baumann taken at Camp Lyndhurst, Augusta County, Virginia, by a traveling photographer, November 1945. Note the W—as in PW—painted on the sleeve of his army field jacket.

On 15 November Karl Baumann borrowed a ragged scarf from another prisoner and wrapped it around his neck to hide the undershirt beneath his U.S. Army fatigue jacket, on the sleeves of which the letter P was emblazoned on the right arm and W on the left. For the price of admission to the ad hoc studio, Karl sat for his formal portrait. Some days later he received the postcard-sized photograph and was quite pleased with the likeness of a healthy looking, fresh-faced young man who bore a slight smile. He could have mailed the portrait home to *Oma*, to his father, or to Anneliese; but he was uncertain about its safe delivery there. Four official PW letters he had mailed from Camp Lyndhurst to Brambauer had never elicited a response. Perhaps the mail services had not been fully restored, he thought. Maybe the war had displaced his loved ones from their homes. Perhaps everyone had been killed in bombing raids or during ground combat. Karl finally resolved the matter and presented his portrait to Galen and Mary Heatwole as a token of his appreciation for the strong bond of friendship that had developed over the past seven months.

Several days later Karl noticed a group of prisoners crowded around the camp's bulletin board before a posted notice of apparent significance. When he finally was able to read the special notice he discovered that a group of about fifty prisoners had been relieved henceforth from further work assignments. The prisoners listed at the bottom of the notice were to appear two days later for a special roll call at the camp gate, and were instructed to pack all their belongings into their duffel bags. Karl scanned the notice and found his name included. He was being transferred somewhere, that was certain; but just where he did not know, and the notice offered no clues. His abrupt release from all work details prevented him from speaking one last time with the Heatwoles. He profoundly regretted he could not say goodbye to the Mennonite farmers and their families who had shown unreserved kindness, respect, and understanding toward a lowly German prisoner of war and made his captivity infinitely more endurable.

The authorities at Camp Lyndhurst never explained how they had selected the prisoners for earliest repatriation to Germany. Though it was not always the case, camp commanders typically took the first opportunity to rid themselves of prisoners who by reason of serious wounds were unable to work or plagued by illness, or those they had deemed recalcitrant. Karl may have been selected because of the very noticeable wound that caused great distress from time to time, especially when he chopped wood. Captain Calafiura most likely considered Karl a troublemaker and was glad to return him to Camp Pickett, where he could cause trouble for some other PW camp commander.

On the appointed day as the notice instructed, Karl and forty-nine other selected prisoners answered their final roll call at Camp Lyndhurst. The well-oiled bureaucratic procedures to transfer prisoners of war had been completed. During the seven months he was confined at Lyndhurst, Karl had deposited spare change from his daily pay into a bank savings account the Army maintained for each prisoner. With his transfer imminent, the Americans had closed his savings account and that morning presented a cashier's check to him, drawn on the First National Bank of Waynesboro, for more than sixty-five dollars.

Several Army trucks and a military police escort arrived during the morning, and now the men climbed aboard with their duffel bags and found seats on the slatted wood benches. Karl Baumann's long journey home began when the small convoy pulled away from the gate and left Camp Lyndhurst in its dusty wake.

9

Returnee

The convoy with its guard escort rolled through the Shenandoah Valley farmlands and the central Virginia piedmont to Camp Pickett, where the prisoners' files were updated and final orders were completed to return the men to Europe through the New York Port of Embarkation. The former Lyndhurst prisoners then joined a large number of returnees selected from other branch camps and the base camp at Camp Pickett. With duffel bags in hand, the homebound Germans boarded a train at the camp depot and settled into the comfortable passenger cars for their nighttime journey to New York City. Many were the contemplative passengers whose emotions clashed with a confusing mixture of anticipation and dread for what they would find when they returned to their homes and families. Many had just cause to fear the devastating losses that awaited them.

The train pulled into a prison camp on the outskirts of New York City the following morning, where the Virginia arrivals congregated with other prisoners to wait out their departure for the long ocean voyage to Europe. Files processing consumed the remaining hours of the day, so early the next morning the five hundred Germans were transported by train to the Port of Embarkation in New York harbor. The train eased to a stop on a sidetrack near a dock where a small U.S. Navy cargo ship was moored. A cold, pounding storm had begun to pour rain down upon the weary PWs as they emerged from the train. Armed guards organized the prisoners into a long column, which then crossed the dock to the gang-plank of the tub, as the slow and ungainly cargo ships were known both affectionately and derisively.

The prisoners boarded the ship and settled into a large lower hold. An adjoining hold was stacked high with crates of food and other commodities destined for American occupation troops. The storage hold and the main deck were off-limits to the prisoners. Sheets of rain pummeled the tub as her crew cast off her mooring lines and she edged away from the dock. The little ship crossed New York harbor, but before she headed out to the open sea her captain ordered the crew to drop anchor. The storm front extended far out into the Atlantic and the raging ocean was no place for the 9,000-ton vessel that carried nearly six hundred men but few lifeboats. Several rapidly produced cargo vessels actually had split in half in treacherous seas during the war years. The ship remained anchored at the harbor entrance for two days while the slow-moving storm whipped the Atlantic waves into whitecaps. Time in the hold passed as slowly for Karl as the most monotonous hours had aboard U-953.

The tub hauled anchor on the morning of the third day and plunged into still-rough ocean waters. Scores of prisoners soon became ill as the ship heaved and bucked with the waves. Karl long ago had become acclimated to the violent motion of ships. Though he felt sorry for the landlubbers who suffered seasickness' manifold miseries, mainly he was glad to be immune to the malady. During the first day at sea two U.S. Navy stewards appeared at the doorway to the prisoners' hold and asked for volunteers to work on the ship. Baumann and another man quickly approached the sailors to offer their help and immediately were escorted from the hold. The two Germans were granted freedom of movement and access to areas otherwise off-limits to PWs. Work outside of the prisoners' hold made the slow transatlantic voyage more bearable, though the tasks the men tackled required few analytical or technical skills. Among other chores, they bolted down tables that the rough sea had tossed askew and re-stacked hundreds of heavy supply crates that had spilled over in disarray inside the cargo hold.

An American steward became fast friends with Karl when he learned that the PW had served with the Kriegsmarine before his capture. As fellow sailors they had much in common. The American, who limped with every step, offered to give his two prisoner helpers a supply of cigarettes at the end of the voyage for their excellent work to put the cargo hold back in order and for other jobs they performed. Farther into the voyage, however, Karl told the steward he had been an *Ubootfahrer* during the Battle of the Atlantic. Then and there the expressions of kinship between the two seamen abruptly ceased. Baumann soon learned from another steward the sailor with the limp had been badly injured when a U-boat torpedoed his ship. The American refused to speak to the German during the remainder of the voyage, and the promised cigarettes never materialized. Nonetheless, Karl was grateful to be able to move about the ship rather than remain in the prisoners' hold during the tub's fourteen-day struggle to cross the Atlantic. He also was gratified the war was over, because any local U-boat running under full diesel power easily could have overtaken the slow cargo vessel and sent her to the bottom with a single torpedo launch.

The tub finally sailed into the French harbor at Le Havre on the Normandy coast early in December. The Germans waited anxiously in their hold for the ship to dock and signal the end of their wearisome voyage. After many months of confinement in the United States and two laborious weeks aboard ship, the prisoners were happy to step again onto European soil. They eventually emerged from the vessel's hold and were ordered to file across a gangplank onto the dock, where a contingent of U.S. Army guards awaited them. Prisoners wondered aloud when, where and how they would be released from captivity; the war had ended six months earlier, so they presumed arrangements were in place for them to be transported directly home to the *Vaterland*. They were badly mistaken.

The five hundred prisoners were formed into a marching column and escorted to a railroad track amid the ruins of Le Havre. A freight train with a long row of empty boxcars sat waiting for them. The German column halted in front of the cars, where groups of forty men were counted out and ordered to board each car. Karl found the dark interior of the car stifling and somewhat unnerving with the men pressed closely together. Their duffel bags were stuffed into a separate boxcar, after which the doors slid closed and were locked from the outside. The train jerked to a start and began to roll slowly across the flat Normandy plain toward Paris, six hours distant, then onto a railway station at Compiegne. The old town was famous for being the site where, in an SNCF (French National Railway) passenger car, the Armistice was signed to end the First World War; and where in the same carriage in 1940 the defeated and humiliated French government surrendered its army and its sovereignty to Adolf Hitler.

GI guards unlocked each of the boxcars' doors and the prisoners jumped onto the ground, stiff and exhausted from the limb-numbing rail trip. Ordered into yet another marching formation, the prisoners began a thirteen-mile march across the northern rim of Compiegne Forest to a giant fenced enclosure near the town of Attichy. The Germans were hungry and thirsty, but received precious little to prepare them for the forced march. As the column proceeded through the French countryside, Baumann observed American guards on motorcycles who appeared to prevent French people from giving water to the parched Germans. An Army truck followed slowly at the end of the marching column to carry prisoners who no longer could proceed under their own power. During the tiresome march, Karl's thoughts continually took him back to Augusta County, Virginia and the many kind acts he had received from Galen and Mary Heatwole, Ruel Driver and other Godly members of the Mennonite community.

Night had descended upon the column of prisoners when a vast expanse of barbed wire came into view. The appearance of the huge prison camp, built on the site of a former Luftwaffe airfield, sent chills though hardened men when they entered the gate. Masses of disheveled and disconsolate German soldiers, sailors and airmen milled about three separate compounds, each of which held over five thousand prisoners. The camp appeared to be operated by the U.S. Army, but some of the guards were fearsome-looking characters in black uniforms—probably Ukrainians who once had been pressed into service with the Wehrmacht. The five hundred new arrivals were directed through a sea of large tents to ten empty ones that awaited them. The men were counted off in groups of fifty for each tent, inside which they would sleep on bare ground except for thin layers of straw that lay scattered about.

A truck delivered the evening meal, which consisted of large barrels of salt herring packed in brine. Hungry prisoners gratefully tore into the herring before they realized they had no water to drink. Karl's mouth and throat soon burned with the salt brine he had swallowed, and in no time his temples throbbed with a tremendous headache. Men shortly became desperate for something to slake their thirst. Inside each tent, a bucket of water sat ready to extinguish an accidental fire that might flare up from the small coal stove that provided heat. The water had been made non-potable to prevent prisoners from drinking the fire suppressant. Baumann began an almost frantic search throughout the compound for a water supply, and eventually stumbled onto a faucet that was guarded by one of the black-uniformed Ukrainians. The prisoner held up his mess tin and pleaded for a drink of water.

"*Keine Wasser heute!*" the guard snapped, his dialect barely understandable.

"No water today? For what possible reason on earth?" Karl was incredulous and nearly distraught as he watched the faucet release tiny drops of water into a large tub that caught the runoff to prevent the area from becoming a mud pit. He *had* to have water, he thought, regardless of the consequences he might suffer as a result. An instant later, before the guard could push him away from the faucet, the prisoner plunged his mess tin into the tub of grimy swill that held the residue from dirty mess kits and filthy hands. Baumann brought the tin up to his lips and gulped down the putrid liquid while the guard watched with bemused silence. The sickening brew at least helped wash away some of the burning brine he had carelessly ingested, but the salt that lingered in his throat made sleep that first night a cumbersome affair.

The next morning the new arrivals were ordered to assemble in an empty field near their tent city. While the men in black uniforms stood guard, several trucks dumped the prisoners' duffel bags onto the ground. When each PW had located his bag he was ordered to empty its contents in front of the guards, who helped themselves to whatever clothing, soap, shaving lotion, trinkets, forks and knives, and parts of mess kits they chose to take. Germans seethed with anger but stood quietly, not daring to challenge the Ukrainians, who soon relieved the prisoners of almost all of their already-meager belongings.

A bizarre ritual was played out each day during the two weeks Karl remained at the Attichy compound. In the morning all prisoners were required to leave their tents and form into a long column. A two-pound loaf of bread—and sometimes a small portion of cheese—was distributed to each fourth man to share with the three PWs next to him. The men then ate their ration throughout the morning while they walked en masse, continually and aimlessly, around the inside perimeter of the compound. Prisoners were not allowed to remain in their tents or stand still, seemingly to prevent organized outbreaks of either local or widespread disruptions or violence. The Germans reported to their tent city for lunch where, with a one-quart tin can nailed onto a stick, each man ladled a dipper of soup into his mess kit. The ritualistic walk began anew after lunch and continued until 17:00 in the evening. Such was Karl's monotonous, mind-numbing routine at Attichy.

Several weeks after he had arrived at the French compound, Karl's contingent of PWs was ordered to form up one morning for medical examinations by a team of American, German, and French military doctors. The physicians' task was to select healthy prisoners for work details to help with the massive cleanup of the war-devastated cities, towns, villages, and countrysides throughout France. The PWs quickly ascertained the purpose of the examinations and fretted over being diverted from their long journeys home to be pressed into work gangs for an indeterminate period of time. The doctor who performed Baumann's rudimentary exam closely scrutinized the prisoner's large healing wound and summarily declared he was not acceptable for labor service. The former *Ubootfahrer* for once was silently grateful for the debilitating wound he had received a lifetime ago aboard U-953, and thankful as well to the doctor who declared him unfit for further service as a prisoner of war. Karl was ordered to join a group of other undesirable PWs who likewise were unable to perform hard labor to help rebuild Europe. He never looked back when a short time later the undesirables were marched through Attichy's main gate, leaving behind the despicable prison compound to board a train bound for the French border.

The men carried the last of their paltry possessions as they slogged, some with great difficulty, a short distance to a nearby train stop. GIs distributed a loaf of bread and a can of corned beef hash to each man before he climbed into a boxcar for the final leg of his repatriation to Germany. The prisoner-laden freight train began rolling and soon tacked onto a northbound heading toward the Low Countries. Severe damage to the railway systems lengthened the trip to Münster, the train's final destination, from a few hours under prewar schedules to two days. Along the route the caravan of bedraggled undesirables slowly rolled through a Belgian town and halted at the local station, where the men were disembarked to stretch their legs on solid ground. A sizeable crowd of locals watching a soccer match in a field across from the station soon realized the men standing beside the tracks were Germans. The locals then turned their full attention onto the prisoners, with shouts and jeers and violent hand motions that symbolized throats being slit.[1] Karl was shaken by the hatred he saw in the townspeople's faces. To the Belgians, the PWs were reminders of the brazen German commandos who had captured fortress Eban Emael to conquer Belgium in 1940, or Wehrmacht troops who had ruthlessly administered their occupied homeland throughout most of the war. The dejected and defeated Germans still represented the massive columns of men and tanks that crashed through American lines across the Ardennes in December 1944 to mercilessly destroy Belgian towns, villages, and people who impeded Hitler's desperate attempt to capture Antwerp. The prisoners scrambled back into the boxcars while their American guards ordered the train out of the station and away from the angry crowd.

The train finally crossed the German border and rolled through the rubble of Aachen, the first German city to be captured by American troops in October 1944 after a vicious six-week street-by-street battle. A pall of gloom swept over the men who saw for the first time the ghastly destruction of total defeat that had befallen the former *Reich*. En route to Münster, a number of Germans jumped off the slow moving train as it plodded through or near their home communities. Those who jumped later would discover that they would not be eligible to receive sanctioned food and clothing rations without official discharge papers from the occupation authorities in Münster.

One of the prisoners who disappeared along the route to Münster was a man who had sailed with Karl aboard the cargo ship from New York. The PW was notable for the guitar he had carried and played during the long voyage to Le Havre, through Attichy, and on the train to Germany. His music both entertained and comforted fellow prisoners, and helped divert melancholy thoughts from the slow and dreary passage of time. The guitar player became animated with excitement when the train pulled into the battered railway station at his hometown. The

---

1.   Karl Baumann, interview with David Benevitch, 18 April 1991.

prisoner leaned out of the freight car's open door and called out to a civilian walking along the track.

"Could you go tell my parents that I am here at the station, but have to go on to Münster to be released?"

The walking man obtained the prisoner's name and home address, then hurried off to a nearby street. A short time later he returned with sobering news: a bomb had destroyed the guitar man's home and killed all the family members who lived there. Karl overheard the news when it was relayed to other prisoners, but neither he nor anyone else had the heart to tell the orphaned guitar man. Everyone's heart ached for their *Kamerad* and each understood the man's anguish when a lone PW finally gathered the strength to gently break the devastating news. Each worried he might be greeted with the same terrible truth. The disconsolate guitar man later jumped off the train somewhere before Münster and was not seen again. Karl hoped the young soldier somehow would find solace simply by having survived the war, and one day make a new life for himself. At night he vividly imagined the man walking aimlessly in his grief, with guitar in hand but no longer playing his happy music.

The prisoners arrived at the remains of the Münster train station at the end of the two-day ride in the cold, rocking freight cars. The tired and unkempt men jumped out of the boxcars to stretch the soreness out of their aching muscles and stiffened limbs. They milled about only for a moment before they were ordered to form up into another marching column. While they stood by the boxcars a British Army troop train passed by slowly on an adjacent track. Many Tommies leaned out of the passenger car windows to gaze upon the sorry spectacle of defeated Germans. While the disparate groups eyed one another with curiosity and suspicion, a Tommy tossed a bag of pastries down onto the ground that landed squarely at Karl's feet. Before Baumann could lean down to pick up the bag, another prisoner drove his foot onto the pastries and ground them into the coal black soil. Hungry as he was, Karl immediately understood that his *Kamerad* had denied him the pastries to refuse the Brits an opportunity to see Germans grovel for food.

The PWs were marched to an old artillery *Kaserne* where their overseers had arranged for them to sleep overnight on the cold barracks floor. Along the way the miserable column passed through Münster's narrow streets. Doors and windows creaked open as residents leaned out to watch the melancholy procession below, perhaps to search for a long lost but familiar face in the crowd. Though their cupboards were all but bare, townspeople sometimes tossed a piece of bread or a slice of bologna into the marching column. Karl once looked up from the pavement to see a slice of bread sail toward him from an upper-story window. He reached out to catch the meager slice, but it hit the heel of his hand instead and tumbled onto the ground. An instant later, four or five famished men lunged to the pavement to struggle for the soiled scraps.

The following morning the cold and hungry men, some of whom wore American prison fatigues and others mere remnants of once-proud Wehrmacht uniforms, were assembled outside the *Kaserne*. Then and there, without ceremony, the prisoners learned they had been released from military service and now were free to return to their homes. The men were handed official discharge papers, after which some turned and walked away into the desolate wilderness of the new and unfamiliar world that lay before them. Others, with their papers in hand, simply stood motionless as if they had no place to go or could not think what to do next. Suddenly free, but with little formality to mark their passage from captivity, the former prisoners began the next chapter of their lives with little else but hope. Many felt strangely vacant of relief or gladness for anything other than having survived the wretched war that collectively had left them with nothing but the bitterness of vain sacrifice and abject defeat.

Those who wished were permitted to board several British Army trucks headed for the town of Arnsberg, about seventy kilometers from Dortmund. Karl wrapped his remaining spoon, half of a mess kit, and a bar of soap in his musty blanket and climbed aboard one of the lorries. Throughout the day the little convoy ground through town after destroyed town. Depression and quiet desperation registered on the faces of people who walked along the roadways in search of food, a place to stay, and perhaps the familiar faces of loved ones or friends. The trucks slowly rolled south and into Arnsberg around 18:00 in the evening. When the riders dismounted from the truck, Baumann asked the German driver which direction he was going to take to return to Münster.

"I can go through Dortmund if you like," the driver said, "but it is going to cost you something."

Karl was quietly incredulous; mere survival had cost him almost everything he owned, but he unrolled his blanket and looked forlornly at his very last possessions. His $65 cashiers check had been lost or stolen somewhere along the long route of his repatriation, so his most prized remaining possession was the bar of soap that he now held out to the driver. The man took it and invited him to sit in the cab. The truck then rumbled into the evening toward Dortmund, and within two hours arrived on the outskirts of the city. Karl directed the driver through still familiar residential neighborhoods on the edge of Brambauer until they approached a street corner where his great-aunt Berta Klode lived. He prompted the driver to stop, thanked him for making the roundabout trip to deliver him so near his home, and jumped from the cab's doorway onto the street. The scene around Aunt Berta's was eerily silent; only the growl of shifting gears and the lorrie's slow acceleration in the background distracted his attention as the driver pulled away into the night. Karl gazed upon the front of his aunt's house and observed the surrounding neighborhood. The townscape was now a shell of its former self. Battle damage was everywhere; the stark remains of blasted buildings stood vaguely silhouetted against the dark sky and created a nightmare scene that would grow only more terrible in the light of day.[2] Aunt Berta's house was scarred by shrapnel from the lethal ordnance that had plowed up the ground all around; ugly chunks had been gashed out of the exterior walls, but the home stood in better condition than most in the neighborhood.

Karl stepped up to the front door and wearily knocked; a moment later the door creaked open. The aging woman who peered out from the doorway at first did not recognize her young caller; then a few seconds later Aunt Berta's face registered surprise and then the warm glow of complete recognition. Looking into her eyes, he felt as if he had returned from the dead. Aunt Berta warmly greeted him and ushered him inside, where her daughter Hetwig and son Wilhelm soon appeared and welcomed their nephew home as well. The young veteran expected to see his great uncle Martin seated in his favorite chair inside the kitchen where the family soon made its way, but found the elderly man's chair strangely empty. Suddenly the warm kitchen took on a chilly, vacant feeling.

Karl took a seat at Aunt Berta's table, and suddenly realized he was incredibly tired, physically drained, and emotionally spent; his myriad experiences in peace and war had taken their toll. His long journey to sea as a *Schiffsjunge*, a young *Matrose* and *Ubootfahrer* had ushered him into adulthood. He had survived direct participation in the greatest and most destructive war in history, and had witnessed a lifetime of terror and cruelty. He also had experienced intense wartime comradeship as a member of the elite Ubootwaffe. In a searing instant he had suffered a nearly devastating wound that had altered, and would redirect, the course of his life. Transported to the United States as a prisoner of war, he had come to know the great hope of millions before him who saw the seemingly endless possibilities for a better future in America. Karl already contemplated emigrating there some day to live peacefully among the Mennonite people. He had returned home to a land that now lay devastated and barely recognizable. His country-

---

2.   Overy, 132. 54 percent of the built-up area of Dortmund had been destroyed during nine major bombing attacks.

men—those who still were alive—had been left utterly destitute through the failed fanatic designs of Adolf Hitler to create a Thousand Year *Reich* at the expense of all humanity.

Karl Baumann's longest patrol finally was over. The overwhelming emotions of life, love, and loss at last proved too much for the former U-boat gunner to bear. He buried his face in his hands—and cried.

10

Veteran

The ravages of war mitigated Karl Baumann's happiness at his return home and to loved ones. When he inquired of Uncle Martin's whereabouts, Aunt Berta sadly explained that during the last months of the war her husband had been shot dead nearby, probably by a sniper, when he ventured outside their local bomb shelter during a lull in the combat that had raged throughout the area. Their son Erich also had not returned from the war; he had been killed in Norway, one of 4,200,000 German soldiers, sailors, and airmen for whom there would be no homecoming reception.[1]

Karl was immensely relieved to learn that *Oma*'s house was undamaged and she was safe. One of her sons had been badly wounded during the horrors of the Russian campaign, but would survive. Karl was terribly anxious to see his grandmother. He had thought so often about her during the darkest hours of his life, when he would have given nearly anything for her to reassure and comfort him once again, and hold him safely in her embrace.

"I will take you down to my sister," Aunt Berta happily declared. "It is curfew time, but I will take you there anyway." She anticipated that British military police patrols would not bother an elderly woman during curfew hours, even in the company of a young German male. Later that night she accompanied her great-nephew to *Oma*'s house.

"*Karlchen!*" *Oma* exclaimed immediately after she answered an unexpected knock at her door. She swept her grandson into her arms and pulled him into her house. Karl rejoiced in the outpouring of love that surrounded him amid the horrid aftermath of war and defeat.

---

1. A. J. P. Taylor, *History of World War II* (London: Octopus, 1974), 279. Estimates of total deaths from all nations during World War II had for most of the postwar era been set at more than 37,000,000. Also, Author's Note: The opening of Soviet archives after 1991 have caused subsequent estimates to exceed to more than 50,000,000.

The young veteran was shocked by the severity of the damage that had resulted from the relentless Allied aerial bombing campaign and ground warfare that turned German cities, towns, and villages into wastelands. Soon he too would realize firsthand that, as Allied armies encircled the *Reich*, essential supplies of food, clothing, and shelter for the population were reduced to far less-than-adequate levels. Months after the end of fighting, few basic commodities had been made available for the German people. The difficult years Karl envisioned for Germany's rebirth convinced him of the need to emigrate to the United States as soon as he would be permitted to do so—to leave behind the land of want for the land of plenty.

Karl was reunited with Anneliese the following day. *Fräulein* Samhuber was a war survivor herself in every respect. She had experienced heavy bombing raids from a subterranean shelter near her Brambauer home and knew the fear of actually being a target of an air attack. One day during the last months of the war, while Anneliese and a friend walked with a group of Hermann Göring *Werke* employees through a field on the way to the factory, a fighter plane bearing American markings blazed into view from the low horizon. The throaty roar of the low-flying aircraft increased with frightening intensity as the plane bore in on the civilians at low altitude. Men and women, young and old alike scattered and ran in panic as fast as their legs would carry them across the open field. Seconds later the ground erupted with sod, soil and rock shards as scores of large fifty-caliber machinegun rounds stitched multiple lines of manmade geysers between the terrified civilians. Anneliese and her girl friend flung themselves onto the ground when they heard the plane's machineguns chatter behind them and the aircraft itself scream directly overhead a second later. She raised her head to watch the fighter plane streak off into the distance and disappear, and soon realized that no one had been wounded or killed during the attack. The *Fräulein* concluded that the pilot probably had intended only to scare the people out of their wits instead of killing them; otherwise, he would have left a field of bloody corpses.

Anneliese had received no word from or about Karl since Herbert Raschewski's troubling letter had arrived in November 1944. Karl had mailed four official prisoner of war postcards to her from Camp Lyndhurst, but none had reached Brambauer.[2] Nonetheless, the couple quickly resumed their relationship, which was cultivated further through shared hardship and times of near desperation. Their long acquaintance and the affection that had endured during the

---

2.   All four postcards were delivered to the addressee several months after Karl's repatriation to Germany.

war had steeled their resolve to understand and appreciate each other while they worked cooperatively toward a better future. Karl Baumann and Anneliese Sam-huber were married on 3 August 1946. The mutual decision to leave their native land, families, and friends to emigrate to the United States had been fully understood and agreed to as a precondition for marriage.

Karl and Anneliese Baumann, wedding portrait; Germany, 1946.

For a number of months following their wedding day, Karl and Anneliese struggled with the rest of the civilian population to obtain enough food to survive almost at subsistence levels. They bicycled far and near to search for wherever commodities rumor or factual information had indicated was available in an outlying town or village. A small supply of cabbage might be found in one village, while potatoes were available elsewhere. The newlyweds were happy to purchase something—anything—to eat after their long bike journeys. They vied for scarce foodstuffs with equally desperate neighbors and transients. Searches sometimes required great effort that produced only frustration. During some long treks through the countryside the couple bedded down at night among thick stands of dark forest.

Oma approached Karl one day with a solemn request. The family dog had become a burden to keep and feed. With everyone struggling to find sustenance to survive, there was not enough food left to share with the household pet.

"Will you get rid of the dog for me?" *Oma* asked, and her grandson nodded. Karl quietly took the dog into the back yard. Desperation often forces men and women into extraordinary decisions that in normal times would be unthinkable. Karl's family now had reached the point of despair that he knew what he had to do, like it or not: the dog would be sacrificed, prepared and eaten by the family.

Karl Baumann obtained employment as an apprentice bridge builder within two weeks of his homecoming. He studied the bridge-building trade for two years, then passed the written examination that allowed him to work in the factory's layout department, where bridge sections were built and used as models for mass duplication. He later transferred to the factory's steel mill and powerhouse as a repairman. During his term of employment Karl learned how gigantic steel production machinery operated and how to repair the heavy equipment. In early 1951 he became a foreman at the steel factory, but his dreams, plans, and goals still were directed westward to the United States.

While he still was a prisoner at Camp Lyndhurst, Karl had declared to himself that he would return to Virginia as soon as possible to begin a new life as a free man. The positive influences he realized from the close-knit religious community in Augusta County far outweighed the adversity he had experienced as a prisoner, and formed an irrepressible desire in him to live among the Godly people who demonstrated their faith in every aspect of their relationships with others.

Karl began to correspond with Galen Heatwole soon after he was repatriated to Germany, but five years passed before he and Anneliese obtained permission from the German and American governments to travel to the United States. Galen and Mary Heatwole kept their 1945 promise to help the former prisoner of war return to Virginia, and in 1951 they sponsored the Baumann's transatlantic journey to the couple's new home.

The couple arrived at New York Harbor aboard the United States Line passenger ship *S.S. American Harvester* on 14 July 1951. They carried with them only the possessions they could pack into two suitcases each. Galen and Mary Heatwole stood dockside to meet and greet them. The arrival of the four at the Heatwole farm was highlighted by a warm reunion with many of the neighboring farmers and their families.

Karl began work on the Heatwole farm the following day. He earned a weekly salary of fifteen dollars, plus food commodities that included one quart of milk per day, three dozen cracked eggs per week, and two hogs per year. Karl and Anneliese sold one of their first swine to help repay the Heatwoles $410.00 for their passage to the United States. During the nearly four years Karl worked on the farm, he and Anneliese developed their English language skills to fluency. Karl attributed his language education to what he called Chicken House English, a reference to the instructions Galen Heatwole issued while they attended the poultry flocks on his farm. During the same period, the immigrant couple developed a deep and abiding spiritual foundation within the Mennonite Church. Karl ultimately became an ordained minister and assistant preacher for several congregations.

Karl and Anneliese on the Galen Heatwole farm; Stuarts Draft, Virginia, 1951.

The Baumanns' spiritual lives intensified over the years and expanded beyond the tenets of the Mennonite faith. Karl and Anneliese eventually embraced the teachings of the Assembly of Yahweh, a Christian denomination that adheres to strict interpretations of the Bible. The enduring couple lives every day with studied dedication to their faith, which they rely upon steadfastly for continual guidance and enlightenment. They are wholly dedicated to Yahweh, to each other, and to their adopted country.

With the United States embroiled in war in Korea, Karl Baumann was ordered to report for a physical examination at the Selective Service Induction Center in Roanoke, Virginia. As a resident alien he was eligible for conscription into the U.S. Armed Forces. During the interview process an induction official learned the prospective recruit had been a member of the Kriegsmarine during World War II. When the official inquired about Karl's discharge from the Wehrmacht, former *Ubootfahrer* mistakenly declared that he had been dishonorably discharged. He believed the Allied occupation government had given dishonorable discharges to all members of the German armed forces in the wake of Germany's unconditional surrender in 1945. By virtue of his war wound, and perhaps by his discharge declaration, he never was ordered to report for induction.

The American Safety Razor Company in Verona, Virginia hired Karl as a machine tool builder in April 1955. He remained employed at ASR until he retired in 1985. Social security, retirement benefits, and a small pension from Germany provide a quiet but comfortable life for the couple.

Karl and Anneliese became the parents of three sons. Lothar, born in 1954; David in 1956; and Michael in 1961, grew to adulthood in a lovingly-strict environment, and all pursued successful careers in education. The elder Baumanns have three grandchildren.

Karl Baumann has built a number of intricate wooden ship models in his basement workshop. He still hears the call of the sea.

Model ship building had become a hobby when Karl was a *Schiffsjunge*, and followed him into the Kriegsmarine and later the fenced enclosure at Camp Lyndhurst. Beneath the camp canteen where he hid while he pursued his craft, he constructed two ships-in-bottles to give away as gifts. The projects allowed him to concentrate his mind upon welcome diversions that helped time pass behind the barbed wire. The numerous ship models he built after the war became more elaborate and complex with the passing decades. Today, several tall sailing ships—beautifully constructed of hand cut wood, adorned with cloth sails, and festooned with precisely knotted lines tied to exacting naval standards—grace large display cases in the Baumann home. The common maladies of aging for a time prevented Karl from finishing one or more large ship models, but renewed determination has seen him through to the successful completion of several more ship projects.

In addition to operating a successful farm and orchard operation, Galen Heatwole worked in manufacturing after the war and later became a businessman and community leader. Galen and Mary Geil Heatwole made possible Karl and Anneliese Baumann's immigration to the United States, and remained good and trusted friends with them for the remainder of their lives. Galen Heatwole died on 13 August 2003, following Mary's death some years earlier.

The irrepressible passage of time has taken its toll on old comrades who escaped the wartime fates of the majority of *Ubootfahrer*. With each reunion, fewer U-953 crew members convene in Germany to answer *Kater's* roll call. Their revered skipper, *Kapitänleutnant* Karl-Heinz Marbach, died 27 September 1995 after a long career as writer and television critic in West Germany. His memoir, *Von Kolberg über La Rochelle nach Berlin* (From Kolberg via La Rochelle to Berlin) was published in Germany three years before his death. Marbach was one of the last U-boat skippers released from captivity after the war, having been confined in a French prison until 1948.

Karl and Anneliese Baumann visited Germany after Karl retired in 1985, but both agree they probably will not travel there again. So much has changed in their native country, and few family members and friends remain to welcome their visit. In all respects, after residing more than fifty years in a small, comfortable ranch house family members and friends built with their own hands, Stuarts Draft, Virginia unquestionably is home.

The veteran seaman and U-boat gunner still maintains contact with a few crewmates in Germany and frequently speaks with Herbert Raschewski, who has visited the Baumann's home in Virginia. In 1984, the two former *Ubootfahrer* met U-953's second skipper, Herbert Werner, at Baltimore-Washington International Airport in Maryland. Werner, a highly successful businessman who now lives in the United States, gained considerable recognition as the author of *Iron Coffins*, a bestselling 1969 memoir of his exploits as the commanding officer of U-415 and U-953. The highly-skilled U-boat commander exercised much more discipline and formality than Marbach; naturally, U-953's original crew never accorded Werner the level of respect that their highly regarded and popular first commanding officer always enjoyed.

In all lives certain issues of long standing remain essentially unchanged and unresolved. Karl still treats the vicious shrapnel wound in his side when it becomes painful. Though he never has been plagued with terrible nightmares that many combat veterans have suffered for decades, he frequently dreams about his early days with the fishing and merchant fleets, and about the men who sailed into war with him aboard U-953 a lifetime ago. In his dreams to this day, young Kuddel stands watch once more on the glistening grey conning tower while the prow slices through rough Atlantic waves. More often now, he dreams about the *Ubootkameraden* who have crossed over the long low Horizon on their eternal voyages.

The massive concrete U-boat bunkers remain on the Biscay coast as stark reminders of the Second World War, a conflict so great in scope that it defies comprehension among those who did not live through it. The bunkers are virtually too large even to be destroyed. Not so the neighboring communities that succumbed to years of bombardment and now have been entirely rebuilt. Brest, almost completely destroyed during the siege in 1944, has a new, post-modern face except for its port, which still is dominated by the largest U-boat bunker ever built. The town of La Pallice suffered less wartime damage and largely returned to its prewar appearance and quiet existence. The U-bunker remains its most well known and dominant feature.

The U-boat bunker at La Pallice still impresses visitors today with its enormous size.

U-953 survived the war, battered but unbeaten, and was surrendered to the Royal Navy in Norway. British naval intelligence teams scoured the boat for any technological innovations the Allies might have found useful in the dangerous world of the Cold War, but man's pursuits to build new and ever more capable engines of destruction soon outpaced the old wartime capabilities of the Type VII-C U-boat. U-953 finally was towed out to sea in 1950, and with the detonation of well-placed explosive charges she was sent to the ocean bottom to join hundreds of her sister boats and the wreckage of many other victims of the Battle of the Atlantic. Karl Baumann is certain the Heavenly Father directly intervened many times to spare U-953 from war's destruction, so that the men who sailed aboard her instead might redeem themselves and dedicate their remaining years in service to Him and to humankind.

William A. Calafiura left the U.S. Army in 1946 and began a long and successful career with the federal government's General Accounting Office. He and his wife Mary Louise lived well in a beautiful home in Shepherdstown, West Virginia, where vestiges of his Camp Lyndhurst experiences seldom crept back into his life. Karl Baumann telephoned the former PW camp commander on 16 June 2000 to speak with the captain for the first time since he was released from solitary confinement in 1945. To his sad disappointment, but not to his surprise, Mr. Calafiura remembered neither the PW nor the incident that had sent him to the stockade with a fourteen day sentence. The work strike still loomed fresh in his mind, however, as did his wartime declaration that the United States had treated German prisoners of war very well—which by and large was unquestionably true, with few exceptions. During the brief conversation Karl explained that he had returned to the U.S. with Anneliese in 1951 and raised three sons whose lives, education, careers and families made the parents exceedingly proud. Calafiura gracefully acknowledged that Karl had lived a good and productive life, but declined a suggestion to meet once again—this time as friends—over dinner at a Shepherdstown restaurant.

"Oh, don't do that," Mr. Calafiura said. Karl Baumann ended the telephone call with a sense of sadness that old confrontations really had not been resolved, but would be put to rest once and for all with the passing of the participants themselves. The following year, on 6 August 2001, William A. Calafiura died in a Martinsburg, West Virginia nursing home.

Camp Lyndhurst is no more. A few concrete foundations and one intact building are the only remnants of the former CCC, CPS and prisoner of war camp that once was situated along a nondescript hillside just inside the George Washington National Forest. The interior area of the camp now is completely overgrown with mature trees; one could never play *Faustball* again on the former volleyball court. The clearing for the soccer field remains, but yields no hint of the tense hours of confrontation during the 1945 work strike that might have turned the field into a killing zone had hot tempers on both sides not waned. The offices, barracks and solitary confinement cells have vanished without a trace, but small vestiges of the camp can be found if one searches carefully. Rock-lined walkways still set straight courses for short, broken distances. Nearby, concrete steps climb to nowhere. A line of healthy trees has grown along the eastern perimeter of the compound fence. Small lengths of heavy barbed wire are bound tightly by the bark that has grown around them—much as the mind holds fast to memories of momentous events that shook the world and men's souls six decades ago.

Glossary of Terms

A

Aale [Ger]—Eels; nickname for torpedoes.

Alarm [Ger]—U-boat commander's order to take the boat into an emergency dive.

Alarmstufe [Ger]—Alert level.

Anschluß [Ger]—Annexation of Austria by Germany into the *Reich* in 1938.

Aphrodite [Ger]—U-boat decoy system to confuse Allied radar tracking attempts.

Arbeitslager [Ger]—Work camp, concentration camp.

Asdic [Brit]—Contraction for the Anti-Submarine Division of the British Admiralty, which initiated development of the sound-ranging system to detect the presense and location of U-boats.

Auf Tiefe gehen [Ger]—"Go to depth," U-boat commander's dive order.

B

Baubelehrung [Ger]—Time period before a U-boat was commissioned, for which the boat's crew was assembled to familiarize themselves with their new boat.

BEF—British Expeditionary Force.

Befelshaber der Uboote, BdU [Ger]—Designation that referred to both *Grossadmiral* Karl Dönitz—the Commander-in-Chief for Submarines—and his headquarters.

Bekleidungskammer [Ger]—Storage facility that housed clothing captured or retrieved from Allied warships and merchant vessels. The clothing was made available for U-boat crewmen without cost.

Bilgekrabbe [Ger]—"Bilge crabs," U-953 sailors' nickname for the boat's technician crewmen.

Blitzkrieg [Ger]—"Lightning war," Wehrmacht strategy that employed a strong, fast maneuvering attack with combined infantry, armored, and air forces to overwhelm an enemy force.

Blood Purge [Ger]—Adolf Hitler's orchestrated murder of political opponents inside the Nazi Party during the Night of the Long Knives on June 29-30, 1934.

Bold [Ger]—U-boat decoy designed to confuse Allied asdic and Sonar systems.

Bootsmaat [Ger]—Kriegsmarine rank equivalent to a U.S. Navy petty officer third class and a Royal Navy petty officer.

Boxe [Ger]—U-boat bunker docking pens that protected one or two boats each, either in drydock or flooded docks.

Bridge—Deck area atop a submarine conning tower, from which maneuvering orders are given while the boat is surfaced, manned by the commanding officer and/or watch officer and members of the bridge watch party.

Bund Deutscher Mädel, BDM [Ger]—"League of German Girls," the female branch of the *Hitler Jugend* (Hitler Youth).

C

CAT gear [Can]—Canadian Anti-Acoustical Torpedo decoy towed by warships.

Catalina, Consolidated—American long range amphibious patrol bomber (PBY).

Conning tower—Small, heavily armored hull extension located directly above a submarine control room, which houses the helmsman's steering station, torpedo data computer, periscopes, and other operations systems.

Corvette—A highly maneuverable armed escort ship, smaller than a destroyer or destroyer escort.

D

Dritte Reich [Ger]—The Third Reich.

Dritte Unterseebootsflottille [Ger]—Third U-boat Flotilla; based in La Rochelle, France.

Drittewache [Ger]—Third bridge watch, both the duty period and the watch party members.

Dumbo [U.S.]—Unofficial nickname of the Consolidated Catalina (PBY) patrol bomber.

E

Eisbär [Ger]— "Polar Bear," codename for a designated U-boat route in the Bay of Biscay.

Elektriker Obermachinist [Ger]—Kriegsmarine rank equivalent to a U.S. Navy and Royal Navy chief petty officer in charge of a vessel's electric motors and electrical system.

Enigma—Kriegsmarine cipher machine used to encrypt and decrypt Ultra-code radio signals transmitted between BdU and U-boats on patrol.

Erste Unterseeboots-Lehrdivision (ULD) [Ger]—First U-boat Training Division; based in Pillau, East Prussia.

Erstewache [Ger]—First bridge watch, both the duty period and the watch party members.

ETO [U.S.]—European Theater of Operations.

F

Fallschirmjäger [Ger]—German paratrooper.

FdU West, Führer der Unterseeboote West [Ger]—Designation that referred to both *Kapitän-zur-See* Hans-Rudolf Rösing—the Commander-in-Chief for Submarines in France—and his headquarters.

Feigling [Ger]—Coward.

Feindfahrt [Ger]—Combat patrol.

Feldpost [Ger]—Wehrmacht postal system, through which each unit (including each U-boat) was assigned a postal number to expedite delivery of mail.

Festung [Ger]—Fortress; designation given to fortress cities, such as *Festung* Brest.

FFI [Fr]—French Forces of the Interior; the French Resistance.

Flak [Ger]—Contraction of *Fliegerabwehrkannonen,* anti-aircraft artillery.

Flakvierling 38 [Ger]—Quadruple-barrel 20mm anti-aircraft gun.

Flakvisier 37 [Ger]—37mm cannon.

Flakzweilling [Ger]—Double-barrel 20mm anti-aircraft gun.

Fliebo [Ger]—Aerial bomb.

Fliegendes Stachelschwein, Das [Ger]—"The Flying Porcupine,"German nickname for the British Sunderland patrol bomber.

Flieger Alarm [Ger]—Warning announcement that a suspected or known enemy aircraft was sighted.

Flotille [Ger]—Flotilla.

Flying Fortress, Boeing—USAAF B-17 long range heavy bomber.

Front boat—A submarine assigned to operational combat duty.

Führer, Der [Ger]—The Leader; namely, Adolf Hitler during the Nazi era.

Führerprinzip [Ger]—Top-down authority that flowed from Adolf Hitler to the lowest official functionary in the Nazi Party.

Funfte Ausbildungsflottille [Ger]—Fifth Training Flotilla; based in Kiel, Germany.

Funfte Schiffstammabteilung [Ger]—Fifth Ship Manning (Personnel) Division; based in Libau, Latvia.

G

G7a [Ger]—Kriegsmarine 7 meter length, compressed-air propulsion torpedo, also referred to as *Ato* and *T-I*.

G7e [Ger]—Kriegsmarine 7 meter length, electrically-driven torpedo, also referred to as *Eto* and *T-III*.

Gare [Fr]—Railway passenger station.

Gauleiter [Ger]—Nazi Party official assigned to govern a specified district or geographic area.

Gefechtswache [Ger]—Watch party assigned to the U-boat bridge during surface combat.

Gestapo [Ger]—Contraction of *Geheime Staats Polizei*, the German secret state police.

GNAT [Brit]—Acronym for German Naval Acoustic Torpedo.

Grid squares—Kriegsmarine system of graduated numbers and measures into which the world's oceans and seas were plotted on naval maps.

Gruppe [Ger]—U-boat wolfpack.

H

Halifax, Handley-Page—British long range bomber employed for anti-submarine warfare.

Happy Time, The—Period from September 1939 to July 1943, when successful U-boat attacks dominated the Battle of the Atlantic.

Hedgehog [Brit]—Mortar-launched projectiles, armed with contact fuses, employed by Allied warships against U-boats.

Heer [Ger]—The German army.

HF/DF [Brit & U.S.]—"Huff-Duff," High-frequency/direction finding system installed aboard Allied ships to locate surfaced U-boats otherwise invisible to detection by asdic.

HJ, Hitler Jugend [Ger]—Hitler Youth.

Hydrophone—Underwater sound detection system employed by U-boats and Kriegsmarine surface ships to locate the presence, bearing and range of other vessels.

I

I.W.O., Erste Wach Offizier [Ger]—The U-boat executive officer, in command of the first bridge watch, and responsible for the torpedoes and their firing systems.

II.W.O., Zweiter Wach Offizier [Ger]—The U-boat officer in command of the second bridge watch, and responsible for all deck and flak guns.

III.W.O., Dritte Wach Offizier [Ger]—The U-boat Navigator (an *Oberfeldwebel,* Chief Petty Officer) in command of the third bridge watch and all helmsmen, and responsible to supply the boat for each mission.

ISU [U.S.]—Italian Service Unit, composed of Italian internees (former PWs) assigned to military bases in the continental U.S.

J

JU 290, Junkers—Luftwaffe long range reconnaissance bomber.

Jungmädelbund, JMB [Ger]—The female branch of the *Hitler Jugend* (Hitler Youth) for young girls.

Jungbahnführer [Ger]—A *Jungvolk* unit leader, a youngster who himself was a *Jungvolk* member.

Jungvolk, JV [Ger]—The branch of the *Hitler Jugend* (Hitler Youth) for young boys.

K

Kamerad(en) [Ger]—Comrade(s).

Kanal Nr 1 [Ger]—Reference name given to original attack orders, issued by BdU to U-boats stationed in Brest on 6 June 1944, to repel Allied invasion forces in the English Channel.

Kapitän [Ger]—Skipper of a civilian vessel.

Kapitän zur See [Ger]—Kriegsmarine rank equivalent to a U.S. Navy and Royal Navy captain.

Kapitänleutnant (KL) [Ger]—Kriegsmarine rank equivalent to a U.S. Navy and Royal Navy lieutenant.

Kaserne [Ger] or *Caserne* [Fr]—Military compound or barracks in an occupied or garrison town.

Kater [Ger]—Tomcat; U-953's radio call sign.

Kolibri [Ger]—Cologne used by U-boat crewmen to mask body odors.

Kölnischwasser 4711 [Ger]—Cologne used by U-boat crewmen to mask body odors.

Kommissbrot [Ger]—Kriegsmarine black "navy bread."

Korvettenkapitän [Ger]—Kriegsmarine rank equivalent to a U.S. Navy and Royal Navy lieutenant commander.

Kostumfest [Ger]—Kriegsmarine ritual where U-boat trainees were ordered, without warning, to change into a different uniform at the fastest possible speed, then withstand inspection scrutiny to the smallest tolerances of comportment.

KPD, Communist Party of Germany.

Kraft durch Freude (KdF) Schiff [Ger]—Passenger liner built and operated under the *Kraft durch Freude* (Strength through Joy) program by the *Reich* before the war, which provided vacation cruises for German workers and their families.

Kriegsmarine [Ger]—The German navy.

Kriegstagebuch (KTB) [Ger]—Literally, War Day Book; daily war diary, ship's log.

L

Lancaster, Avro—British long range heavy bomber.

Landser [Ger]—German field soldier.

Lazarett [Ger]—Military hospital or clinic.

Leichtmatrose [Ger]—Civilian sailor or seaman of lower rank than a *Matrose.*

Leigh Light [Brit]—Powerful, narrow-beam searchlight attached to the underside of the aircraft to spotlight surfaced U-boats in darkness.

Leitender Ingenieur (L.I.) [Ger]—Chief Engineering Officer of a U-boat.

Leutnant zur See [Ger]—Kriegsmarine rank equivalent to a U.S. Navy ensign and a Royal Navy midshipman.

Liberator, Consolidated—American long range heavy bomber (B-24) and ASW patrol bomber (PB4Y-2).

Liberty ship [U.S.]—Small transport ship, manufactured quickly and en masse during the war to ferry troops and supplies from the United States to the world's combat theaters.

Licht, Luft und Nerven sparen [Ger]—U-boat crewmen's admonition to "conserve light, air and your nerves."

Lightning, Lockheed—American fighter plane (P-38).

Luftwaffe [Ger]—German air force.

LuT [Ger]—Electrically driven torpedo programmed to run in wandering, zigzag patterns with regular 180-degree turns; an improved version of the FAT (*Federapparat Torpedo*), that was capable of being programmed to run on a greater number of patterns.

M

Maat [Ger]—Kriegsmarine rank equivalent to a U.S. Navy petty officer third class and a Royal Navy petty officer.

Marinequadrat [Ger]—Unit of measurement used with U-boat navigation that represented approximately 4.25 *Seemeilen* on each side or eighteen square nautical miles.

Matrose [Ger]—Civilian sailor or seaman.

Matrosengefreiter [Ger]—Kriegsmarine rank equivalent to a U.S. Navy seaman second class and a Royal Navy ordinary seaman first class.

Matrosenobergefreiter [Ger]—Kriegsmarine rank equivalent to a U.S. Navy seaman first class and a Royal Navy able seaman.

Metox [Ger]—Radar detection system (FuMB 1) employed by U-boats.

MHJ, Marine Hitler Jugend—Nautical branch of the Hitler Youth.

Mixer [Ger]—Torpedo technician member of a U-boat crew.

Mosquito, de Havilland—British fighter-bomber.

Motorsegeler[Ger]—Motorized sailing ship.

MP—Military Police, military policeman.

N

Nanu [Ger]—"Well, I never!"

Naxos [Ger]—Advanced radar detection system (FuMB 28) employed by U-boats.

Nervenklauen [Ger]—Things that adversely affects one's nerves.

O

Oberbootsmann [Ger]—Kriegsmarine petty officer.

Oberelektrikermachinist [Ger]—U-boat chief electrical motor machinist with Kriegsmarine rank equivalent to a U.S. Navy and Royal Navy chief petty officer.

Oberfeldwebel [Ger]—Kriegsmarine rank equivalent to a U.S. Navy and Royal Navy chief petty officer.

Oberkommando der Wehrmacht (OKW) [Ger]—High Command of the Armed Forces, equivalent to the U.S. Joint Chiefs of Staff.

Oberleutnant zur See (Oblt. z. S.) [Ger]—Kriegsmarine rank equivalent to a U.S. Navy lieutenant (junior grade) and Royal Navy sub-lieutenant.

Obermaat [Ger]—Kriegsmarine rank equivalent to a U.S. Navy petty officer second class and a Royal Navy petty officer.

Obermachinist [Ger]—U-boat chief diesel motor machinist with Kriegsmarine rank equivalent to a U.S. Navy and Royal Navy chief petty officer.

Obersteuermann [Ger]—U-boat navigator with Kriegsmarine rank equivalent to a U.S. Navy and Royal Navy chief petty officer.

Offizier [Ger]—German military officer.

Oflag [Ger]—Contraction of *Offizier-Lager*; a German prisoner of war camp for Allied officers.

Organizatoni Todt (OT) [Ger]—The construction arm of the Wehrmacht that built the U-boat bunkers and other large projects before and during World War II.

P

Patronen [Ger]—Cartridges, such as rifle bullets or cannon shells.

P-Drei [Ger]—"P-3" cleaning fluid used aboard U-953.

Pimpf [Ger]—The lowliest rank in the *Jungvolk*.

PW—Prisoner of War.

Q

R

RAD, Reichsarbeitsdienst [Ger]—Reich Labor Service.

RAF [Brit]—Royal Air Force.

Rake—U-boats of a wolfpack positioned parallel to each other to form a line to intercept and attack approaching Allied convoys.

Reich [Ger]—Empire; the Third Reich of Adolf Hitler's Germany.

Reichsdienstflagge [Ger]—National ensign flown by ships of Germany's merchant fleet, which identified a merchant ship as a government-chartered vessel and her crew as employees of the *Reich*.

Reparationsarbeiter [Ger]—Reparations worker; a German assigned to work in France during the period between the first and second world wars.

Revier [Ger]—Small first-aid clinic operated by the Wehrmacht or one of its branches.

Ritterkreuz [Ger]—Knight's Cross variant of the Iron Cross, issued to Wehrmacht personnel for valor.

Rohr [Ger]—U-boat torpedo tube; also a gun barrel.

S

SA, Sturm Abteilung [Ger]—Storm Troopers.

S-Boot [Ger]—A small, fast, German torpedo patrol boat.

Schiffsjunge [Ger]—Ship's boy or cabin boy aboard a civilian vessel.

Schloß [Ger]—Castle.

Schnorchel [Ger]—Snorkel, U-boat underwater breathing system.

Schußmeldung [Ger]—Written report required to be filed with BdU whenever any of a U-boat's weapons are fired or launched.

Schwerpunkt [Ger]—A meeting point, such as for U-boats, at a given set of coordinates.

Schwimmer [Ger]—Flotation bulb that rode the surface atop the *Schnorchel* breathing tube.

Seefahrtsbuch [Ger]—Official passport that all German civilian sailors were required to possess before they put to sea.

See-Kadett [Ger]—Student enrolled at a German naval academy, equivalent to a U.S. Naval Academy midshipman.

Seemanner [Ger]—Seamen.

Seemännische Bevölkerung [Ger]—Germany's seafaring population, which resided along the country's coastal regions within close proximity to sea.

Seemannsamt [Ger]— Government agency that exercised bureaucratic authority over Germany's civilian sailors.

Seemannsheim [Ger]—Boarding house operated for merchant seamen and their families.

Seemanns-Heuerstelle [Ger]—Official employment agency for merchant seamen.

Seemeile [Ger]—One nautical mile, or knot.

Silvestertag [Ger]—New Year's Eve.

Snort [Brit]—Nickname for the *Schnorchel* (snorkel), U-boat underwater breathing system.

Soldbuch [Ger]—Official identity document issued to each member of the Wehrmacht, which contained detailed and updated individual, medical, and service information.

Sonar [U.S]—Contraction of Sound Navigation and Ranging, a system developed by the U.S. Navy to detect the presence and location of U-boats.

Staatsjugendtag [Ger]—"State Youth Day," typically a Saturday, when Hitler Youth members. were excused from school to contribute a day of training and drill to the state (the *Reich*).

Stabsoberbootsmann [Ger]—U-boat senior chief boatswain's mate, for which there was no directly equivalent U.S. Navy and Royal Navy rank.

Stalag [Ger]—Contraction of *Stammlager*; a German prisoner-of-war camp for ranks other than officers.

Steuermann [Ger]—U-boat helmsman with Kriegsmarine rank equivalent to a U.S. Navy petty officer first class and a Royal Navy senior petty officer.

Sturm Abteilung [Ger] —The private army of the Nazi Party; also known as the SA or Brown shirts.

Sunderland, Short [Brit]—British amphibious patrol bomber used in anti-submarine warfare.

T

Tallboy—British 12,000 lb. bomb designed to destroy German U-boat bunker complexes.

Tether—A heavy cotton belt connected to the inside wall of the conning tower bridge, with the opposite end attached to a security belt worn by a member of the bridge watch to prevent being cast overboard in rough seas or during violent surface maneuvers.

Tommies [Brit]—Nickname for British military personnel.

Torpedoversuchsanstalt, TVA [Ger]—Kriegsmarine torpedo testing center located at Gotenhafen (Gdynia, Poland).

U

Ubootfahrer [Ger]—U-boat crewmen.

Ubootheim [Ger]—Kriegsmarine dining and recreation facility operated at a U-boat crew's home base for both officers and enlisted men.

Ubootkamerad(en) [Ger]—U-boat comrade(s), fellow U-boat crewmen.

Ubootkriegsabzeichen [Ger]—Kriegsmarine dress uniform badge awarded to U-boat crewmembers to recognize their service of at least ninety days on combat patrols.

Ubootwaffe [Ger]—The U-boat arm of the Kriegsmarine.

U-bunker [Ger]—U-boat pens, the massive concrete bombproof bunker or shelter designed to safely house U-boats while in port.

U-flak [Ger]—Kriegsmarine designation for attack U-boats converted to anti-aircraft gunboats.

U-Flotte [Ger]—U-boat flotilla.

U-Gruppe(n) [Ger]—U-boat wolfpack(s).

Ultra—Kriegsmarine code system used by BdU to communicate with U-boat commanders at sea.

Unterseeboot [Ger]—Submarines and submersibles, the contraction of which is U-boot (U-boat).

Unterwassermarsch [Ger]—Underwater course undertaken by a U-boat.

USAAF—United States Army Air Forces.

USN—U.S. Navy.

V

Vaterland [Ger]—The Fatherland; Germany.

Volkschule [Ger]—Public school.

Vorpostenboot [Ger]—Kriegsmarine surface vessel that served as a picket or perimeter patrol boat.

W

Wabos [Ger]—Wasserbomben; depth charges or other explosives launched from a warship.

Wache [Ger]—"Watch" or watch party that manned the bridge whenever the U-boat rode on the surface; designated *Ertse*—(First—), *Zweiter*—(Second—), *Dritte*—(Third—), and *Gefechts*—(combat—) watch.

Wachhaus [Ger]—"Watch house," Sentry box or station.

Wachoffizier (Erste-, Zweiter-, Dritte-, Gefechts-) [Ger]—The officer assigned to command each bridge watch.

Wanze [Ger]—Kriegsmarine radar detector installed on U-boats.

Wehrmacht [Ger]—German armed forces; the army, navy and air force.

Wintergarten [Ger]—Elevated gun platform aft of, and connected to, the conning tower bridge.

Wolf's Lair—Adolf Hitler's Eastern Front advanced headquarters complex in East Prussia.

Wolfpack—Massed U-boat deployment tactic established to overcome the dual problem of single U-boats: inability to located enemy targets and, once located, inability to penetrate convoy defenses to launch attacks.

X

Y

Z

Zaunkönig [Ger]—"Wren," Type V (or T5) acoustic torpedo.

Zentrale [Ger]—Central control room located on the main deck below the U-boat's conning tower.

Zweiterwache [Ger]—Second bridge watch, both the duty period and the watch party members.

Bibliography

Articles

Horn, Daniel. "Coercion and Compulsion in the Hitler Youth, 1933-1945," *The Historian* (August 1979): 639-663.

Moore, John Hammond. "Hitler's Wehrmacht in Virginia, 1943-1946," *The Virginia Magazine of History and Biography* 85 (July 1977): 259-273.

Simpich, Frederick. "The Story of the Ruhr." *The National Geographic Magazine*, May 1922, 553-564.

"Souvenir Savvy; You Can't Take It With You if It's Loaded or Looted." *Yank Magazine*, British Edition, Vol. 3 No. 32, 21 January 1945, 5.

Books

Bluejackets' Manual, United States Navy, 1943. Annapolis: U.S. Naval Institute, 1943.

Führer Conferences on Naval Affairs, 1939-1945. Annapolis: Naval Institute Press, 1990.

Handbook on German Military Forces (Reprint of U.S. War Department Technical Manual TM-E 30-451). Baton Rouge: University of Louisiana Press, 1990.

Atkinson, Rick. *An Army at Dawn; The War in North Africa, 1942-1943*. New York: Henry Holt, 2002.

Ballard, Robert D. *The Discovery of the Bismarck*. Toronto: Madison Press Books, 1990.

Beschloss, Michael. *The Conquerors; Roosevelt, Truman and the Destruction of Hitler's Germany 1941-1945*. New York: Simon & Schuster, 2002.

Blumenson, Martin. *Breakout and Pursuit*, United States Army in World War II; The European Theater of Operations. Washington, DC: U.S. Government Printing Office, 1961.

Buchheim, Lothar-Gunter. *U-Boat War*. New York: Bantam, 1979.

Carter, Kit C. and Mueller, Robert. *The Army Air Forces in World War II; Combat Chronology 1941-1945*. Washington, DC: U.S. Government Printing Office, 1973.

Chance, Peter Godwin. *Before It's Too Late; A Sailor's Life, 1920—2001*. Sidney, BC: Self-Published, 2001.

Chandler, David G. and Collins, James Lawton, Jr., eds. *The D-Day Encyclopedia*. New York: Simon & Schuster, 1994.

Cowdrey, Albert E. *Fighting for Life; American Military Medicine in World War II*. New York: The Free Press, 1994.

Crocker, Mel. *Black Cats and Dumbos; WWII's Fighting PBYs*. Blue Ridge Summit, PA: Aero, 1987.

Desgraves, Louis. *Visiting La Rochelle*. France: Editions Sud Ouest, 1998.

Eksteins, Modris. *Rites of Spring; The Great War and the Birth of the Modern Age*. Boston: Houghton Mifflin Co., 1989.

Elson, Robert T. *Prelude to War*, World War II. Alexandria, Virginia: Time-Life Books, 1976.

Fodor, Eugene, ed. *1936...On the Continent; An Entertaining Travel Annual*. New York: Fodor's Travel Guides, 1986.

Gansberg, Judith M. *Stalag: U.S.A. The Remarkable Story of German POWs in America*. New York: Crowell, 1977.

Garbett, Mike and Goulding, Brian. *Avro Lancaster in Unit Service*. New York: Arco Publishing Co, 1970.

Gilbert, Martin. *The Holocaust; A History of the Jews of Europe during the Second World War*. New York: Holt, Rinehart and Winston, 1985.

Krammer, Arnold. *Nazi Prisoners of War in America.* New York: Stein & Day, 1979.

Lake, Jon. *Sunderland Squadrons of World War 2.* Oxford: Osprey, 2000.

Lewis, LTC George G., USA, and Mewha, CPT John, USA. *History of Prisoner of War Utilization by the United States Army 1776-1945.* Washington: Center of Military History, U.S. Army, 1988.

Miller, David. *U-boats; The illustrated History of the Raiders of the Deep.* Washington DC: Brassey's, 2000.

Overy, Richard. *The Penguin Historical Atlas of the Third Reich.* London: Penguin Books, 1996.

Perret, Geoffrey. *There's a War to be Won; The United States Army in World War II.* New York: Random House, 1991.

Perret, Geoffrey. *Winged Victory; The Army Air Forces in World War II.* New York: Random House, 1993.

Pitt, Barrie. *The Battle of the Atlantic,* World War II. Alexandria, Virginia: Time-Life Books, 1977.

Ponting, Clive. *Armageddon; The Reality Behind the Distortions, Myths, Lies, and Illusions of World War II.* New York: Random House, 1995.

Rich, Norman. *Hitler's War Aims; Ideology, the Nazi State, and the Course of Expansion.* New York: W. W. Norton & Co., 1973.

Salmaggi, Cesare & Pallavisini, Alfredo. *2194 Days of War.* New York: Gallery Books, 1979.

Schmeelke Karl-Heinz and Schmeelke, Michael. *German U-boat Bunkers Yesterday and Today.* Atglen, PA: Schiffer Publishing, Ltd., 1999.

Shirer, William L. *The Rise and Fall of the Third Reich; A History of Nazi Germany.* New York: Simon and Schuster, 1960.

Stern, Robert C. *Type VII U-boats.* London: Brockhampton Press, 1998.

Taylor, A. J. P. *History of World War II.* London: Octopus, 1974.

U-Boat Commander's Handbook. Gettysburg, Pensylvania: Thomas Publications, 1989.

United States Army. *Biennial Report of the Chief of Staff of the United States Army, July 1, 1941 to June 30, 1943, to the Secretary of War.* Washington, DC: Government Printing Office, 1943.

van der Vat, Dan. *The Atlantic Campaign; World War II's Great Struggle at Sea.* New York: Harper & Row, 1988.

Walther, Herbert, ed. *Der Führer; The Life & Times of Adolf Hitler.* London: Bison Books, 1978.

Werner, Herbert A. *Iron Coffins; A Personal Account of the German U-boat Battles of World War II.* New York: Holt, Rinehart and Winston, 1969.

Winter, J. M. *The Experience of World War I.* New York: Oxford University Press, 1989.

Zentner, Christian, ed., *Hitler-Jugend.* Hamburg: Verlag für geschichtliche Dokumentation GmbH, 1978.

Correspondence

Bredow, Horst. Cuxhaven-Altenbruch, Germany. Letter to author, 14 July 2000.

Calafiura, Cpt. William A. Letter to the Commanding General, U.S. Army Third Service Command, Baltimore, Maryland, 2 March 1945. David Benevitch Collection, Buena Vista, Virginia.

Raschewski, Herbert. Lübeck, Germany. Letter to Anneliese Samhuber; Brambauer, Germany, 7 November 1944. Karl and Anneliese Baumann Collection, Stuarts Draft, Virginia.

Reda, Doris. Diez/Lahn, Germany; letter to author, 28 June 2000.

Shenck, Robert J. Mundelein, Illinois. Letter to unknown addressee, July 1969. Joseph Moyer Collection, Waynesboro, Virginia.

Dissertations

Wall, Forest Burnett, Jr. "German Prisoner of War Camps in Virginia During World War II." Ph.D. diss., Carnegie-Mellon University, 1987.

Interviews

Baumann, Anneliese Samhuber. Interviews with author, 13 March 1999-28 December 2004. Stuarts Draft, Virginia.

Baumann, Karl Christian Wilhelm. Interviews with author, 13 March 1999-28 December 2004. Stuarts Draft, Virginia.

Baumann, Karl Christian Wilhelm. Interview with David Benevitch, 18 April 1991. Stuarts Draft, Virginia.

Bechtel, Albert. Telephone interview with Karl Baumann, 1 May 2000. Trier, Germany.

Blair, Charles W. Telephone interview with author, 9 December 2004. Mt. Solon, Virginia.

Branch, Jack. Interview with David Benevitch, 3 January 1991. Interview location not identified.

Calafiura, William A. Interview with David Benevitch, 25 June 1991. Shepherdstown, West Virginia.

Chance, Peter Godwin, Commander, RCN (Ret.). Telephone interview with author, 21 April 2006. Sidney, British Columbia, Canada.

Cooper, Harry. Telephone interview with author, 28 February 2000. Hernando, Florida.

Hartmann, Eduard. Telephone interview with author, 16 November 2000. Chicago, Illinois.

Heatwole, Galen. Interview with author, 1 April 2000. Waynesboro, Virginia.

Moreman, Albert. Interview with David Benevitch, May 1991. Stuarts Draft, Virginia.

Raschewski, Herbert. Telephone interview with Karl Baumann, 8 November 2004. Kassel, Germany.

Schages, Hans. Interview with David Benevitch, 6 May 1991. Stuarts Draft, Virginia.

Steinhoff, Leighton H. Telephone interview with author, 14 April 2006. Kitchener, Ontario, Canada.

Stemmler, Hans. Telephone interview with Karl Baumann, 5 June 2000. Geisenheim-Johannisberg, Germany.

Internet Sources

Facts About Bochum. 1999. www.bochum.de/english/boallg.htm

http://uboat.net/allies/aircraft.sunderland.htm

http://uboat.net/boats.htm

www.angelraybooks.com/diewehrmacht/Kriegsmarine/uwp2.htm

www.deutsche-uboote.de/kommandanten/marbach_karl-heinz.html

www.feldgrau.com/ranks.html

www.naval-history.net/WW2194306-2.htm

www.raf.mod.uk/bombercommand/diary/aug44.html

www.u-boote-online.de/dieboote/u0306.html

www.ubootwaffe.net/crews

www.ubootwaffe.net/ops/boat.cgi

www.ubootwaffe.net/ops/boat.cgi?boat=953

www.uwm.edu/~jpipes/interview6.html. Witter, Robert, ed. *Rudolf Salvermoser, A Grossdeutschland Veteran*; 1999.

www.warsailors/com/singleships/hallfried.html

Microfilm

Kriegstagebuch U-953. Roll 3379, Microfilm Publication T1022. College Park, MD: United States National Archives and Records Administration.

Government Archives

Gorsline, James M. "Annual Narrative Report and Summary of Extension Work in Augusta County, Virginia, 1944." Staunton, VA: Augusta County Extension Service, United States Department of Agriculture.

Prisoner of War Camp, Camp Pickett, Virginia, Enemy POW Information Bureau, Subject File, 1942-1946, Box 2669, Record Group 389. College Park, MD: United States National Archives and Records Administration.

Report of Attack on a U-Boat, 8th June, 1944, HMCS *Skeena*, 12th June, 1944. Record Group 24, Series D-1-C, Volume 6904, File NSS 8910-353/28. Toronto, Ontario: Library and Archives Canada.

Ship's Log: HMCS *Skeena*; Record Group 24, Series D-2, Volume 7861. Ship's Log: HMCS *Restigouche*; Record Group 24, Series D-2, Volume 7795. Ship's Log: HMCS *Qu'Appelle*; Record Group 24, Series D-2, Volume 7762.. Toronto, Ontario: Library and Archives Canada.

Picture Credits

Page 151: Greg Owen
Page 159: Karl-Heinz Patzer
Page 161: U. Eduard Hartmann
Page 167: Karl Baumann
Page 168: U. Eduard Hartmann
Page 173: Greg Owen
Page 194: Greg Owen
Page 198: Greg Owen
Page 212: Greg Owen
Page 220: Greg Owen
Page 242: Clarence Quay
Page 248: U.S. Army Signal Corps photo, via Library of Virginia
Page 259: Clarence Quay
Page 267: Greg Owen
Page 277: Karl Baumann
Page 282: Galen Heatwole
Page 284: Karl Baumann
Page 299: Karl Baumann
Page 301: Karl Baumann
Page 302: Greg Owen
Page 305: Alain Biard

Index

Page numbers in *italics* refer to illustrations

A

Aachen, 292
aerial observations, 62, 64, 108n52
affidavits, 261
Afrika Korps, 237, 243–44
agricultural labor, 223, 243, 245, 264–65, 275
Ahrendholz, Gerhard, 58
air quality. *See also* pressure vacuum; *Schnorchel*
   engines and, 85, 105–6
   hygiene and, 95
   submergence and, 88, 134, 145–46, 199
aircraft
   of American forces, 62–63, 68–69, 101–2, 118, 180
   of British forces, 102, 122–23, 126, 180, 196, 211–13
   Heatwole's, 281–82
   neutral, 150, 153
   observations by, 62, 64, 108n52
   and submarine warfare, 105–6, 107, 128
alcohol, 12, 77, 79, 131–32
Allied forces. *See also* American forces; British forces
   air attacks by, 62, 150, 164–65, 295, 298
   Canadian, 180–90
   Normandy invasion, 1–2, 168–69, 174–94, 206, 226

   as PWs, 260–61
   and submarine warfare, 107, 162, 215
American forces. *See also* Allied forces
   air attacks by, 68–69, 101–2
   aircraft of, 62–63, 68–69, 101–2, 118, 180
   assigned to PW camps, 256–57
   attitudes toward Germans, 288
   detection of U-boats, 91, 178
   food drops by, 246n10
   in France, 210, 213, 215–21, 222
   Navy, 94n32
American Safety Razor Company, 302
anti-aircraft gunboats. *See also* U-boats; U-953
   as decoys, 74, 100, 104
   effectiveness of, 104, 128
   U-953 as, 74–75, *75*, 80
   weapons aboard, 74–75, 95, *103*, 128
anti-aircraft gunners
   in Brest, 211
   duties of, 80, 101, 122–23, 200
   training, 55–56
anti-submarine tactics. *See* detection, of U-boats
Aphrodite countermeasures, 146, 154, 156, 171
Arbeitslager. See concentration camps
artificial illumination, 102, 153, 164, 165n56, 193
artillery, 215–16
Asdic signals, 61, 142, 146, 156
assassination attempts, 209–10
ASV Mk. II radar, 102

333

CPSIA information can be obtained at www.ICGtesting.com
Printed in the USA
BVOW04s2218091114

374368BV00001B/127/P

9 781605 280325